Tributes
Volume 8

Logos and Language
Essays in Honour of Julius Moravcsik

Volume 1
We Will Show Them! Essays in Honour of Dov Gabbay, Volume 1
S. Artemov, H. Barringer, A. d'Avila Garcez, L. Lamb and J. Woods, eds.

Volume 2
We Will Show Them! Essays in Honour of Dov Gabbay, Volume 2
S. Artemov, H. Barringer, A. d'Avila Garcez, L. Lamb and J. Woods, eds.

Volume 3
Probability and Inference: Essays in Honour of Henry E. Kyburg
Bill Harper and Greg Wheeler, eds.

Volume 4
The Way Through Science and Philosophy:
Essays in Honour of Stig Andur Pedersen
H. B. Andersen, F. V. Christiansen, K. F. Jørgensen, and V. F. Hendricks, eds.

Volume 5
Approaching Truth: Essays in Honour of Ilkka Niiniluoto
Sami Pihlström, Panu Raatikainen and Matti Sintonen, eds.

Volume 6
Linguistics, Computer Science and Language Processing.
Festschrift for Franz Guenthner on the Occasion of his 60th Birthday
Gaston Gross and Klaus U. Schulz, eds.

Volume 7
Dialogues, Logics and Other Strange Things.
Essays in Honour of Shahid Rahman
Cédric Dégremont, Laurent Keiff and Helge Rückert, eds.

Volume 8
Logos and Language
Essays in Honour of Julius Moravcsik
Dagfinn Follesdal and John Woods, eds

Tributes Series Editor
Dov Gabbay   dov.gabbay@kcl.ac.uk

Logos and Language
Essays in Honour of Julius Moravcsik

edited by

Dagfinn Follesdal
and
John Woods

© Individual author and College Publications 2008. All rights reserved.

ISBN 978-1-904987-84-0

College Publications
Scientific Director: Dov Gabbay
Managing Director: Jane Spurr
Department of Computer Science
King's College London, Strand, London WC2R 2LS, UK

http://www.collegepublications.co.uk

Original cover design by orchid creative   www.orchidcreative.co.uk
Printed by Lightning Source, Milton Keynes, UK

All rights reserved. No part of this publication may be reproduced, stored in a retrieval system or transmitted in any form, or by any means, electronic, mechanical, photocopying, recording or otherwise without prior permission, in writing, from the publisher.

Preface

This volume arises from a conference in December, 2006 to honour Julius Moravcsik on the occasion of his formal retirement from the Stanford Philosophy Department. The programme was structured around the several areas of philosophical investigation in which the honoree has made highly regarded contributions, and the conference speakers with the exception of Alan Code and István Bodnár were his former students.

After having received his BA and PhD at Harvard Julius began his career at the University of Michigan in the academic year 1959–60. In 1968 he moved to Stanford, which has been his permanent philosophical home ever since. He served as Chair of the Philosophy Department during two periods, 1972–75 and 1983–86. He was also president of the American Philosophical Association, Pacific Division, 1987–88 and President of the Society for Ancient Greek Philosophy, 1989–91.

Most of the papers appearing here were delivered at the Moravcsik Conference. A scant few of the conference papers were pledged elsewhere and could not be included in the volume. On the other hand, we have included papers by some of Julius's students and friends who were not able to attend the Conference.

The Moravcsik volume appears in the Tributes Series of College Publications of London. It is a fitting arrangement. Dov Gabbay is the series editor, and Dov and Julius were Stanford colleagues and occasional co-authors in the 1970s. The editors wish to thank College Publications for participating in this tribute to Julius, and to Julius' Stanford colleagues, Chris Bobonic, John Perry, Patrick Suppes, Kenneth Taylor and Tom Wasow, who together with Dagfinn Føllesdal organized the Conference. The editors, one of whom has enjoyed having Julius as a colleague during all of Julius's 38 years at Stanford and the other having benefited from having had him as a teacher at Michigan are also most grateful for advice and support from Julius' wife, Rita Moravcsik, his sister, Edith Moravcsik, but most of all Julius himself. We value his introductory brief account of his life and we treasure his rich and varied philosophical accomplishments. The editors also warmly thank Claudio Beccari for invaluable technical assistance.

Dagfinn Follesdal
Stanford, California.

John Woods
Vancouver, British Columbia.

Contributors

István Bodnár is associate professor of philosophy at Eötvös University, Budapest, and visiting associate professor at Central European University, Budapest. He first met Julius in the early nineties in Budapest.

Alan Code is a Board of Governors Professor of Philosophy at Rutgers University. He first met Julius Moravcsik over thirty years ago at the APA meetings in New York, and subsequently for many years was a regular member of the West Coast Aristotelian Society that Julius founded and directed with great vigor and collegiality. The paper in this volume continues a line of investigation that he and Julius explored in their jointly taught seminar at Stanford in 1988-89.

Dagfinn Follesdal is C.I. Lewis Professor of Philosophy at Stanford. He first met Julius at Harvard when Julius was a Santayana Fellow there in 1964. This started a friendship that continued when Julius came to Stanford in 1968 and they became colleagues.

Susan B. Levin is Associate Professor of Philosophy at Smith College. She wrote her dissertation under Julius' supervision and received her PhD from Stanford in 1993.

Richard McKirahan has been professor of classics and philosophy at Pomona College since 1973. He met Julius at the West Coast Aristotelian Society soon after arriving at Pomona and learned from Julius at the monthly meetings of the WCAS for over thirty years.

John Malcolm is Emeritus Professor of Philosophy at UC-Davis. He is a charter member of the Aristotelian Society of the West founded by Julius about 40 years ago.

Mohan Matthen is Professor of Philosophy and senior Canada Research Chair at the University of Toronto. He wrote his dissertation *Essentialism and Non-Contradiction: A Study in Aristotle's Metaphysics* under Julius's supervision, and received the PhD from Stanford University in 1976.

Henry Mendell is professor of philosophy at California State University, Los Angeles. He wrote his thesis, "Aristotle and the Mathematicians: Some Cross-Currents in the Fourth Century," under Julius' supervision and received his PhD from Stanford in 1986.

Otto Neumaier is professor of philosophy at Salzburg University. He wrote his PhD thesis on Chomsky's Innateness Hypothesis and critized therein some of Julius' contributions to this topic. When he first met Julius in 1981 at a conference on rationality in Biel (Switzerland) and discussed with him this critique, the "critical attitude" turned out to be a fruitful misunderstanding, and Julius' cordial response stimulated "the beginning of a wonderful friendship" which was deepend by several visits of Julius in Salzburg. It appears to be natural that this friendship brought about the translation of Julius' writings on friendship as well as on some other questions of morality into German, collected in the book *Was Menschen verbindet* which was published with a long introduction by Otto Neumaier in 2003.

Timothy Schroeder arrived at Stanford University in 1993, and within the week was attending Julius' course on Plato. He is now Associate Professor of Philosophy at Ohio State University, but remains embarrassed by his paper for Julius on the Gorgias.

Nicholas D. Smith is the James F. Miller Professor of Humanities at Lewis and Clark College in Portland, Oregon. He completed his doctoral dissertation, *The Similes of Light in Plato's Republic*, under Julius Moravcsik's direction at Stanford in 1975.

Scott Soames is Professor and Director of the School of Philosophy at the University of Southern California. He was an undergraduate at Stanford where he took several classes from Julius in 1970-1971. It was Julius who introduced him to the philosophy of language, and advised him to study philosophy and linguistics at MIT. They have remained friends throughout the years.

Voula Tsouna is Professor of Ancient Philosophy at the University of California, Santa Barbara. She has published on Hellenistic and Roman philosophy, the Herculaneum papyri, and Plato.

John Woods. Julius Moravcsik and John Woods arrived at Michigan in September, 1959, Julius as Assistant Professor and John as a PhD student. In the next three years, John took every course that Julius offered. They have been friends ever since. John is now Director of The Abductive Systems Group at the University of British Columbia and the Charles Peirce Professor of Logic in the Group on Logic and Computational Science at Kings College London.

CONTENTS

Preface **Dagfinn Follesdal and John Woods**	iii
Contributors and their association with Julius	v
A Brief Account of My Intellectual Life **Julius Moravscik**	1

Part A. Language

Meaning, Implicature and Assertion **Scott Soames**	9
Moravcsik and the Contents of Consciousness **Timothy Schroeder**	19

Part B. Aesthetics

Pictures and the Feeling of Presence **Mohan Matthen**	37

Part C. Ethics

Why Are We Morally Responsible for Ourselves? **Otto Neumaier**	49

Part D. Plato

Platonic Metaphysics and Semantics: The *Cratylus*' Ties to the *Sophist* and *Politicus* **Susan Levin**	73

Julius, the Late-learners and (a section of) *Sophist* 255c12-13   99
John Malcolm

Moravcsik on Plato on Radical Reorientation of One's Life   109
Nicholas D. Smith

Part E. Greek Science

Plato by the Numbers   125
Henry Mendell

Part F. Greek Philosophy

The Eipcureans on Anger and the Desire for Revenge   163
Voula Tsouna

Philoponus' Account of Theses, Hypotheses, Postulates and   181
Definitions in his Commentary on Aristotle's *Posterior Analytics*
Richard McKirahan

Part G. Aristotle

Sophistic Elenchis 176a 10-12: Many Questions for Julius   211
Moravcsik
John Woods

Aristotelian Colours as Causes   221
Alan Code

Aristotle's Planetary Observations   229
István Bodnár

A Brief Account of My Intellectual Life

JULIUS MORAVSCIK

I was born in 1931 on the 26th of April in Budapest, Hungary. My first years were filled with surgeries. Fortunately, I survived these. My first "friends" were toy animals and this was so for a long time. Things changed when I started to spend time in the nearby zoo. Here my "friends" were live animals. I came to know them by name.

Early on, I was taken to the opera house by my parents. First I was exposed to easy pieces, including some Mozart. At home, my older brother and I were allowed to play make-believe in the morning: we were animals from Rudyard Kipling's stories. We were exposed a lot to animals and to classical music at a very early age and this stayed with us all our lives.

With this came also the sense of mystery and the beginning of an understanding of religion. Christmas was a very important festivity in the family's life. My father brought a Christmas tree to the apartment and there were gifts exchanged. Years later, with my father in Europe and me in the USA, I asked my father if my favorite ornament was still in place. My father was very happy that I still retained memories of those Christmases.

We had very nice summer vacations outside the city. At one of the places where we went several times, there was an old church served by several generations of Lutheran ministers all coming from our family. This church is protected today as a historical monument.

But then the war broke out and life became difficult. I was given the task of buying food for the family with the food coupons and bring it home all by myself. This was so because I was the only family member who was old enough to carry food but young enough not to be in danger of being forced to join the army. The authorities could have taken both my brother and my father.

Some serious incidents occurred. One day, a grenade exploded next to me. At another time we found thirty dead bodies in our garden – these were all soldiers. At yet another time, I had to witness two soldiers being killed for no reason at all. On another occasion, we had to kill a horse for his meat to eat but unfortunately, there was no trained butcher available and so amateurs did the work. The slaughtering took a long time; it was terrible. I couldn't watch all of it because I fainted.

Many people say that you should forget your negative experiences and that this can be done. But I think it is easier for adults to forget terrible things; for young people, it is much more difficult. In my mind, these scenes remained stuck.

When the war came to an end, my father and I ventured down into the city from our summer home in the hills of Buda. As we got to our house, it looked as if it was in good condition when viewed from one side. We then walked to the other side and saw that the building was completely destroyed. The family had to move to a different part of the city: new place, new people, some communists, some not.

After the war, it took a long time before the news of the horrible events came to light; for example, Churchill wiping out so many German civilians for no reason and, of course, the killing of the Jews. The latter case affected me very personally because four very close relatives died in terrible ways. When the first pieces of news started to reach other countries, people thought that these things were impossible. Eventually, however, the evidence emerged and people reported what happened: it was sheer horror. The 19th-century German writer Georg Büchner wrote: "Mensch ist ein Abgrund." 'Man is an abyss.' If we try to peer into it, we recoil. I always thought that trust had to be the main element that brings us all together, but after what we had seen and heard, how can one hope for the unity of all mankind?

During the postwar years, I did not spend much time on politics. Three things occupied my attention. Two of them were Russian writers: Fyodor Dostoevsky and Leo Tolstoy. The third was a book by the great Danish philosopher Søren Kirkegaard. This book was very interesting to me. Although later on my philosophical interests changed, a rapport with Kirkegaard's thought remained with me. This was my first encounter with philosophy. After that, my main interest shifted to ancient Greek philosophy. This was fueled to a large extent by my father Gyula (Julius) Moravcsik, who was an expert in this field. His enthusiasm inspired me in this direction.

Around the same time, a remarkable person entered my life. He was a Lutheran bishop, an incredible speaker; he also inspired me very much. His name was Lajos Ordass; he eventually became a leading figure of the Lutheran church in Hungary. But he couldn't achieve much because the communists incarcerated him three times. His sermons were wonderful and his bravery as he stood up to the communists touched me deeply. He was a marvelous example of courage. It was easy for me to have contact with him because his son was a classmate of mine: we sat in adjacent seats.

As time passed, the situation in Hungary became confused and my mother wanted her two sons to leave the country for America. This led to a long debate in the family, which my mother eventually won. This is how my brother and I came to the US. We first went to Boston because we had an uncle living there and we continued our education there. My brother ended up at Harvard and I entered a Protestant private school.

On our way from Hungary to the US, we spent several months in Paris. I had hardly any knowledge of English and I decided to study this language. As the place of my study, I chose one of the towers of the Cathedral of Notre Dame, where I spent several months poring over my English grammar book.

Paris is a city with a charm of its own. Art - past and present – is an excellent source of learning. I saw the city of course through the eyes of a 17-year-old. It was my first glimpse at a big Western city. The opera was very good and my brother and I often attended performances. Others in my age group ran around in Paris and had a good time just playing around but I never partook in such activities. Today I don't feel at all that I missed anything important. I have been back in Paris a couple of times giving lectures but for me the city has become less interesting because it has become more modern.

After several years in the US, my life became easier.

My first work in Greek philosophy was at Harvard under Professor Raphael Demos. I was later also introduced through Professor Roderick Firth to modern epistemology, which I found very interesting. However, I ended up staying mostly with Greek philosophy.

At Harvard, I also encountered Professor John Austin, who was visiting from Oxford at the time. His lectures were inspiring to me even though very few people attended them. This did not discourage me and later my lectures mirrored Austin's lectures to some extent. At that time, I also took some courses with the classicist Professor Werner Jäger. I also made the acquaintance of two very inspiring people. One was the psychologist Daniel N. Osherson and the other, Israeli philosopher Jonathan Stavi. I introduced Osherson to Chomsky and that changed Osherson's aims in his work. Osherson was interested in establishing self-supporting colleges with revolutionary programs. This outstanding person ended up in the Department of Psychology at Princeton University. With Stavi, though he is a logician, we talked about ethics. We examined cases that you could analyze either through Kantian ethics or through hedonistic ethics.

The next important event in my life was that I received a Fulbright fellowship. It helped me go to Oxford for a whole year. This was marvelous for my coming to understand different ways of doing philosophy. When I started my studies at Harvard, there was hardly any interest in Greek philosophy but then I went to Oxford where the atmosphere encouraged me to talk to a large number of people. One of these was Gilbert Ryle, a member of the generation of British ordinary language philosophers. He kindly invited me to his office every week for a philosophical chat. Why and how I ended up having this great opportunity, I don't know. At Corpus Christi College, the humanities could keep even. Willard Van Orman Quine was admired but his views and techniques did not dominate the whole field. In this freedom it was easy to dive deeper into Greek philosophy. Sir Bernard Arthur Owen was my tutor and I saw him every day. I continued my relationship with him and we kept up our correspondence. Eventually, Owen and I parted ways because I was more philosophical and he was more philological but my admiration for him did not cease.

When I returned to the USA, I devoted myself to teaching. It went quite well. Besides liking philosophy, I came to like teaching philosophy as well. I could look up to Professor Firth, who I knew in my earlier years at Harvard and who then became an example for me.

Then came a period when I was invited to give lectures in different countries. This had some good effects but not always. Once I had to give three different lectures in three different places on three different subjects in the space of a single week. This may have had a bad effect on me because afterwards I often mixed up words within a sentence from different languages. Ironically, the first person who discovered this during one of our conversations was one of the great linguists of our time: Noam Chomsky!

As time passed, I did more and more lecturing in different countries. I ended up with 22 foreign places where I gave lectures. This reminds me of an earlier matter. At the end of my high school studies in the US I got a 99 in English. This was quite an accomplishment since I started speaking English only in the beginning of that year.

One of the most stimulating visits abroad was my stay in South Africa. These were still very difficult times in that part of the world. The military kept me under constant surveillance. Another highly rewarding visit was my teaching in Singapore for four months – a quite different situation. The students were excellent. I was sad to leave them and apparently, that feeling was mutual. It was impressive to see their work. Although there were differences, Plato was the common denominator.

It was during one of my trips to Israel that I met Jonathan Stavi, whom I mentioned above. Jonathan and I forged a very close friendship. A logic expert told me that Stavi was one of the three best logicians of his generation. I was also very much moved by his character. He took very fine care of his old aunts. He brought them food when they were not able to go shopping anymore; he brought them their meal every day. He was also very kind to animals: he used to go around town and helped stray animals. His ways of looking at things really made a big difference in my take on things. Nobody could find a better friend.

Around this time, I had the privilege of meeting the Norwegian philosopher Dagfinn Follesdal, an expert in the philosophy of language and several other areas of philosophy, who, like I, had studied under Quine at Harvard. I also got acquainted with a wonderful group of philosophers in Salzburg. I had new chances to enjoy music and philosophy there. My best friend in the group was Otto Neumaier. Later came several other opportunities for interesting discussions. These include four months of teaching in Singapore mentioned above and a period in Australia. There were also two trips to Russia. I visited Iran to lecture there as well but I don't wish to discuss the details of that trip.

I also met some very fine philosophers in Germany. Günther Patzig, an expert in ancient philosophy, and others showed me many things that I had not encountered in the US or in England.

Returning to the USA, I had the privilege of being able to receive some comments on my work by Georg Kreisel. This Austrian-born British philosopher specialized in the philosophy of mathematics was one of the best philosophers of that time. I also had conversations with Hilary Putnam. Later I became chairman of the Philosophy Department at Stanford. I recruited very good philosophers, among them J. O. Urmson and Stuart Hampshire from England and the Canadian philosopher Ian Hacking. It was a very good department but later, unfortunately, several members left for personal reasons. I received a lot of different comments from different places. Given my experiences and those of others who did not suffer during the war, we seemed to see the world differently, and along with it philosophy as well.

Due to WWII, a sense of hostility developed against certain countries. However, I felt that we should not have such feelings. With the help of the department, I managed to invite some German and Russian philosophers as visitors. Some people were surprised because they knew that my family had suffered in the war but I felt we should get over this. I shook hands with the Russians as well. Professor Patrick Suppes secured funds for an exchange program between Russian and Stanford philosophers.

At Stanford, I had many excellent students; Scott Soames was perhaps the best. It was here that I started the West Coast Aristotelian Society. This society has survived for thirty-four years. Its origin was in England. It began two generations earlier. I kept up my broad interest in different parts of philosophy outside Aristotle as well because I was convinced that this was the way the Ancient Greeks did it and this was how we should do it today. Being very narrow-minded may be an advantage in some fields but it does not help much in philosophy.

Let me now turn to my position in philosophy. I am a Platonist but with a pragmatic flavor. I believe that abstract structures are most important for understanding the world but I also realize that our way of looking at the world has a certain humane angle to it. At Stanford, I inaugurated new courses such as one in the philosophy of friendship. I grappled with difficult questions, such as how we know when an explanation is really deep. I am still looking for ways of reaching out for new concepts. I agree with Cambridge philosopher Frank P. Ramsey that we have not explained sufficiently the relationship between subject and object but I think we should not give up. My views have not been shared by many and at times they were not understood. This led to a conversation with Noam Chomsky. He said to me: "People will not understand you." My reply was: "You know, one cannot have everything in life."

I really would like to have my thinking turn to everyday problems but so far I have not succeeded. But of course I will keep on trying.

Part A
Language

Meaning, Implicature, and Assertion
SCOTT SOAMES

Thanks to the organizers I have the privilege of being back at my *alma mater* to pay tribute to my teacher, Julius Moravcsik. In addition to Julius, two of the organizers — Dagfinn Follesdal and Pat Suppes (or rather Pat's computer) — taught me at Stanford. Dagfinn had the dubious pleasure of reading my weekly essays for a tutorial on Husserl. It is to him — Dagfinn, not Husserl — that I owe the best advice I have ever been given about writing philosophy. As I was struggling through the *Ideas*,[1] he advised me "to write in such a way that someone who knows the subject can immediately tell if you are wrong" — advice for which my critics have been grateful ever since.

I met Julius in the 1970-71 academic year — the same year that Pat's computer in Ventura Hall taught me logic. In the fall, Julius introduced me to Tarski, Chomsky, and philosophy of language. In the winter I learned what little I know about Plato from him. In the spring, he organized a pair of seminars given by David Kaplan and Barbara Partee, to which I was graciously admitted, despite not yet being a graduate student. That was my first introduction to direct reference, about which I was then dubious, and to the systematic study of syntax and semantics, about which I was not. The next year, following Julius's advice, I went to MIT to study philosophy and linguistics. In that final year at Stanford, it was Julius who set me on the path I have followed, with his encouragement, ever since. My freshman English teacher at Stanford had told me that the aim of education was to allow one to recognize a good man when one saw him. When I met Julius I knew he was right. One of the great benefits of my education has been a lifetime association with the profoundly good man we honor today. There is no one from my early days in philosophy to whom I owe more.

My topic today picks up one of the threads of Julius's 1990 *Thought and Language*.[2] There, he argued that the meanings of many descriptive words, like 'emergency', specify necessary, but not sufficient, conditions for application. Determinate extensions for such words — and determinate propositions expressed by sentences containing them — arise only when the abstract, and incompletely specified, application schemas provided by their meanings are filled in with contextually salient information. This general idea — that the semantic contents of sentences often constrain, without fully determining, what propositions are expressed and asserted

---
[1] Edmund Husserl, *Ideas*, translated by W.R. Boyce Gibson, (London: Allen and Unwin), 1931.
[2] Julius Moravcsik, *Thought and Language*, (London and New York: Routledge), 1990.

by those who use them — has gathered steam over the last sixteen years. From the relevance theorists' insistence on the contribution of conversational maxims and contextual information to what sentences are used to say, to Kent Bach's conversational implicitures, Crimmins' and Perry's unarticulated constituents, and my own pragmatic enrichment of sentences containing names, descriptions, and propositional attitude constructions, the idea that solutions to many of the vexing problems in philosophical semantics require a new understanding of the relationship between semantics and pragmatics is one whose time has come. Today I will use it to illuminate the distinction between meaning and implicature, and explain how the incomplete meanings of sentences containing bare numerical quantifiers combine with Gricean conversational maxims to generate the propositions asserted by uses of such sentences.[3]

How many? Implicatures and What is Said

I begin with sentence (1).

1. I have two children.

If I utter this in answer to the question "How many children do you have?", I assert that I have two, and only two, children. How much of this information is part of meaning, and how much is due to implicature? Does the sentence literally mean that I have exactly two children, or does it mean that I have at least two, while generating the conversational implicature that I have at most two as well? Matters become clearer when we look at related examples. Suppose someone interested in having a quick beer with me asks "Do you have two beers in the fridge?" It is clear that my guest wants to know whether I have at least two bears. Hence, when I answer, by uttering (2)

2. (Yes) I have two beers,

and he goes to the fridge and sees I have six, it won't occur to him that I have said anything false, or even misleading. Since he could reasonably think this if (2) meant, and I asserted, that I have exactly two beers, (2) doesn't unambiguously mean this — in which case surely (1) doesn't unambiguously mean that I have exactly two children.

In a different conversational setting, the information conveyed would be richer. Had my guest, wondering whether I had enough for a party, asked, "How many beers do you have?," I would have taken it as a request for the precise number. My utterance, "I have two beers," would then be understood as asserting that I have exactly two. Assuming that the meaning of sentence (2) doesn't change from one conversation to the next, one is tempted to conclude that, in general, sentences of the form (3) *mean* (3a), and that the extra information — that I have at most,

---

[3]The discussion in what follows in this paper distills, in greatly reduced form, the main ideas of my "Drawing the Line Between Meaning and Implicature — and Relating both to Assertion," *Nous*, 2:3 (2008), 529–554.

and hence exactly, two Fs — is conversationally implicated when, and only when, it is conversationally relevant precisely how many Fs I have.

3. I have n Fs.

    3a. I have at least n Fs,

    3b. I have exactly n Fs

However, this explanation is doubtful. Utterances of (3a) have different conversational implicatures from those of (3). If I assertively utter (3a) in a context in which it is relevant, not just that I have a minimum of n Fs, but also how many Fs I have, my utterance *will not* implicate that I have at most, and hence exactly, n. Rather, it will implicate that, for all I know, I have more than n. Mary asks, "How many children do you have?" I answer, "I have at least two." In so doing, I don't communicate that I have exactly two children. Instead, I state that I have a minimum of two, and implicate that I am uncertain whether I have more. The explanation of this is simple. The Gricean maxim of quantity requires me to make the strongest, relevant statement I can. Thus, I will make the weaker claim expressed by an instance of (3a), instead of the stronger (relevant) claim expressed by the corresponding instance of (3b), only when I am uncertain whether I have more Fs than those I know about, and hence lack sufficient evidence for (3b). If (3) meant the same as (3a), something similar should be true of utterances of (3). But it isn't. To make a long story short, the analysis of (3) as meaning the same as (3a) saddles us with three daunting problems — (i) explaining why the implicatures that typically result from utterances of (3a), *do not* result from utterances of (3), (ii) explaining how the implicatures needed by this analysis of (3) *are* generated, despite the fact that they are not carried by utterances of its supposed synonym, and (iii) explaining how the needed implicatures end up contributing to what is *asserted* by utterances of (3) — rather than being mere suggestions about what a cooperative speaker must believe, and intend to communicate, given what he or she has chosen to assert. To avoid these problems, we need another analysis.

Why Ambiguity is Not the Answer

At this point, a simple thought is likely to occur. Perhaps (3) is semantically ambiguous, having one reading in common with (3a), and one in common with (3b). The Gricean injunction to make the strongest, relevant statement one can might then be seen as selecting the stronger reading when it is conversationally demanded. However, this won't do either. Although the view can accommodate the cases so far considered, it can't accommodate utterances of (4), which are often understood as asserting the propositions expressed in (5).

    4.   a. Matriculated students are allowed to take five courses.

         b. The sedan was designed to carry five passengers.

         c. The car seats five adults.

      d. John is capable of eating five hamburgers at one sitting.

      e. The navy can withstand the loss of five carriers without jeopardizing its mission.

5. a. Matriculated students are allowed to take up to five courses.

    b. The sedan was designed to carry up to five passengers.

    c. The car seats up to five adults.

    d. John is capable of eating up to five hamburgers at one sitting.

    e. The navy can withstand the loss of up to five carriers without jeopardizing its mission.

Let's look at the pair (4a/5a), utterances of which are naturally understood as asserting that matriculated students may take any number of courses from one to five. This result cannot be gotten by assigning (4a) the readings of (6a) and (6b).

6. a. Matriculated students are allowed to take at least five courses.

    b. Matriculated students are allowed to take exactly five courses.

I assume that [A is allowed to take at least / exactly / up to five Fs] is equivalent to [It is allowed that A take at least / exactly / up to five Fs]. (Here and in what follows, I use 'A' and 'F' as metalinguistic variables.) Since these sentences include numerical quantifiers in clauses to which the operator "it is allowed that" is attached, scope ambiguity is possible. On the wide-scope readings of the quantifiers, (6a)/(6b) are equivalent to (6aw)/(6bw).

6. aw. At least five courses x are such that matriculated students are allowed to take x.

    bw. Exactly five courses x are such that matriculated students are allowed to take x.

These sentences stipulate that the courses that admit matriculated students are at least, or exactly, five in number. However, they don't count the number of courses that may appear on the schedules of matriculated students. Thus, we may put these readings aside.

The narrow-scope readings, (6an)/(6bn) do count the number of courses that may appear on student schedules.

6. an. It is allowed that: matriculated students take (a total of) five or more courses — i.e. (some) scenarios in which matriculated students take (a total of) at least five courses are permitted.

    bn. It is allowed that: matriculated students take (a total of) exactly five courses — i.e. (some) scenarios in which matriculated students take (a total of) exactly five courses are permitted.

Whereas these readings don't entail the corresponding narrow-scope readings of (6c),

6. c. Matriculated students are allowed to take at least one / two / three / four courses.

the reading of (5a) we are looking for does — as does the proposition asserted by utterances of (4a) in contexts in which (5a) can be substituted for (4a). This suggests that the ambiguity theory must posit another meaning.

With this in mind, consider (6d).

6. d. Matriculated students are allowed to take at most five courses.

The relevant reading of (6d) is one that specifies five as the highest number of courses that students are permitted to take. This is not the wide-scope reading, since that reading doesn't count the number of courses on permissible schedules. Nor is it the narrow-scope reading, which is equivalent to (6dn).

6. dn. It is allowed that: matriculated students take (a total of) n courses, for some $n \leq$ five — i.e., (some) scenarios in which matriculated students take (a total of) five or fewer courses are permitted.

Rather, it is a reading equivalent to (6d*).

6. d*. Five is the largest number n such that it is allowed that: matriculated students take (a total of) n courses.

A corresponding reading of (6b) is equivalent to (6b*), which differs from (6bn) in ruling out course schedules with more, or fewer, than five courses.

6. b*. Five is the only number n such that it is allowed that: matriculated students take (a total of) n courses — i.e., five is the only number n such that (some) scenarios in which matriculated students take (a total of) n courses are permitted.

The reading of (5a) we are after is equivalent to (5a*).

5. a*. For any number n up to five, it is allowed that: matriculated students take (a total of) n courses — i.e. one, two, three, four, and five are each numbers n such that (some) scenarios in which matriculated students take (a total of) n courses are permitted.

This reading is distinct from (6b*) in two respects: (i) unlike (6b*), (5a*) doesn't entail that schedules with more than five courses are disallowed, (ii) also unlike (6b*), (5a*) does entail that course schedules with less than five courses are allowed. More generally, the truth conditions of (5a*) differ from those of the any of the readings of (6a), (6b), and (6c).

The crucial argument can now be made. Utterances of (4a) can be used to assert a proposition equivalent to (5a*). We have already seen that this can't be explained by assigning (4a) the readings (6an) or (6bn). The same is obviously true for the *readings of (6a) and (6b). We, therefore, conclude that (4a) is not ambiguous between (6a) and (6b). If the phrase ⌈n Fs⌉ is ambiguous, it must be at least three ways ambiguous — between ⌈at least n Fs⌉, ⌈exactly n Fs⌉, and ⌈up to n Fs⌉.

Even that's not all. Utterances of (7a) would typically assert the proposition expressed by (7b) — which has truth conditions, (7c), permitting three, four, and five course loads, while prohibiting one or two course loads.

7. a. Matriculated students are required to take *three courses*, and allowed to take *five courses*.

    b. Matriculated students are required to take *at least three courses* and allowed to take *up to five courses*.

    c. No scenarios in which matriculated students take fewer than three courses are permitted, while (some) scenarios in which they take (a total of) three, four, or five courses are permitted.

How is this possible? We saw that one who utters (5a) — which corresponds to the second conjunct of (7b) — often asserts that matriculated students are allowed to take *any number of courses from one to five*. This might lead one to think that ⌈A takes up to n courses⌉ is true iff the total number of courses taken by the individual designated by A is less than or equal to the number designated by n. But if that were so, the second conjunct of (7b) would permit (some) one-course, and (some) two-course loads – thereby contradicting the first conjunct of (7b). Since (7b) isn't contradictory, ⌈up to n Fs⌉ doesn't mean what we first imagined.

Instead, its meaning is equivalent to that of ⌈from k up to n Fs⌉, where k designates a contextually supplied lower bound (with a default setting of 1, unless otherwise indicated). When (7a,b) is uttered, the first conjunct sets the lower bound at three, giving us the non-contradictory proposition asserted. Since the phrase ⌈up to n Fs⌉ is context sensitive, and since the ambiguity theory must posit its meaning as one of the readings of ⌈n Fs⌈, the theory must treat ⌈n Fs⌈ as *both* ambiguous and context sensitive. However, this is overkill. Once we have context sensitivity, ambiguity can be eliminated.

The Contributions of Meaning and Conversational Maxims to Assertion

Let's return to instances of (3) — ⌈I have n Fs⌉. As in our other examples, the position occupied by the numerical quantifier can be syntactically expanded in various ways: ⌈at least n Fs⌉, ⌈exactly n Fs⌉, ⌈up to n Fs⌉, ⌈as many as n Fs⌉, ⌈up to n but more than m Fs⌉, and so on. Call the contents of these completions *possible pragmatic enrichments* of the semantic content of the quantifier. The semantic content of (3) is free of any such completion, and so is nonspecific about how the constituent [n Fs] should be modified. Nevertheless, it plays an important role in constraining what is asserted. What is asserted is required to be an obvious and relevant pragmatic enrichment of the semantic content of the sentence uttered.[4] When this content is a complete, truth-evaluable proposition, and hence a candidate for assertion, we let the proposition itself count as one of its own possible enrichments. In cases like (3), in which the semantic content is not truth-evaluable, non-vacuous enrichment is required in order for anything to be asserted. Either way, the semantic content of a sentence can be thought of as a set of conditions that constrains what is asserted by utterances of it. When these constraints fall short of determining a complete, truth-evaluable proposition, pragmatic enrichment is required. When they do determine a complete proposition, enrichment is optional.[5] When the option is taken, the proposition semantically expressed by a sentence (in a context) itself counts as asserted only when it is an obvious and relevant consequence of the enriched proposition that it is the speaker's primary intention to assert.[6]

Pragmatic enrichments are influenced by a variety of factors, including the direction and purpose of the conversation, remarks previously made, salient information about the context, background assumptions shared by speakers and hearers, and Gricean maxims. In addition to generating conversational implicatures, over and above what is asserted, the maxims help determine what an utterance asserts by narrowing down the class of possible enrichments to those that most effectively advance the conversation. When several enrichments are feasible, the maxims dictate

---

[4] I assume that such enrichments are always enrichments of the semantic contents of one or more of the constituents of the sentence. See, my "Naming and Asserting," in Z. Szabo, ed., *Semantics vs. Pragmatics* (Oxford: Clarendon Press) 2005, and "The Gap Between Meaning and Assertion," in my *Philosophical Essays, Volume I* (Princeton and Oxford: Princeton University Press), 2009.

[5] Cases of obligatory enrichment are discussed in (i) "Naming and Asserting," where it is noted that the semantic contents of sentences containing possessive noun phrases only weakly constrain, without determining, the asserted relationship between the denotation of the possessor NP and the denotation of the possessed NP, and (ii) "The Gap Between Meaning and Assertion," where it is argued that some descriptions require contextually supplied temporal information. Cases of optional enrichment involving names, definite descriptions, and attitude ascriptions are also discussed in my "Why Incomplete Descriptions do not Defeat Russell's Theory of Descriptions," *Teorema*, Vol. XXIV, No. 3, 2005, 7-30.

[6] Sometimes optional enrichment — though not required to obtain a complete proposition — is needed to make the speaker's remark relevant and informative. Two instructive examples are given by Robyn Carston in "Implicature, Explicature, and Truth-Theoretic Semantics," in Ruth Kempson, ed., *Mental Representation: The Interface Between Language and Reality*, (Cambridge: Cambridge University Press) 1988. They are: 'The park is some distance from where I live', and 'It will take us some time to get there'. The distinction between cases in which enrichment is required to secure a complete proposition, and those in which it is optional, parallels Kent Bach's distinction between *conversational implicitures* that complete semantically underdetermined sentences and those that merely expand propositions that are semantically expressed. See Bach "Conversational Impliciture," *Mind and Language* 9, 124-62, 1994, and, "You don't say?," *Synthese*, 127, 11-31, 2001.

that one select the strongest, relevant proposition among them for which one has adequate evidence. In this way, the maxims play a role in determining what is asserted, and thereby contribute to the truth conditions of utterances.

Our earlier examples illustrate this. In the case of my utterance of (1) — 'I have two children' — the precise number of my children is relevant. Since I would violate the maxim of quantity by saying too little, if I were to assert only that I had at least two children, the stronger enrichment, that I have exactly two, is selected. In the case of (2) — when I say, 'I have two beers' in response to your request to have a have a quick drink with me before leaving — it is only relevant whether I have at least two beers. Since, I would be giving extraneous information, if I were to assert that I have exactly two, the conceptually stronger — but conversationally irrelevant — pragmatic enrichment is rejected, and the weaker enrichment is selected in its place.

Next consider (4a) — 'Matriculated students are allowed to take five courses'. Here, the possible enrichment 'at least five courses' would result in an assertion that was silent on the permissibility of the most interesting schedules — those involving one, two, three, or four courses — while bizarrely pronouncing schedules with many more courses than students could possibly take — as permissible. The possible enrichment 'exactly five courses' isn't much better. To learn that matriculated students are allowed to take exactly five courses is to learn that schedules with five courses are permitted — with either no indication of whether schedules with any other number are permitted (the narrow-scope reading), or the rather strange implication that schedules with either more, or fewer, courses are impermissible (the *interpretation). Although there may be situations in which the former, very weak assertion, or the latter, unusually strong one, is what is wanted, such situations are well outside the norm, and don't readily spring to mind.

By contrast, when the enrichment is 'up to five courses', the resulting proposition — understood as allowing student schedules of one, two, three, four, and five courses — is strong, natural, and relevantly informative. Thus, adherence to the Gricean maxims leads us to expect what we, in fact, find — namely that utterances of (4a) are naturally understood as making assertions equivalent to (5a*). For the same reason, it is no mystery why, when a truncated version of (4a) occurs as the second conjunct of (7a) — 'Matriculated students are required to take three courses, and allowed to take five courses' — the contribution of that conjunct to the proposition asserted is not the proposition that would often be asserted if (4a) were uttered on its own. If that proposition were its contribution, then the proposition asserted by uttering the conjunction would violate the Gricean maxim against saying what one knows to be false. Thus, a different pragmatic enrichment is selected which — in conformity with the maxims — yields the strongest, most informative and relevant statement for which the speaker has sufficient evidence. In this way, the theory accommodates our examples.

In all these cases, semantic content is incomplete, and conversational maxims help determine contextually complete assertions. These cases contrast with classical conversational implicatures. In classical cases, one says or asserts one thing, and, as a result, implicates something else that is not part of what one asserts. In Grice's famous example, a professor writes a recommendation for a job candidate in philosophy: "Dear Sir, Mr. X's command of English is excellent, and his attendance in class has been regular. Sincerely ..." In so writing, the professor implicates, but does not assert, that the student is no good at philosophy. Here, no completion of the semantic content of the sentence used is needed to arrive at a complete proposition, and no elaboration of that content by expansion of its constituents could possibly yield the implicature. As a result, the implicated proposition is not asserted, but merely suggested by what is.

The Nature of Our Theories

I started by considering ⌈I have n Fs⌉. Speakers who understand these sentences are reasonably reliable judges about what *they*, and other speakers, mean and assert by utterances of them in various situations. However, they don't have reliable intuitions about what these sentences mean. They don't know whether ⌈I have n Fs⌉ means the same as ⌈I have at least n Fs⌉, ⌈I have exactly n Fs⌉, or ⌈I have up to n Fs⌉. They don't know whether it means the same as one of these three, is ambiguous between them, or whether it means something else. They certainly don't know that the meaning of ⌈I have n Fs⌉ constrains what it is used to assert, without fully determining a truth-evaluable proposition. Like many correct statements about linguistic meaning, this is a theoretical truth to which the practical ability to speak and understand the language gives one no privileged access.

For the same reason, speakers are often not able to separate out, from the total information carried by a particular utterance, the information contributed by the conventional meaning of the sentence uttered, and distinguish it from that which is added by taking conversational maxims and other contextual factors into account. It is obvious that speakers don't consciously go through Gricean reasoning in all relevant cases. Nor should we jump to the conclusion that they do so unconsciously. There are, of course, complex cognitive processes at work when we produce and interpret utterances. However, it is a mistake to suppose that in constructing semantic and pragmatic theories, we are making substantial psychological claims about them. Instead, we are constructing an idealized, normative model that gives a rational reconstruction of our ability to identify what is asserted and conveyed by an utterance. As input, the model takes a sentence uttered, a representation of the context of utterance, and the semantic content assigned to the sentence by our semantic theory. From this, idealized speaker-hearers in the model abstract information using conversational maxims, plus propositions representing what they take to be common conversational knowledge. Conclusions about what has been asserted, implied, and suggested are inferred. The model is validated by showing that these conclusions match those of real speakers.

The relationship between meaning and implicature falls out of this picture. When we show that some part of the information conveyed by an utterance results from the application of conversational maxims — as opposed to the meaning of the sentence uttered — we show that such information is rationally extractable from the utterance, together with a defensible conception of meaning, *even if real, non-idealized speakers don't follow this route either consciously or unconsciously.* The needed conception of linguistic meaning is minimalist. Meaning is a kind of least common denominator. *It is information associated with sentences and other expressions that must be mastered by a rational agent — over and above the agent's ability to reason intelligently, and engage in cooperative linguistic behavior — in order to be able to communicate with other members of the linguistic community.* The point is *not* heuristic, but constitutive. *This is what meaning is.* If this conception is correct, then no matter what idiosyncratic psychological processes we actually use to interpret utterances, what our sentences mean — and what part of that which is asserted and conveyed by an utterance is due to meaning — is a matter of rational reconstruction, not cognitive psychology.

Moravcsik and the Contents of Consciousness[1]

TIMOTHY SCHROEDER

There is a doctrine in the theory of consciousness known as *representationalism*, or *intentionalism*. According to this doctrine, what it feels like to be in a particular state of consciousness — the qualitative character of that state — is *identical* to the content of some mental representation(s). For instance, the state of consciousness I am enjoying just now as I see a pattern of sunlight and shadow falling on my wall is, in part, a state of consciousness that presents to me a patch of light grey shadow just there, straight ahead of me and just above eye-level. According to representationalism, what it is like to be in this very specific state of consciousness is for it to seem to me that there is a patch of light grey shadow *there*, straight ahead of me and just above eye-level. And for it to seem so to me is just for that to be the content of one of my mental representations.[2]

Representationalism gives a central role to content when explaining consciousness. What content *is*, though, is contested. For every theory of content on offer, there can be generated a corresponding representationalist theory of consciousness. In a series of publications, Julius Moravcsik has defended a novel theory of meaning that a representationalist can take as a theory of the content of consciousness.[3] In this paper, I investigate the possibility of the representationalist doing just this. Is this a hostile co-optation of Moravcsik's theory of meaning? Is it a friendly extension of Moravcsik's theory to a new domain? Or something more equivocal? This particular question I leave to one side. But there are a number of interesting consequences of investigating the intersection of representationalism and his theory of meaning in any case, as I hope to show in what follows.

1 Representationalism

I begin by saying more about representationalism.

The doctrine I have in mind is the strongest form of the various doctrines that are gathered under the heading of 'representationalism' or 'intentionalism' in theorizing

---

[1]Thanks to both John Woods and Julius Moravcsik for the opportunity to contribute this essay. Thanks are also owed to Ben Caplan, with whom I have worked out a number of related ideas.

[2]Michael Tye is perhaps the most active contemporary representationalist, but others have also defended the view, or closely related views. See, e.g., Dennett (1991), Dretske (1995), Harman (1990), Lycan (1987), Tye (1995).

[3]Moravcsik (1990; 1998).

about consciousness. According to the doctrine I have in mind, the qualitative character of a state of consciousness is a content of consciousness, and this content is strictly *identical* to the content of some mental representation or representations. What it feels like to see a red quilt, feel a kiss on one's forehead, or taste a ripe chokecherry is that P, that Q, that R for various contents of consciousness P, Q, and R, and these contents are identical to the contents of particular mental representations.

Weaker doctrines in the neighbourhood hold that the qualitative character of consciousness is *determined* by the contents of particular mental representations, or that the qualitative character of consciousness *supervenes* upon the contents of particular mental representations, for instance. Other weakenings of the doctrine allow that the details of the functional role played by a mental representation can make a difference to the details of the qualitative character of consciousness, or allow that representationalism accounts for some but not all of the kinds of states of consciousness that exist; and so on. But the doctrine I have in mind accepts no such weakenings.

Representationalism of the sort that interests me accepts no weakenings because its goal is not merely to give necessary and sufficient materialistic conditions for the existence of particular states of consciousness.[4] Its goal is to *explain* how it is that consciousness arises from a materialistic world.[5] To do so, giving necessary and sufficient conditions is a start, but it is far from the end. The end is to give necessary and sufficient conditions such that it is *clear* — clear from the armchair — why satisfying those conditions, and only those conditions, would generate the particular states of consciousness that they do.

Representationalism requires a number of supporting theses for its truth, and the most prominent of these should be itemized, explained, and perhaps given enough of a defence to justify a minimum of interest in the doctrine. Three supporting theses stand out.

(1) Representationalism requires the existence of mental representations. There has been a substantial movement since at least the beginnings of functionalism in the philosophy of mind to hold that there are entirely materialistic mental representations, and to hold that the mental representations posited by philosophers are also posited by branches of psychology (especially cognitive psychology), neuroscience (especially cognitive neuroscience), computer science (especially artificial intelligence), and linguistics (especially syntax and semantics).[6] According to this movement, mental representations are mental particulars — and in animals like us, neural particulars as well – each having its own causal role. Mental representations can be conscious or unconscious, available to the whole mental economy (e.g., those used in occurrent thought) or restricted to some special sub-personal realm within

---

[4]The assumption of the representationalist is that it will be relatively easy to give a materialistic theory of mental representation.
[5]I.e., to bridge Levine's (1983) "explanatory gap."
[6]See, e.g., Fodor (1975).

that economy (e.g., those that serve to prepare grammatical sentences for speech). They are also generally thought to be structured: a mental representation that A is to the left of B is thought to employ the distinct capacities to represent A, to represent B, and to represent one thing's being to the left of another. All this is sufficiently familiar that I will not belabour it; these reminders will have touched upon everything needed later. Arguments in defence of these various claims have been made at length elsewhere; I will presuppose that some of them at least are successful, and that mental representations exist in something like this form.

(2) Representationalism requires (approximately) that every representation that P within a subject makes a difference to that subject's consciousness – a difference that can be well characterized as making the conscious subject feel (experience, consciously think...) that P. The doctrine is threatened by any case in which it appears that there is a mental representation that P without that representation making a difference to consciousness. An obvious candidate is that of one's standing beliefs and desires. A belief that London is vibrant, for instance, involves a mental representation that London is vibrant. I have the mental representation even when I am not actively thinking that London is vibrant, it seems, for it is the basis of my disposition to answer "yes" if someone asks "do you find London a vibrant city?" Yet, when I am not actively thinking that London is vibrant, it does not seem that my representation that London is vibrant is making any difference at all to my consciousness. Similar points could be made about my representation that my dad is healthy, a representation that sets the content of my desire that my dad be healthy. It seems that, when I am not conscious of this desire, the representation of my dad's health makes no difference to what it feels like to be me.

In response, the representationalist has various strategies available. Well-known representationalists have taken the view that representationalism holds only of certain mental representations — those with nonconceptual contents.[7] Those mental representations with conceptual contents — beliefs, desires, and other propositional attitudes — do not make a difference to consciousness.

There are good reasons to be dissatisfied with this approach, however. First, it would appear to vitiate the goal of explaining consciousness, a goal that is the whole point of the very strong doctrine I am calling 'representationalism'. The representationalist typically begins to explain consciousness through suggesting that there is nothing more to experiencing the world than taking it to be some way or other, i.e., representing it to be some way or other. Or the representationalist holds that consciousness of the world is simply awareness of it, and awareness is simply representation. To be parts of successful explanations, these opening explanatory gambits cannot make use of an equivocal notion of representation, nor can they make use of an arbitrary notion of representation. No successful explanation can rely on equivocally or arbitrarily deployed notions, after all. But once the representationalist introduces two sorts of representations — the conceptual (those that make a difference to consciousness) and the non-conceptual (those that

---

[7]E.g., Dretske (1995), Tye (1995).

do not) — the representationalist has invited charges of equivocation or arbitrariness. Either the representationalist has conceded that there is a sense in which representations make no difference to consciousness (in which case, why concede that non-conceptual representations are of a sort that make a difference to consciousness?), or the representationalist has conceded that there is an arbitrary distinction between kinds of representation (Why does the involvement of concepts bar a representation from making a difference to consciousness?). Neither horn of this dilemma is inviting, and there is a danger of being impaled on both at once.

The second reason to be dissatisfied with any attempt to write off beliefs, desires, and the like as irrelevant to consciousness is that it just seems a mistake, phenomenologically speaking. Thinking need not use verbal or visual (or any other sort of) imagery in order to make a difference to consciousness: I can be consciously thinking of something before I can put into words or images what it is that I am thinking about, it seems to me. I will have more to say about this later. For now, I hope it will suffice to say that this view is not wholly idiosyncratic: a number of contemporary philosophers of mind (not, for the most part, representationalists — but that does not matter for the purposes of theory-building) have recently embraced the idea that occurrent thought has a qualitative character such that distinct thoughts have distinct qualitative characters, and these philosophers have likewise held that these qualitative characters do not reduce to sensory experience or imagery.[8]

Given the reasons that there are for the representationalist to hold that all mental representations — conceptual or not — make a difference to consciousness, something different needs to be done with the problem cases. I represent London to be vibrant, but ordinarily this representation makes no difference to my consciousness. How can this be? One option representationalists have not much explored is simply to be dispositionalists about these attitudes, and so about these mental representations. My unconscious belief need not be thought of as an unconscious but occurrently tokened mental representation that London is vibrant. It can instead be thought of as a disposition to occurrently token such a mental representation under prompting. My unconscious belief, then, is not something that involves a representation that London is vibrant at the moment at which it is unconscious. It is only when the belief is brought to consciousness that there is a concrete mental representation that London is vibrant — and this is just when the idea that London is vibrant suffuses my consciousness. Notice that the representationalist can also allow for borderline cases: in a borderline case of the tokening of a given representation, there will be a borderline case of the representation making a difference to consciousness — this might do well at handling certain cases of perception at the edge of awareness, ideas lurking at "the back of one's thoughts" and the like. The strategy under consideration fares well against the worries just raised in the two previous paragraphs, and it also fits neatly with some of the current ideas we see in neuroscience about representation, on which the tokening of

---

[8] E.g., Horgan and Tienson (2002); Siewert (1998).

a representation requires elevated (and so necessarily temporary) activity in some relevant neural structure. If my unconscious belief that London is vibrant were merely a disposition to form this representation, then that would be compatible with the view that my brain need not be continuously active (or active at all) in order to maintain my belief that London is vibrant.

So far, transiently unconscious mental representations have been the focus of concern. But one might also object that there are permanently unconscious mental representations that do not make a difference to consciousness. For instance, there are representations in primary visual cortex that do not seem to make a difference to consciousness, and likewise there are representations of the syntactic structure of the sentences we see and hear that are not among the contents of consciousness either (much to the sorrow of professional linguists). If every mental representation makes a difference to consciousness, and these are mental representations, why do they not (or so it seems) make any difference to what it is like to be me?

The conventional answer of the representationalist here is more compelling. The representationalist generally holds that, for the content of a mental representation to be one of the contents of consciousness, it is necessary either that the mental representation be having widely distributed downstream effects on the processing of other representations, or that it at least be poised or available for the generation of these effects.[9] The rationale for requiring these widely distributed effects — "fame in the brain" as Dennett[10] puts it — is that no state of consciousness is "naked," as it were. Every state of consciousness is some person's state of consciousness (or, if we are not to count dogs, owls, and the like as persons for this purpose, then some *intelligence's* state of consciousness). And for a state of consciousness to belong to a person — and not merely to reside within a person, the way one brain might be lodged between the lobes of another within a single skull — it is necessary that the mental representation that makes up one state of consciousness is functionally integrated into a complete psychology. Since there are good *a priori* credentials to the thought that every state of consciousness is some person's state of consciousness, this restriction is not arbitrary and does not threaten to vitiate the explanatory hopes of representationalism.

(3) Representationalism also requires that every feature within a subject's consciousness be some content of consciousness that might plausibly be the content of some representation. There have been a number of challenges here, and a number of able responses.

Christopher Peacocke was among the first to argue that there are problems here.[11] When we experience two trees of the same height, one nearby and one far away, we experience them as being of the same height, and yet we also see one (the nearby tree) as "bigger" in some sense. Peacocke pointed out the problem this seems to raise for representationalism long before the doctrine itself was philo-

---

[9]This is the view of Dennett (1991), Dretske (1995), and Tye (1995), for instance.
[10]Dennett (1991).
[11]Peacocke (1983).

sophically popular. The fact that we experience them as being of the same height corresponds to our representing them as having the same height, Peacocke allowed. But the fact that we experience the trees as different in some size-like way does not correspond to our representations of their size. Here, representationalists such as Michael Tye have retorted that we represent the nearby tree as occluding more of the world behind it, and of occupying a larger perceiver-relative visual angle — and this is just how it looks.[12]

Even if this response is successful, there are many other arguments that have been launched to show that the variety of consciousness exceeds the expressive capacities of representations. I do not intend to give a full survey of all the arguments that have been made and the best responses to them. I hope it will suffice to raise one particularly salient pair of objections, and show that it is not beyond hoping that representationalism has the resources to deal with them.

Pain and the experience of orgasm are two states of consciousness that have received significant discussion as apparent counter-examples to representationalism.[13] Pain has a sensory component (nociception) that is credibly representational, but it also has a subjective awfulness that does not appear to be necessitated by, much less identical to, anything as banal as a representation of tissue damage. Likewise, the experience of orgasm seems to have a sensory component that is credibly representational, but also a subjective wonderfulness that appears to go beyond representational contents featuring stroking, spasmodic contraction, and the like.

Michael Tye has made some moves in this debate,[14] but he has perhaps not gone as far as one should to meet the challenge, and here I propose my own solution to this problem.[15] Pleasure and displeasure should themselves be thought of as sensory states within a sense modality. Feelings of hedonic tone, as it can be called, run from intense pleasure, through neutrality, to intense displeasure along a continuum. These feelings represent net change in intrinsic desire satisfaction. In a word, they represent how much better or worse things are going just now. In crude outline, the case for this view is easily sketched. First, pleasure and displeasure tend to correlate well with change in apparent net desire satisfaction: getting more of what one wants tends to please, while getting less of what one wants tends to displease. Second, we treat pleasure and displeasure as if they had contents that might misrepresent the world in just the required ways: some pleasure is inappropriate in virtue of the world not actually going well for us (e.g., feeling everything is fine — when it clearly isn't — simply because one is drunk), and some displeasure is inappropriate in virtue of the world not actually going badly for us (e.g., feeling everything is terrible — when it clearly isn't — simply because one is depressed). And third, the neuroscience of pleasure and desire suggests that changes in desire satisfaction are a standard cause of changes in

---

[12]Tye (1995).
[13]E.g., Block (1996).
[14]E.g., Tye (1996).
[15]For a fuller treatment, see Schroeder (2004), chapter 3.

hedonic tone. If all of this is right, then pleasure and displeasure do have credible representational contents. The distinctive content of pain that is its awfulness is that things are going awfully: the awfulness of the feeling is just the feeling that things are going awfully. Likewise, the distinctive content of the feeling of orgasm that is its wonderful quality is that things are going wonderfully: the wonderful quality of the feeling is just the feeling that things are going wonderfully.

These brief remarks are far from sufficient to convince the reader that every variation in qualitative character will have a corresponding variation in representational content, but I hope that these particular examples have at least begun to make the case that the representationalist is not without resources here. And this is where I will leave the matter.

At this point, I hope that the doctrine of representationalism is reasonably clear, and at least passably credible in the eyes of the reader. It is time to turn to the point at which the theory meets Moravcsik's theory of meaning.

2 Representationalism and Content

What theory of content is best suited to the representationalist's purpose? There are various theories on offer; does it even matter which one the representationalist prefers? It matters quite a bit, as it turns out. For the representationalist holds that the contents of one's mental representations (those that are available to influence, or actually influencing, downstream cognitive processing) are identical to the contents of one's consciousness. And from this it follows that whatever access we have to our own consciousnesses we also have to the content of mental representations. We can, in short, *introspect the nature of mental content*, if representationalism is correct. Not infallibly, if introspection is less than infallible. But we can introspect the nature of mental content as well as we can introspect the experience of seeing light grey shadows on a white wall, and so on, and this is — so it seems — quite an excellent level of introspective access. So representationalists must limit their choice of theories of content to those theories compatible with phenomenology.

According to Julius Moravcsik, there are actually three levels of content (I interpret Moravcsik's 'meaning' as equivalent to 'content' as understood by the typical representationalist). These are what can be called the Millian level of content, the Fregean level of content, and the Moravcsikian level of content. How well is each suited to being the content of consciousness?

The Millian level of content is that brought back to the attention of philosophers of language by Kripke, Putnam, and others. At this level of content, representing that Vancouver is pretty is the same thing as representing that Vancouver est belle, for just the same objects and relations are involved, and there is no change in the condition required of the world for the representation to be true. Likewise, if I am in Palo Alto, then at this level of content the representation that Tim is in Palo Alto has the same content as the representation that I am here.

Most representationalists work, by default, with the idea that the Millian level of content is the level relevant to representationalism. But, as I have argued with

Ben Caplan, this cannot be correct.[16]

To see the problem that Millian contents pose for representationalism, consider a few mental representations.

1. A representation that there is a ringing bell behind me.

2. A representation that there is a light flickering now.

3. A representation that Hesperus is Phosphorus.

Each of these representations has a Millian content that does not respect the phenomenology of the state of consciousness realized (according to the representationalist) by its tokening.

Begin with (1). When I mentally represent that there is a ringing bell behind me, how am I presented to myself by this representation in consciousness? Three answers seem available, when one is focused on the Millian level of content.

To begin, one might say that I am not presented at all by the mental representation: the mental representation is just of a ringing bell in the behind direction. This seems wrong, however. Phenomenologically, it seems clear that the bell is located *behind*, and as a location *behind* requires something with a front for the bell to be behind. And further, phenomenologically, it seems clear that the bell is located behind *me*. The bell is not behind just any object or person, according to my state of consciousness, but behind one particular person: me. (If the bell were behind Nora but in front of me, I would be having an illusory experience — misrepresenting.) So I must be presented by the mental representation that there is a bell ringing behind me.

But now, how am I presented? At the Millian level of content, perhaps I am presented as an individual. One can say that I represent that there is a ringing bell behind Tim. If Nora were to have heard the bell behind her, then she would have represented that there is a ringing bell behind Nora — a different particular individual. But this is where a new problem arises. For there is no *phenomenological* reason to believe that my identity as Tim gives me one experience of the bell ringing behind me, while Nora's distinct identity gives her a qualitatively different experience. On the contrary, if we are similar enough in our ears and brains, then Nora and I should have exactly the same qualitative state of consciousness when we hear a bell ringing behind us. The objection here can be presented this way also: imagine identical twins Terry and Tracy who have lost their memories of which is Terry and which is Tracy. The twins can hardly answer this question by introspection of their auditory experiences, with Terry hearing some events as happening behind Terry, not Tracy, while Tracy hears some events as happening behind Tracy, not Terry. This is not what the content of consciousness is like.

Finishing off, consider the possibility that I am presented via some Russellian device of definite description. Perhaps my mental representation is that there is

---

[16]Caplan and Schroeder (2007).

a ringing bell behind the man who is typing at a laptop computer just now, or something of this sort. But again it is clear that this will not do. First, there is no plausible description through which each experience of mine represents me. And second, even if we imagine some such description, there is the danger that it will have too many satisfiers, and then my experiences will count as veridical if there is a ringing bell behind some *other* person satisfying my description, which is certainly not what makes an experience veridical! (And how can this possibility be blocked, except by tying the description to particulars, returning us to the previous problem?) My experience specifies that the ringing bell is behind *me*, not behind just any man satisfying some description that I satisfy.

Continuing on with (2), one can see exactly the same problems arising for time that arose for location. We experience things as happening *now*, a specific time, because states of consciousness put constraints on when events could have happened: a candle I experience as flickering now must now be flickering (not have flickered or be about to) if my experience is to be veridical. So time must be represented in some way in the content of consciousness. The representation of each moment — now — cannot be as an individual, however, or else it would be possible to determine through introspection that now is T1 or T2 for some given particular moment in time. And again, time cannot be represented through a description of the moment in time, for any description not tied to particulars will be satisfiable by more than one moment in time, and yet my consciousness of a flickering light requires that the light flicker *now*, and not just at some moment that is descriptively exactly similar to now.

Looking at (3) a slightly different problem arises, for (3) deals with a conscious thought rather than with a sense experience. But in spite of this difference, (3) poses problems that are, by now, becoming familiar just the same. The conscious thought that Hesperus is Phosphorus is phenomenologically different from the conscious thought one would most naturally record as 'Hesperus is Hesperus', yet the Millian content of these two thoughts is the same. Again, the Millian level of content is distinct from the level making up consciousness.

Given the overwhelming evidence, representationalism should reject the idea that the relevant content of mental representations — relevant to consciousness — is the Millian level.

What about the Fregean level of content? The Fregean level of content is, of course, that articulated by Frege in "On Sense and Reference" under the heading of 'sense' or *Sinn*. It is hard to know exactly what Frege took sense to be: a mode of presentation for a referent, yes, but what exactly is a mode of presentation? Something descriptive? Sometimes, so it seems, but not clearly in every case.

However we understand the details of Frege's notion of sense, the level of content that we might draw from it obviously fares better with (3). The thought that Hesperus is Phosphorus and the thought that Hesperus is Hesperus have distinct contents at the Fregean level, after all, just as the thoughts have different qualitative characters when one thinks them.

Unfortunately, the Fregean level of content does not do any better than the Millian level with respect to (1) and (2). Take (1) first. Because Fregean sense *determines* reference, the Fregean content of a mental representation that a bell is ringing behind me must be such as to uniquely determine the person, Tim, behind whom the bell is ringing. But phenomenologically, this definiteness is lacking in consciousness. My experience of a bell ringing behind me does not suffice to determine that I, Tim, exist. It suffices to determine that someone exists, of course, and I *am* that someone, but no matter how I introspect my experience of the bell ringing behind me I do not find anything sufficient to determine that it is Tim rather than his identical twin, or some other person, having the experience. Anyone could have an experience qualitatively identical to mine, it seems. Returning to the twins Terry and Tracy: nothing about the introspectible quality of Terry's experience of a bell ringing behind her determines that it is Terry, and not Tracy, having the experience.

Time is no better than location for the Fregean level of content, and so (2) is handled no better than (1). I see the light flickering at T1, but nothing introsectible determines that it is at T1 that I see the light flickering: I might be seeing the light at any time at all, so far as the qualitative character of my consciousness is concerned.

The Moravcsikian level of content is perhaps less familiar, and could use an extended description before its evaluation here. What is this level of content? It is a level of "explanatory schemes," according to Moravcsik. A minimum of two and a maximum of four sorts of explanatory schemes are part of the Moravcsikian content of each element in the lexicon. These are the four factors of Moravcsikian content:

> i. The constitutive factor — that is, the necessary link between the given word and a domain within which the denotation ranges must be located.
>
> ii. The structural factor. This consists of necessary principles of individuation and persistence, if any, and those necessary distinguishing properties that are required by at least individuation and necessary functional requirements.
>
> iii. The agential factor. This obviously does not apply to all items; for instance, abstract entities do not have necessary causal powers attached to them. This factor includes those necessary causal properties of items within the denotation range that partially determine origin, causal powers involved in producing successors (e.g., modes of procreation) and those causal powers that are necessarily linked to how items in the denotations should function.
>
> iv. The functional factor. This includes those functional properties that are necessarily parts of the meaning of the word; for example, that under normal conditions a knife functions to cut, and a

cleaning establishment to clean.

(Moravcsik 1998, 97).

Though the theory is framed as a theory of linguistic content, it is not hard to see how to transpose it into a theory of the content of mental representations. Each capacity to represent some item in the "mental lexicon" — each concept, in other words — will have at least the first two of these factors as its Moravcsikian content, and many concepts will have all four factors. These factors are clusters of features, modeled on Aristotle's four causes (four types of explanation, really — hence their relevance to a level of content that forms an explanatory scheme).

An example will help to make things clear. Following Moravcsik's account, the third level of content for the concept BIRD would include (i) it is a spatially extended thing; (ii) it is a biological organism; (iii) it is a natural entity with its own mode of procreation; (iv) its functions are performed by flying, moving around on the ground, and so on (Moravcsik 1998, 112).

If Moravcsikian content were the level of content that is identical to the content of consciousness, then it would be possible to introspect and find it there. So, following the example, consider the thought that geese are birds. Is anything like Moravcsikian content for the concept BIRD part of one's consciousness when one thinks this thought?

Superficial introspection might suggest that the answer is 'no'. In my own case, auditory imagery dominates when I think the thought that geese are birds. It would be easy to jump to the conclusion that this auditory imagery is all that makes up my consciousness when I think this thought. If I would leap to this conclusion, I would have to conclude that Moravcsikian content is irrelevant to consciousness: since Moravcsikian content for words does not include the sounds of the words, its counterpart content for mental representations cannot be held to include the auditory image of the sounds used to express the concept.

Superficial introspection might also suggest that the answer is 'yes'. Sometimes when I introspect I find I also have visual imagery of geese. On these occasions, thinking the thought that geese are birds gives me visual imagery that makes it clear that they are birds, and this visual imagery presents (i) a spatially extended (ii) biological organism (iv) flying in formation for migration. The visual image is also lacking in certain details — the texture of the feathers, the sound of the geese, their location, the terrain over which they are flying — that would not feature in any part of the Moravcsikian content of the thought that geese are birds. So the visual image substantially corresponds to the Moravcsikian content of the thought, at least in gross outline.

What is wrong with both superficial approaches to introspection is that they focus on sensory imagery of one sort or another rather than on the thought itself. Sometimes thoughts are accompanied by sensory images, and sometimes these images present things that are linked to the Moravcsikian content of the thought, while other times they do not. But thoughts are one thing, and sensory images we might or might not entertain at the same time are something else.[17] The contribution that a thought makes to consciousness should not be confused with the contribution that sensory images caused by the thought might make.

More careful introspection must separate conscious thoughts from the sensory images that can be linked to such thoughts. When I force myself to hold the thought that geese are birds firmly in mind *without* relying on auditory imagery, *without* generating visual imagery, I find myself in a distinctive state of consciousness. What is *it* like? Because it is not in any way a sensory state of consciousness, it cannot be described in sensory terms. It is not as though I am looking at anything or listening to anything. It is most simply described as being in that state of consciousness in which it is vivid to me that geese are birds.

To tease out the subtle features of this state of consciousness, ask yourself a certain sort of question. Would this state of consciousness be different if...? If you were thinking that tomorrow is a holiday? Surely the answer here is 'yes'. Thinking that geese are animals? Again, it seems clear that the answer is 'yes'. The state of consciousness in which one is thinking that geese are birds is a distinctive state, different from the state of consciousness enjoyed when one thinks other thoughts. But now, what about this: would this state of consciousness be different if you thought that geese were, like penguins, naturally incapable of flight? Would it be different if you thought that geese were machines, and not biological organisms at all? Would it be different if you thought that geese were temporally extended events rather than spatially extended objects? If your answers here incline to 'yes', then it seems that your state of consciousness when you think the thought that geese are birds is one that has features sensitive to the Moravcsikian level of content.

Introspection at this level of subtlety is not so reliable that I am confident of my own answers. But so far as I can tell, my conscious thoughts *are* sensitive to a number of the considerations at stake here. Moravcsik's factor (i) distinguishes between concepts for things that are grasped as spatial entities and things that are grasped as temporal entities. If my consciousness when thinking the thought that geese are birds is sensitive to factor (i), then it would be different if I took geese to be temporal sequences of time-slices, say. And this seems right. Insofar as I can tell, my commitment to geese as spatial objects rather than temporal processes is introspectible in the thought that geese are birds. Moravcsik's factor (ii) sets minimal principles of individuation one must use to have a concept (to have mastery of a word, in the original formulation), and Moravcsik's example suggests principles such as *birds are biological organisms* as being at the appropriate level of generality. (We might grasp the concept BIRD while thinking that the birds include everything with wings, and simply be making a mistake about insects and bats. But if we think a thought that we are inclined to express with sentences like 'birds are a kind of furniture made from metal' then we do not grasp the concept at all.) Again, I am inclined to think that introspection reveals this in

---

[17]But see Prinz (2002) for an argument to the contrary.

my thought that geese are birds: it is introspectible that I am not thinking about metal furniture when I think such a thought, even though the auditory image of the thought is an auditory image that might, for all of *its* intrinsic properties, be an image of a thought meaning that metal furniture is nice on patios. Still, the thought is clearly a thought of living things. What about factor (iv), the factor that takes into account what would count as well-functioning or malfunctioning for a thing? Here my introspection lines up less well with Moravcsikian content: I do not have the feeling that my conscious thought would be different in any way if geese were, like rheas, naturally flightless birds. Thinking that geese are birds and that rheas are birds does not seem, to me at any rate, to be thinking thoughts that include in themselves anything about the natural flightedness or flightlessness of the creatures in question.

Grant that at least a substantial part of Moravcsikian content appears in consciousness when one thinks a thought, and what follows? We are not yet in position to conclude that the Moravcsikian level of content is identical to the content of consciousness, and in fact we have good reason to worry that it is not. Returning to mental representations (1) through (3) discussed earlier, we see that mental representations (1) and (2) have distinctive features that involve indexicality in some way. (1) represents location as behind *me*, and (2) represents flickering as happening *now*. And the Moravcsikian level of content is not designed to be the level that provides a theory of indexicals.

Taking the concepts ME and NOW, what might we say about their Moravcsikian contents? (Here I am speculating somewhat freely. Reader be warned!) The concept ME is clearly a concept of a spatially extended thing, while NOW is of a temporal extent. This is factor (i) within Moravcsikian content. Factor (ii), the necessary principles of individuation and persistence, should be such as to tie ME to its thinker, and NOW to its moment of being thought, without specifying particular individuals or times. Thus, the principle of individuating a thing as the Millian content of ME is that the extended thing is the thinker of the thought, while the principle of individuating a duration as the Millian content of NOW is that the duration is the moment of the thought. The concept ME perhaps has elements of factor (iii), the factor expressing agency, and it might be said that an individual who is ME is an agent of thoughts; but neither ME nor NOW is tied to conditions of well-functioning, and so factor (iv) does not apply.

If this extension of Moravcsikian content to the concepts ME and NOW is not taking excessive license with the theory, then it would seem that Moravcsikian content has the features needed for mental representations (1) and (2). The thought that there is a bell ringing behind me is one that makes it clear, just in its thinking, that the bell is located relative to *me*, without identifying me as anything other than the thinker of the thought. Any other thinker of the thought would also have the same Moravcsikian content, but only the thinker of the thought satisfies the Moravcsikian content at the time of thinking it, and this is just what was wanted to deal with this case. Similarly, the thought that there is a light flickering now is one that makes it clear, just in its thinking, that the moment of flickering is *now*, without identifying this time as anything other than the moment of thought. Again, this is what we get from the Moravcsikian content of the thought. We get a content that could be correctly deployed at any other time, and so which does not specify an individual moment in time, and yet we also get a content that, given its context of deployment, is satisfied only by the moment of time at which it is thought.

What of mental representation (3), that Hesperus is Phosphorus? Here we seem to encounter a problem. Factor (i) is unobjectionable: it gives us that the Moravcsikian content of both HESPERUS and PHOSPHORUS requires that both be spatially extended objects, and this seems right. But factor (ii) is problematic. What are the individuation conditions for satisfiers of the two concepts? It seems that they will be the same, if they are to remain general enough to be the things that anyone must grasp if that person is to have a grasp of the concept. For instance, to grasp the concept HESPERUS it does not seem compulsory that one believe that Hesperus is seen in the evening; one might be minimally interested in astronomy and simply know that Hesperus is one of those heavenly bodies that shines like a distant star. To require more is to put severe constraints on who will grasp any given concept, with only expert users of the concept counting as grasping it at all. This is contrary to Moravcsik's very notion of the third level of content, which is meant to explain such things as *variations* in competence with a concept, and so is not meant to be the sort of thing that only perfect users of the concept might have as contents. As for factors (iii) and (iv), since Hesperus and Phosphorus are not conceived of as agents or as things with functions they might fail to perform, factors (iii) and (iv) do not apply. So there is nothing to distinguish the concepts HESPERUS and PHOSPHORUS except for factors (i) and (ii), and neither actually distinguishes them. Thus, the Moravcsikian content of the thought that Hesperus is Phosphorus will be the same as the Moravcsikian content of the thought that Hesperus is Hesperus, which is not, phenomenologically speaking, how it feels.

3 Conclusion

After considering the Millian, Fregean, and Moravcsikian levels of content, not one is perfectly suited to being the content of consciousness that is required for representationalism. The Moravcsikian level would appear to come closest, and to add some surprising insights into what it is like to think a thought, but not one of these levels has all the properties required by the representationalist theorist of consciousness.

Some would see this as a reason to despair of the prospects of representationalism. But as a representationalist sympathizer, I suggest a different moral: finding a theory of content that will serve the representationalist's purposes might be hard, but it is probably not impossible! In fact, Moravcsikian content is a fairly close approximation to what the representationalist seeks. The right lesson to take away is that it is time for the representationalist to pay more attention to possible theories of content with Moravcsikian features, and see what can be done.

BIBLIOGRAPHY

[Block, 1996] Block, N. 1996. "Mental Paint and Mental Latex." *Philosophical Issues* 7, 19-49.
[Caplan and Schroeder, 2007] Caplan, B. and Schroeder, T. 2007. "On the Content of Experience." *Philosophy and Phenomenological Research* 75, 590-611.
[Dennett, 1991] Dennett, D. 1991. *Consciousness Explained.* Boston, MA: Little, Brown & Co.
[Dretske, 1995] Dretske, F. 1995. *Naturalizing the Mind.* Cambridge, MA: MIT Press.
[Fodor, 1975] Fodor, J. 1975. *The Language of Thought.* Cambridge, MA: Harvard University Press.
[Harman, 1990] Harman, G. 1990. "The Intrinsic Quality of Experience." *Philosophical Perspectives* 4, 31-52
[Horgan and Tienson, 2002] Horgan, T., and Tienson, J. 2002. "The Intentionality of Phenomenology and the Phenomenology of Intentionality." In D. Chalmers (ed.), *Philosophy of Mind: Classical and Contemporary Readings.* New York: Oxford University Press, pp. 520–532.
[Levine, 1983] Levine, J. 1983. "Materialism and Qualia: The explanatory gap." *Pacific Philosophical Quarterly* 64, 354-61.
[Lycan, 1987] Lycan, W. 1987. *Consciousness.* Cambridge, MA: MIT Press.
[Moravcsik, 1990] Moravcsik, J. 1990. *Thought and Language.* London: Routledge.
[Moravcsik, 1998] Moravcsik, J. 1998. *Meaning, Creativity, and the Partial Inscrutability of the Human Mind.* Stanford, CA: CSLI Publications.
[Peacocke, 1983] Peacocke, C. 1983. *Sense and Content.* Oxford: Oxford University Press.
[Prinz, 2002] Prinz, J. 2002. *Furnishing the Mind.* Cambridge, MA: MIT Press.
[Schroeder, 2004] Schroeder, T. 2004. *Three Faces of Desire.* New York: Oxford University Press.
[Siewert, 1998] Siewert, C. 1998. *The Significance of Consciousness.* Princeton, NJ: Princeton University Press.
[Tye, 1995] Tye, M. 1995. *Ten Problems of Consciousness.* Cambridge, MA: MIT Press.
[Tye, 1996] Tye, M. 1996. "Orgasms Again." *Philosophical Issues* 7, 51-4.

Part B
Aesthetics

Pictures and the Feeling of Presence
MOHAN MATTHEN

It is one of philosophy's scandals that in Book X of the *Republic,* Plato expresses a trenchant and unyielding disapproval of painting, poetry, and tragedy — arts that employ *mimesis*. So little understood is this episode that in 1979, Julius and Philip Temko organized a pathbreaking conference to explore, as they say in the Preface of the ensuing volume, "how Plato, the philosopher who used poetic images more than anyone else, could talk about art the way he did." In truth, Plato — like many other philosophers — was, as Julius implies in his contribution to that volume, sometimes much stronger in his analytic powers with regard to art than in taste or judgement. For when one peers under his perverse reaction to art and literature, one finds a surprisingly acute analysis of *mimesis*. In this paper, I explore a problem that arises out of Plato's treatment.

1

Let us start with a puzzle of interpretation. Plato famously held that couches made by craftsmen are copies of the Ideal Couch. And he claimed that pictures of couches are copies of the former. This led him to consign pictures to a third and inferior domain of reality — a realm ontologically even further removed from Ideal reality than artifacts. The implication is that the three domains are mutually exclusive — the inferiority of the painter and of the poet is predicated on the supposition that he provisions only the most evanescent of the three. Is this justified? Why can't a copy of a copy be a copy?

Plato is not working with a causal theory of copying in *Republic* X. His point is not that a picture of a couch does not causally originate from the Form of the Couch and is not in *this* sense a picture or copy thereof — in the sense that when I take a photograph of a blue square it is a photograph of *that* blue square, not of others, however indistinguishable, and a photograph of a photograph of a blue square is not a photograph of the blue square because it did not originate from the latter in the appropriate way. His point is rather that products of art are less faithful to the Forms than worldly things. And though commentators seem to assume that this conclusion accords with intuition, it does not seem to follow from the characterization given. For fidelity in copying, though not transitive, does not seem to be *in*transitive either. A fine copy of Leonardo's Mona Lisa — a copy of Leonardo's copy — may be truer to Lisa Gherardini, Madam Gioconda, than a daub executed in her presence. Similarly, one would expect that an extremely realistic painting of a truly superb couch might capture the reality of the Ideal Couch better than a Lillberg loveseat purchased from Ikea and hastily assembled by a clumsy freshman in her dorm room — even though the latter is directly derived from the form.

You might think that this argument is immediately defeated by the fact that the artifact that the freshman produces is actually a couch, while a painting however good is not — just as da Vinci's masterpiece is not, for all of its virtues, a woman. But Plato does not appear to give this particular argument much credence, for he says (596e) that in a way the painter *also* makes a couch — in the precise sense that he too makes the appearance of one. And in any case, why couldn't a painter make a painting directly from his apprehension of the Form? In his essay on the topic, Julius says that "Plato regards the lack of understanding of function and purpose [of couches] a flaw in the artist." True, that's what Plato implies, but isn't he being a little ungenerous? After all, he claims that understanding of artifacts flows from using them, and surely *some* artists must have been rich enough to own and use couches. Why could they not have put the understanding they derived from this aspect of their lives to work in their artistic endeavours?

2

Plato's argument (598a-b) is actually much better than the one suggested by the copy-of-a-copy terminology. He says: "A couch is the same as itself regardless of which side you view it from, but it appears different from different angles." Plato does not explicitly articulate the contrast with pictures. Myles Burnyeat gives this account of it: "the picture shows only how the couch appears when viewed from a particular angle." But surely this is true of the couch as well: on any given view, it only shows itself from a particular angle. True, the couch is capable of revealing itself from different angles, but then it is also capable of being depicted from different angles. I mean one could have pictures of the same couch from different angles; any given picture is *of* the couch, isn't it, just as any given view is of the couch? What exactly is the difference, then, between couches and pictures of couches?

I suppose it must be this: a painting of a couch from one side is different *in content* from a painting of the same couch from a different side. When you look at a couch from the back, you are looking at the same couch from a different angle; however, a picture of a couch from a different angle is a different picture. Since the pictorial content of pictures from different angles is different, the couch cannot be their content. Plato concludes that a painting is not an imitation of a couch, but an imitation of the sensory appearance of a couch. It doesn't, and doesn't try to, capture the multifaceted reality of the couch, but only, as he says, "a small part" of it.

This argument shows why the copying relation has to be intransitive for Plato. When a carpenter makes a couch, he attempts to capture the essence of the Ideal Couch. He makes imperfect realizations of this essence — imperfect couches. But the painter — and the poet also, though I will not attempt here to say why — only attempts to capture the sensory form of worldly couches. He makes, if you will, a visual couch — or at least this is the form of expression that Plato suggests when he says that the painter too makes a couch, since he makes the appearance of one. This is why the painter does not need to know the reality of the things he paints: all he needs to know is how to capture their visual forms. Moreover, the painter *cannot* copy Forms, because Forms have no visual form. This is why the pictorial copy of an artifact cannot be a copy of the Form. Painting is an epistemically challenged field, Plato suggests — it applies one and the same body of knowledge to things that are quite diverse in essence.

Plato's analysis of pictures is clearsighted. It does not — as many accounts did, until recently — appeal to intrinsic similarity as the root of the relationship of pictorial representation. Rather it appeals to a relational form of similarity — to how the human sensory system responds similarly to pictured things and to the pictures of these things.[1] For according to Plato, the artist exploits what he (Plato) takes to be a weakness in human nature: "that things of the same magnitude look to be of different size from different distances ... Scene-painting in its exploitation of this weakness in our nature falls nothing short of witchcraft ..." (602d).[2] A painter deliberately paints two equal lines unequal if they are to be seen at different distances. Thus, he creates an image that bears no intrinsic similarity to what he is depicting — the image is a picture of something because it evokes the same sensory response. Plato sees this as falsification and hence as intellectually inferior and even corrupting — and this is a perverse judgement, as I said earlier. However this may be, modern studies of pictorial representation and of sensory response in general would have done better to focus, as Plato did, on the human sensory faculty, rather than worrying about similarity as such. In the last thirty years or so, thanks largely to the work of Richard Wollheim, Plato's approach to pictorial representation has become the standard theory. It hasn't always been.

3

Plato's treatment of pictorial representation creates a puzzle. How can we tell the difference between something seen in a good picture and the same thing seen in three-dimensional reality? On the unqualified similarity view, it might seem, this is not a problem. For if the resemblance of a picture to its model is always less

---

[1] Julia Annas suggests that Plato's account applies only to *trompes d'oeil*. This is wrong. Perhaps she is misled by the talk of mirror images at 596d — but Plato does not say there that mirror images are pictures, merely that they belong, with pictures, in the class of things that capture appearance.

[2] Myles Burnyeat thinks that Plato is merely making the point, familiar from the *Protagoras*, that sensory appearance is at odds with what reason tells us. "[W]e know perfectly well that the painting is flat with no depth to it," Burnyeat writes, "But knowing this does not stop . . the painting seeming to have depth." Plato does, of course, rely on this point, but this is true of *all* the situations in which we use our senses. It has nothing special to do with pictures. (By the way, it is not the painting that seems to have depth, but the scene it represents.) The interesting thing *here* is that Plato is claiming that the painter exploits the mendacity of the senses.

than perfect, then the non-similarity might itself be taken to explain how we make the distinction — in particular, pictures are two-dimensional, and this marks an obvious point of dissimilarity when the model is three-dimensional.

This quick response brings out, however, a main deficiency of the similarity account. The picture is, of course, two-dimensional; it is a marked surface. A painting, for instance, is on canvas; it is perhaps 3 ft by 3 ft; it is enclosed in a frame; it has brushstrokes on its surface, and so on. And what is portrayed by the picture is none of the things mentioned above. Thus, the picture fails to resemble what is depicted. But this is really irrelevant, because the question we want answered is not whether *the picture* resembles what it depicts, but whether *the object we see in the picture* resembles what it depicts. It is not right, for example, to think that one of the dissimilarities between Lisa Gherardini and da Vinci's painting of her is that in the latter there are brushstrokes on her face. The brushstrokes belong to a different object; they belong to the picture. What is more, they are not *seen* as belonging to her: it is actually hard to see both the brushstrokes and her complexion in a single act of visual attention, or, perhaps, in a single act of vision. When you look at *her* in the picture, your visual state is as of a three-dimensional woman. The issue for theories of depiction is not whether the painting resembles her, but whether the woman you see in this way resembles Lisa Gherardini. You might respond, of course, that there is, literally, no woman that you see when you look at the Mona Lisa. But this is precisely the issue that Plato finesses by asking whether the picture has a similar effect on the human visual system as Gherardini herself, and whether looking at the painting is like looking at her. His theory allows us to replace the existentially loaded reference to a woman in the picture with a more circumspect statement about the effect that the picture has on your visual system.

But now the question arises with fresh force: if one really does see a woman in the painting — i.e., if your visual experience really is similar to that when you are looking at a three-dimensional woman — how do you tell that it is a painting of a woman you are looking at, not a woman? A painting is supposed to evoke in us a visual state similar to that evoked by the depicted object. And while it is clearly impossible for the *painting* to resemble its object in all respects, it seems entirely possible that the picture should evoke exactly the same effect in a viewer as a three-dimensional object, especially on the traditional treatment of vision. After all, the retina is two-dimensional, and geometrical optics suggests that a two dimensional surface like a picture could, at least in principle, evoke exactly the same two-dimensional effects as a three-dimensional one. And one could say: this is the art that painters attempted for centuries to perfect: how to make this happen.

Plato says something very valuable about this puzzle. Recall his observation that three-dimensional objects are the same no matter where you view them from. And we may add: not just this, but they look as if they are the same object. That is, when you view a three-dimensional object over time, its continuity and sameness manifest themselves in your visual states. Nearby objects reveal themselves at different angles when you even move your eyes or head. With objects that are further away, it is true, *you* have to move about to discover these different aspects. What both of these temporally extended observations share is a visually experienced continuity of the object you are looking at. As you move around a room with your eyes fixed on a table, the table does not look as if it were merely a succession of temporal stages; rather, it presents the look of the same object through this extended experience — the tracking experiments of the Gestalt psychologists, and now of Zenon Pylyshyn, prove this. The things you see in a picture do not behave in this way. As you move about, they continue to reveal the same aspect. Over time, then, and with movement, they don't look like three-dimensional objects. As long as you think that perception has a temporally extended aspect, it is no mystery how they look different from the things depicted therein.

These phenomena of continuity force one to be aware, as noted before, of looking at two things at once — a picture and what is depicted in the picture. The picture looks like a single three-dimensional object when one moves around. But the woman in the picture looks quite different: she does not look like a single three-dimensional woman as you move around. This is what Wollheim calls the "twofoldness" of pictorial seeing: "On the one hand I recognize a face", he says, "on the other hand, I am visually aware of the surface of the picture." This twofoldness tends to support the three levels of reality view — viewing a picture is always looking into it as well as looking at it; willy-nilly, one is aware of two different things, one of which looks different in a fundamental way.

Plato does not seem fully to have understood the implications of this, however. For as Julius remarks: "If art — even "good" art — captures our attention and does not move us to go beyond it, and seek understanding on higher levels, then Plato regards its enjoyment as harmful to our souls." The point that Plato neglects in arriving at this view is his own: that when we look at a picture we are subject to the same experience as that which we have when we look at the thing that it depicts. In a number of other dialogues, Plato seems to hold that visual experience of worldly things can impel us towards an understanding the Forms. The famous ascent passage in the *Symposium* (210a-212a) that Julius has written about is one such. Here, Plato claims that a person's delight in individual beautiful things — presumably sensory — lead her on to an appreciation and understanding of the Beauty beyond. Similarly, in the sticks-and-stones passage of the *Phaedo*, sensory experience of equal sticks and stones reminds us of equality itself. Plato is held up here by the equal lines that one sees in pictures not always being really equal. He fails, however, to distinguish between the lines that one sees in a picture, and the lines that depict them; the visual experience that the latter unequal lines create is the same as that which truly equal lines create. It follows that a picture of equal lines should be capable of leading one to understanding in exactly the same way as sensible equal lines. Plato overlooked this: he writes as though one could *never* go through pictures to knowledge and understanding. It was his insight that painters seek to mimic the appearance of things; it was his failure that he didn't appreciate that by doing so, they get you, in the relevant way, to see the thing itself.

4

Though temporally extended experiences are important to understanding the difference between looking at a thing in the round and looking at it in a picture, they cannot be the whole story. For our attention is often not on such differences. In watching a gripping baseball game — if there is such a thing — on television, one may very well fail to be aware of one's own inability to change one's point of view; one may also be unaware of characteristics of the picture itself — the reflections on the screen, the fact that it does not occupy the whole of one's field of view, and so on. In this situation, you attend only to the events taking place in the picture. Good art is often, perhaps always, a deliberate exploitation of twofoldness — but it is nonetheless true that quite often pictures are presented in a way that directs our attention solely to the depicted things. But even in such cases, one's experience is not the same as when one sees the depicted thing in real life. Why is this?

As it happens, there is another way that pictures strike us differently from real life. This difference lies in the recently discovered fact that we have not one, but two visual systems. One of these, which I shall call *descriptive vision,* provides us with awareness of colours, shapes, motion, and so on — sense qualities that we attribute to objects that we see. The other, which I call *motion-guiding vision,* is responsible for guiding our limbs — for example, our hands when we grasp something, or our feet when we walk around or over an obstacle.[3]

Briefly, the important point here lies in the different effect that these two visual systems make on consciousness. Descriptive vision works through visual consciousness; it informs us of sensory qualities through visual qualia. Colours, for instance, look a certain way: that is, when vision determines that a particular thing is yellow, it makes that determination available to us by making that thing look a certain way. Descriptive vision presents its data in terms of a sensory map: for each property that descriptive vision attributes to a thing, there is a quale that stands in the corresponding place in the visual field and indicates that property. Motion-guiding vision does not rely on visual consciousness in this manner: rather, it relies on a direct link between the parts of the brain in which visual information are processed and the parts of the body that it controls. If, for example, you reach out to pick up a cup or a pen, your body does not rely on conscious visual feedback of the relationship between your hand and the cup; rather it proceeds by the use of a visual pathway that is independent of conscious vision.[4] Our ability to act on ob-

---

[3]What I am calling "descriptive vision" and "motion-guiding vision" are entitled ventral-stream and dorsal-stream vision by neurophysiologists. I prefer not to get involved in the neuroanatomy of these visual systems, hence my non-standard terminology.

[4]The evidence for this claim lies in the following: even when the conscious visual feedback is distorted in certain ways, motion-guiding vision proceeds as if unimpaired. It is known, for example, that motion-guiding vision is not susceptible to visual illusions of size. Those visual illusions occupy the whole of our visual consciousness, yet the fingers make no mistake — they

jects does not depend on a consciously available map in which their qualities are represented.

Descriptive vision presents us, if you will, with an *image* — a matrix of visual qualia each of which gives us a reason to attribute a sensual quality to an object in the scene. Motion-guiding vision operates more surreptitiously. It enables us to come into contact with and act upon objects in the scene *without* going through qualia. It is not the point of motion guiding vision to make things look any way, or to provide us with reasons for believing anything; the point is rather to enable us to make contact with things in your vicinity. Kevin O'Regan and Alva Noë put it well: motion-guiding vision *perceptually couples* you with objects in your vicinity.

Let me summarize this in slightly different terms. Vision provides you with two different capacities with regard to objects around you. The first capacity, mediated by visual qualia, has to do with the qualities that you attribute to the seen object. The second capacity, unmediated by visual qualia, has to do with making contact with and physically manipulating the object. Because this second quality is unmediated by visual qualia, it is not linked with any quality you could explicitly attribute to the object, or with your awareness of any such quality. In this sense, it is a primitive form of contact with the object.

Now, the crucial point with regard to pictures is this. Pictures themselves — the objects that are attached to the marked surfaces that we look at with so much interest — engage *both* descriptive *and* motion-guiding vision. If one had to move a painting from one place to another, or straighten it on the wall, or paint over a part of it, one's hands and arms would have no difficulty accomplishing these tasks. They would not be in the blind. And of course, one does see pictures themselves three-dimensionally: one sees that they have marked surfaces, that they are a certain size, and so on. On the other hand, the objects *in* pictures engage descriptive vision but not motion-guiding vision. When one tries to touch the objects depicted, one's hand will be carried to the surface of the painting, but not in ways that correspond to how one would move if one were attempting to touch or manipulate the corresponding object. If one tries to grasp a depicted arm or a hand, for example, one will have difficulty sizing one's grip appropriately — one can do it, but only with the skills of a mime. Thus the things in the picture will *look* much like real-life objects; the qualities one ascribes to these objects on the basis of one's visual consciousness will be much the same. But the capacity to manipulate these objects will be missing.

5

Traditional views of visual awareness do not capture the kinds of differences between pictorial vision and three-dimensional vision that I have been talking about here. For these views make visual states temporally non-extended and wholly qualia-based. They take it, first of all, that a visual state is a momentary state,

---

are not operating by courtesy of the visual qualia of size that dominate our awareness of objects.

and that visual awareness over a period of time is simply a sequence of temporally punctate visual states. I am claiming, however, that one sort of difference between pictures and three-dimensional seeing is evident only over time, as one moves around the world relative to the things that we see. Over time, one becomes aware of the spatial relations between objects that form an essential part of one's visual perception of the three-dimensional world. But that sort of awareness is embedded in our visual states at every moment. At every moment we are aware of objects as three-dimensional and as continuous with those that we see at other times. This implies that what one is aware of at a moment traces to information that one receives over a period of time. Our awareness of things over time is not reducible to awareness at moments of time.

Wollheim, it will be recalled, insisted that we see objects in pictures. I have been agreeing with this, but now I want to add that we see these objects in a quite different way — the content of our pictorial states is different in kind from that of our states of ordinary three-dimensional vision. One immediate difference is that there is a spatial disconnection between yourself and the things you see in pictures. There is a space in the picture, but that space is different from the space that you occupy. Think for instance of a photograph of two men shaking hands, with a car in the background. These three objects are related to each other in their space: one man is to the left of the other, and both are in front of the car. But what is their relation *to you?* Are the men ten feet away? It might seem intuitive that there has to be an answer to this question. You might think, for instance, that the size of the objects tells you how far away they are just as it does in the three-dimensional world. But is this so? Do the men look further away if the photograph is smaller? No. So this account does not work. Maybe you think that the men look as far away from you as the photograph is. Aside from the intrinsic implausibility of supposing that two grown men are shaking hands at your fingertips, this would imply that if you moved closer to the picture the men should appear closer to you — indeed that you should appear to approach them at the same speed as you are moving. But this is not what happens. In fact, there is a peculiarly static feel about the depicted men — you move toward them, but they don't seem to get any closer. In large part this is, of course, because as you walk toward them you still see them from the same point of view; what is more, their relationship to the car does not change — they do not obscure or cover up parts of it that were previously unhidden. The result is that when you are looking at a picture your visual awareness is of things that are spatially related to each other, but not to you. There are two spaces in pictorial vision, the space of the viewer and the space of the depicted things. In a picture gallery, there may indeed be several spaces — one for each picture that is in view.

There is another difference between how you see things in pictures and in the round. I speculated before that objects in pictures do not create in you the feeling that they are *there* to be touched or manipulated. Your hands have no guidance when you try to contact pictured objects: if you try to put your arm on the far shoulder of one of the men in the photograph that I have been imagining, you will not move in a natural manner. This second difference is actually something that pictorial vision shares with visual imagery. During visual imagery, as in when we see an object in a picture, motion-guiding vision is not engaged. Visually guided reach towards objects is not supported in pictorial seeing: it is also not supported when we *visually imagine* a scene.

Motion-guiding vision is insensitive to the illusions that pictures use in order to mimic three-dimensional efects; it is also not engaged by visual imagery, which comes directly from the descriptive portions of the visual system. Both of these activities involve only the descriptive visual system, and both exclude motion-guiding vision.

This difference between pictured objects and real ones accounts, I believe, for something to which some recent authors have attached much metaphysical freight — the supposed stativeness or facticity of vision, the phenomenological feeling that it is providing you with something that is real and present. I believe that this phenomenon has a quite simple explanation in the terms that I have been exploring,.

Suppose that you are looking at a some object, a piece of furniture say, and it looks to you as if it is black. Now suppose that you entertain an image of the very same object, but in a different colour — you imagine it reupholstered in brown, say. Simply by switching from an image that engages both descriptive and motion-guiding vision to one that is confined to descriptive vision, you entertain an image that does not engage motion-guiding vision. The image you now entertain is one to which you are not perceptually coupled — you have no ability to touch it or manipulate it.

I would like to suggest that this lack of ability entails a corresponding lack of ability to use a spatial demonstrative for this image — you cannot use terms like 'there' in a perceptually grounded way. Of course, there is nothing stopping you from closing your eyes and entertaining an image of a thing that is "there" with respect to you. But this image will not support the demonstrative in the proper way. If you take a step or two in its direction, your proprioceptive sense of motion and changes in the image will not be properly coordinated. You can perhaps *will* a correlation, but such an act of willed imaging lacks the sense of feedback from the image. All in all, these acts will require effort, will be felt as emanating from one's own mental activity, and will therefore lack the normal feeling that is required to support a perceptual demonstrative.

Go back to the black couch that you are imagining as brown. When you look at it, you are in a visual state that might be parsed roughly thus:

(1) [There] Black Couch.

When you entertain the counterfactual image of the same couch in brown, the spatial demonstrative is missing. Thus:

(2) [...] Brown Couch (same).

Now, the important point here is that *seen* visual images support spatial demonstratives of this type. On the other hand, merely imagined and pictorial images have no such capacity. This accounts for their supposed facticity. The felt facticity of seen images resides, I would suggest, in the spatial demonstratives that are embedded in them, and this in turn relates to their temporally extended and motion-related aspects.

The received view of visual states makes them temporally punctate and wholly qualia based. Plato's reflections on pictures suggest that this view has grave limitations. I have been arguing that starting from his reflections on pictures, and using certain results from the psychology of vision, one might arrive at a rather different notion of visual states — one that makes them temporally extended and dependent on non-qualia based spatial demonstratives. It is a mystery to me that Plato could have been so profoundly suggestive in his brief analysis of depiction and yet so wrongheaded in his assessment of their value. What is it about philosophy that allows it to be so one-sided?

Part C
Ethics

Why Are We Morally Responsible for Ourselves?

OTTO NEUMAIER

The question *why* we are morally responsible for ourselves presupposes a positive answer to another, more fundamental question, that is, *whether* we are morally responsible for ourselves. We shall not call this into question, however, because, although some people might doubt that we are morally responsible for ourselves, or responsible at all, from a moral point of view we have to take for granted that there is at least *some* moral responsibility for ourselves, for the reason alone that the denial of this fact would cut the ground from any moral reasoning. So, the question of moral responsibility for ourselves is mainly directed towards the *reasons* that are necessary in order to be justified in attributing moral responsibility to people, where the notion of responsibility has to be understood in the sense of a *moral duty* they have *to themselves for their own sake*.

The assumption that we are morally responsible for ourselves, that is, that we have moral duties to ourselves for our own sake, is put forward, for instance, by Immanuel Kant (1797: 237) who emphasizes that "man has duties only to men (himself or other men)." It is particularly the German philosopher and psychologist Eduard Spranger (1963: 63f.), however, who reduces our moral responsibility ultimately to "the one great responsibility for ourselves and in the eyes of ourselves," that is, to the imperative that we ought to take care of ourselves. According to Spranger, we are not *also* responsible for ourselves as well as for many other beings, but rather *first of all*, that is, we are not responsible for ourselves because we are responsible for other beings (and could not satisfy this responsibility without taking care of ourselves at the same time), but *for our own sake*. We owe to ourselves as a moral duty that we take care of ourselves.

This very thesis is in the focus of the following considerations. Starting from the assumption endorsed by Kant and Spranger *that* we are morally responsible for ourselves, we will have to ask for the reasons *why* this is the case. In order to answer this question we will first have to clarify shortly at least two points: on the one hand, we have to point out the conditions that are generally necessary in order to be justified in attributing responsibility to someone, and we have to discuss some fundamental moral principles, on the other, because this is a prerequisite for distinguishing moral duties form other kinds of responsibility.

1 Conditions for the Attribution of Responsibility

Responsibility can basically be regarded from two points of view, that is, from a *subjective* and an *objective* one. In many cases we *feel*, or are held to be, responsible for something although no reasons are, or could ultimately be, given in order to show why it is justified to make us responsible; in many other cases, however, we are inclined to expel any thought of being responsible from our consciousness, although it is objectively justified to ascribe responsibility to us. Indeed, the subjective feeling of being responsible is interesting in psychological or sociological respects, but it is only of secondary value for ethics. From a moral point of view the objective reasons that can be referred to in order to be justified in ascribing responsibility to someone are much more important than some vague or urgent feeling that we, or someone else, be responsible for something — or than the wish that this be not the case. If it is possible to refer to good reasons, we can bring responsibility into play even in cases in which we would like too much to make recourse to excuses; on the other hand, if no good reasons can be brought about, we have to refrain from ascribing responsibility to someone (including ourselves) independently of what our feelings are in this respect.

In many cases in which it is said that someone is responsible for something we ascribe responsibility to the person in question. The attribution of responsibility can be understood in at least two ways that are connected, but not identical, that is, descriptively or normatively. As has been observed already by Hans Kelsen (1941, 1954), the attribution of responsibility in the *descriptive* sense is related to *causal explanations* of the kind "If A is the case then B is the case." To ascribe descriptively responsibility to someone amounts to asserting that some *empirical* state of affairs exists. The expression 'responsibility' is used in this way, for instance, when some expert says in a trial that the culprit is responsible for his or her deeds and hereby means that he or she is provided with certain physical and psychological capabilities which are necessary for holding him or her *accountable* for those deeds. Similarly, responsibility is ascribed descriptively when we say that a certain minister of the Austrian government is responsible for the environment and thereby mean that he is *in charge* of the environmental agenda of this country. We are also confronted with this kind of attributing responsibility when someone's action is identified as the *cause* of a certain event — and, thus, the person in question is determined as its *causer*. Therefore, when it is said that some doctor is responsible for the death of a patient this possibly amounts to nothing more than the assertion that there is a causal connection between the doctor's acting and the patient's death.

As a matter of course, people who call some doctor responsible for a patient's death *can* mean more than just a statement about some causal connection and, as a matter of fact, many people probably understand such a statement in a *normative* way. The assertion of a causal connection does in itself *not necessarily* imply moral or legal claims, although it is in many cases necessary in order to be justified in ascribing to someone moral or legal responsibility in a normative sense. Already the attribution of responsibility in a descriptive sense depends on certain conditions, however. For instance, in law as well as in ethics, the assertion of someone's causal responsibility is usually carried out *counterfactually* according to the rule that it is justified to regard someone as the originator of some state of affairs only if there are good reasons for assuming that the state of affairs in question would not occur (or would not have occurred) if that person would not perform (or would not have performed) a certain action (where the notion of action includes also the omission of some act).

The attribution of responsibility in a normative sense is *a fortiori* bound to certain conditions, in particular to the condition that it is justified to ascribe descriptively responsibility to someone. Hence, the normative attribution of responsibility always implies some kind of descriptive attribution of responsibility, but not vice versa. When it is said in a normative sense, for instance, that parents are responsible for their children, this often amounts to claiming that they have the *duty* to do certain things (and to omit some others), *because* they are the parents of the affected beings. This includes not only that they are *capable* of creating those beings, of taking care of them, and of being called to account under certain circumstances, but also that they are, as a matter of fact, the *causers* of the existence of those children and that they are in charge of their well-being as long as the children cannot take care of themselves to a certain extent. The normative attribution of responsibility amounts to asserting or declaring the validity of a norm directed towards the person in question, and this is done under the supposition that some other conditions are fulfilled, particularly the conditions which are necessary for being justified in attributing responsibility in a descriptive sense. According to Kelsen, the *normative* attribution of responsibility can be formulated as "If A is the case (that is, if certain conditions are fulfilled), then B *should* be the case."

So, the normative attribution of responsibility is in some relevant sense similar to promises. Both speech acts imply obligations in accordance with some rules that are presupposed by the members of a linguistic, cultural, or moral community. As is argued by Searle (1969: 57–61), promises cannot be given arbitrarily, at least insofar as it depends on several conditions whether they are *valid*. What is decisive in this context is the following instance: If all conditions which are necessary for the validity of a promise are fulfilled, it is justified not only to regard some sentence as a valid promise, but also to claim that someone *commits* himself or herself to do something by uttering the promise, that is, in this case it is objectively justified to claim that the person who promises something *ought to do* what he or she promises.

The conditions to be sketched below have to be understood in the light of the *presumption of innocence*, that is, the normative attribution of responsibility is *not justified* as long as there are not good reasons to assume that *all* of these conditions are fulfilled. So, the burden of proof rests with those who would like to ascribe responsibility to someone and not with those to whom responsibility is ascribed. Although the attribution of responsibility is ultimately intended to be normative, this language game includes the assertion of certain empirical states of affairs that are to be ascribed to someone in a descriptive sense. In short, the normative attribution of responsibility is justified only if the following conditions (which are discussed in some more detail in Neumaier, 2008, 66–103) are fulfilled:

(i) *Accountability*, that is, the person who is subject to the attribution of responsibility is provided with certain physical and psychological abilities that are necessary in order to understand and to do what is ascribed to him or her as his or her responsibility. It may happen, for instance, that someone causes some harm; if there are reasons to assume that he or she lacks the psychological prerequisites that are necessary for understanding the action and its consequences as well as the norms that come into play, then it is pointless to direct any moral or legal claims to the subject in question. In such cases the normative attribution of responsibility lacks any plausibility because the *Ought-Can Condition* is violated according to which it is justified to claim that someone ought to do something only if he or she can do it. This principle underlies also the second condition for the attribution of responsibility.

(ii) *Freedom of acting*, that is, it is possible for someone to choose between at least two alternatives in order to exert some causal influence upon some state of affairs which is under consideration for being attributed to the person in question as something he or she is responsible for. In a *subjective* sense, this condition is not fulfilled, for instance, when someone is forced to perform a certain action by some inner constraint (like a neurosis), although he or she is perfectly able to understand what the right alternative would be. Freedom of acting can also be prevented by objective conditions, however, for instance by some outer compulsion (like being threatened to death by someone else) or by some situation in which no alternative at all is available to exert some causal influence. If in an airplane all steering instruments break down, for instance, so that the pilot has no possibility anymore to control the flight, then it is not justified to hold him or her responsible for a crash and its consequences.

(iii) *Causality*, that is, there are reasons to assume that a certain state of affairs that is under consideration for being attributed to someone as something he or she is responsible for does causally depend from a specific action of the person in question. For instance, someone could not only intend to kill another person, but also be able to do that and even do everything in his or her power in order to cause that person's death, but without "success." If the other person nevertheless dies, but without any "help" of the subject in question, then it is not justified to hold him or her responsible whatever his or her intentions, capabilities, and possibilities were. As has been pointed out already by Fritz Heider (1958: 112ff.), however, there are a variety of answers to the question under which conditions it is justified to say that some state of affairs causally depends from someone's acting, and consequently, a variety of forms or degrees of responsibility can be attributed to someone:

(a) Strictly speaking, it is justified to regard someone as the causer of some state of affairs only if it can be *demonstrated* that the state of affairs in question would not occur (or would not have occurred) if that person would not perform (or would not have performed) a certain action. In many cases this condition cannot be fulfilled, however, so that we have to recourse to the weaker assumption that there are *good reasons* for assuming that some state of affairs would not occur without someone's acting. Since the condition is weaker, the same holds for the responsibility that can plausibly be attributed to someone. On the other hand, there is no *rational* justification for the attribution of causal responsibility if some state of affairs can only be *somehow* related to the subject in question (for instance, by his or her living in a certain era, being the member of a certain family, and the like).

(b) In many cases someone is held to be responsible for some state of affairs that *as a matter of fact* is a causal consequence of his or her acting — independently of whether it is possible for him or her to foresee this consequence. In other cases responsibility is attributed to someone only if the state of affairs in question is objectively *foreseeable* as a causal consequence of his or her acting. In particular, someone is held responsible for a state of affairs, however, which he or she *intends* to bring about by his or her acting. To some extent, the role of causality for the attribution of responsibility depends on the presupposed norms (to be discussed in the next section). As far as responsibility is regarded as a *moral duty* we have *primarily* to refer to the consequences of actions that are objectively foreseeable or even intended by the person in question, because it is not justified to obligate someone to consider in his or her decisions consequences which he or she neither intends nor is able to recognize. To be sure, factual consequences are *secondarily* relevant for the attribution of moral duties, however, that is insofar as the insight of having unintentionally or ignorantly done some harm to others by all means can be a reason for the commitment to recompense the damage.

(iv) *Concern of others*, that is, there are reasons to assume that some being (other than the acting person) is *affected* by some state of affairs that is causally connected with a specific action of the person whose responsibility is at stake. To cause some state of affairs does not necessarily amount to thereby affect someone. Let us assume, for instance, that some hiker batters a heap of pebbles with his or her walking stick so that the stones are blown away. If nothing more happens than just that, there is no reason at all to think about any responsibility of this hiker. The situation is different, however, if that heap of pebbles happened to be a "rock cairn" which served as a way marker to other hikers or — even more so — if other people are hit by one of the stones and wounded. Under this condition it appears justified to say that someone is affected by the state of affairs that is caused by someone's action.

(v) *Normative relevance*, that is, there are reasons to assume that due to some norm the fact that some being is affected has to be regarded as something the person in question has to take into account when he or she exerts some causal effect upon a state of affairs. In fact, not any kind of being affected calls for responsibility. It is not the same, for instance, whether some action of mine restricts someone's convenience or whether it threatens his or her life. Thus, it is necessary to evaluate the *interests* of the beings who are affected by some state of affairs with regard to their weight or relevance. The evaluation of interests is a matter of the *norm system*, however, that is presupposed in the attribution of responsibility. It is not the same whether we refer to legal, moral, religious, or other norms. Consequently, when moral responsibility is at stake, in particular moral responsibility for ourselves, we have to point out the *moral principles* upon which the attribution of responsibility is based.

2 Principles of Morality

The conditions presented in the previous section are formulated in view of the attribution of moral responsibility, although they are not restricted thereupon, but play also some role in the attribution of other forms of responsibility which, like for instance legal, political, or professional responsibility, differ from moral responsibility in some respect or the other. As *citizens* of a certain country we are politically responsible, whereas national and international law regulate to what extent and in which respect we are *legal subjects* and therefore subject to legal responsibility. By contrast, *every human person* who is, according to our first condition, able to understand his or her actions and their moral status is a candidate for taking moral responsibility. Moral accountability includes, however, the ability to understand the *universal* claim of moral norms, that is, to understand that, for instance, some moral norm according to which a specific action is marked as right or wrong at the same time characterizes *all* actions as morally right or wrong which are similar to that action in the relevant respects, or that the interests of *all* beings which are alike or similar to each other in some relevant respect have to be taken into account in the same way (granted that there are reasons to assume that the interest in question has to be taken into account at all). If Piaget (1932: 195ff.) is right, children at the age of ten to twelve years develop what he calls *autonomous morality*, including the concept of justice, that is, of the universal claim of moral norms. Consequently, this is the earliest stage for regarding humans as morally accountable in the proper sense, even if children exhibit some consciousness of the consequences of their doing already before.

What was initially introduced as a feature of the moral accountability of subjects is at the same time an objective element of the attribution of moral responsibility, that is, of what can be attributed to someone as the object of his or her moral responsibility under the condition that he or she is in principle able to understand it. So, the attribution of moral responsibility is basically guided by the *Principle of Equal Consideration of Interests* which is propagated in contemporary ethics particularly by Peter Singer (1993: 23, 25f., 38f.) and a more general formulation of which is the *Principle of Equal Treatment of Equal Cases*. This principle goes ultimately back to the *Golden Rule*, that is, to the rule that we should treat others as we would like to be treated. A more general and abstract formulation of this rule is Richard Hare's (1955) *Principle of Universalizability* from which it can be derived that whatever beings have to be treated alike as far as they are alike in some *relevant respect*. Thus, it is not justified to take into account as beings upon whom no pain should be inflicted mischievously only humans because they alone could be rational or self-conscious; what is relevant with regard to the wanton causation of pain is rather *sentience*, including the ability to experience pain. If it is not allowed to inflict any torment wantonly upon me because of my sentience, then the same applies to all beings who are able to experience pain like me.

Although the Principle of Equal Consideration of Interests is fundamental for moral reasoning, it is not sufficient for being able to judge in concrete situations whether a certain action is morally right, alone for the reason that equal or similar interests of various beings can clash with each other. If the only possibility for saving one's life is, for instance, to sacrifice the life of another person, I am doomed to act immorally under the provision of just this principle, because at any rate the life of one of these persons is disregarded, and they are not treated equally in the equal respect. The situation gets even more complicated when, as it is usually the case, most different interests of various beings who are in some way or the other affected by some action have to be taken into account and *weighed* against each other. As was mentioned in the context of the concern of others, some state of affairs might be of *vital* interest to some being, whereas it makes living for another being only somewhat more *convenient*. It seems to be plausible to assume that interests concerning life and survival, and everything that is necessary for a certain quality of living, are *primary* relative to other interests, and it should also be possible (although difficult) to order interests on a scale from the primary ones, which are fundamental for the life of a being, to more and more secondary ones. Then, we could assume a *Principle of Priority of Primary over Secondary Interests*, according to which some more fundamental interest is more important for moral reasoning than a less fundamental one.

This principle, which conforms to the *quality* of interests, ranks before the frequently mentioned *Principle of the Priority of the Common Welfare over the Individual Well-Being*. If we reversed this preference, it would be morally justified to prefer *any* interests of a majority of beings to the interests of a minority, even in case these are of fundamental nature for the lives of the affected beings, whereas those are most secondary. On the other hand, the *quantity* of interests is not totally irrelevant with regard to the ascription of moral responsibility, but it comes rather into play in cases in which the interests that have to be weighed are equal or quite similar to each other. If some state of affairs caused by someone's action affects relevantly similar, but conflicting interests of two groups of beings, it seems to be justified to prefer the interest of the major group to that of the minor one. This consideration seems to have an undesirable consequence, however, namely that it is justified, for instance, to sacrifice the life of a person (or of a smaller group of people) if this is the *only* possibility for saving the lives of a greater group of people. We must admit that such a situation is anything else but ideal, and neither is its solution by reference to the principle mentioned above. Unfortunately, the only alternative at hand would be even more problematic, that is, to sacrifice the lives of more people in order to save the lives of a smaller number of people. The crucial point seems to be whether the sacrifice of someone's life is really the *only* alternative at hand (and maybe Werfel's hero Jacobowsky is right in assuming that there are *always* two possibilities...). This amounts to admitting that a great deal of investigation has still to be devoted to the clarification of the freedom of acting and the question of available alternatives that have to be considered in moral judgments about someone's responsibility (not to mention conceptual and other more fundamental questions that have first to be answered in this context).

As a matter of fact, our behavior usually follows a totally different rule of priority as we are inclined to prefer the interests of beings who are in some respect or the other *closer* to us, in particular the interests of members of the family, partnership or some other "core community" we live in, to the interests of beings who are more distant to us. So, we do not so much consider the quality or quantity of interests which are affected by our actions irrespective of who is the affected being, nor is it the gravity of the consequences of our actions which matters mainly to us, but the spatial, temporal, genetic, or personal *closeness* of the affected beings. Indeed, it is possible to *explain* this behavior biologically, psychologically, or sociologically, because in *most* cases the beings who are closest to us are also the ones who are most probably affected by our doing. This does not amount to saying, however, that such a behavior is *morally justified* in every case, because it may happen that some more distant being is more severely affected by some action of ours than our closest relatives.

From the point of view of universalistic ethics, behavior ruled by the *Principle of Priority of Closeness* cannot *per se* be justified, because, as Hare (1981) argued with regard to the consideration of future beings in moral reasoning, it amounts to *discounting* and, thus, *devaluating* what is more remote compared to what is closer. According to this principle, it is justified to valuate one and the same consequence of our actions less if it affects beings who are spatially, temporally, genetically, or personally farer to us, than it would be valuated if beings who are spatially, temporally, genetically, or personally closer to us are affected. It seems, however, that it is not morally justified, for instance, to expect of future generations of humans to live under conditions which we are not willing to put up with for ourselves, or to "export" readily tons of toxic waste to people living in the "Third World", because we would not like to have it in our own environment due to the risks for our health.

To reject the discounting of the more distant amounts to deny, of course, that the closeness of some being could be a primary criterion for moral judgments about the consequences of our actions. The rejection of discounting is motivated not only by the prospect of a high degree of *injustice* if equal interests are not treated equally, but also and even more by the fact that, according to the Principle of Priority of Closeness, it is justified to prefer ultimately *our own* interests generally to the interests of any other beings, because we are always closest to ourselves. Hence, if we want to exclude radical egoism from the set of ethical positions, we have to begin with

evaluating the interests of *all* beings who are affected by our actions, including ourselves, according to other criteria than that of closeness. On the other hand, this does not amount to assuming that closeness is completely irrelevant for moral reasoning. We can rather refer to it if we have already considered all other moral principles at hand, but without having come to any result in some concrete situation. That is, if *all other things are equal* and if we have nevertheless to decide what to do (or to judge which action is morally responsible), then it seems to be morally justified to take the spatial, temporal, genetic, or personal closeness of a being as a criterion in order to be able to act at all. If two beings A and B are to be treated equally in all other respects which are relevant for our decision, and if we have nevertheless to decide in favor of A or of B, then it appears to be justified to prefer, say, A because A is closer to us than B. Consequently, we have to think about whether we are willing to concede that it is morally justified, for instance, to kill an animal that menaces the life of my child, or another human person who threatens my life. Apparently, we have to accept this consequence at least under the condition that this is the *only* possibility for saving our own lives.

For moral judgments on actions not only interests have to be weighed but also the gravity and the extent of their *consequences* as well as the *knowledge* which to attribute to us can be justified. The consequences of our actions have to be judged in at least two respects:

(i) According to condition (ii) mentioned in the previous section, the attribution of responsibility presupposes that it is possible for us to exert some causal influence on a situation by having at least two alternatives at our disposal. Each of the available alternatives has a variety of consequences which have to be considered in several respects: The consequences that some alternative has for the various beings affected by the relevant action have to be weighed *against each other* with regard to their impact on the *interests* of *all* affected beings, and they have to be compared with the entirety of the consequences of all *other available alternatives*. As has been pointed out already by Frankena (1973: 14), according to any moral system that contains a teleological element, "an act is *right* if and only if it or the rule under which it falls produces, will probably produce, or is intended to produce *at least as great a balance of good over evil* as any available alternative; an act is *wrong* if and only if it does not so." Hence, we are not only responsible to act in this way, but it is also justified to ascribe moral responsibility to us solely under this condition. It might be the case that some action of mine has overall rather evil consequences, but if there are reasons to assume that from all available alternatives I have chosen one the foreseeable consequences of which are at least not worse than the consequences of any other alternative, then it is not justified to morally blame me for this action, because the consequences of every other alternative would not have been better (or would have been even worse) for the whole group of affected beings (including myself).

(ii) In accordance with the *presumption of innocence* mentioned above, we have to be regarded as morally responsible in the *positive* sense as long as there are no reasons to assume that the totality of consequences of some action of mine does not produce a greater evil than the other available alternatives of acting. Waiving this assumption would have disastrous consequences for moral reasoning, because then it would be justified to regard everybody as morally *guilty* as long as he or she could not demonstrate of *every* action of his or hers that its consequences are altogether at least not worse than the consequences of some other available alternative. The effort to do that would be *infinite*, however. On the other hand, it seems that the presumption of innocence can be applied without difficulty only in cases in which we know at least to some degree *which* consequences the various available alternatives have. This is by far not always the case; we have rather to reckon particularly nowadays that it is probable *that* certain actions will have some *severe, irreversible consequences* without being able to tell those consequences in advance. If we adhered to the presumption of innocence under this condition, we would have to regard countless actions as morally right, even if the probability of particularly grave and irreversible consequences is relatively high. Consequently, there would be no possibility to attribute to anybody the moral *duty* to refrain from a certain action of which it is impossible to say with certainty *which* consequences it has.

As a matter of fact, the presumption of innocence is often mentioned as an argument against the postulate that people living in highly industrialized countries should change their behavior in some way or the other. If it is claimed, for instance, that they should renounce from using fossil combustibles or substances containing certain chlorofluorocarbons because they have *probably* irreversible negative effects on the world climate, it is countered that we do *not really know* enough yet about these correlations so that we can go on with our behavior until we will have certainty. In this case, because of the gravity of the consequences, the presumption of innocence appears to be inappropriate so that it has to be superordinated by a *Principle of Prudence* of the kind proposed by Føllesdal (1981: 396) according to which we should refrain from performing a certain action if there are not *very good reasons* to assume that the probability of negative consequences of this action are very low. Such a principle has to be applied to situations with a relatively high probability of particularly severe and irreversible consequences; the gravity and constancy of negative consequences offer always a sufficient reason to act prudently — and to mark some action as morally problematic even if the probability of such consequences is relatively low. Only if we understand the consequences of our actions to a sufficient extent or if there is no evidence at all for the probability of severe, irreversible consequences, we can pass over to the presumption of innocence.

In addition to principles for priorities with regard to the consequences of actions and the interests of affected beings, we need also moral principles for the *succession of actions*. Eventually, we have usually to choose what we should do first. Should our first concern be, for instance, to revolutionize agriculture by new technologies in order to have enough nutrition for a constantly growing number of people when the areas of cultivable land shrink at the same time, or should we rather aim at recompensing the damage caused by the failures made so far in the exploitation of natural resources? Presumably, these are no strict, or even real, alternatives so that one approach does not exclude the other one, but it might yet be meaningful to proceed in a certain succession of actions ruled by principles. One possibility is, for instance, to apply a principle proposed by Hans Jonas (1979: 34) according to which we should first attempt at removing and preventing unacceptable evil and harm before considering the increase of welfare and happiness; in Jonas' words, the "prognosis of doom" has greater weight than the "prognosis of bliss," because we can live without the greatest good, but not with the greatest evil. If we accept this principle, we have to admit that our moral responsibility includes the duty to remove first evil that we recognize as unacceptable (for whomever), before we can think of creating new goods or augmenting human happiness.

The introduction of such principles is an attempt at clarifying the content of the conditions for the normative attribution of moral responsibility mentioned above and, thus, at determining more exactly the domain of moral responsibility. Those principles are not sufficient, however, for achieving this task. In order to distinguish moral responsibility from legal or other forms of responsibility, we have rather to refer also to the *Principle of Personal Causality* that goes ultimately back to Aristotle, but is explicitly formulated by William Stern (1918). According to this principle, it is justified to hold persons morally responsible only for states of affairs on which they can exert *by themselves* some causal influence. In contrast, a natural or legal person can be held legally responsible for something that is not causally connected with some action of his or hers (think, for instance, of product liability). Indeed, this practice contradicts the precept mentioned above that causal responsibility should be attributed counterfactually, but it is motivated by other reasons, in particular by the endeavor of the legislating persons to protect the victims of some event, for instance those who are affected by a defective product or by some damage caused by it. In such a case the producer is held liable even if the damage cannot be causally connected with the production process.

This practice seems to be inappropriate when *moral* responsibility is at stake, that is, for the following reason: It is possible to speak *meaningfully* of responsibility only if it can be distinguished from something that is *not* responsibility, that is, from phenomena that are not connected with moral, legal, or other demands, or from cases in which it is not justified (or not meaningful) to attribute responsibility to someone. If it is impossible to "define" responsibility in this sense and to delimit guilt or blameworthiness from other forms of responsibility (like liability), we are left with three rather unattractive alternatives, namely to feel *constantly guilty for everything*, to *delete* the conception of responsibility totally from our lives, or to use the expression 'responsibility' at best *metaphorically* only. In order to have a clue what we are responsible for and what we are not responsible for, we have to delimit the range of responsibility, whether by restricting the array of states of affairs, of actions, and of beings that form the domain or *object* of our responsibility, or by referring to additional *principles* or *criteria*, like the Principle of Personal Causality.

Although there are reasons to assume that the legal order is to some extent also an *open system of norms*, we have to admit that in spite of this openness its domain is much more exactly defined than that of a moral system which, in contrast to it, does not contain any regulations or limitations with regard to the array of beings, states of affairs, or actions for which we are held to be morally responsible, not to mention some information on the sanctions that were to be imposed on someone because of some wrongdoing. Due to the universal claim of morality it is impossible to restrict the attribution of responsibility in a similar way like in law, but moral principles apply to a potentially infinite number of cases. Therefore, the domain of moral responsibility is fundamentally open, and it is necessary to determine by reference to *other* criteria when it is justified to attribute moral responsibility to someone. One possibility is to rely on the Principle of Personal Causality according to which we are to be held morally responsible only for something upon which we can exert some causal influence by ourselves. Thus, as was recognized already by H.L.A. Hart (1968: 225f.), the assumption that we could be held responsible for something upon which we can exert no causal influence at all contradicts the concept of morality.

3 Moral Responsibility for Ourselves

From the notion of morality sketched in the previous section (which is discussed in more detail in Neumaier 2008, 105–172) it follows that we have the right and the duty towards ourselves to act morally, that is, to act correctly in accordance with the moral principles. This implies that it is justified to prefer our own interests to those of other beings if and only if the result of morally considering the various interests affected by our doing is in favor of ourselves (including the possibility that the comparison of interests does not result in any preference so that it is justified to prefer our own interest). This has nothing to do, however, with the question whether we are responsible for ourselves, because what is at stake are the prerequisites for responsible, or morally correct, behavior in general. As was mentioned above, someone acts responsibly in the moral sense only if he or she chooses from all available alternatives one the consequences of which are, for all affected beings including himself or herself, altogether at least not worse than the consequences of the other alternatives. In fact, it is *possible* that the result of comparing consequences and interests is to our own favor, but moral responsibility can also amount to subordinating our own interests.

Whenever we have to respect the interests of other beings who are affected by our actions, we bear also responsibility for ourselves, however, because this is a necessary condition for satisfying our responsibility with regard to those beings. In this respect, the moral responsibility we have for ourselves is positively *prior* to any other form of responsibility so that we can follow Spranger and say that moral responsibility always implies the imperative of taking care of ourselves. On the other hand, this does not amount to assuming that moral responsibility could be generally reduced to this imperative, nor do we know thereby *why* we are morally responsible in all these cases.

The thesis that we are morally responsible for ourselves, because this is a necessary condition for observing our responsibility for other beings, means not more than that self-responsibility is a *means* for achieving the real task of our moral responsibility, that is, the appropriate consideration of the interests of *all* beings (including ourselves) affected by some action of ours. We can hardly dismiss such an *instrumental* justification of moral self-responsibility, but this is not the answer given by Kant and Spranger to the question why we are morally responsible for ourselves. From their point of view, we are not so much morally responsible for ourselves in the instrumental sense but, rather, because we owe it *to ourselves for our own sake* to take care of ourselves. Which reasons could be referred to, however, for justifying that we have moral duties towards ourselves for our own sake?

In Kant's view (1797: 63), we have moral duties only to beings who have moral rights to us, and to have a moral right amounts to having the "*capacities* for putting others under obligations." Since "from all our experience we know of no being other than man that would be capable of obligation," a human person has, according to Kant (1797: 237), no duty to any beings other than "men (himself or other men)." Thus, Kant endorses some form of moral *anthropocentrism* according to which only humans have moral rights, because they are the only beings who are capable of putting someone under obligation. This anthropocentric view of Kant's does not, however, provide humans with a *carte-blanche* to treat, for instance, animals as they like, because, as is emphasized by Kant (1797: 238), "violent and cruel treatment of animals is far more intimately opposed to man's duty to himself, and he has a duty to refrain from this; for it dulls his shared feeling of their pain and so weakens and gradually uproots a natural predisposition that is very serviceable to morality in one's relation with other men." Thus, Kant condemns cruelty to animals because it leads to the brutalization of humans.

On the other hand, it is, in accordance with Kant's argumentation, by all means allowed to cause harm to animals *if* this provides a possibility to preserve or protect *human* life, because our compassion for harm to other humans weighs more than the compassion for harm to animals. One reason for that is, according to Kant (1924: 239) that *animals* "are there merely as a means to an end," because they "are not self-conscious," whereas humans are the end, in which case we can no longer ask: "Why does man exist?" Therefore, we have no direct duties to animals, but those alleged duties are, rather, indirect duties to humankind. In Kant's (1797: 237) view, we may have duties "*with regard to* other beings" than humans, but no duties "*to* those beings." The duties we have with regard to animals are just indirect duties we have to humans (including ourselves).

One of our duties to humans (including ourselves) is the preservation and protection of our lives if this is within the range of our possibilities of acting. Another duty is that we refrain from using any humans as a means to attain those ends. This follows from the Categorical Imperative which is paraphrased by Kant (1785: 36) as a *practical imperative* of the following form: "Act in such a way that you treat humanity, whether in your own person or in the person of another, always at the same time as an end and never simply as a means." Consequently, Kant assumes not only that humans are the only beings who have rights, but also that they are the only beings who have duties, and that they have these duties to all humans including themselves and for their own sake.

When Kant says that a human person "has duties only to men (himself or other men)," he does not say explicitly that we have duties to ourselves for our own sake, but primarily includes us into the group of those beings who have rights towards us and to whom we have duties. The assumption that we have duties to ourselves for our own sake is implied, however, by the practical imperative mentioned above, because it demands that I have to treat humanity also in *my own person* "always at the same time as an end and never simply as a means." And at another place, Kant (1797: 214) emphasizes explicitly that we are primarily under obligation to ourselves, "for I can recognize that I am under obligation to others only insofar as I at the same time put myself under obligation, since the law by virtue of which I regard myself as being under obligation proceeds in every case from my own practical reason; and in being constrained by my own reason, I am also the one constraining myself."

This idea appears by all means to be plausible in view of Kant's inclination to bind duties to the capability of obligating and being obligated. Furthermore Kant is right in assuming that among all humans I am first and foremost the one who is able to put myself under obligation. If we do not feel constrained to act morally by ourselves, or *autonomously*, it is highly improbable that we are in any way impressed by the attempts of other humans to put us under some moral obligation. This assumption raises the following problems, however:

(i) Kant's formulation that a human person has duties *to* "men (himself or other men)" is *ambiguous*: On the one hand, it can mean that we are only responsible in the sense of a moral duty *for* ourselves and other human beings, because only humans are capable of putting us under moral obligation, but on the other hand, it can also mean that we are morally responsible only *in the eyes*, or *in front*, of ourselves and other human beings, because only humans are capable of calling themselves or others to account. According to Kant, humans are thus not only the *objects* of their moral responsibility, but also the *moral authorities* who attribute moral responsibility to people (including themselves), control whether it is satisfied, and call people (including themselves) to account if this is not the case. Apparently, Kant's (1797: 233) primary concern is to show that we are basically the moral authorities for assessing our own moral responsibility, for he emphasizes that the human person is "his own innate judge." This thesis is totally different, however, from assuming that we are the primary objects of our own responsibility. And the fact that we are morally responsible to (that is, in the eyes of) our own conscience does not exclude in any way that we do not have moral duties to ourselves for our own sake, but merely in the *instrumental* sense, that is, insofar as this is necessary in order to satisfy our moral responsibility to (that is, for) other beings.

(ii) Kant's remark that we would not accept any duties to other people if we would not feel obligated to ourselves is arguably aimed at the assumption that we are willing to consider the claims of others only if we accept moral norms due to our *conscience*. This raises the question whereof the conscience of a human person consists and how it comes into being. If the German philosopher Hans Lenk (1986: 44ff.) is right in assuming that conscience is a "product of education and self-interpretation, ... an internalized concept" of socially given rules of conduct, then the conscience of some individual does not exist before the moral claims of the community he or she lives in, but is the *result* of being confronted with, and having internalized, those claims. Consequently, a human person is not "his own innate judge," but he or she has at best socially become his or her own judge.

(iii) Even if we were primarily responsible in the eyes of ourselves, this would not amount to assuming that we are also primarily responsible for ourselves, that is, that we have moral duties *to* ourselves and not only with regard to ourselves. As a matter of fact, we have to ask whether it is even meaningful to assume that we have any rights or duties to ourselves. That is to say, we can speak of rights and duties *meaningfully* only if some being A to whom some right is ascribed is not identical with the person B towards whom A has the right in question. If A and B are identical, then there is no point of asking for rights or duties. Let us imagine, for instance, that Cassius Clay declares to have some rights or duties towards Muhammad Ali. Depending on our attitude, we would experience such a remark as strange or funny, because those two names refer to one and the same person. It is almost the same situation as the one indicated by Wittgenstein (1953: § 268) by asking "Why can't my left hand give my right hand money?" Similarly, we have to admit that we have indeed moral duties with regard to ourselves, because we have duties to other human beings, but it seems to be impossible to justify that someone could have a moral duty to himself or herself *only*. Seen in this light it doesn't seem to be by chance that Kant (1797: 214) circumscribes the possibility of putting myself under obligation also in such a way that I am always "the one constraining" myself with regard to myself...

According to Kant's own criteria, we are therefore not responsible for ourselves for our own sake, but with regard to ourselves, that is, in some *instrumental* way. This does not amount to treating ourselves as a means only and, thus, violating Kant's practical imperative; it is rather said that the responsibility we have for ourselves can be *justified* as a *moral duty* not for our own sake, but only instrumentally, that is, with regard to the fact that it is necessary that we take care of ourselves in order to satisfy the moral duties we have to others.

4 Moravcsik's way

A main concern of Julius Moravcsik's contributions to ethics is to point out the close connection of morality with the *human condition* and, consequently, to demonstrate that ethics encompasses a greater variety of phenomena than we would presume because of the contemporary restriction to questions of *justified, correct conduct* which are usually answered by referring to some *moral laws* or rules that determine our *duties and rights*. Philosophers like Plato and Aristotle, who are in the focus of Moravcsik's philosophical investigations, directed their moral considerations to many other instances of individual and social life, like friendship and other interpersonal relationships, as well as care, respect, trust, and other attitudes that tie human beings to each other. This broader concept of morality and ethics offers also some possibilities for a deeper understanding of why we are morally responsible for ourselves.

To begin with, we could try to "save" the assumption that we are morally responsible to ourselves insofar as we have moral duties to ourselves for our own sake, that is, by justifying the attribution of a moral duty that a person A has to a person B, not by referring to a moral right B has towards A, but by assuming that B has some *intrinsic value* in the sense of Moore (1903; 1922). The fact that something is valuable in itself, or for its own sake, is also a good reason to assume that I am committed to consider it in my actions. In contrast to moral rights I am not obliged to bring some intrinsic value into being if it does not (yet) exist, but I have anyhow the moral duty to take existing moral values into consideration and to refrain from some action that would impair or destroy them. So we could think, even though we do not have moral duties to ourselves due to some right we would have towards ourselves, there is still the possibility left that we have moral duties to ourselves because our own life has some intrinsic value which we have to respect.

Indeed, the life of every human being is not only instrumentally valuable, that is, insofar as he or she can contribute with his or her actions to the welfare of other humans (as well as non-human beings), but the life of every individual seems also to have some value in itself, or for his or her own sake. From this we could conclude that we have at least the moral duty to ourselves to omit actions that could impair or destroy such a value. Before drawing this conclusion we should try, however, to answer the question what it is that bestows such an intrinsic value upon our life. Now, as has been argued by Moravcsik (1988a), the value of an individual's life is not only based on his or her natural dispositions, or "qualitative properties" (like capabilities or character traits), but also on his or her "relational properties," that is, on personal structures which are internalized representations of the essential relationships someone cultivates with other beings and the experiences resulting from such relationships (like friendships, family ties, or other social relations).

The notion of a human person implies the assumption of relational properties, because it is impossible to conduct a personal existence without any relationships to other persons. If being a person basically amounts to being able to reflect and to experience oneself *as* oneself, then it is plausible to assume that being a person presupposes a *social* life from which we gain some information on the world and ourselves which is not contained in our genes and enables us to regard ourselves, as it were, from the outside, virtually like someone else, that is, to develop what Helmuth Plessner (1928) calls the "eccentric positionality" of persons. In short, we could not conduct a life as human persons if we would not live in the community of other human persons. Thus, the assumption that the life of a human person has some intrinsic value is to a great extent based on the relationships this person cultivates with other persons and essentially refers, therefore, to his or her relational properties. Consequently, Moravcsik (1988b) argues that human individuals as well as the communities they live in and constitute have both an intrinsic value and an instrumental value for each other.

Conducting a personal life includes, amongst other things, that the person in question cares for the humans who form a community with him or her, that he or she respects them, is interested in them, and takes the moral responsibility arising from situations in which the other members of such a community are affected by some action of the person in question. As far as moral *responsibility* is at stake, the main question is not, however, whether we cultivate relationships with other human persons but, rather, to what extent and in what respect other beings, particularly persons, are *affected* by our actions. As is mentioned above, in many cases the beings who are closest to us, that is, the beings with whom we cultivate our essential relationships that are internalized as relational properties, are also the ones who are most probably affected by our actions. So, in many cases the concern of some being results from a relationship, and the same holds for the moral responsibility we have for such a being.

Indeed, we usually have also essential relationships to ourselves, but what matters more in this context is the fact that nobody could conduct a life as a human person if he or she would not cultivate any social relationships to other human persons at all. If, because of some catastrophe, only one human person had survived, his or her life would have lost a great deal of its intrinsic value. Although the life of such a person would not be totally valueless, since its value could be based not only on relational properties, but also on qualitative ones, it would at least be much more difficult to justify that one's life has an inherent value in such an extreme situation and, *therefore*, to require that he or she had the *moral duty* to live on in spite of his or her radical loneliness.

Consequently, such extreme situations delimit the plausibility of Kant's (1785: 10) thesis that it is everybody's duty "to preserve one's life", and to do that in particular "if adversity and hopeless sorrow have completely taken away the taste for life, if an unfortunate man, strong in soul and more indignant at his fate than despondent or dejected, wishes for death and yet preserves his life without loving it." Indeed, a human person who preserves his or her life without loving it is not to be blamed for doing that. We can admit this, however, without assuming at the same time that preserving one's life in a situation of "adversity and hopeless sorrow" were a *moral duty* for every human person. How could the validity of such a duty be justified if there is no other being on the whole world for whom a human person could be morally responsible than this very person himself or herself?

But do duties represent the only moral category that is relevant for the question why we are morally responsible for ourselves? According to Julius Moravcsik (1980; 2004), this is definitely not the case, and he has argued that ethics should start with an account of *human nature* that includes as an essential component a conception of a human *ideal*, that is, of the kind of person we *should* like to be; this ideal comprises also certain *emotions* and *attitudes* which are subject to rational critique, but cannot be justified within a moral theory, because they do not fall under moral laws or rules. Moravcsik (1980) argues for the importance that attitudes and emotions have for morality by referring to some examples of "moral blindness" which may lead the members of one moral community to accept certain practices as morally immaculate that are vehemently rejected by the members of another moral community, although they all acknowledge the same moral principles. Moravcsik's examples are the practices of slavery and of staking prisoners of war, but we could also think of the sexual abuse of children or of cruelty to animals (which is regarded by people living in the "enlightened" world as immoral, whereas many of them regard animal experimentation which serves the development of remedies for humans or just of cosmetics as morally irreproachable).

To get back to the question of why we are morally responsible for ourselves, we can consider the possibility that moral responsibility for ourselves might not be a *moral duty* we have to ourselves for our own sake but that it is nevertheless *morally good* to take responsibility for ourselves and, for instance, to preserve our life as long as just *any* value inheres to it. As a matter of fact, the expression 'responsibility' is often used in order to say that it is morally good to perform certain actions and to omit other ones, without claiming that we would violate some duty by refraining to perform (or to omit) such actions. Unlike Hans Jonas (1979: 6f.) who argues that we are morally responsible for the preservation of the whole biosphere in the sense of a *duty*, we can rather assume that moral responsibility for the preservation of the whole biosphere is not so much a case of moral duty, but of acting morally well: It is certainly not morally bad to perform actions that serve the preservation of the biosphere, but human persons would be morally overburdened if they had the moral duty in the strict sense to do that. The precept of acting morally well can at best mean that everything we do should be morally good, but not that we should do everything that is morally good, because there is an infinite number of morally good actions, and it would be absurd to require from humans to perform infinitely many morally good actions.

The moral responsibility we have for ourselves can also be seen in the light of this consideration, that is, not as a moral duty, but as some kind of *meritorious* or *supererogatory* acting, as it is called by philosophers like Kant (1797: 53, 194f.) or Bolzano (1834: III 212; 1837: IV 69f.). Viewed from this point of view, it is morally good to take moral responsibility for ourselves, although we do not violate any moral duty to ourselves for our own sake by omitting some relevant action. Inasmuch as moral responsibility for ourselves has to do with moral duties, they have to be regarded as *instrumental*, that is, we are responsible for ourselves in the sense of a moral duty, because this is a necessary condition for meeting the duties we have to other beings who have rights towards us. It does not seem plausible to assume, however, that we have duties or rights towards ourselves for our own sake. The assumption that we have duties only *with regard* to ourselves, that is, in the instrumental sense, does not amount to saying that we are not at all morally responsible for ourselves; it is rather the case that we are always *also* morally responsible for ourselves because of our moral responsibility in general. If we would not take care of ourselves, we would violate our moral responsibility to others. Therefore, it is "only" with regard to the context of *emergence* that the moral responsibility we have for ourselves is *prior* to any other kind of responsibility — in contrast to the question how responsibility in the sense of a moral duty is to be *justified*.

In Kant's own words, we do not so much have moral duties *to* ourselves, but moral duties *with regard* to ourselves. This does not reduce the importance of moral responsibility for ourselves, although in another respect than Kant had in mind: As much as we do have, according to Kant (1797: 238), a moral duty to refrain from any "violent and cruel treatment of animals," because this practice dulls our "shared feeling of their pain and so weakens and gradually uproots a natural predisposition that is very serviceable to morality in one's relation with other men," as much do we have a moral duty to take care of ourselves, because otherwise nobody would have any reason to trust that we behave responsibly towards him or her — irrespective of whether it is justified to attribute some moral duty to us. Thus, by not taking care of ourselves, our sense for morality as well as the basis for the living together of humans would also be weakened and ultimately uprooted

— the result being some general form of "moral blindness" as it is pointed out by Moravcsik (1980). From his considerations we can also conclude that the quest for moral duties might not be the main issue when moral responsibility for ourselves, and in general, is at stake. Apparently, what matters more is the question whether we have reasons to trust in each other with regard to some common moral basis of conduct. Our common interest in preserving this basis of morality and community does not offer any theoretical *justification* that we are responsible for ourselves in the sense of a moral duty we have *to* ourselves, but it provides at least a good *motivation* to argue for such a *moral duty in the instrumental sense*.

BIBLIOGRAPHY

[Bolzano, 1834] Bolzano, Bernard (1834): *Lehrbuch der Religionswissenschaft*, Sulzbach: Seidel.
[Bolzano, 1837] Bolzano, Bernard (1837): *Wissenschaftslehre. Versuch einer ausführlichen und größtentheils neuen Darstellung der Logik*, Sulzbach: Seidel.
[Føllesdal, 1981] Føllesdal, Dagfinn (1981): Einige ethische Aspekte der DNS-Rekombination, in: Morscher, Edgar/Neumaier, Otto/Zecha, Gerhard (Eds.): *Philosophie als Wissenschaft. Essays in Scientific Philosophy*, Bad Reichenhall: Comes, 393–411.
[Frankena, 1963] Frankena, William K. (1963): *Ethics*, 2nd ed., Upper Saddle River/NJ: Prentice Hall, 1973.
[Hare, 1955] Hare, Richard M. (1955): Universalisability, in: *Proceedings of the Aristotelian Society* 55: 295–312.
[Hare, 1981] Hare, Richard M. (1981): *Moral Thinking. Its Levels, Method and Point*, Oxford: Clarendon.
[Hart, 1968] Hart, H.L.A. (1968): *Punishment and Responsibility. Essays in the Philosophy of Law*, Oxford: Clarendon.
[Heider, 1958] Heider, Fritz (1958): *Psychology of interpersonal Relations*, New York: Wiley.
[Jonas, 1979] Jonas, Hans (1979): *The Imperative of Responsibility. In Search of an Ethics for the Technological Age*, transl. by Hans Jonas with the collab. of David Herr, Chicago: University of Chicago Press, 1984.
[Kant, 1785] Kant, Immanuel (1785): *Grounding for the Metaphysics of Morals*, transl. by James W. Ellington, 3d ed., Indianapolis: Hackett, 1993.
[Kant, 1797] Kant, Immanuel (1797): *The Metaphysics of Morals*, transl. by Mary Gregor, Cambridge: Cambridge University Press, 1991.
[Kant, 1924] Kant, Immanuel (1924): *Lectures on Ethics*, transl. by Louis Infield, London: Methuen, 1979.
[Kelson, 1941] Kelsen, Hans (1941): *Vergeltung und Kausalität*. Den Haag: van Stockum (Reprint: Wien: Böhlau, 1982).
[Kelsen, 1954] Kelsen, Hans (1954): Kausalität und Zurechnung, in: *Österreichische Zeitschrift für Öffentliches Recht* 6: 125–151.
[Lenk, 1986] Lenk, Hans (1986): Verantwortung und Gewissen des Forschers, in: Neumaier, Otto (Ed.): *Wissen und Gewissen. Arbeiten zur Verantwortungsproblematik*, Wien: VWGÖ, 35–55.
[Moore, 1903] Moore, G.E. (1903): *Principia Ethica*, rev. ed., ed. by Thomas Baldwin, Cambridge: Cambridge University Press, 1993.
[Moore, 1922] Moore, G.E. (1922): The Conception of Intrinsic Value, in: Moore (1903), 280–298.
[Moravcsik, 1980] Moravcsik, Julius (1980): On What We Aim At and How We Live, in: Depew, David J. (Ed.): *The Greeks and the Good Life*, Indianapolis: Hackett, 198–235.
[Moravcsik, 1988a] Moravcsik, Julius (1988a): The Perils of Friendship and Conceptions of the Self, in: Dancy, Jonathan/Moravcsik, Julius/Taylor, C.C.W. (Eds.): *Human Agency. Language, Duty, and Value. Philosophical Essays in Honor of J.O.Urmson*, Stanford/CA: Stanford University Press, 133–151.
[Moravcsik, 1988b] Moravcsik, Julius (1988b): Communal Ties, in: *Proceedings and Addresses of the American Philosophical Association* 62: 211–225.

[Moravcsik, 2004] Moravcsik, Julius (2004): *The Ties That Bind*, Budapest–New York: Central European University Press.

[Neumaier, 2008] Neumaier, Otto (2008): Moralische Verantwortung. Beiträge zur Analyyse eines ethischen Begriffs. Paderborn: Schöningh.

[Piaget, 1932] Piaget, Jean (1932): *The Moral Judgment of the Child*, transl. by Marjorie Gabain, London: Routledge & Kegan Paul.

[Plessner, 1928] Plessner, Helmuth (1928): *Die Stufen des Organischen und der Mensch. Einleitung in die philosophische Anthropologie*, Berlin–Leipzig: de Gruyter.

[Searle, 1969] Searle, John R. (1969): *Speech Acts. An Essay in the Philosophy of Language*, Cambridge: Cambridge University Press.

[Singer, 1993] Singer, Peter (1993): *Practical Ethics*, 2nd ed., Cambridge: Cambridge University Press.

[Spranger, 1963] Spranger, Eduard (1963): *Menschenleben und Menschheitsfragen. Gesammelte Rundfunkreden*. München.

[Stern, 1918] Stern, William (1918): *Die menschliche Persönlichkeit* (= Person und Sache, 2). Leipzig: Barth.

[Wittgenstein, 1953] Wittgenstein, Ludwig (1953): *Philosophical Investigations*, transl. by G.E.M. Anscombe, Oxford: Blackwell.

Part D
Plato

Platonic Metaphysics and Semantics: The *Cratylus*' Ties to the *Sophist* and *Politicus*

SUSAN B. LEVIN

1 Introduction

The nature and extent of the *Cratylus*' ties to other Platonic dialogues is hotly contested, and commentators have stressed what they take to be its isolated position. On my interpretation, the *Cratylus* may be tied differently and more closely than hitherto recognized — on both metaphysical and semantic grounds — to the *Phaedo*, on the one hand, and to the *Sophist* and *Politicus*, on the other. First and foremost, the *Cratylus* criticizes what Plato views as inadequate conceptions of "nature" (*phusis*) and "correctness" (*orthotês*) in the application of "words" or "names" (*onomata*) to their referents. While the *Cratylus*' emphasis is critical, Plato provides clues there regarding the content of his own stance. Those hints are developed in the *Phaedo*, which articulates Plato's conception of naturalness in the presentation of his theory of Forms and uses eponymy to provide the semantics of the Form-participant relation (i.e., that framework in terms of which judgments of terms' appropriateness are made). The Method of Division (*diairesis*) as such does not figure in the *Cratylus*. In addition, links to the *Sophist* and *Politicus* do not center on the problem of falsehood; the mere fact that in the *Cratylus*, as in the *Euthydemus*, falsehood is claimed to be impossible does not in itself justify assertions of a close kinship with the *Sophist*. I maintain that, as is the case with the *Cratylus* and *Phaedo*, the most fundamental and tightest connections involving the *Cratylus* and these two late dialogues center on the concepts of naturalness and appropriateness.[1] It is thus not the notion of Forms or division itself that constitutes the closest link between the *Cratylus* and key dialogues from both the middle and late periods but rather concepts that are treated extensively in light of Forms and division, respectively, in those writings to which connections are made.[2] Due to a shift in the locus of common ground, a single interpretation of the *Cratylus* can forge close ties to key dialogues in both periods. I present briefly here my

---

[1] While a final determination regarding the *Cratylus*' position is impossible, in Levin [2001] I locate it near the beginning of that group of dialogues comprising the *Symposium*, *Phaedo*, and *Republic*; for this view see also, e.g., Kahn [1973; 1986]; Ross [1955]; Méridier [1931]; and von Arnim [1912]. Although some have linked it with the *Theaetetus*, Luce [1964] and Calvert [1970] offer grounds for adhering to the earlier date; cf. Brandwood [1990] and Kahn [1996].

[2] For a recent account tying the *Cratylus* to Plato's treatment of *diairesis*, see Barney [2001, 44–45, 94, and 100–101].

central conclusions regarding the *Cratylus* and *Phaedo*, which I develop at length elsewhere, then turn to Plato's handling of naturalness and appropriateness in the *Sophist* and *Politicus*.[3]

2 *Cratylus*

In earlier work on the *Cratylus*, I argued that the Greek literary tradition constitutes the most direct and central opponent of the dialogue's critical treatment of etymologizing, above all of proper names, for the sake of revealing their referents' natures.[4] In the course of the *Cratylus*, Plato rejects both the notion that etymological analyses can disclose *phuseis* and the guiding assumption of literary practice that natures belong first and foremost to individuals. Plato's critique of etymological praxis transpires via the *technê* framework, highly normative in character, that he had articulated in the *Gorgias*, whose central criteria for this elevated status were the subject-matter, understanding, and goodness conditions.

At the outset of the *Cratylus*, when purporting to treat etymologizing as a truly expert endeavor, Plato speaks as though one could, if properly oriented, recover the original intentions of one *nomothetês*, who later in the dialogue becomes the *onomathetês* through a linguistic ploy (388e-389a); on this alleged model, the dialectician judges the namegiver's constructions to ensure that terms' semantic constitution properly reveals their referents' natures. As it becomes clear that Plato has no genuine interest in uncovering original semantic intentions in the positing of *onomata*, the *onomathetês* loses his normative veil, and the dialectician — now jobless in connection with naming thus construed — vanishes from the discussion as Plato crushes its claim to *technê* status.[5] Having rejected this status for naming qua etymologizing, with its attendant machinery of the double expert, Plato glances briefly toward his own stance regarding the notions of naturalness and appropriateness (438-440), his own revamped conceptions of which undergird the *Phaedo*.[6]

---

[3]I intend this discussion to broaden the terms of debate that have been further enriched by the recent treatments of Sedley [2003] and Barney [2001], which assert different connections and interpretive foundations than I do here involving the *Cratylus* and other dialogues.

[4]See Levin [2001, chaps. 1–3]. The authors on whom I concentrate there are Homer, Hesiod, Pindar, the three tragedians, and Herodotus.

[5]In this critique, the understanding and subject-matter (*peri ti*) requirements on genuine *technai* are in the foreground (for discussion see Levin [2001, 82–89]). The goodness criterion is, however, also relevant insofar as audiences' affective responses can be shaped or enhanced by particular analyses of names' descriptive content. Moreover, an occupation with the goodness condition helps to make intelligible Plato's stress on the possibility that *onomata*, and analyses thereof, can be manipulated to accommodate whatever interests the creator or user happens to have. By the close of the dialogue, it is evident that those who shadow *onomata* in their quest to grasp reality will be deceived, and hence suffer harm, by failing to identify and pursue those *eidê* whose apprehension secures human flourishing (see Levin [2001, 129–131]). Hence, all three of the major conditions are operative in the *Cratylus'* rejection of the *technê* status of naming qua etymologizing. For a different view of Plato's concern to recover namegivers' intentions, see Sedley [2003].

[6]For a defense of these claims, see Levin [2001, 94–98 and chap. 4]. *Pace* the many interpreters who contend that Plato's remarks concerning etymology or phonetic constitution (i.e., *prôta*

Although the *Cratylus* rejects the view that naming qua etymologizing qualifies as a *technê* — which wrongheaded stance deprives the dialectician of a normative role in matters of naming — it suggests (439d) that judgments of terms' correctness, if grounded on a sound metaphysics and semantics, would be an important component of philosophical practice. In elaborating his own theories elsewhere, Plato will in fact show how the evaluation of terms' appropriateness, while not itself a *technê*, indeed falls within the province of philosophy, the *technê* par excellence.

3 *Phaedo*

At the heart of Plato's metaphysics in the middle dialogues is a dichotomy between reality and appearance.[7] The concept of "nature," in whose treatment Plato diverges both from literature and from Presocratic natural philosophy, plays an essential role in his theory. What is natural for Plato is a certain articulation of reality into objective and theoretically important unities, which are granted the status of Forms; the key is to identify elements whose interrelations yield the order and harmony that he construes as paradigmatic (the most central cases of this being entities in the realm of values and of mathematics). The *Phaedo* offers direct linguistic testimony to the centrality of naturalness, as when Plato emphasizes that the opposite itself can never become opposite to itself, "neither that in us nor that in nature (ἐν τῇ φύσει)" (103b5). Later in the dialogue, he invokes "the true earth" (ἡ γῆ αὐτή), plus the superior quality of what issues from and belongs to it, as an allegory for the realm of Forms and the qualitatively higher status of its constituent entities (109a-114c).[8]

This metaphysical picture raises a new and important semantic question: what is the connection between the employment of a term (e.g., beautiful) with reference to a Form and its use as an ingredient in a series of complex predicates (i.e., how is one to represent the semantics of the Form-participant relation)? For this

---

onomata) reflect serious philosophical commitments on his part (see most recently Sedley [2003] and Barney [2001]), I continue to maintain that while Plato's philosophical intentions in the *Cratylus* are quite sincere, they do not result in his provision of a positive account of *orthotês onomatôn* therein. For earlier work claiming to find in the long etymological portion of the dialogue evidence of a positive stance, see Kretzmann [1971; 1967]; Silverman [1992]; Weingartner [1973]; Kato [1986]; Grote [1867]; Lorenz and Mittelstrass [1967]; and Steinthal [1890/1961, 99, 108]. For accounts that foreground Plato's discussion of phonetic constitution, see Jowett [1892, 259–262] and Leky [1919/1967, 54].

[7] Material in this and the following paragraph is drawn from Levin [2001, 106–110]. In contrast to Notomi [1999, 141–162], who argues that Plato's construction of "appearance" in the *Sophist* is *no longer* merely negative, I would suggest that while, epistemologically speaking, appearances can certainly lead one astray earlier on (see, e.g., the lovers of sights and sounds in *Rep.* 476a-c), they also clearly stimulate the process of recollection in both the *Phaedo* and *Symposium* — notwithstanding the fact that in the former, the negative side of Plato's bidimensional judgment is so fervently expressed as to sometimes divert interpreters from giving core acts of perceptual recognition and judgment their proper due.

[8] For pertinent terminology see also *Symp.* 210e4-5; *Rep.* 490a8-b3, 501b2-3, and 525c2-3. Unless otherwise noted, citations of OCT, vol. 1, are from the 1995 edition of Duke, Hicken, Nicoll, Robinson, and Strachan.

purpose neither synonymy nor homonymy will do; Plato chooses, instead, eponymy, which had been prominent in Greek literature, revamping it as needed to suit his metaphysics centering on Forms and *metechonta*. Through its provision of a framework for offering philosophical judgments of correctness when *onomata* of Forms and their participants are at issue, the *Phaedo* realizes the possibility, suggested at the *Cratylus'* close, that the praxis of naming, if properly construed, could assume a valuable role in the conduct of philosophy. Although the manner of terms' assignment to entities reflects and expresses certain general facts about natures — namely, whether the referents of the *onomata* in question are *phuseis* in the primary sense or derivatively — for Plato, *onomata* themselves do not reveal those natures.

Turning now to the *Sophist* and *Politicus*, we see that the key notions of naturalness and appropriateness that weld the *Cratylus* to the *Phaedo* also tie it closely to these two late writings. Possible appearances to the contrary notwithstanding, Plato does not resurrect in the *Sophist* an alleged concern with etymological praxis. Instead, his recourse there to considerations of semantic constitution is in strict keeping both with the *Cratylus'* rejection of the philosophical merit of etymologizing and with Plato's limited use of such analyses as a kind of literary device outside that dialogue.[9] Although the philosopher's work in the domain of naming does not expand along those lines, Plato's discussions of *onomata* in the *Sophist* and *Politicus* illustrate that the philosopher of the late dialogues will not only, as in the *Phaedo*, make judgments regarding the proper application of existing *onomata*; she will also, where necessary, delete terms from the lexicon and add those that are required to designate elements of reality that have yet to be graced with *onomata*. In this way, while the philosopher does not collaborate with or function as *onomathetês* in the precise sense that Plato had derided in the *Cratylus*, Plato's concern with naming comes full circle, in the end, by placing both evaluation and construction — properly construed — in the philosopher's repertoire.

4   *Sophist* and *Politicus*

While Plato's technical discussions in the middle period focus on individual Forms and on the Form-participant connection, he obviously maintains the existence of ontological links between Forms. As Moravcsik [1973b, 325–326] has noted, although Plato is committed to the existence of such ties and aware of their importance, he does not incorporate the consequences of this realization in the fabric of his metaphysical theory as set out at this juncture.[10] There is thus a gap between

---

[9] For a different interpretation of the *Sophist*, according to which the *Cratylus* leaves open the possibility that the naturalistic conception of language is correct, see Notomi [1999, 136].

[10] My own discussion of *diairesis* in the *Sophist* and *Politicus* is strongly influenced by this magisterial essay. That in the middle dialogues Plato espouses ontological ties between Forms is evident in his treatment of the virtues of soul in the *Republic* (Book IV, preceded by *Meno* 71-80); the relation between the Form of the Good and other Forms (*Rep.* VI-VII); and his remarks on connections between mathematical entities in the *Phaedo*'s last argument for immortality (103a-107b).

Plato's theory as he actually presents it, on the one hand, and his own application of it and description of the content of *dialektikê*, on the other (i.e., as movement "by means of Forms, through and to Forms, and culminating with Forms" [εἴδεσιν αὐτοῖς δι' αὐτῶν εἰς αὐτά, καὶ τελευτᾷ εἰς εἴδη, *Rep.* 511c1-2]).

Plato can close this gap only by developing the theory further. While Plato's basic ontology remains the same in the *Sophist* and *Politicus*, the focus of his technical discussions shifts from individual *eidê* and the Form-participant relation to the issue of mutual ties between the elements of reality themselves. In this context, *diairesis* plays a salient role, and in the *Sophist* and *Politicus* Plato uses it to explore how certain indivisible Forms (the specific concepts of sophistry and statesmanship, respectively) are connected to a network of other more generic Forms or kinds.[11] *Diairesis* — most fundamentally the notions of naturalness and appropriateness that are central to its employment — constitutes the focus of the present inquiry.

In the *Phaedo*, Plato introduced a strong notion of what I call "ontological naturalness" to distinguish it from the familiar semantic rubric of *orthotês onomatôn*. He retains this notion in the late dialogues, employing it in connection with those specific cuts gleaned in reality in the process of division. Plato first treats *diairesis* theoretically and as a methodology of broad relevance in the *Phaedrus*.[12] There

---

[11] The dialectician is explicitly assigned responsibility for division into kinds: see the introduction of this view in the *Phaedrus* (266b-c), along with its reiteration and development in the *Sophist* and *Politicus* (253b-e and 284e-285c, respectively). In the late writings, there are certain expansions of the scope of reality, a notable example being the fact that a pursuit like sophistry, relegated in the *Gorgias* to the class of *empeiriai*, is now admitted as a *technê*, that is to say, as part of reality. Such activities are, however, viewed as bad insofar as they are capable of wringing grave harm on people's souls, as may be discerned clearly in the case of *sophistikê* from the particular sequence of intermediate Forms, or kinds, through which the *Sophist*'s investigation moves. Hence, Plato's attitude toward such practices in the late dialogues remains as fervently hostile as before although the expression of that condemnation takes a somewhat different form. On *diairesis* as moving through Forms, see Cornford [1957, 269–270] and Skemp [1952, 73–74, 76]. According to Moravcsik [1973b], what is at issue are more and less generic Forms (the latter of which are kinds), even if not all differentiae issuing from *diairesis* themselves represent such entities. On the view of Sayre [2006, chap. 12], though kinds in the *Sophist* are equivalent to *eidê* construed as Forms (227) and divisions in the *Politicus*, too, must be made "according to Forms" (229), what results from the process in the latter are kinds construed as classes rather than Forms themselves (229). My own sympathies lie with the general stance of Moravcsik [1973b] concerning Forms and kinds. For the purposes of the present study, however, one may note that notwithstanding this scholarly disagreement on whether all products of division are Forms, the process of *diairesis* is in any case ultimately Form-dependent from start to finish.

[12] See 265d-266c and 277b. While Plato employs a scheme of classification in the *Gorgias* (463e-466a, cf. 454e) to suit the demands of a particular context, there is no indication that he consciously views the approach as having broad or general applicability, as he clearly does from the *Phaedrus* onward. For a recent, illuminating account of the *Phaedrus* that treats *diairesis* — first anticipated, then introduced expressly — as the dialogue's unifying principle, see Dorter [2006]. On the *Phaedrus* as the juncture of division's introduction, cf. Sayre [2006, 36, 125]; Notomi [1999, 5]; and Moravcsik [1973b, 325–327]. For a different view see Barney [2001, 44–45, 94, 100–101]; Shorey [1903, 51]; and Dodds [1959, 226].

Some (e.g., Kretzmann [1971, 130]) attribute significance vis-à-vis *diairesis* to the mention of "cutting" (τέμνειν) and "burning" (κάειν) in *Cra.* 387a-b, whereas, in fact, the medical role of

he describes the process of division by analogy with a natural body and its limbs, where language of "naturalness" is used to emphasize the objective character of proper delineations (see 265e1-266a3).[13] Having expressed his tremendous esteem for those able to draw the relevant distinctions (266b5-7), Socrates labels individuals with this capacity διαλεκτικοί (b8-c1).[14] Plato employs the same analogy in the *Politicus,* as for instance early on when the Eleatic Stranger asks whether he and Young Socrates might discover a natural break or division (τις διαφυή; literally, a joint) in ἡ γνωστική (259d10-11).[15] Reinforcing the point as they prepare subsequently to enumerate those *technai* that must be distinguished from statesmanship and that resist simple bifurcation, the Stranger notes that they must divide them "according to their natural divisions as we would carve a sacrificial victim" (Κατὰ μέλη τοίνυν αὐτὰς οἷον ἱερεῖον διαιρώμεθα, 287c3).[16] The analogy with natural bodies, both here and in the *Phaedrus,* is felicitous because it highlights the fact that there are objectively correct and incorrect places to make "cuts," or "breaks," in reality.[17]

In the *Cratylus,* Plato concludes that naming does not itself qualify as a *technê*

---

these activities was well known prior to Plato and is at issue there (cf. Luce [1965, 32]). For pre-Platonic occurrences, see Heraclitus, DK 58, and Aesch. *Ag.* 848-850; for the medical sense in Plato prior to the *Cratylus,* see *Grg.* 456b4, 476c3-d2, 479a9, 480c6-7, and 521e8. Notably, *temnein* does not appear at all in the passage in which classification is under discussion (*Grg.* 463e-466a); in fact, with the *Cratylus'* early provision of a shuttle analogy in view, it is worth observing that *temnein* with a medical sense, weaving, and an instance of classification are all present in the *Gorgias* without being linked together. It is not the case that the technical sense at issue in *diairesis* replaces the non-technical (in this regard see *Pol.* 293b2 and 298a4-5, where τέμνειν, conjoined with κάειν, has its familiar medical sense). The former meaning does, however, come strongly to the fore (see, e.g., *Sph.* 219e4, 227d1; and *Pol.* 261b11). Instances of *temnein* in a mathematical setting (especially the participle and cognate noun in *Rep.* 509d6-7) may well have a transitional or intermediate status but are not equivalent to the technical sense involved in *diairesis.*

[13]For cuts as involving natural kinds, see Moravcsik [1973b, 330, 339, 344, and 345]. The right-hand division in the *Phaedrus* arrives at a type of ἔρως with the same appellation as (ὁμώνυμος with) the other, yet of a wholly different nature, specifically, divine; the idea that *onomata* are potentially misleading, developed and exemplified further in the *Sophist* and *Politicus,* is pertinent here.

[14]As Robinson [1953, 70] has observed, Plato utilizes *dialektikê* and its cognates to designate his favored philosophical method, " '*whatever that may be,*' " at a given juncture.

[15]The noun *diaphuê* occurs only twice in the Platonic corpus. In the other, earlier, instance, Plato uses the term in its literal and more familiar sense (*Phd.* 98c8).

[16]Plato views it as advantageous to divide evenly, i.e., down the middle, wherever possible (*Pol.* 262a-c and 265a). Though, as seen in *Pol.* 287c, the structure of reality does not always permit simple bifurcations (cf. *Phil.* 16c10-d7), one must aim to reach the smallest number of ontologically legitimate "cuts" therein; on Plato's use of nondichotomous divisions, see Sayre [2006] and Notomi [1999]. Unless otherwise noted, translations of the *Sophist* and *Politicus* are those of White [1993] and Skemp [1952], respectively.

[17]For imagery of a biological and genealogical variety, see, in addition, *Sph.* 268d3-4. The notion of there being objectively right and wrong places to make cuts emerges abundantly elsewhere, as when Plato emphasizes that at all points below that of the generic Form (e.g., *technê* or *arithmos*) one must arrive at a *meros* that is also an *eidos*; while all such *eidê* are also *merê,* the reverse is not necessarily the case (*Pol.* 263b). This view is strongly prefigured at *Phdr.* 265e1-3.

though, as we saw, this is compatible with its being integral to the conduct of *technai*, specifically, dialectic. The role of the dialectician in matters of naming remains central to Plato's reflections, evolving in the late writings as befits shifts there in his handling of Forms and their individuation.[18]

Plato sets as the goal of *diairesis* arrival at the most disclosive characterization (*logos*) possible of that indivisible Form toward which inquiry is in each case directed (see *Sph.* 217b2-3).[19] As in the middle period, answers to the *ti esti* question never comprise the mere provision or exploration of a single *onoma*.[20] In fact, at *Sophist* 261d-262c Plato announces in no uncertain terms his continued adherence to the view that *onomata* by themselves never indicate the nature of anything (see especially 262c2-5, where Plato insists that οὐδεμίαν... οὔτε οὕτως οὔτ' ἐκείνως πρᾶξιν οὐδ' ἀπραξίαν οὐδὲ οὐσίαν ὄντος οὐδὲ μὴ ὄντος δηλοῖ τὰ φωνηθέντα, πρὶν ἄν τις τοῖς ὀνόμασι τὰ ῥήματα κεράσῃ). While this observation is made in comments about syntax, it involves a claim about the status of *onomata* that is of general pertinence. In the remark's broader context, the term ὄνομα is first used generically, in the sense of "word" (see 261d2 and 4). In what follows, ὀνόματα thus construed are divided into ὀνόματα and ῥήματα (261e4-262a1). Given the sequence of these remarks, the claim that no ὄνομα is nature-revealing (262c) thus stands regardless of whether one has the term's generic or more specific sense in view. *Phuseis* are always revealed at the level of *logoi* since such disclosures must indicate the explanandum's relation to other concepts, which is something no *onoma* — and only a limited set of *logoi* — can accomplish.[21] This is not to say that individual *onomata* are inessential to the enterprise; Plato's interest in them, however, concerns

---

[18]In Plato's treatments of division in the *Sophist* and *Politicus*, *logoi* "replace the earlier unique characterizations that were achieved by means of the peculiar nature-revealing singular references" [Moravcsik, 1973b, 326]. These singular references (e.g., *auto to kalon*) do not, of course, reveal through their descriptive content, as in etymologizing, but instead point one in the direction of natures. As we will see, a distinction between descriptive content and descriptive force is pivotal to conceptualization of the *Cratylus*' intricate connection, as regards semantics, to the *Sophist* and *Politicus*.

[19]For *logoi* as more and less revealing rather than true or false, see Barney [2001, 174–175] and Moravcsik [1973b, 332–333, 345]. Though a central form of inquiry, *diairesis* is employed in conjunction with other methodologies to address questions about *phuseis*. One may acknowledge this fact of supplementation without reaching Ryle's conclusion [1965, 141, 143; see also 1966, 135–142, 261–262, 285–286] that *diairesis* is not used or even usable for serious philosophical inquiry. For a recent account underscoring the methodological import of division to philosophical conduct and education, see Sayre [2006, 110–111, 205, et passim].

[20]For the specification of a response to this query as the goal of inquiry regarding sophistry, see *Sph.* 218b7-c1.

[21]This is evident from Plato's use of *onomata* and *logoi* in his treatment of angling, sophistry, and statesmanship in the *Sophist* and *Politicus*. All acceptable *logoi* must specify whole-part relations with regard to the object of investigation in a combination that singles it out from all other Forms or kinds (cf. Moravcsik [1973b, 340-341]). In a given case, more than one *logos* may meet the aforementioned requirement; the seventh and final *logos* is conveyed as the best answer to the *ti esti* question posed at the outset (268d3-4). Cornford maintains that the seventh division in the *Sophist* yields the only seriously intended and correct account of *sophistikê*, while the preceding six serve as a disguised collection [1957, 173, 175–177, 187, and 324]; he thus fails to draw a key distinction between relative and absolute differences in value.

their role in compound descriptions that focus on whole-part ties involving Forms.

In the *Cratylus*, Plato contests the view that individual *onomata* are themselves sources of insight, and he never subsequently withdraws this rejection. In the *Sophist* and *Politicus*, the investigation of natures begins with a shared *onoma*, that given by convention. In keeping with the *Cratylus'* outcome — which foregrounds the inability of etymologies themselves to disclose *phuseis* and the highly manipulable character of proferred analyses — at the start of the *Sophist* Plato underscores that having an *onoma* in common is merely a prerequisite for an inquiry that in no way centers on it (218b6-c5).[22] Operating simply with a shared *onoma* is compatible with inquirers' having varying beliefs about the nature of its referent. As the *Cratylus'* ending made clear, one cannot decide between such opinions by appeal to the *onoma* itself but must instead pursue an independent, rational inquiry into the *phusis* of the explanandum.[23] In the case at hand, the indivisible Form under investigation is sophistry. Plato has already elucidated, most concertedly in the *Gorgias*, both that and why he repudiates sophistry, and his articulation of the theory of Forms in the middle dialogues, combined with remarks targeting the sophists (e.g., the ship-of-state analogy at *Rep.* 488a-489d, with 492a-494a), permits one to grasp how the *Gorgias'* critique via the framework of *technê* may be expressed with Forms in view. Despite Plato's ongoing, essential clarity on what is so flawed and deleterious about the practice of sophistry, he has yet to reformulate his stance based on adjustments to the theory of Forms, and hence to the content of dialectic, in the late writings. Moreover, there remained widespread confusion on the part of others in Plato's time regarding the true character of sophistry and hence its essential difference from philosophy, as signaled vividly by Theaetetus' naïve optimism about the *onoma* in the *Sophist* (with the Stranger's comment at 218c1-5) and Young Socrates' lack of clarity about sophistry at the outset of *Politicus* — notwithstanding the fact that the latter had been present at the morning's discussion as chronicled in the former dialogue (see *Sph.* 218b).[24] The all-important goal of inquiry in the *Sophist*, therefore, is to pinpoint the nature of *sophistikê* in that *logos* which best captures its unique relation to other Forms or kinds. Only a procedure of this type can elevate one beyond mere beliefs, both

---

[22]See also 221a7-b2 where, following a discussion of angling, the Stranger observes that "now we're in agreement about the angler's expertise, not just as to its name; in addition we've also sufficiently grasped an account concerning the thing itself" (Νῦν ἄρα τῆς ἀσπαλιευτικῆς πέρι σύ τε κἀγὼ συνωμολογήκαμεν οὐ μόνον τοὔνομα, ἀλλὰ καὶ τὸν λόγον περὶ αὐτὸ τοὔργον εἰλήφαμεν ἱκανῶς). Cf. the clear distinction between an ὄνομα and τῆς οὐσίας ὁ λόγος in *Leg.* 895d1-9 (also cited by Stenzel [1940, 121] to buttress his point that in the late writings, "Λόγος οὐσίας... takes the place of λόγος αἰτίας").

[23]For φύσεις expressly identified as the goal of inquiry in the cases of sophistry and statesmanship, see *Sph.* 264d-265a and *Pol.* 275c, respectively.

[24]For an illuminating account of how much was at stake for Plato, as regards the legitimation and stature of philosophy, in offering such a delineation of sophistry, see Notomi [1999]. Notomi's work there on the *Sophist*, combined with scholarship, including Levin [2001], on this same concern with respect to poetry, yields a fuller picture than before of the depth and persistence of Plato's concern to debunk the authority of his two main non-philosophical classes of rival to philosophy's status as the ultimate arbiter of human values and flourishing.

true and false, concerning *phuseis*. As in the middle period, *onomata* themselves do not reveal natures.

In the *Sophist*, in fact, Plato emphasizes that using a term's descriptive content as a guide to its referent's nature can be seriously misleading and deems it inappropriate procedure. He lays the foundation for making this point at the start of the dialogue, when Theaetetus appeals to it to resolve the question of whether the object of inquiry, in this case sophistry (σοφιστική), qualifies as a τέχνη (221d1-4).[25] At this juncture, Theaetetus exhibits an unreflective optimism about the disclosive power of the term's constitution — alluding to its ties to σοφός — that the ensuing discussion will show to be quite unjustified.[26] He here misapplies the result of the foregoing treatment of angling. There the Stranger states that they have agreed "about the angler's expertise" (221a7, cf. 218c) *before* he suggests, at the close of the synoptic *logos*, an etymology of the term ἀσπαλιευτική as combining ἀνά with σπᾶν ("to draw up," 221c).[27] The etymology's provision at the end of this *logos*, which only in its entirety specifies a nature, combined with Plato's warning at *Sophist* 220c10-d4 not to attach oneself to the descriptive content of particular terms, makes clear that he stands by the *Cratylus'* conclusion — illustrated most dramatically by dual etymologies there of the crucial term ἐπιστήμη from divergent ontological perspectives (412a and 437a)[28] — that analyses of *onomata* are not, indeed cannot, themselves be nature-revealing. In my view, Plato's playful associations outside the *Cratylus*, in the *Sophist* as elsewhere, function not to disclose *phuseis* but at most reinforce philosophical points made on independent grounds (see, e.g., his supposed derivation of πόλις from πολλοί at *Rep.* 369c).[29]

Plato's assessment of the sixth division constitutes an important juncture in the movement away from a reliance on the *onoma* in delineating its referent's nature. This characterization, according to which sophistry employs refutation (ἐλέγχειν) to teach humility, does not actually capture the proper denotation of the term *so-*

---

[25] Although Plato locates the dialogue's analysis in the framework of *technê*, he often speaks in terms of practitioners — of sophists rather than sophistry. For πολιτικός and πολιτική as interchangeable, see *Pol.* 258b2-c3 and 259d4-5. Following Plato's lead, in the ensuing discussion of the *Sophist* I treat the pertinent locutions as such.

[26] On the tie to σοφός, cf. *Prot.* 312b7-c6, especially Hippocrates' naïve comment at c5-6 following Socrates' request to be told what the former thinks a sophist is. See also *Pol.* 258b-c, where, as Sayre [2006, 16–17] discerns, Young Socrates' avowal that the sophist, like the statesman, operates with *epistêmê* indicates that he has failed to absorb the outcome of the morning's investigation, according to which the sophist lacks insight, possessing only opinion (*doxa*), and produces merely imitations (for the *Sophist*'s culminating emphasis on this unexalted cognitive state, see 267d-268c).

[27] As White [1993, ad loc.] observes, the actual derivation of the noun is unknown; Plato thus speculates "fancifully" in keeping with the context at hand. Both in the *Cratylus* and elsewhere, where etymology is at issue, Plato, like Greek literary authors, is not concerned with what we would call philological accuracy.

[28] While the former derivation of *epistêmê* purports loyalty to the flux ontology, the latter alleges to document that stasis prevails.

[29] For further discussion of this point, see Levin [2001, 92–93]. For a different view see Sedley [2003].

phistikê; instead, it wrongly makes the referent a good part of reality by assigning it too elevated a function (Μὴ μεῖζον αὐτοῖς προσάπτωμεν γέρας, 231a3). In actuality, as has often been noted, the description applies not to sophistry but instead to the Socratic elenchus.[30] This account illustrates just how awry an inquiry can go if it purports to grant independent credence to the descriptive content of *onomata*. At this juncture it is said merely that the *logos* captures a certain likeness of the explanandum; no attempt is made to ground ontologically or otherwise specify what the points of common ground and divergence consist in (a4-b1). Noteworthy here is Theaetetus' observation of resemblance, promptly followed by the Stranger's caution to be on guard against likenesses (ὁμοιότητες) because underlying them may be important differences in natures. This is indeed the state of affairs with regard to sophistry since the emphasis on similarity masks the genuine relation of good to bad. The comment about dogs and wolves (a6), which look alike but differ markedly in their dispositions, illustrates these points effectively. Despite any superficial parallels between Socratic methodology and sophistic praxis, on all essentials the divergence is fundamental and ineradicable.

As they resume the seventh division following a prolonged investigation of not-being and falsehood, the Stranger suggests that he and Theaetetus now have the necessary preparation for its completion. Once the final "cut" is made, and having labeled one type of insincere mimic as the demagogue, the Stranger asks what they should call the other, "wise, *or* a sophist?" (σοφὸν ἢ σοφιστικόν; 268b10).[31] Theaetetus, now moving properly from the results of rational inquiry to the consideration and assignment of *onomata*, responds: "We can't call him wise, since we took him not to know anything. But since he imitates the wise man he'll obviously have a name derived from the wise man's name (δῆλον ὅτι παρωνύμιον αὐτοῦ τι λήψεται). And now at last I see that we have to call him the person who is really and truly a *sophist*" (b11-c4).[32] Only the foregoing investigation made it possible to draw the important distinction involved in this use of *parônumios*, which would

---

[30] See, e.g., Cornford [1957, 177]. For an alternative stance see Notomi [1999, 64-68].

[31] The emphasis is mine. The disclosure in 233c10-11 (with 234e7-235a7) that the sophist lacks genuine insight adumbrates and sets the stage for the disjunction articulated in 268b10; for detailed consideration of the arguments by which Plato supports his denigration of sophists' cognitive state as the dialogue progresses, see Notomi [1999]. The *peri ti* requirement on *technai* also plays an important role since the sophist purports and is reputed by some to have understanding of all subjects (232e1-233c7). This all-inclusive construction of "subject matter" will not, however, allow the practice of sophistry to meet the *peri ti* condition in the sense at issue for estimable *technai* — in sharp contrast to philosophy, which is, as Plato argued in the *Republic*, the *technê* par excellence (for a defense of this view, see Levin [2001, chap. 5]); although to argue such here would take one far afield, I believe that Plato maintains this view of philosophy in the *Sophist* and *Politicus*. While failure to meet these two *technai* requirements articulated in the *Gorgias* contributed heavily to sophistry's being dubbed there a mere *empeiria*, it is treated in the *Sophist* as part of reality, albeit one that is highly infelicitous from the perspective of human flourishing. On the *technê* issue as salient for Plato from early on through the *Sophist* and *Politicus*, see also Kato [1995, 165].

[32] At this juncture, as before, the notion of imitation is introduced — μιμητὴς δ' ὢν τοῦ σοφοῦ (268c1) — but now the contrast with what is genuine is ontologically grounded. The halt at 236e is occasioned by the fact that the foregoing investigation had divided μιμητική into εἰκαστική and

wholly escape one unfamiliar with its progression. Had the *Sophist*'s inquirers relied on allusions to descriptive content — a procedure toward which Theaetetus was initially inclined — the *phusis* of the activity of sophistry would never have clearly emerged.

In order to see more distinctly the relationship between Plato's handling of the term *sophistikê* — above all the nature of its application to those who self-consciously, even self-aggrandizingly, appropriated the appellation *sophistês* for themselves in the second half of the fifth century[33] — and his concern with *orthotês onomatôn* in the middle dialogues, it will be necessary to situate Plato's remarks in the *Sophist* in the broader context of his treatment of this topic.

By comparison with his predecessors, both literary and philosophical, Plato introduces conceptual distinctness, that is to say, delineates species of a genus that one might call "wordplay" (see Levin [2001, 70–71]), provided one remains attentive to situations in which this "play" is, for Plato, in some way a quite serious endeavor. His clear distinctions, in contrast to the literary tradition, between etymology and eponymy in the *Cratylus* and the *Phaedo*, and, contra Heraclitus, between semantic and phonetic constitution in the *Cratylus*, are perhaps the two most striking instances of this earnestness.

The case in the *Sophist*, as concerns the relationship between *sophos* and *sophistikê*, involves descriptive content though it is not just the same as the etymological analyses offered in the *Cratylus*.[34] In fact, it does not fall unqualifiedly into any distinct type of concern with the appropriateness of *onomata* that is available to Plato based on either his predecessors' efforts or his own. As concerns the latter, although the term *parônumios* appears in this passage, there is no Platonic notion of paronymy in the corpus, technical or semi-technical, on a par with eponymy.

If one cannot look straightforwardly back before Plato or to Plato himself in order to elucidate what transpires here, perhaps one may look ahead: the fact that Plato employs here the term *parônumios* might lead one to wonder about possible ties to Aristotelian paronymy, introduced in the *Categories* (1a12-15, 6b11-14, and 10a27-b11). Perhaps Platonic usage points ahead to Aristotelian-style paronymy, offering what might be considered a harbinger thereof. This is not the case, however, if, as I believe, Ackrill [1963/1989] is right to maintain that Aristotle's concern with respect to paronymy, as in his tenfold classificatory scheme, is foundationally

---

φανταστική without its yet being evident that the latter has a denotation in the sense at issue for Plato. Before Plato can address this issue, he must establish the possibility of τὸ... φαίνεσθαι τοῦτο καὶ τὸ δοκεῖν, εἶναι δὲ μή, καὶ τὸ λέγειν μὲν ἄττα, ἀληθῆ δὲ μή (236e1-2). Since it is under the latter intermediate Form, or kind, that Plato wishes to place sophistry, division cannot proceed until he establishes that the referent of the term φανταστική is properly unified. Once the twofold division of μιμητική is deemed natural, *diairesis* may resume (266d-267a).

[33]For the influence of the sophists in Athens during the last third of that century, see Ford [2001, 89–90].

[34]The most straightforward cases in the *Cratylus* (those, e.g., of Ἅγις from ἄγω, 394c; Πλούτων from πλοῦτος, 403a; and Παλλάς from πάλλειν, 406d-407a) bear the closest similarities, as concerns the character of proposed derivations, to the relationship involving descriptive content that is considered in the *Sophist*.

about the world, that is to say, non-linguistic entities, rather than about *onomata* themselves.

Aristotle, by his own lights, extends conceptual clarity regarding distinct *onomata* and their interrelations. For him, doing so involves divergence from Plato on key notions such as eponymy, which, based on his belief that the theory of Forms falls prey to the TMA (see the *Peri Ideôn* 84.21-85.3 and *Metaph.* 1039a2-3), Aristotle persists in labeling either synonymy or chance homonymy:[35] he never acknowledges a distinct philosophical conception of eponymy as treated by Plato and hence never recognizes it as in salient respects an antecedent for his own notion of homonymy involving related natures where *pros hen legesthai*, or "focal meaning" (following Owen [1986]), specifically — as distinct, say, from analogy and metaphor — is at issue.[36]

Ackrill [1963/1989, 72] is correct to say that the paronymous relationships at issue in the *Categories* are "not etymological" in the sense that Aristotle, at any rate, does not appear to *intend* them in this light. Just as Plato moves clearly beyond literary practice by distinguishing among three species of *orthotês onomatôn* — etymology, eponymy, and assessments of "functional terms"[37] — Aristotle ventures beyond Plato by separating judgments of appropriateness when etymology is at issue, on which he comments in *De Interpretatione* 2, from what he takes to be true cases of paronymy as treated in the *Categories*. Not only is this distinction not found in Plato, but — in contrast to his teacher — Aristotle employs paronymy, as he does subsequently the notion of focal meaning, to underscore semantic ties between *onomata* based on non-linguistic relationships of varying nature and complexity among their referents.

In Aristotelian paronymy, as previously noted, entities themselves are primarily at issue, and on the foundation of their non-linguistic ties, one moves derivatively to connect *onomata*. Quite notably, Aristotle assumes that, in the case of terms' deriving from one another in the pertinent way (e.g., "grammarian" from "grammar" or "brave" from "bravery" in *Cat.* 1), the root *onoma* applies *correctly* to the referent of the derivative usage.

Plato uses *parônumios* twice in the corpus: once in the *Sophist* and on a second occasion to distinguish between two senses of equality (*isotês*) in the *Laws*. While

---

[35]The text of the *Peri Ideôn* is cited from Fine [1993]. For other Aristotelian criticisms of Plato's theory of Forms, see *Metaph.* I.9, XIII.4-5, and *EN* I.6. Regarding synonymy see *Metaph.* 987b7-10. *Metaph.* 991a2-8, which is repeated virtually verbatim at 1079a33-b3, offers an interpretive choice between synonymy and homonymy depending on how one views Forms' tie to the pertinent entities in the spatiotemporal realm. Eponymy's semantic plausibility entails participation's being a fruitful notion, but Aristotle is adamant that it is not (see *Metaph.* 992a26-29 and 1079b24-26).

[36]Detailed consideration of these issues would take one far afield for present purposes. For discussion of Aristotle's interpretation of eponymy and of common ground between Platonic eponymy and focal meaning — regarding, above all, the non-semantic foundation of the tie in question — see Levin and Ward [2000]; we argue there that focal meaning is a particular kind of homonymy among those types that, in contrast to chance homonymy, involve shared natures.

[37]For discussion of functional terms in *Republic* V, see Levin [2001, 119–126]. The *onomata* at issue there involve the domains of kinship and ruling.

superficially, at any rate, the prior instance abides closer to what Aristotle has in view in the *Categories* — since in the former case two related *onomata* rather than two purported senses of a single term are at issue — I maintain that in fact both Platonic instances diverge markedly from Aristotelian usage insofar as what is ultimately at issue for Plato in the *Sophist* and *Laws* is fundamental, that is to say, natural, *opposition* between the referents of the terms in question. Due to this striking clash, in both cases Plato employs the term *parônumios* to ground strongly implied judgments that, since the natures of the terms' referents are at odds, the *onomata* in question are *inappropriately* assigned to their non-primary referents, that is, to sophistry and equality qua strict parity, respectively.

Although Plato's use of *parônumios* in the *Sophist* does not fall directly under etymology or eponymy as treated in the middle dialogues, it bears certain similarities to both. One common element between etymology and the case at issue here is that, as with respect above all to proper names as treated by the Greek literary tradition, the *onoma* is preliminarily assumed — at any rate by Socrates' interlocutor — to be nature-revealing, and Plato's investigation in the *Sophist*, as in the *Cratylus*, therefore takes the *onoma*'s descriptive content as its point of departure. By comparison with many cases addressed in the *Cratylus*, the identity of the derivation in the *Sophist* is — linguistically speaking — straightforward.[38] Plato wants to stress, however, that even where the etymological tie at issue between *onomata* (here, *sophistikê* and *sophistês* from *sophos*) is evident, one must nonetheless undertake an independent investigation into the nature of the derivative term's referent instead of simply assuming that the designation is fittingly assigned. On the basis of this common ground, at this preliminary juncture one may deem *sophistikê-sophos* to be a case of what one might call quasi-etymology.

As in the case of Platonic eponymy, ascertaining what are proper derivative designations, if any, hinges on one's also achieving, or having attained, clarity about the criteria under which the primary designation, here, *sophos*, is fittingly made. Putting the point in the form of a query, what are the grounds on which the descriptive force of the term *sophos* may be said to apply to a given referent? In paradigmatic cases of Platonic eponymy, the same term (e.g., *kalon*) is at issue in both primary and secondary applications (e.g., *auto to kalon* vs. *ta kala*). Although in nonparadigmatic instances this is not the case (e.g., *ta isa* from *isotês*), there is always a standard designation, for instance, *auto to ison* rather than *isotês*, that serves as the touchstone and ultimate reference point for semantic ends.[39]

---

[38] Perhaps the most elaborate is δίκαιον (412c-413d), but see also, e.g., Κρόνος (396b), Ἑστία (401b-d), and βλαβερόν (417d-418a).

[39] For αὐτὸ τὸ ἴσον, see *Phd.* 74a12, c4-5, e7, 75b6, and 78d3 (cf. αὐτὸ τὸ ὅ ἐστιν ἴσον at 74d6); the variant ἰσότης appears at 74c1. Although the Recollection Argument in the *Phaedo* singles out equality for the purposes of illustration, Plato makes clear that the account applies just as much to all other relevant cases, including values such as αὐτὸ τὸ καλόν and αὐτὸ τὸ ἀγαθόν (75c-d); for a pointed, subsequent generalization, see 100c6 (καὶ πάντα δὴ οὕτως λέγω). For αὐτὸ τὸ καλόν in the *Phaedo*, see also 78d3 and 100c4-5; in the latter case, Plato distinguishes it expressly from τὰ καλά (100d7-8). For αὐτὸ τὸ καλόν in the *Symposium*, as distinguished from τὰ καλά (210e3),

For present purposes, it is important to distinguish between descriptive content, which is at issue in etymology, and descriptive force, which characterizes eponymy. The case of *sophistikê-sophos* might seem, at first blush, to threaten a blurring of this distinction. As the foregoing discussion makes clear, individual *onomata* can combine in both the middle and late writings — in strictly eponymous primary designations and in *logoi* singling out one indivisible Form from all others, respectively — without themselves being modified or revised, to yield locutions with descriptive force.[40] In cases of etymology, in contrast, where descriptive content, or semantic constitution, is at issue, the term whose appropriateness is under investigation is always derived from, and a modified version of, another. The *onoma* under consideration here, *sophistikê* or, alternately, *sophistês*, stems from *sophos* with the suffix *-istikê*, or from *sophos* plus *-istês* indicating a practiced agent, in order to signify that a specific kind of activity involving expertise is at issue.

It is crucial to stress, in addition, that in contrast to Aristotelian paronymy, the linguistic ties involved in Plato's use of *parônumios* in the *Sophist* mask fundamental *differences* in nature such that, as a proper understanding of what it means to be *sophos* is achieved, it becomes clear that the terms *sophistikê* and *sophistês* are inappropriately applied to the activity and practitioners, respectively, that have been a crucial Platonic opponent from his earliest writing. Something quite similar in the pertinent respect is true in the *Laws*, where Plato states that two constructions of *isotês* are homonymous but opposed in effect (ὁμωνύμοιν μέν, ἔργῳ δὲ εἰς πολλὰ σχεδὸν ἐναντίαιν, 757b2-3): from his vantage point, only distribution to each based on merit counts as *genuine isotês* (τὸ κατὰ φύσιν ἴσον ἀνίσοις ἑκάστοτε δοθέν, d4-5). "Equality" and "justice" are used paronymously (τούτοις παρωνυμίοισί...προσχρήσασθαι, d6), in contrast, concerning the allocation of shares and opportunities that are literally the same. Although the locutions at issue in the *Sophist* are not *homônumoi*, one finds a basic opposition in natures there as well since the philosopher turns out to use *mimêsis* in a wholly contrasting way from the sophist, whose skill is ultimately placed under *phantastikê*.[41] As the dialogue shows, the two diverge fundamentally in nature based above all on their radically opposed cognitive states: since practitioners of *sophistikê* are not *sophoi* — quite the opposite — the designations *sophistikê* and *sophistês* are incorrectly applied to them.

Although the locutions in the *Sophist* do not fall neatly into any existing Platonic category of semantic relation, recourse to historical background surrounding use of the term *sophistês* helps to reinforce the aforementioned distinction between descriptive content and descriptive force, with the result that the case at issue there may be seen to tilt more clearly toward a concern with the former as dis-

---

see 211d3 and e1; cf. 211c7-8 (αὐτοῦ ἐκείνου τοῦ καλοῦ) and 211e3 (αὐτὸ τὸ θεῖον καλόν).

[40] While derivative eponymous designations (e.g., *ta kala* from *auto to kalon* due to participants' dependency on the *eidos* for their derivative and partial possession of the feature in question) as such involve a multiplicity, insofar as *metechonta* in any Form are always potentially a plurality, the linguistic shift from singular to plural does not count as a change of the type at issue here.

[41] For extensive discussion of Plato's argument in this connection, see Notomi [1999].

played by etymology — which, as the *Cratylus* makes vividly clear, leaves room for inappropriate designations (see 394d-e) — than toward any other notion.

At the outset of the *Protagoras*, Socrates recounts how Hippocrates roused him at the crack of dawn in a state of great excitement concerning the presence in Athens of Protagoras, whom Hippocrates takes to have "a monopoly on wisdom" (310d5-6).[42] Reinforcing the point when pressed by Socrates to specify just what a sophist is — and here tying the point expressly to the descriptive content of the term *sophistês* — Hippocrates replies, "I think that, *as the name suggests*, he is someone who has an understanding of wise things" (Ἐγὼ μέν, ἦ δ' ὅς, ὥσπερ τοὔνομα λέγει, τοῦτον εἶναι τὸν τῶν σοφῶν ἐπιστήμονα, 312c5-6).[43] In the ensuing discussion between Socrates and Protagoras, Plato has the dialogue's eponymous sophist indicate that while *sophistikê* is an ancient art (*technê*), he is the first to "acknowledge that *I am* a sophist (ὁμολογῶ τε σοφιστὴς εἶναι) and that I educate men" (317b4-5) — an admission that Socrates later singles out as reflecting tremendous self-confidence, not to say hubris, on Protagoras' part (348e5-349a4).[44] On Protagoras' account, others, including the poets Homer, Hesiod, and Simonides, had shied away from designating *themselves* as sophists due to their fear of opprobrium (316d-317a); in fact, while the appellation of sophist was applied to poets by others, the fifth-century contemporaries of Socrates were the first to appropriate the term self-consciously for themselves. In what follows it becomes evident that, in Protagoras' view, not only were ancient poets the first, albeit not self-identified, sophists, but crucial to education is one's being "in command of poetry," which Protagoras construes more specifically as expertise in poetic interpretation (338e-339a).[45] As one might well expect given the competitive aim of the practice in general and particular exhibitions thereof, emphasized by Guthrie [1971], the ensuing exegesis of Simonides (339a-341e) exhibits Protagoras' confidence that sophistic activity in fact surpasses the poetic insofar as the latter requires hermeneutical displays of the

---

[42] Cf. Socrates' carefully qualified comment on this point at 309d1-2 (especially, εἴ σοι δοκεῖ σοφώτατος εἶναι Πρωταγόρας); translations of the *Protagoras* are from Lombardo and Bell [1997].

[43] In this and the following quotation, the emphases are mine.

[44] Tr. Lombardo and Bell, slightly modified. Keenly aware of this self-promoted lofty reputation, Socrates presses Hippocrates to learn the actual nature of sophistry, for "if you are ignorant of this, you don't know whether you are entrusting your soul to something good or bad" (312c2-4). For Protagoras' assertion that, through his tutelage, Hippocrates' soul will improve and that, due to his own goodness, Protagoras is uniquely qualified to assist others in this regard, see 318a and 328a-b, respectively. For lengthy discussion of the pertinent history of usage and terminological development from *sophos* to *sophistês*, see Guthrie [1971, chap. 3]. The familiar view, exemplified by Guthrie, that there is a stepwise, substantive progression in constructions of what it means to be wise is challenged by Kerferd [1976; cf. 1981, 24]. See Ford [1993] for a position diverging in salient ways from both approaches; in his view "the history of wisdom... may be seen not as an evolution in the direction of the spiritual, but rather as a gradual paring away of particular skills (such as carpentry and, one may add, poetry) from the archaic 'inspired ability' in many kinds of activities" (35).

[45] Concentrating on sophistic remarks about and engagement with poetry, Ford [2001] argues, contra Guthrie [1971], that the sophists profess above all to impart a linguistic or rhetorical *technê*. While Ford's goal is clearly to understand the sophists' interpretation of their own praxis, my own concern is with Plato's construction of their activity and its import.

former's brilliance for the realization of its full value to the soul.[46]

Commenting on *Sophist* 221d, White [1993, ad loc.] says that *sophistês* is "etymologically related" to *sophos*, "and so can be taken to connote knowledge and expertise." As we have seen, that is indeed what the sophists believed and what many others, too, assumed. Already at this early juncture in the dialogue, however, Plato identifies the sophist as akin (συγγενῆ), not to the philosopher, but rather to the angler (221d8-9). While this particular claim of its bond with angling will turn out to be false, Plato's initial adumbration that sophistry and philosophy are not *suggenê* will pan out in spades. Indeed, it is not sophistry, but instead rhetoric, generalship, and judging, that Plato claims in the *Politicus* to be most closely akin (συγγενῆ) to statesmanship (303d-304a) — which activity remains, as in the *Republic*, part and parcel of the philosopher's task.[47]

The *Sophist* shows that, from Plato's perspective, those clever speakers who had, through sheer hubris, appropriated the term "sophists" for themselves are not, strictly speaking, entitled to this appellation; that is to say, his investigation yields the conclusion that since the *sophistês* is not *sophos*, the term "sophist" is inappropriately applied to him, hence the *disjunction* σοφὸν ἢ σοφιστικόν in 268b10.[48] As we saw, sophistic sleight of hand was powerful, such that many bought into the sham that the terms *sophistikê* and *sophistês* were nature-revealing. Indeed, linguistically, that is to say, on the level of philological accuracy, no controversy exists. But here, as elsewhere, philological accuracy is not Plato's concern. Thus interpreted, *parônumios*, properly contextualized in the *Sophist*'s discussion, ges-

---

[46] Cf. both the *Apology* (22a-c) and the *Ion* (533d-535a), where Plato stresses poets' incapacity to speak with illumination regarding the meaning of their own compositions. On the centrality of sophists' competitive intentions vis-à-vis the poets, see also Ford [2001, 102–103]: "if the revered Homer can be shown to have made such errors in expression [as attributed to him by Protagoras at Arist. *Poet*. 1456b and *Soph. El.* 173b], Protagorean wisdom must be very powerful indeed."

[47] As concerns the *Sophist*, see Notomi [1999] for an argument against the widespread view among commentators that a separate dialogue, the *Philosopher*, was actually intended. I accord with Notomi that, in seeking the nature of the sophist there, Plato is at one and the same time working to delineate the philosopher's nature (on this point cf. Ford [1993, 39–41]). In fact, Notomi does an exemplary job of foregrounding the interwovenness of Plato's investigations of sophistry and philosophy such that clarification of the nature of the former requires coinvestigation of the latter. The *Gorgias* had excoriated both rhetoric and sophistry as mere *empeiriai*; in fact, the dialogue's direct emphasis was on the former. The *Politicus*, in contrast — drawing on the *Phaedrus*' depiction of rhetorical skill as an aid to philosophy (276a-278d) — identifies rhetoric as one of three *technai* that are akin (συγγενῆ, 303e9) to statesmanship and valorized as such (see 303d-304d; cf. Skemp [1952, 218-219n1]).

[48] Through *diairesis*, of course, Plato also develops a contrast between sophistic and Platonic *logoi* — including, as concerns the former, Gorgias' *Encomium of Helen* on the bewitching power of *logos* as one defense of Helen against the charge that she was ultimately responsible for the onset of the Trojan War (cf. Guthrie [1971, 50–51]). As Guthrie observes, this work of praise is a prime exemplar of how one might go about making the weaker argument appear to be the stronger, which Protagoras exalts as a key strength of sophistic practice and education; on sophistic *logoi*, see also Guthrie [1971, 44–45]. Thus, Plato debunks sophists' entitlement to their *onoma* and approach to *logoi* through one and the same argumentative process in the *Sophist*. For express, prior recognition, albeit one whose context is unknown, that one dubbed a *sophistês* may not in fact be *sophos*, see Eur. frag. 905, Nauck[2] (also cited by Ford [1993, 36]).

tures most directly toward an etymological tie, and this late dialogue reinforces the *Cratylus'* conclusion that analyses of terms' descriptive content cannot as such reveal natures and that it is quite dangerous to the souls of those who aim to flourish to behave as though *onomata* did or could function in this capacity.

Following the exchange in *Sophist* 268b10-c4 — which cements the outcome of philosophical discrimination as to precisely how and why *sophos* fails to apply with descriptive force to practitioners of *sophistikê* — the dialogue concludes with a recounting of the *logos* that best answers the *ti esti* question with regard to sophistry. This *logos* is "naturally correct," not in the *Cratylus'* sense of imitation via semantic or phonetic constitution, but merely in a derivative way insofar as it richly discloses the *phusis* of the explanandum. More specifically, each part of the *logos* (i.e., every *onoma*) denotes a natural, or objective, unity, and these *onomata* are combined so as to yield the complex of denotations that most effectively locates sophistry, the object of inquiry, on the map of *technai*. Notably, Plato does not operate by providing etymologies of the characterization's parts, correlating terms' descriptive suggestions — whatever they may be — with the nature of sophistry. According to Barney [2001, 197], the *Sophist* "does not exclude the mimetic account of the *Cratylus*, but adds to it a new level of explanation." Similarly, in the view of Sedley [2003], the *Cratylus* endorses the claim that " 'for *any* name, its success as a tool for communication depends, at least largely, on its imitative powers' " (145), and analysis "will remain a vital...element in [Plato's] semantics right to the end" (86). On the interpretation presented here, there is, indeed, strong continuity between the *Cratylus* and *Sophist*. It stems, however, above all from the fact that, having rejected the view in the *Cratylus* that terms' descriptive *content* is nature-revealing, Plato develops an account of eponymy in the *Phaedo* that distinguishes between two levels of terms' application — the form of strict designations on its primary tier (e.g., *auto to kalon* vs. *ta kala*) pointing one toward natures proper — through descriptive *force*. In the *Sophist*, in turn — selective gestures toward descriptive content notwithstanding — Plato reaffirms his commitment to the *Cratylus'* conclusion that the descriptive force of *logoi* (on the strong interwovenness of whose elements see below), and not a version of mimesis à la the *Cratylus*, is the operative notion.

Central to Plato's treatment of *sophistikê*, and salient, though in a distinct and less explicit way, to his handling of *politikê* in the *Politicus*,[49] is thus the idea that one cannot draw legitimate conclusions about natures by gliding directly from par-

---

[49]Since the character of statesmanship hinges on the nature of the *polis* in which it operates, one whose focus is on *politikê* risks being misled if she operates with the wrong view of such a community (275a8-10, cf. 278e9-11). In the *Politicus*, the discussion is strongly prescriptive insofar as Plato is concerned with what the term *polis*, and hence *politikê*, *should* refer to (301c6-e4). This difference in approach between the *Sophist* and *Politicus* is in no way accidental: the title "statesman" is a banner of praise for one measuring up to an ideal, not, as with "sophist," a term of censure. Crucially, however, as in the *Sophist* (268b-c), the invocation of descriptive content would be unhelpful, even misleading, to one unfamiliar with the course of the inquiry conducted therein; for one acquainted with it, in contrast, such an appeal amplifies nothing.

ticular *onomata* to reality. As we have seen, one cannot but start with those terms provided by convention; one who gives excessive weight to them, however, risks being seriously deceived. In the *Sophist* and *Politicus*, the *onomata* in question, *sophistikê* and *politikê*, were viewed as misleading not for their ultimate failure to mark off genuine unities but instead for encouraging a false conception thereof. In the *Politicus*, Plato also investigates the prior issue, insisting that one cannot automatically infer from the mere existence of a general term that its referent constitutes an actual kind. The philosopher's responsibilities concerning judgments of fitness in the *Sophist* and *Politicus* hence include not just working with *onomata* already in use but encompass both the deletion of philosophically-extraneous terms and *onoma*-construction to fill gaps that *dialektikê* reveals.[50] The latter tasks represent a key elaboration of the dialectician's duties as arbiter of *orthotês onomatôn* by comparison with Plato's conclusions regarding *onomata* in the *Cratylus* and his articulation of eponymy in the *Phaedo*.[51]

If one judges ordinary language from the vantage point of *diairesis*, one will discover superfluous *onomata*, that is, terms failing to mark off natural unities. This becomes evident early in the *Politicus*, when the Stranger characterizes the error made in the preceding treatment of statesmanship as

> the kind of mistake one would make if, seeking to divide the class of human beings into two, he partitioned them into Greeks and barbarians. This is a division most people in this part of the world make. They separate the Greeks from all other nations, making them a class apart; thus they group all other nations together as a class, ignoring the fact that it is an indeterminate class made up of peoples who have no dealings with each other and speak different languages. Lumping all this non-Greek residue together, they think it must constitute one real kind

---

[50]Plato pursues linguistic innovation with philosophical aims in mind in the middle dialogues, too — as in his novel combination of familiar *onomata* to designate Forms (e.g., *auto to kalon*) — though he does not specify *onoma*-construction as a *task* of philosophy. There Plato also invests existing terms (e.g., *metechein*) with technical or semi-technical meanings when articulating his view of reality. Subsequently, as we have seen, he does the same with terms such as *temnein* and *diaphuê* in the context of *diairesis*. As to Plato's treatment of naming in the late writings, most striking in terms of invention is his explicit contention that there may be *merê* qualifying as *genê* that have yet to be marked off as such, and hence assigned *onomata*, and that the discovery of such is integral to philosophical practice.

[51]This extension in the late writings occurs with respect to *onomata* construed specifically as what we would call general terms. The *Cratylus*, purporting initially to endorse proper names' descriptive content as nature-disclosing, raises the matter of negative merit when noting that Theophilus, for instance, would be an improper appellation for a bearer who turned out to be impious (394d-e); at this early juncture in the dialogue, however, the working assumption is that a name whose semantic constitution did convey the proper message — in the above example, negative divine affect toward its referent — would be nature-revealing. More to the point here — since, on my interpretation, the *Cratylus* categorically rejects the notion that referents of *onomata* qua proper names actually *have phuseis* strictly construed — the issue of inappropriate designation tout court from an ontological standpoint is already in a limited manner pertinent at this earlier juncture.

because they have a common name 'barbarian' to attach to it (βάρβαρον μιᾷ κλήσει προσειπόντες αὐτό, διὰ ταύτην τὴν μίαν κλῆσιν καὶ γένος ἓν αὐτὸ εἶναι προσδοκῶσιν). (262c10-d6; tr. Skemp, with modifications)

Plato's handling of *barbaros*, like that of *sophistikê* and *politikê*, highlights the fundamental error of unreflective movement from *onomata* to reality. This case, however, differs from those of sophistry and statesmanship insofar as here an entity's very status as a natural unity is in question. In fact, one operates mistakenly on the assumption that the referent of the term *barbaros* constitutes a natural, or objective, whole. Because no strong principle of unity links members of this group together (ἀπείροις οὖσι καὶ ἀμείκτοις καὶ ἀσυμφώνοις πρὸς ἄλληλα, d4), it constitutes a *meros* that is not also a *genos*. Although popular belief accepted a sifting of humankind into Greeks and barbarians, according to Plato this "division" is untenable.[52] Parallel to the case of eponymy, a technical or semi-technical version of which he introduces in the *Phaedo*, Plato is not contesting the use of philosophically-inappropriate *onomata* for ordinary purposes;[53] his point is, rather, that from the standpoint of one committed to uncovering the nature of reality, the existence of the *onoma* in question is illegitimate.[54]

In the case of *barbaros*, one is deceived into thinking that its referent is a genuine

---

[52]Thus, from a theoretical standpoint not every abstract property can function as a natural unit. In the cases of barbarian and number other than 10,000, discussed in the *Politicus* (262c10-e1), one confronts assemblages with some principle of unity — both include only human beings and numbers, respectively — which is why their constituents may be grouped together at all. While this is a sufficient condition for a group's falling under the generic concept of human being or number, any subdivisions of either *eidos* that are themselves to count as kinds must share a comparatively significant but more specific property that binds them in a strong internal way that is not signified merely by negation (i.e., the property of not being Greek and that of not being 10,000); cf. Moravcsik [1973b, 341]. Such "bifurcations" do not yield fruitful theoretical outcomes but rather stifle them; as in the middle period, explanatory power, while not formally proving objective unities' existence, is pertinent as either indirect proof or confirmation of another type (on the scope and import of Forms' explanatory force in the middle dialogues, see the still-classic discussion of Cherniss [1965]).

[53]Plato was not concerned to challenge familiar usage of eponymy as long as it was restricted to its proper sphere and its importance not overestimated. Plato's disinterest in revising or eliminating nonphilosophical employment thereof is evidenced by the fact that he never criticizes nontechnical usage and by his recourse to it even after his introduction of a revamped version in the *Phaedo* to provide the semantics of the Form-participant relation; see, e.g., *Leg.* 626d3-5, where Plato offers the derivation (familiar from Soph. *OC* 107-108; Eur. *Ion* 8-9, 29-30, 1555-1556) of "Athens" from "Athena." In the middle dialogues, Plato's revisions of conventional usage aim solely at that range of cases, above all those involving mathematical entities and values, in which a term's primary referent must be separate from the spatiotemporal realm. In the present case, too, Plato is not contesting the use of philosophically-inappropriate *onomata* for ordinary purposes: he does not believe that people must stop using the term "barbarian," for instance, in ordinary discourse since it is useful for expressing distinctions that they may wish to voice in its conduct. In fact, Plato himself continues to employ the term *barbaros*, which occurs numerous times in the *Laws*, as for example in Book X, where the Athenian divides humankind into Greeks and barbarians (887e4; cf. Clinias' remark in 886a4-5).

[54]Similarly, one should not infer straightaway from the existence of a certain number of *onomata* that the same number of genuine unities exist (see *Sph.* 217a).

genos on account of (διά) the presence of a single appellation in the existing lexicon (further stress is added by Plato's repetition of the phrase μία κλῆσις). One might, in addition, be misled by the fact that a term can be constructed for a supposed unity into fancying that this "unity" must exist (262d6-e3). While one can invent or posit (θέμενος, e2) an *onoma* for the group containing all numbers other than 10,000, this is far from sufficient grounds for concluding that the group qualifies as a kind. It is noteworthy that Plato here introduces the notion of appropriateness explicitly, to illustrate the reverse of the approach he has in view. Once again he highlights the causal sequence that gives primacy to the *onoma*: in this case, as with that of "barbarian," one moves illegitimately from the existence of an appellation (διὰ τὴν κλῆσιν) to the conclusion (αὖ) that a certain group merits (ἀξιοῖ) the rank of *genos*; here ἓν ὄνομα, διά, and αὖ combine to make the point quite emphatically.[55] The proper sequence, in contrast, as illustrated repeatedly in both late dialogues, is to use the results of rational inquiry as decisive grounds for concluding that a group, if also a Form or kind, in fact deserves an *onoma*. Everything hinges on whether one discerns the proper "cuts" in reality; as in the *Cratylus* (see Plato's culminating statement in 438-440), the correct approach thus involves a complete reversal of that causal progression evident in the above two examples.[56]

While individual *onomata* do not yield satisfactory answers to the *ti esti* question, kind names designating objective unities must exist since they are the constituents of those *logoi* that do disclose *phuseis*. In this context, terms are fittingly assigned if they mark off Forms or kinds and inappropriately assigned if they do not. In undertaking divisions, the dialectician working with the prevailing lexicon may, as we have seen, discover serious defects from a philosophical point of view, and she remedies these shortcomings as they come to light.

Previously emphasized was the fact that from a philosophical perspective, the Greek lexicon contains superfluous terms. Plato makes clear that ordinary language may also lack a range of necessary terms when assessed against the structure of reality. In fact, notable among the variations in Plato's late-period treatment of *onomata* is the fact that *onoma*-construction, in which he did not evince a genuine interest in the *Cratylus* and *Phaedo*, is expressly invested with a measure of importance alongside proper use.[57] As we saw in Section 2, *onoma*-construction, on

---

[55] Plato had offered explicit judgments of fitness on many occasions in the *Cratylus*; at issue there, too, from his perspective is movement from *onomata* to elements of reality without one's having undertaken an independent investigation of the latter. For such terminology in the *Cratylus*, see, e.g., ὀρθῶς: 392e2, 394e9, 395b3, c2, d4, 396a9, c3, 6, 397b7, c6, 398c3, 399c5, 400c4, 401c7, 404d4, 405c1, 406e1, 407a5, 409c6, 412e2, 413a5, 415d4, e2, 416d8; δικαίως: 406c6 (δικαιότατ'), 408b1, 409c1 (δικαιότατ'), 410b7, c9, 418e2, 419d7 (τὸ δίκαιον); ἀληθῶς: 397e2, 400b6; and καλῶς: 390d6, 396a1 (παγκάλως), b8, 400b1, 401d7.

[56] Other instances include the relation between ποιητική and κτητική in the *Sophist* (219a-d) and Plato's comments on musical sound in the *Philebus* (17c-e).

[57] From the fact that divisions had not been carried out prior to Plato (*Sph*. 267d-e; cf. *Pol*. 285a), one has as much reason for inferring the existence of extraneous terms as one does the absence of *onomata* where they are needed. As previously observed, the *Cratylus* purports interest,

the one hand, and terms' evaluation and use, on the other, were linked to different "experts" — the *onomathetês* and dialectician, respectively — at the outset of the *Cratylus* when Plato purported to grant *technê* status to naming qua etymologizing. Adhering to the *Cratylus'* closing suggestion, developed in the *Phaedo*, that making judgments of appropriateness on legitimate ontological grounds falls solely to the philosopher, in the *Sophist* and *Politicus*, Plato makes both jobs the exclusive responsibility of this figure.[58]

Plato insists that only one motive for production is philosophically acceptable. From the perspective of dialectic, the need for construction arises when rational inquiry yields previously unnamed abstract entities that constitute genuine unities. In the *Sophist*'s final division, the Stranger distinguishes two types of mimicry but finds himself at a loss for terminology by which to designate them (267d4-5). Since current vocabulary reflects the ways in which reality has been construed to date and no one prior to Plato truly attempted to break reality down into its constituent unities, the process of *diairesis* may reveal elements of reality that, because previously unrecognized, have yet to be assigned *onomata* (hence Plato's observation that "we necessarily lack a good supply of names" [καθὸ δὴ τῶν ὀνομάτων ἀνάγκη μὴ σφόδρα εὐπορεῖν, d8-9]). At such junctures the dialectician is called upon to remedy the lack, and in so doing she may take descriptive content into account. Hence terms' semantic constitution is never investigated in its own right but comes under discussion solely in the conduct of *diairesis* as the dialectician seeks to relate a given explanandum to other Forms in the same conceptual field. Notably, here, as elsewhere, one does not move from *onomata* to entities but identifies the activity and property in question *before* construction occurs. Moreover, such kind names break down easily into their descriptive components, so "deep" structural analyses — of the sort that allowed Socrates great interpretive latitude in the *Cratylus* (for examples see n. 38) — have absolutely no role in the process.

Finally, and most fundamentally, the semantic constitution of *onomata* is never itself nature-revealing since it fails to indicate the referent's connection to other Forms. As in the middle dialogues, issues of denotation always take precedence, and Plato never identifies or conflates any descriptive suggestions that *onomata* may (be supposed to) contain with answers to the all-important *ti esti* question. That Plato is concerned to downplay the import of individual *onomata* is evident, moreover, from his depiction of the final *logos* as an *interweaving* of *onomata* (268c5-6 [συμπλέξαντες] with 259e4-6 [συμπλοκήν]; cf. 253b-c on *genê* specifically [συμμείγνυσθαι, μείξεως, συμφωνεῖ]). This, conjoined with Plato's recourse to the alphabet analogy in the *Theaetetus* (202e-206a), *Sophist* (253a), *Politicus* (277e-278e), and *Philebus* (17a-b, 18b-d), foregrounds his conviction that — as with paradigmatic expressions of Forms' natures via eponymy — the most disclosive

---

for a time, in the genesis or construction of *onomata* already in existence, whereas in the late dialogues the issue is construction of terms where they do not yet exist. For neologisms in the *Sophist* and *Politicus* themselves, see Notomi [1999, 75–76] and Sayre [2006, 105–110, 208].

[58] On the dialectician and *onoma*-construction, cf. Derbolav [1972, 146–147].

logoi are always more than mereological sums.⁵⁹

Plato's procedure alone makes clear that the ground of terms' appropriateness must be sought ultimately in their having *genê* or *eidê* as denotations; from a philosophical standpoint, only where such unities exist may one speak of an *onoma* as fittingly assigned. In addition, he provides numerous linguistic manifestations of this stance toward appropriateness. The *Politicus*' treatment of "number other than 10,000" utilizes such terminology, in that case ἀξιοῖ (262e3), to render a judgment of inappropriateness. As concerns the provision of positive assessments, at *Sophist* 219b, for example, Plato maintains that a group of activities can fittingly (δικαιότατ') be called by a single appellation and offers an account of how this judgment was reached. *Poiêtikê*, along with *ktêtikê*, is the most generic intermediate Form, or kind, arrived at in the *Sophist*'s discussion. The kind name is properly assigned not because its descriptive content reveals the natures of these *technai* but because the activities in question, for instance, agriculture and the assembly or molding of vessels — whatever their own unique relations to other *technai* — are branches (based on function)⁶⁰ of this more generic Form or kind (note the inferential force of τοίνυν in b11). While not itself nature-revealing, the term *poiêtikê* will be one component of the *logos* at which one arrives when investigating the nature of any more specialized *technê* that shares this feature.

Terminology of appropriateness appears on numerous occasions elsewhere, with judgments of fitness based ultimately in each case on considerations of denotation. For instance, and similar to what transpires in the case of *poiêtikê*, Plato stresses in the *Sophist* (224a) that, due to their shared purpose, one may properly apply the term "wholesaler" (ἔμπορον ὀρθῶς ἂν λεγόμενον παρασχεῖν) not just to one who dispenses wares aimed at the body's sustenance but also to one whose products are directed toward the soul (as in the case, e.g., of music). The issue of a common task surfaces again with the Stranger's observation that a range of *technai*, including "filtering," "straining," and "winnowing" (226b5-6), all possess the function of discrimination (Διαιρετικά που τὰ λεχθέντα εἴρηται σύμπαντα, c3).⁶¹ Since all are branches of a single, more generic, *technê*, they are appropriately assigned one *onoma*: Κατὰ τὸν ἐμὸν τοίνυν λόγον ὡς περὶ ταῦτα μίαν οὖσαν ἐν ἅπασι τέχνην ἑνὸς ὀνόματος ἀξιώσομεν αὐτήν [i.e., διακριτικήν] (c5-8); here the truth of the subordinate clause implies the veracity of what follows. Plato thus makes explicit the ground of this judgment of fitness. The *onoma*'s descriptive content reflects a function common to all, and the term in question would be one component of that *logos* answering the *ti esti* question for each; the *onoma* by itself, however, is not nature-

---

⁵⁹On the notion that pertinent *logoi* in the late writings transcend their aggregated parts, without this point's being applied to the topic under investigation here, see Moravcsik [1973a, 165]. Aristotle recurs to the alphabet analogy when he illuminates the character of substantial unity by differentiating between the syllable and the heap (see *Metaph.* 1041b11-19).

⁶⁰For an emphasis on commonality of function in naming kinds of *technê*, cf. Moravcsik [1973a, 161-162].

⁶¹With Burnet I prefer Διαιρετικά to Διακριτικά here.

revealing.[62] One may contrast the aforementioned treatments of correctness, which involve movement from denotation to judgments of fitness involving *onomata*, with that instance, discussed above, in which the reverse sequence is wrongly pursued — καὶ τῷ λοιπῷ δὴ παντὶ θέμενος ἓν ὄνομα, διὰ τὴν κλῆσιν αὖ καὶ τοῦτ' ἀξιοῖ γένος ἐκείνου χωρὶς ἕτερον ἓν γίγνεσθαι (*Pol.* 262e1-3) — that is to say, where one infers the presence of a genuine unity from the mere existence of an appellation that purports to point thereto.

5 Conclusion

In the past, interpreters doubted the *Cratylus*' seriousness of intent and deemed it largely insignificant to the unfolding of Plato's thought. Taylor [1960], for instance, designates the *Cratylus* a "minor Socratic dialogue" (75) that affords "a picture of Socrates in one of his more whimsical moods" (78). According to Fowler [1926, 4], it "cannot be said to be of great importance in the development of the Platonic system, as it treats of a special subject somewhat apart from general philosophic theory." An extreme version of the stance that the dialogue simply does not fit well in the corpus is evident in the work of one nineteenth-century German commentator, who maintained that, due to what he alleged to be its idiosyncratic style and content, the *Cratylus* simply could not have been written by Plato.[63] To this day, many others (see n. 6) — focusing on the opening section of the *Cratylus* and on Plato's treatment of etymology or phonetic constitution — have maintained that the dialogue makes serious philosophical proposals. On my interpretation, such commentators rightly emphasize the sincerity of Plato's intentions in the *Cratylus*. These intentions do not, however, result in the elaboration there of substantive positive notions. Instead, following a protracted investigation of the purported *technê* status of naming qua etymologizing, Plato rejects approaches to the notions of naturalness and appropriateness that are based on the constituency of *onomata*. Although the dialogue's emphasis is critical, Plato provides indications in 438-440 of the direction that his positive theorizing will take.

Ongoing attempts, most recently by Sedley [2003] and Barney [2001], to locate the *Cratylus* in the body of Plato's work are welcome and have been highly illuminating. My interest here has been to contribute to the rich, long-standing

---

[62] For the primacy of denotation where judgments of appropriateness are at issue, see also δικαιότατα (*Sph.* 224b5, *Pol.* 288b5); δικαίως (288c4); ἄξιον (*Sph.* 223a6); ἀξίαν (229d6); and ἀξιωθῆναι (*Pol.* 275b6, cf. ἀξίαν in 276b3). In *Pol.* 305e2-6, Plato offers an account of the *technê* that προσαγορεύοιμεν δικαιότατ' ἄν... πολιτικήν. That denotative considerations are foundational here is evident not only from the general course of the dialogue's inquiry but also from the immediate context (e8-10); in addition see δικαίως as employed in 305d10 regarding the *technai* of oratory, generalship, and judging. Plato uses participial forms of πρέπειν to modify the term ὄνομα directly (for πρέπον ὄνομα, see *Sph.* 225a10 and 267d4-5); see also the optatives διαπρέψειεν and διαπρέποι at 219c8 and 9, respectively, and the functionally-equivalent προσήκει at 226e6. Here, too, an appellation is never itself viewed as naturally correct along the lines of the *Cratylus*' rejected etymological construction of *orthotês onomatôn*; instead, the judgments offered take the same form as the others, with the merit of *onomata* based on fitness of denotation.

[63] See Schaarschmidt [1865].

discussion of this enigmatic dialogue, which shows no sign of abating, by situating it in a novel and alternative manner within the corpus: most specifically, the foregoing investigation, which began by tracing Plato's metaphysical and semantic focus in the *Cratylus* and *Phaedo*, allows one to see the former dialogue as playing a salient role in the development of two concepts, those of naturalness and appropriateness, that are crucial to Platonic metaphysics and semantics not merely at the juncture when the theory of Forms is first articulated but also in two pivotal late works, the *Sophist* and *Politicus*, in which that theory is subject to scrutiny and further elaboration. The result is that the *Cratylus*, whose status within Plato's corpus has long puzzled interpreters, may be granted a different, firmer, and more central spot than before among his writings.

Acknowledgements

An earlier version of this paper was presented at the Third International Conference on Ancient and Medieval Philosophy, Fordham University, October 2006. In addition, I benefited greatly from prior discussion of *diairesis* in late Plato with Julius Moravcsik, and it is with pleasure and gratitude that I dedicate this essay to him.

BIBLIOGRAPHY

[Ackrill, 1963/1989] J. L. Ackrill, tr. *Aristotle's "Categories" and "De Interpretatione."* Clarendon Aristotle Series. Reprinted from corrected sheets of the first edition, Oxford: Clarendon Press, 1963/1989.
[Arnim, 1912] H. von Arnim. *Sprachliche Forschungen zur Chronologie der platonischen Dialoge*. Sitzungsberichte der Kaiserlichen Akademie der Wissenschaften in Wien, Philosophisch-historische Klasse, 169/3: 1-235. Vienna: Alfred Hölder, 1912.
[Barney, 2001] R. Barney. *Names and Nature in Plato's "Cratylus."* New York: Routledge, 2001.
[Brandwood, 1990] L. Brandwood. *The Chronology of Plato's Dialogues*. Cambridge: Cambridge University Press, 1990.
[Burnet, 1900–1907] J. Burnet, ed. Plato, *Opera*. Vols. 1-5. Oxford: Clarendon Press, 1900–1907.
[Calvert, 1970] B. Calvert. "Forms and Flux in Plato's *Cratylus*." *Phronesis* 15: 26-47, 1970.
[Cherniss, 1965] H. Cherniss. "The Philosophical Economy of the Theory of Ideas." In *Studies in Plato's Metaphysics*, 1-12. Ed. R. E. Allen. New York: Humanities Press, 1965.
[Cornford, 1957] F. M. Cornford, tr. *Plato's Theory of Knowledge: The "Theaetetus" and the "Sophist" of Plato*. New York: Macmillan Publishing Company, 1957.
[Derbolav, 1972] J. Derbolav. *Platons Sprachphilosophie im "Kratylos" und in den späteren Schriften*. Darmstadt: Wissenschaftliche Buchgesellschaft, 1972.
[Diels, 1951/1992] H. Diels. *Die Fragmente der Vorsokratiker*. Ed. W. Kranz. Vol. 1. 6th ed. Reprint, Zürich: Weidmann, 1951/1992.
[Diggle, 1981/1986] J. Diggle, ed. Euripides, *Fabulae*. Vol. 2. Reprinted with corrections, Oxford: Clarendon Press, 1981/1986.
[Dodds, 1959] E. R. Dodds, ed. Plato, *Gorgias*. Oxford: Clarendon Press, 1959.
[Dorter, 2006] K. Dorter. "The Method of Division and the Division of the *Phaedrus*." *Ancient Philosophy* 26: 259-273, 2006.
[Duke et al., 1995] E. A. Duke, W. F. Hicken, W. S. M. Nicoll, D. B. Robinson, and J. C. G. Strachan, eds. Plato, *Opera*. Vol. 1. Oxford: Clarendon Press, 1995.
[Fine, 1993] G. Fine. *On Ideas: Aristotle's Criticism of Plato's Theory of Forms*. Oxford: Clarendon Press, 1993.
[Ford, 1993] A. Ford. "Sophistic." *Common Knowledge* 1.5: 33-48, 1993.
[Ford, 2001] A. Ford. "Sophists without Rhetoric: The Arts of Speech in Fifth-Century Athens." In *Education in Greek and Roman Antiquity*, 85-109. Ed. Y. L. Too. Leiden: Brill, 2001.

[Fowler, 1926] H. N. Fowler, tr. *Plato*. Vol. 4. Loeb Classical Library. Cambridge, Mass.: Harvard University Press, 1926.
[Grote, 1867] G. Grote. *Plato and the Other Companions of Sokrates*. Vol. 2. 2d ed. London: John Murray, 1867.
[Guthrie, 1971] W. K. C. Guthrie. *The Sophists*. Cambridge: Cambridge University Press, 1971.
[Jaeger, 1957] W. Jaeger, ed. Aristotle, *Metaphysica*. Oxford: Clarendon Press, 1957.
[Jowett, 1892] B. Jowett, tr. *The Dialogues of Plato*. Vol. 1. 3d ed. London: Oxford University Press, 1892.
[Kahn, 1973] C. H. Kahn. "Language and Ontology in the *Cratylus*." In *Exegesis and Argument: Studies in Greek Philosophy Presented to Gregory Vlastos*, 152-176. Ed. E. N. Lee, A. P. D. Mourelatos, and R. M. Rorty. New York: Humanities Press, 1973.
[Kahn, 1986] C. H. Kahn. "Les mots et les formes dans le *Cratyle* de Platon." *Cahiers de philosophie ancienne* 5: 91-103, 1986.
[Kahn, 1996] C. H. Kahn. *Plato and the Socratic Dialogue: The Philosophical Use of a Literary Form*. Cambridge: Cambridge University Press, 1996.
[Kassel, 1965/1966] R. Kassel, ed. Aristotle, *De Arte Poetica Liber*. Reprinted with corrections, Oxford: Clarendon Press, 1965/1966.
[Kato, 1986] M. Kato. *Techne und Philosophie bei Platon*. Frankfurt am Main: Peter Lang, 1986.
[Kato, 1995] S. Kato. "The Role of *Paradeigma* in the *Statesman*." In *Reading the Statesman*, 162-172. Proceedings of the III Symposium Platonicum. Ed. C. J. Rowe. Sankt Augustin: Academia Verlag, 1995.
[Kerferd, 1976] G. B. Kerferd. "The Image of the Wise Man in Greece in the Period before Plato." In *Images of Man in Ancient and Medieval Thought*, 17-28. Ed. F. Bossier et al. Leuven: Leuven University Press, 1976.
[Kerferd, 1981] G. B. Kerferd. *The Sophistic Movement*. Cambridge: Cambridge University Press, 1981.
[Kretzmann, 1967] N. Kretzmann. "Semantics, History of." In *The Encyclopedia of Philosophy*, vol. 7, 358-406. New York: Macmillan, 1967.
[Kretzmann, 1971] N. Kretzmann. "Plato on the Correctness of Names." *American Philosophical Quarterly* 8: 126-138, 1971.
[Leky, 1919/1967] M. Leky. *Plato als Sprachphilosoph: Würdigung des Platonischen "Kratylus."* Reprint, New York: Johnson Reprint Corporation, 1919/1967.
[Levin, 2001] S. B. Levin. *The Ancient Quarrel between Philosophy and Poetry Revisited: Plato and the Greek Literary Tradition*. New York: Oxford University Press, 2001.
[Levin, 2000] S. B. Levin. "Comparative Reflections on Aristotelian Focal Meaning and Platonic Eponymy." Coauthor, Julie Ward. Paper presented at the 19th Annual Conference cosponsored by the Society for Ancient Greek Philosophy and the Society for the Study of Islamic Philosophy and Science, SUNY Binghamton, October 2000.
[Lloyd-Jones and Wilson, 1990] H. Lloyd-Jones and N. G. Wilson, eds. Sophocles, *Fabulae*. Oxford: Clarendon Press, 1990.
[Lombardo and Bell, 1997] S. Lombardo and K. Bell, trs. Plato, *Protagoras*. In *Plato: Complete Works*, 747-790. Ed. J. M. Cooper. Indianapolis: Hackett Publishing Company, 1997.
[Lorenz and Mittelstrass, 1967] K. Lorenz and J. Mittelstrass. "On Rational Philosophy of Language: The Programme in Plato's *Cratylus* Reconsidered." *Mind*, n.s., 76: 1-20, 1967.
[Luce, 1964] J. V. Luce. "The Date of the *Cratylus*." *American Journal of Philology* 85: 136-154, 1964.
[Luce, 1965] J. V. Luce. "The Theory of Ideas in the *Cratylus*." *Phronesis* 10: 21-36, 1965.
[Méridier, 1931] L. Méridier, ed. and tr. *Platon: Œuvres complètes*. Vol. 5. Paris: Société d'édition "Les belles lettres," 1931.
[Minio-Paluello, 1949] L. Minio-Paluello. Aristotle, *Categoriae et Liber De Interpretatione*. Oxford: Clarendon Press, 1949.
[Moravcsik, 1973a] J. M. E. Moravcsik. "Plato's Method of Division." In *Patterns in Plato's Thought*, 158-180. Ed. Moravcsik. Dordrecht: D. Reidel Publishing Company, 1973.
[Moravcsik, 1973b] J. M. E. Moravcsik. "The Anatomy of Plato's Divisions." In *Exegesis and Argument*, 324-348. Ed. E. N. Lee, A. P. D. Mourelatos, and R. M. Rorty. New York: Humanities Press, 1973.
[Nauck, 1889] A. Nauck, ed. *Tragicorum Graecorum Fragmenta*. 2d ed. Leipzig: Teubner, 1889.

[Notomi, 1999] N. Notomi. *The Unity of Plato's "Sophist": Between the Sophist and the Philosopher.* Cambridge: Cambridge University Press, 1999.
[Owen, 1986] G. E. L. Owen. "Logic and Metaphysics in Some Earlier Works of Aristotle." In *Logic, Science, and Dialectic: Collected Papers in Greek Philosophy,* 180-199. Ed. M. Nussbaum. Ithaca: Cornell University Press, 1986.
[Page, 1972] D. Page, ed. Aeschylus, *Tragoediae.* Oxford: Clarendon Press, 1972.
[Robinson, 1953] R. Robinson. *Plato's Earlier Dialectic.* 2d ed. Oxford: Clarendon Press, 1953.
[Ross, 1955] D. Ross. "The Date of Plato's *Cratylus.*" *Revue internationale de philosophie* 9: 187-196, 1955.
[Ross, 1958/1989] D. Ross, ed. Aristotle, *Topica et Sophistici Elenchi.* Reprinted with corrections, Oxford: Clarendon Press, 1958/1989.
[Ryle, 1965] G. Ryle. "Plato's *Parmenides.*" In *Studies in Plato's Metaphysics,* 43-60. Ed. R. E. Allen. New York: Humanities Press, 1965.
[Ryle, 1966] G. Ryle. *Plato's Progress.* Cambridge: Cambridge University Press, 1966.
[Sayre, 2006] K. M. Sayre. *Metaphysics and Method in Plato's "Statesman."* New York: Cambridge University Press, 2006.
[Schaarschmidt, 1865] C. Schaarschmidt. "Über die Unechtheit des Dialogs *Kratylos.*" *Rheinisches Museum für Philologie,* n.s., 20: 321-356, 1865.
[Sedley, 2003] D. Sedley. *Plato's "Cratylus."* Cambridge: Cambridge University Press, 2003.
[Shorey, 1903] P. Shorey. *The Unity of Plato's Thought.* Chicago: University of Chicago Press, 1903.
[Silverman, 1992] A. Silverman. "Plato's *Cratylus*: The Naming of Nature and the Nature of Naming." *Oxford Studies in Ancient Philosophy* 10: 25-71, 1992.
[Skemp, 1952] J. B. Skemp, tr. Plato, *Statesman.* London: Routledge and Kegan Paul, 1952.
[Steinthal, 1890/1961] H. Steinthal. *Geschichte der Sprachwissenschaft bei den Griechen und Römern.* Vol. 1. Reprint, Hildesheim: Georg Olms Verlagsbuchhandlung, 1890/1961.
[Stenzel, 1940] J. Stenzel. *Plato's Method of Dialectic.* Tr. and ed. D. J. Allan. Oxford: Clarendon Press, 1940.
[Taylor, 1960] A. E. Taylor. *Plato: The Man and His Work.* 7th ed. London: Methuen, 1960.
[Weingartner, 1973] R. H. Weingartner. *The Unity of the Platonic Dialogue.* Indianapolis: Bobbs-Merrill, 1973.
[White, 1993] N. P. White, tr. Plato, *Sophist.* Indianapolis: Hackett Publishing Company, 1993.

Julius, the Late-Learners and (a Section of) *Sophist* 255c12-13

JOHN MALCOLM

At *Sophist* 236e the sophist is presented as a purveyor of false statements. He (or, as many are currently reprogrammed to say, she) counters this by denying that there are any such things. The basis of this contention is that falsehood is defined in terms of *what is not* or *non-being* (240d-241a) and, since *what is not* cannot be thought or uttered (238c), falsehood is inconceivable and *a fortiori* non-existent. The main thrust of the dialogue is to disarm this doctrine, but, the better to represent an exemplary specimen of Julius' significant contribution to the exegesis of the *Sophist*, I shall downplay expressing the inexpressible *non-being* and shall concentrate on the so-called constructive section beginning at 251a. It has been preceded by an introductory segment, 216a-236e, for the most part of mind-numbing tedium. (Any who find this area of primary interest should more carefully monitor their medication.) This wasteland, admittedly with an occasional oasis,[1] is followed by the problem-raising portion, 236e-250e, where it is shown that the understanding of both Being and Not-Being is fraught with confusion. Many find positive Platonic doctrine in this part of the dialogue, but I take the statements at 250de to the effect that what has resulted is utter perplexity (*aporia*) to preclude this.[2]

---

[1] Two such passages:
(i) The two kinds of evil in the soul corresponding to two such in the body at 227e ff. Wickedness (*ponēria*) is to disease (*nosos*) as ignorance (*agnoia*) is to deformity (*aischos*). The cures are given at 229a. As medicine (*iatrikē*) is to gymnastic (*gumnastikē*), so correction (*kolastikē*) is to instruction (*didastikē*).
(ii) The distinction between two forms of image (*eidōla*)-making, the likeness-making (*eikastikē*) and the appearance-making (*phantastikē*) given at 236c 6-7, to be picked up at 266d 8-9 and used in the final definition of the sophist at 268c8 ff.

[2] There is general agreement that Plato is concerned only with raising difficulties in the sub-section on non-being as inexpressible (236e-239b) and also at 242c-245e on the number of Being, whether many or one. A majority of scholars, however, tend to see a significant revision of Plato's earlier doctrines when the Friends of the Forms are forced (at 248e-249b) to accept both motion (in the soul as knower) and things moved (with the Forms as known) into their realm of true reality. But the result of this discussion is that the Friends acknowledge that the real contains both what can act and be acted upon. This principle, "Whatever has real being can act or be acted upon" cries out to be related to that accepted by the materialists (247de), "Whatever can act or be acted upon has real being (*ontōs einai*)." Now this latter, if taken as a biconditional definition of real being (247e3), contains the Friends' dictum as one of its components. I conclude that, far from giving us his own metaphysics, Plato is here showing that, if subject to some

Let us return to 251a ff. Plato's first move in supporting the thesis that there *are* false statements is to block the suggestion that there are no statements at all. The latter is the teaching of the so-called "late-learners" who maintain that we cannot call one thing by many names. For example we can call a man "man," but nothing else, such as "good" or "old." So all we can get is naming, but no *statements* of ascription or classification. Here I am prudently following Julius ("Being and Meaning in the *Sophist*", 58-9).[3] Others have understood the late-learners to admit identity statements, e.g., "Man is man," but the preponderance of evidence is against this[4] and, as we shall eventually see, Owen and Frede, two most highly respected commentators, err in this fashion and are thereby led to advance interpretations of the most striking implausibility. Since their writings in this regard are subsequent to the aforementioned "Being and Meaning", this shortcoming is inexcusable.

The late-learners are refuted at 252c where it is shown that their principle prevents its very formulation which, of course, is a statement (see note 4, above) and, with a gesture to any who still persist in granting them identity statements, a non-identity statement. The way words combine to form the now-allowed statements (reflecting the status of their ontological correlates) is made more accessible at 253a by an analogy with the way letters unite to form words. Just as vowels combine consonants, so certain forms, the vowel forms, act as uniters of other forms. This is revealed in statements by their linguistic equivalents. (It would seem from 252d, where the well-formed statement "Motion is at rest" is precluded, that a combination of forms ensures not only a statement but indeed a *true* statement. Let us pretend that we do not notice this and proceed.) At 254de Plato limits us to the 5 greatest kinds: Motion, Rest, Being, Sameness and Difference. ("Motion" is here applied to all change and not just to locomotion. This word has been used since it is the conventional opposite to "rest.") The most straightforward (and doubtless over-simplified) way to take these five kinds is to see Motion and Rest as consonant forms, represented linguistically by the subject or predicate terms of a statement, whereas the vowel forms Being, Sameness and Difference unite the

---

dialectical encouragement, the doctrines of the two leading, and at first violently opposed, parties may appear consonant to a very high degree. The inference to be drawn is that there is a great deal of puzzling, if not paradoxical, uncertainty about Being as there was earlier about Non-Being. This is the position emphasized at the subsequent 250d3-e4.

[3] From now on only page references will be given for the works listed in the bibliography.

[4] Despite 251b1 "*we* [my italics] not only say 'He is man' (*anthropon auton einai*)," the late-learners are surely those who deny *any* intermingling, hence none with Being (251d5-6). "Being" is one of the forbidden items cited at 252c2 where they are represented as self-refuting since, to propound their principle that everything is by itself apart from the others, they must unite the verbal expression of Being together with "apart," "by itself" and "from the others" in a non-naming capacity. One has to grant that the example explicitly rejected at 251b4-5 by the late-learners ("good" said of man) involves an "accidental," but they may be seen as treating "Being" as a name only, as in the earlier anti-dualist arguments at 243de which precluded any *determinate* pluralism. This was so because, if to avoid monism you say "Being" names something *different* from any of the n things to which it equally applies in "N things are," you will recursively end up with n+1 things.

subject with the predicate. Being, at the very least, underwrites the copula, Sameness the identifying "is" or "*is* the same as" and Difference the differentiating "*is* other than" (the latter two, as emphasized, helped along by Being.) It is hardly a fortuitous accident that, with Being and Difference, we find already introduced the components of the eventual recasting (completed by 258d) of non-being as the non-problematic *being different from.*

Sophist 254d to 255e undertakes to establish that the five greatest kinds are distinct. (It is assumed that Motion and Rest differ as do Sameness and Difference.) Motion and Rest are distinguished from Being, Sameness and Difference on the basis that Motion and Rest cannot be predicated of each other, but Being, Sameness and Difference can be predicated of both Motion and Rest. It is worth stressing that in the constructive section of the dialogue it is only the function of Motion and Rest as exclusive opposites that is exploited. Their ontological status is irrelevant. This is not surprising since we are concerned here with false statement and are in logico-linguistic territory and are not doing metaphysics. Characteristics of Forms *qua* Forms, such as Motion considered as an unchanging Form and hence being at rest (a condition rejected at 252d), are totally extraneous.[5] On the other hand, since ontology is *pre*cluded by the very subject matter, there are no grounds for *con*cluding that Plato has modified his earlier view of the Forms as paradeigmatic exemplars.

It is time further to explore the benefit of adopting Julius' interpretation of the late-learner's thesis. This advantage obtains in an examination of the much disputed argument at 255cd to the effect that Being and Difference are distinct. Yet, before we turn to this, our central concern, it is crucial to emphasize that in the text immediately preceding, at 255bc, Being and Sameness are differentiated. The reason given is that to apply Being to Motion and Rest is not to apply Sameness to them. Now, if we are to read Being here as Existence, the argument is straightforward. To say two things exist is not to say they are the same. But for those of us who, following Frede and Owen, take Being predicatively, i.e., as "being *something*", the argument is often dismissed as fallacious, for, if we complete "Motion and Rest are" in the same way as we would "Motion and Rest are the same," it fails, since "Motion and Rest are each other" does not clash with "Motion and Rest are the same as each other." (See, for example, Bostock, 91).

One may be tempted to try to rehabilitate Plato's argument as it stands by urging that the same property may be ascribed to both Motion and Rest without their thereby becoming the same instance of that property. For example, their both being Forms does not imply that they are the same Form. But, to consider (counter?) the observation that they are the same *qua* Form, we are at least forced to concede that the differing ways of being the same (e.g., in number, in species, in genus, etc.) suggest that it might have been preferable had Plato anticipated

---

[5] So much for the years of effort spent by Gregory Vlastos in the preparation of his paper "An Ambiguity in the *Sophist*", pp. 270-317 in his *Platonic Studies*. Here I am in agreement with van Eck, 2000, p. 5.

his strategy for distinguishing Being from Difference and (arguably) given us a contrast between the non-relative and the relative where Being belongs in both classifications, Sameness in the latter only. (Admittedly, the controversy, into which we are about to enter, concerning the interpretation of the Being/Difference dichotomy may moderate our enthusiasm for this proposal.) In any case, all we need for present purposes is to re-emphasize that Sameness and Being have been presented as separate in the *Sophist before* we come to the differentiation of Being and Difference at 255cd. In the latter case the type of treatment applied to Being and Sameness will not even *appear* to work. One cannot maintain that Being cannot be Difference on the grounds that, if they were the same, then, since Motion and Rest both are, Motion and Rest would (counter-factually) be different! Another sort of consideration must be introduced.

At 255c12-13 the text reads, "Of beings ("existents" at 260a5) some (are) in themselves (*auta kath'hauta*), others are always said with relation to other things (*pros alla*). This dichotomy is used to distinguish Being from Difference, since to be different is always to be different with respect to something else and this restricts Difference to the second half of the dichotomy, whereas Being extends to both. Let me refer to these two ways of being as KH(*kath'hauto*)-being and PA(*pros allo*)-being. Some see KH-being as existence and PA-being as predication (Moravcsik, 54; Bostock, 93-4). Both parts of this way of reading the contrast may be questioned. With respect to KH-being it highlights Being as Existence, but Existence is not Being's main import in the constructive section of the *Sophist*. This is seen in Being's function as a vowel form, usually the copula, as exemplified in its crucial role as the "being" in "being other than," the reformulation of *not-being*, and in its appearance at 256e5 where, for each kind, Being is many, i.e., each kind has many true positive predications. As for PA-being, this account takes it as predication *simpliciter* and hence lands in the somewhat forced position of claiming that to attribute any property to a subject is to express that subject's being in relation to something else, a venture well beyond the surface grammar of the passage in accordance with which "being other than" should, at the very least, be restricted to relatives (two(+)-place predicates). This leads us to the so-called "traditional" version where KH-being is that supplied by non-relatives (one-place predicates), PA-being that presented by relatives. This is close to the account I favor, but it has been severely savaged by Owen and Frede on the grounds, which I share, that if we take PA seriously, we cannot allow it to cover relatives as such because that would admit Sameness as a relation to something *else* (Owen,256; Frede, 1967,17).

Owen (256-7) takes KH-being as that expressed by identity statements, PA-being that in predications. This puts Sameness safely out of PA thus preserving the latter's connotation of *Difference*. My initial reservation with Owen's interpretation has been given just above. If we follow the most straightforward strategy and stick to the surface grammar of the passage, we are unlikely to cast *all* non-identifying predicates in the role of being other than their subject. We are rather to see PA as limited to relatives, assuming that we can give an account of Sameness which would keep it from PA.

Owen has two motivations for his reading. (1) It supports his thesis that the "is" of existence does not play a significant part in the constructive section of the *Sophist* by banishing existence from the interpretation of KH. But, as we shall see, one can readily do this by following a more traditional version. (2) He (256) intriguingly views the *KH as identity/PA as predication* distinction at 255c 12-13 to be Plato's reply to the late-learners whom he takes as regarding all admissible statements as identities. But Julius has taught us that this is not so. All the late-learners can get is a string of names. For them "Being" would have no verbal function. In any case, the late-learners have been rebutted earlier at 252c where, as we have already seen (p.112, above), it is shown that, if their principle is accepted, it cannot be formulated. So Owen's move is unnecessary. It is also insufficient. An identity/predication distinction would not impress them since they accept neither component. Furthermore, for Owen, positive identities are KH, but negative identities, i.e., "X is other than Y" are obviously PA, since that is what PA *means*. So the KH/PA contrast is not an identity/predication distinction as such.

A final jab at Owen. He claims (257) that his interpretation shows why a different argument was needed earlier to distinguish Being from Sameness since, for him, Sameness is not in PA, to be contrasted with Being in PA *and* in KH. But on Owen's interpretation one would *not* need a different argument for Sameness since it is limited to KH and Being covers KH and PA. In fact, as noted on p. 114, above, it is because the argument for Being vs. Sameness does *not* work for Being vs. Difference that the KH vs. PA item is introduced. One could not suggest that Being cannot be Difference because then, if Motion and Rest both were, they would be different! Owen has it backwards! Let us go forward to Frede.[6]

Frede (1992, 400-1) Takes KH/PA as two ways of being (something) which are reflected in two uses of the incomplete "is." X can be something either "by itself" (KH) or "with reference to something else" (PA). Fortunately time constraints prevent me from even trying to do justice to this deservedly much-discussed interpretation. Let me begin by mentioning a paradoxical result thereof. "Sameness is different from Difference" is PA for Frede, but the "equivalent" "Difference is different from Sameness" (a *self*-predication) is KH.[7] Another anomaly obtains when we note that Frede sees his account as telling against the late-learners. He

---

[6] My two main points against Owen have been anticipated by Bostock; that regarding the late-learners at pp. 99-100, my "final jab" at pp. 93-4.

[7] Frede may deny this attribution to KH, for he says, remarkably, (1992, p. 402) that "The Same is the same as itself" would be *pros allo*. It is not easy to reconcile this with the strict sense of *pros allo* as implying *otherness* which is crucial to Frede's rejection of the traditional reading of *pros alla* as applying to relatives as such. (See Silverman, p. 174.) This move also complicates Frede's representation of self-predications as *kath'hauta* (1967,31), a problem not definitively resolved by merely remarking (402) that we can "distinguish different kinds of self-predications." Frede (401, n. 5) attributes his view to Owen. For Owen, however, KH-being is identity whereas Frede goes to some length (402) to disassociate identity from KH-being.

(400) grants that these persons are concerned with rejecting certain statements about *individuals*. They deny that we can say of *a* man that he is good. For Frede their misunderstanding about statements is being addressed at 255c12-13. However, for him, (1967, 31; 1992, 402) only Forms can be subjects for KH predication. Anything said of *individuals* is in PA since it will introduce a Form, obviously something other than the individuals. "Theaetetus is Theaetetus" and "Theaetetus is young" are equally PA. How then can a distinction *between* KH and PA help the late-learners see the difference between essences and non-essences,with Frede, (or, indeed, that between identities and predications, with Owen)? In any case we can recall the moves we made against Owen in this regard. To begin with, no rejection of the late-learners is needed, since they were already refuted three Stephanus pages earlier. Secondly, how can a KH/PA distinction affect them anyway since they will not accept it? To focus on Frede, a contrast between two *verbal* uses of "being" will not impress them, since, from their point of view, both are equally mistaken.

Had Owen and Frede followed Julius' convincing portrayal of the late-learners' doctrine they would have been spared what may be termed a "background motivation" for their versions, the supposition that the KH/PA distinction as applied in understanding statements would be an effective move against the earlier targets. Let me now, in conclusion, turn to deal with their primary concern. This is that the traditional view, to the effect that PA covers all relatives, cannot account for Sameness if, as we should, we take literally the *otherness* of PA-being. Given that we are excluding Sameness from PA, I shall propose a minor adjustment to the usual reading of the "surface-grammar-friendly" traditional interpretation. This will permit us to adopt the most obvious differentiation of Being and Difference.

For such an approach to work, PA must be taken as a sub-class of relatives, now that Sameness is no longer therein. Where then has Sameness gone? If the KH/PA dichotomy is taken to be exhaustive, Sameness must be in KH. But, in contrast to Owen, for whom Sameness was not only in KH, it *was* KH, KH-being must now include all non-relational predicates as well. While this alternative would certainly distinguish Being from Difference, it has, as far as I know, no supporters and, what is worse from our present perspective, by including Sameness therein, it precludes the traditional reading of KH as containing one-place predicates only.

But suppose the KH/PA division is taken as non-exhaustive?[8] Distinct advan-

---

[8] Frede (1967, 36) suggests that a non-exhaustive disjunction of *ta men ... ta de* would go against the usage (*Sprachgebrauch*) of these expressions. This impression is readily reinforced by the prevalent contexts of dichotomous division, but there are passages where the contrast is not limited in this way. Notably at *Rep.* 338d7-8 we find "of cities some (*hai men*) have tyrannical rule, others (*hai de*) democratic, others (*hai de*) aristocratic." Then, taking up the thesis that each form of government makes laws for its own advantage, the text continues (e2-3), "... democracy (makes) democratic laws, tyranny tyrannical and the others (*hai allai*) likewise ... ." The plural, "the others," shows that the original tri-partite division need not be read as exhaustive, leaving room for timocracy and oligarchy which appear at 545b6 and 545c1 respectively. Other likely cases are to be found in Aristotle: (1) At *Meta.* 1042b15 ff. where he lists various ways of *forming* sensible substances. These are presented as a non-exhaustive list of examples (*hoion ta men ...*

tages follow. In the first place, Sameness does not have to be accounted for at 255c12-13. Not only are we spared the complexities attendant upon trying to accommodate it to an "either KH or PA" classification, but, in addition, its absence fits best with the dramatic development of the dialogue, for Sameness has already been differentiated from the other greatest kinds *before* we get to our passage. Hence there is no reason to think that Plato had to propose a classificatory schema which would have to take account of it. Furthermore, now that the basis for the alternatives of Owen and (arguably) Frede is undercut, we are justified in reading KH/PA in a natural and straightforward non-exhaustive way. This involves a twofold modification of the one-place (non-relative)/two-place (relative) traditional interpretation. Each component is to be restricted. KH-being is what something possesses in virtue of its essence (as at *An. Po.* 73a35-6). This excludes one-place "accidental" predicates. PA-being excludes the relation of sameness. In each case the sought-for contrast is readily apparent from the grammatical surface structure of the sentences expressing the two ways of being. "Man *is* animal" is KH. "Man *is* other than dog" is PA. Hence Being ≠ Being other. Q. E. D.

Ironically, the very examples we want in each case are to be found in Diogenes Laertius who is by no means a customary source of penetrating insights into the thought of the many figures he covers. At III, 108-9, he echoes the *Sophist* with a two-fold division of beings (*tōn ontōn*). The first, labeled *kath'heauta*, ranges over natural kinds, "man, horse and other animals." The second, and contrasting, group is represented linguistically by comparatives, "greater," "quicker," and "more beautiful." This is exactly what we would expect if these items were representatives of PA-being, taken in the restrictive literal sense of always introducing something different than that to which they are ascribed. Diogenes, however, does not divide ways of being into KH and PA. His second label is *pros ti* or "in relation to *something*." Let this be designated as PT-being. What we have then, as far as terminology is concerned, is the traditional division into non-relatives (KH) and relatives (PT).[9] Nevertheless, whether by luck or design, Diogenes has interpreted these two components more narrowly and in exact conformity with our understanding of KH/PA at *Sophist* 255c12-13. Purposively or not, he has omitted accidents from KH and his type of items in PT will not accommodate Sameness. So, despite his nomenclature, he has not in fact fully represented the established one-place/two-place exegesis of KH/PT. Yet his acceptance of the "wider" terminology, perhaps a reassurance to those who justifiably have reservations as to his acuteness, gives us an opportunity to rehabilitate Sameness by dividing PT-being into (1) PA-being, where something is (something) in relation to something else (*pros allo*), and (2) PH-being, where something is (something) in relation to itself

---

ta de... ta de...). (2) At *Meta.* 1053b15-16 there is a non-exhaustive list of "physicists." The text reads, "...of these the one (*ho men*) ..., another (*ho de*) ..., another (*ho de*). These counter-examples should not surprise those hesitant to accept a non-exhaustive reading at 255c12. After all, it does not read (as, e.g., at *An. Pr.* 43a25) "of *all* beings, some are..., others are."

[9] For KH/PT as the usual contrast, see Fine, chapter 12.

(*pros heauto* – found for example, at 256b1).[10] Plato *could* have distinguished Being from Difference at 255c8ff. by contrasting KH with PT and then noting that PA was a sort of PT. But, given that the other component of PT, PH, had just previously been dealt with at 255b8-c7, he accentuates his concern with Difference by using PA alone, a move which in no way compromises his basic purpose which, after all, was not to distinguish non-relational being from relational being as such.[11]

It may be worth speculating why my "simplistic" approach to the passage has not prevailed. A possible explanation may be that the KH/PA dichotomy has been regarded as *conceptually* exhaustive. Something must be (something) either *in* itself or in relation to something else. I suggest this may be challenged, for we can also have something *in relation to* itself. This option is not to be included in KH when, as I am assuming, KH is restricted to non-relatives.[12] But if, in the interest of exhaustiveness, self-identity is then put into PA, PA has lost its essential otherness and the original basis for an apparently exhaustive self/other contrast is removed.

Finally, there is the question, "Is the wider KH/PT dichotomy exhaustive?"[13]

---

[10] This is obviously *not* the sense of PH used by Meinwald in her commentary on the *Parmenides* where (p. 75) *pros heauto* in that dialogue is taken to have the force of *kath' hauto* in the *Sophist* and "signals that the predication reveals the structure of the subject's own nature" (p. 74). She explicitly rejects my version (p. 55) as "the most simple-minded way" of following "the hint of the surface grammar" and finds it philosophically unfruitful for the *Parmenides*. Be that as it may, it is, I submit, adequate for the *Sophist*.

[11] Admittedly, *pros ti* and *pros allo* are sometimes taken as equivalent (e.g. *Categories* 6a 36-7). But this is not necessarily the case. At *Meta.* 1021a9-10 Aristotle has sameness (overlooked in the *Categories* passage) as a *pros ti*, but, fortunately, with no indication of its being *pros allo*. One may wonder why I have turned to Aristotle for my references. There are two places in Plato where a KH/PT distinction is made. Neither, however, is at all helpful for our *Sophist* passage. In the *Theaetetus* we find the dictum of Protagoras that things are not anything in themselves (*auto kath'hauto* at 152d3), but always in relation to a perceiver (*pros ti & tini & tinos* at 160b9). This is (a) not Plato's view, (b) not logico-grammatical, but metaphysical, and (c) if applied to the *Sophist*, would impair a Being/Difference distinction since it *excludes* KH-being.

As far as terminology is concerned, the *Philebus* may seem more promising. At 51c6-7 certain items (geometrical figures, colors, sounds) are presented as beautiful *kath'hauta* and not *pros ti*. Indeed, at 51d7-8 these are beautiful *auta kath'hauta* and not *pros heteron* – the latter a possible conflation of PT and PA. But, even if we *could* get a clear view of the distinction being offered here, it would be a major challenge to see it as helping us choose between the competing exegeses of 255c12-13. This consideration holds *a fortiori* for 53d3-4 where the contrast is made between something *auto kath' hauto* and something "with a view to something else" (*ephiemenon allou*), exemplified at 54ab as ships vs. shipbuilding.

As Fine (174) has emphasized, the moral of all this is that there is no standard application in Plato of KH vs. PT (PA). The interpretation of the dichotomy is to be gained from the context in which it is found – a procedure I have endeavored to follow in this paper. (A manifest example of the need to view the various "*kata*" and "*pros*" expressions as "non-rigidly designating" is to be found at *Topics* 142a28 where the double is *kath'hauta pros ti*, in accordance with *Meta.* 1017a22, 26 and 1021b3-4!).

[12] Putting PH in KH *along with* one-place predicates was mentioned on p. 117, above.

[13] So it would appear in (the unreconstituted) D.L. who ascribes KH-being to "as many as do not need a further explanation" (*hermēneia*)" and PT-being to "as many as *do* need such an explanation."

What of "Socrates is wise"? If KH is to be fully determined on a "one-place predicate" criterion, this example fits therein, but one might transcend mere grammar and urge that so-called accidentals are improperly described as belonging to something in virtue of its own nature.[14] To avoid getting into this issue, I have adopted a blatantly non-exhaustive interpretation of a one-place/two-place dichotomy, restricting the former to sortals, and the latter to a sub-class of relatives. Yet this approach remains adequate to fulfill its function, that of differentiating Being from Difference.[15]

I conclude on a personal note. At *Sophist* 241d the Eleatic Stranger describes his challenge to Father Parmenides' prohibition of non-being as patricide. Since I have studied *under* both Vlastos and Owen and, extensively, *with* Frede, (though not on Greek philosophy) this paper is an attempt at both patricide *and* fratricide, a doubly soul-enhancing undertaking.[16]

BIBLIOGRAPHY

[Bostock, 1984] Bostock, David. 1984. 'Plato on "is not"' *Oxford Studies in Ancient Philosophy* 2: 89-119.

[Fine, 1993] Fine, Gail. 1993. *On Ideas: Aristotle's Criticism of Plato's Theory of Forms.* Oxford: Clarendon Press.

[Frede, 1967] Frede, Michael. 1967. *Prädikation und Existenzaussage.* Hypomnemata 18. Göttingen: Vandenhoeck und Ruprecht.

[Frede, 1992] Frede, Michael. 1992. 'False Statements in the *Sophist*.' In *The Cambridge Companion to Plato*, ed. Kraut. Cambridge: Cambridge University Press:397-424.

---

[14] Note that those who include predicates such as "large" in PA, as, for example, Szaif, 353,n.31, and Vlastos, 288,n.44 (*via* Hermodorus), are not using a *grammatical* one-place/two-place predicate distinction to contrast KH and PA. Against the tendency to take Plato as regarding "large" as a relative see White, 1992, pp. 285-7 and 1993, pp. xxiv-xxv.

[15] A possible way of dealing with one-place "accidentals" at the grammatical level would be to make use of the concept of KA(*kat'allo*)-being where something is something "according to" or "with respect to" something else. Then one could proceed as follows. First divide Being into KT (*kata ti*)-being (where something is (something) with respect to *something*) and PT(*pros ti*)-being. Then divide the former into KH(*kath'hauto*)-being and KA(*kat'allo*)-being to parallel the division of PT-being into PH(*pros heauto*)-being and PA(*pros allo*)-being. KH-being, as we would expect (cf. *An.Po.* 73a35), would apply to essential attributes. KA-being in turn, would then account for the one-place accidentals. Support for this might be gained from such passages as *Topics* 134a 20-25 where a body is colored (*kat'allo*) because its surface is colored. Analogously, Socrates is to be designated as wise with respect to, or in accordance with, (*kata*), something else, i.e. wisdom. He is not wise, however, *in relation to* (*pros*) wisdom. (Nor is wisdom, unlike the surface, which is also colored, itself to be characterized as wise.) Also at *Meta.* 1020b11 when substances change in quality they are called "F" *kata* F-ness. The fundamental division between "being something with respect to something (*kata ti*)" and "being something in relation to something (*pros ti*)," with its correspondingly symmetrical components, would seem to have a better claim to be exhaustive than do either the KH/PT or the KH/PA alternatives. Let me insist, however, that the material contained in this footnote is speculative in the extreme and of a sort usually to be found only in works published at the expense of their authors.

[16] This present offering may be seen as a sequence to my "A Way Back for *Sophist* 255c12-13" in *Ancient Philosophy* 26 (2006). It relies heavily on the earlier work, but includes several revisions, most notably additional evidence in support of its key claim – the non-exhaustiveness of the KH/PA dichotomy at 255c12-13.

[Malcolm, 2006] Malcolm, John. 2006. 'A Way Back for *Sophist* 255c12-13' *Ancient Philosophy* 26: 275-89
[Meinwald, 1991] Meinwald, Constance. 1991. *Plato's* Parmenides. Oxford: Oxford University Press.
[Moravcsik, 1962] Moravcsik, Julius. 1962. 'Being and Meaning in the *Sophist*' *Acta Philosophica Fennica* 14: 23-71.
[Owen, 1970] Owen, G.E.L. 1970. 'Plato on Not-Being' in *Plato I*, ed. Vlastos. New York: Doubleday Anchor: 223-267.
[Silverman, 2002] Silverman, Allan. 2002. *The Dialectic of Essence*. Princeton: Princeton University Press.
[Szaif, 1998] Szaif, Jan. 1998. *Platons Begriff der Wahrheit*. 2nd edn. Karl Alber: Munich.
[van Eck, 2000] van Eck, Job. 2000. 'Plato's Logical Insights: On *Sophist* 254d-257a' *Ancient Philosophy* 20: 53-79.
[Vlastos, 1973] Vlastos, Gregory. 1973. *Platonic Studies*. Princeton: Princeton University Press.
[White, 1992] White, Nicholas. 1992. 'Plato's Metaphysical Epistemology.' In *The Cambridge Companion to Plato*, ed. R. Kraut. Cambridge: Cambridge University Press: 277- 310.
[White, 1993] White, Nicholas. 1993. *Plato: Sophist*. Indianapolis: Hackett

Moravcsik on Plato on Radical Reorientation of One's Life

NICHOLAS D. SMITH

1 Introduction

On page 299 of *Plato and Platonism*, Julius Moravcsik characterizes what he sees as a central feature of the kinds of ethical confrontation we find in Plato's dialogues:

> The typical encounter in the ethically oriented dialogues is not between people who calculated the good things and appropriate interactions in the right way and those who were mistaken in their calculations, but between those like Socrates who had the right ideal and others who embraced misguided ideals like hedonism, inordinate power, the desire for domination and such like. Plato asks of such people not only that they accept new rules of conduct, but also that they reorient their whole lives around a new ideal.

In Moravcsik's view, Plato's understanding of how human beings can adapt to new ideals requires a significant "plasticity" of human nature, for the radical reorientation that is required presupposes that we not only replace one ideal with another, but also come to have new beliefs, desires, and preferences. I believe Moravcsik is exactly right to understand Plato as requiring hedonists and would-be tyrants to undergo radical reorientation of their lives. But I shall argue that the way in which Moravcsik has represented Plato's view of moral transformation requires at least significant clarification, and perhaps significant modification.

Just as he was about to engage in the most searching criticism of another scholar's views, the late Gregory Vlastos set the tone of his criticism with these words: "[O]nly those who are strangers to the ethos of scholarly controversy will see anything but high esteem in my critique" (Vlastos 1991, 39 n.2). It precisely this sort of high esteem that I provide in the argument of this paper.[1] I will argue that Plato regarded our nature as far more fixed than the way Moravcsik represents it, and that what Moravcsik sees as an "extremely plastic" conception of our nature is to be understood, instead, as Plato's view, in the first place, of just how difficult our natures are to fathom, and in the second, how the efforts Moravcsik sees Plato

---

[1] And, indeed, the very sort of high esteem I was trained by Moravcsik himself to bestow on his and other scholars' work, when he was my dissertation director.

calling for are really efforts to bring our fixed natures into full realization in good lives.

Moravcsik's depiction of Plato's view conceives of the options as two: either one can ask how one should live, given one's actual beliefs, desires, and preferences, or else one can ask whether one's actual beliefs, desires, and preferences are the best ones, and then, given a negative answer to that question, reorient one's life around the very different set of goals and preferences such an inquiry would reveal. I have two problems with this picture — one based on the Platonic texts, and one more generally philosophical. Briefly, my textual concern derives from various texts in which Plato has Socrates seem to point to fixed natures within himself or his interlocutor, but whose settled characteristics are not easily accessible, or even opaque, to those whose natures they are. My philosophical concern is that Plato's answer, as I understand it, to the question "How should I live?" is better motivated and more motivating than the answer Moravcsik provides on Plato's behalf. In the remainder of this essay, then, I shall first pursue the textual issue, and will close with a few remarks about the philosophical point.

2 Test Passage #1: Socrates v. Polus (*Gorgias* 471e-479d)[2]

For confirmation (or disconfirmation) of Moravcsik's characterization of Plato's view, it makes sense to look at cases in which Socrates is depicted as confronting interlocutors whose beliefs, desires, and preferences are characterized quite clearly as seeming to be very much out of line with those Socrates himself advocates. One such interlocutor is Polus, in Plato's *Gorgias*, who admires the tyrant Archelaus of Macedon, on the ground that Archelaus managed to usurp the throne and put several innocent people to death, all with impunity. Socrates, however, refuses to say that Archelaus is happy, and Polus accuses him of feigning disagreement simply to avoid being refuted (471e). Socrates responds by making a distinction between rhetorical refutation — in which one can be counted as refuted if a great number of witnesses testify against one — and the sort of refutation that Socrates himself practices, according to which the only witness that matters is the interlocutor himself (471e-472b). So in this passage, Socrates says that he will produce *Polus himself* as a witness against the view that Polus has expressed.

One of the aspects of what Vlastos called the "problem of the elenchus" is Socrates' insistence that his interlocutors provide sincere responses to his questions — responses that articulate the interlocutors' own views. Different characterizations of this requirement have appeared in the literature,[3] but the requirement itself is familiar enough, appearing, as it does, in a number of our texts (see, e.g. *Euthphr.* 9d7-8; *Cri.* 49c11-d1; *Prt.* 331c4-d1; *La.* 193c6-8; *Rep.* I.349a4-8; *Grg.* 458a1-b1, 495a5-9, 499b4-c6, 500b5-c1; [*Alc.* I] 114d11-e9). Now, there are dif-

---

[2]He arguments I develop in the next two sections are the product of my collaboration with Thomas C. Brickhouse. See Brickhouse and Smith 1994, 73-91.

[3]See, e.g. Benson 2000, 38-39; Benson 2002, 105; Brickhouse and Smith 1994, 16; Brickhouse and Smith 2002, 147-149; Irwin 1993; Vlastos 1994, 7.

ferent ways in which one might understand this requirement, for after all, many of the things that interlocutors actually say, when questioned by Socrates, contradict others things they have said. But Socrates' requirement seems to indicate something stronger than a supposition that skillful questioning can induce others to give the sorts of answers Socrates himself seeks, because he explicitly indicates that insincere answers are out-of-bounds. But let us look more closely at what Socrates takes to be the significance of getting Polus to testify against himself.

The argument between Socrates and Polus concerns whether doing wrong is worse than suffering it, and escaping just punishment is better than incurring and suffering it. Polus often insists that Socrates actually agrees with Polus's own expressed position, but in each case, Socrates immediately turns the tables on the young sophist.

Socrates: For I know how to produce one witness in support of my statements, and that is the man himself with whom I find myself arguing; the many I dismiss: there is also one whose vote I know how to take, whilst to the multitude I have not a word to say. See therefore if you will consent to be put to the proof in your turn by answering my questions. For I think, indeed, that you and I and the rest of the world believe that doing wrong is worse than suffering it, and escaping punishment worse than incurring it.

Polus: And I, that neither I nor anyone else in the world believes it. You, it seems, would choose rather to suffer wrong than to do it.

Socrates: Yes, and so would you and everyone else. (*Grg.* 474a5-b8[4])

Socrates and Polus do not seem to agree about very much, in this debate, but what they do agree about is why people would say the things that they do when standing as witnesses in the sort of debate in which they are now engaged. Socrates promises to get Polus to testify in favor of the very view Polus most vehemently denies. Polus is convinced that he will *not* provide such testimony, precisely because he thinks that neither he nor anyone else actually *believes* what Socrates has forecast as Polus's eventual testimony. Socrates, on the contrary, seems very confident that Polus will end up providing the testimony he has forecast, precisely because he supposes that "you and I and the rest of the world believe that doing wrong is worse than suffering it, and escaping punishment worse than incurring it." But notice, it is not merely that Socrates takes everyone actually to *believe* the very position Polus has opposed — including Polus himself — Socrates actually goes on to make the very same case for the *preferences* that people have: Polus archly scoffs at Socrates for being committed to choosing suffering wrong to doing it, and Socrates again turns the tables on Polus in the most general way on this matter of preference: "Yes, and so would you and everyone else."

Of course, Socrates actually does manage to get Polus to testify against the very position Polus had earlier advocated, but when the young sophist has given the very testimony Socrates had forecast, once again, Socrates makes it very clear what he takes the significance of Polus's answers to be:

> Socrates: Then would you rather have the evil and foul when it is more than when it is less? Do not shrink from answering, Polus; you will get no hurt by it: but submit yourself bravely to the argument, as to a doctor, and reply yes or no to my question.
>
> Polus: Why, I should not so choose, Socrates.
>
> Socrates: And would anyone else in the world?
>
> Polus: I think not, by the argument at least.
>
> Socrates: Then I spoke the truth when I said that neither you nor anyone else in the world would really choose to do wrong rather than suffer it, since it really is more evil.
>
> Polus: Apparently.
>
> Socrates: So you see, Polus, that when one refutation is contrasted with the other they have no resemblance, but whereas you have the assent of everyone else except myself, I am satisfied with your sole and single assent and evidence, and I take your vote only and disregard the rest. (475d4-476a1)

---

[4] All translations of the *Gorgias* given herein are those of W. R. M. Lamb, from the Loeb Classical Library edition.

Along the way, as Socrates calls forth his witness, he also seems to grant that Polus does not *only* believe what Socrates says he (and everyone else in the world) believes — despite Polus's own resistance, but also concedes now and again that Polus *also* believes what Polus claims to believe (for example, at 472d1-6 and 473b1-2). So Socrates' view is not that Polus simply *lies* or misrepresents his actual opinion, but rather that Polus seems unaware of the fact that he *also* holds the *opposite* opinion from the one Socrates disputes, and the way in which he holds that other opinion — the one he is so aggressively *dis*avowing — is in some sense deeper and more stable than the other opinion that he so aggressively avows. I say that it is in some sense deeper and more stable, because once he is put into a position of becoming aware that he actually does hold the opinion he has been disavowing, he ends up testifying *against* the opinion he had earlier avowed. When Polus comes to realize that he holds both of a pair of contradictory beliefs, we discover which of them he is more committed to by watching which one of the pair he ends up avowing. As Socrates predicted, Polus ends up avowing the opinion that Socrates claims we all share.

In Socrates' discussion with Polus, accordingly, we *do* find Socrates bidding the younger man to undergo a fundamental ethical change. But the nature of this change is not from an ideal that he does hold to one that he does *not* hold, as Moravcsik's view of the plasticity of human nature would seem to have it. Instead, Socrates clearly characterizes the change as a change to what Polus himself has really believed all along, but has not seemed to realize that he does.

3 Test Passage #2: Socrates v. Callicles (*Gorgias* 481c5-482c3)

In the entire Platonic corpus, only the exchange between Socrates and Thrasymachus can rival the friction one finds in the debate between Socrates and Callicles in the *Gorgias*. In Callicles, surely, Socrates finds an interlocutor who is plainly characterized as devoted to the wrong ideals, and as holding the wrong beliefs, desires, and preferences. Callicles enters the dialogue simply incredulous at what Socrates has said to Polus (481b10-c4), and then — once Socrates has given his first reply — calls Socrates a demagogue (482c5), and faults Gorgias and Polus for their failures in discussion with Socrates for allowing shame to overcome them (482d1-e2). Callicles enters the argument with Socrates, apparently, bent on shamelessness. Callicles goes on to praise those who can break the bonds of convention and become lawless and despotical (484a2-b1). He sneers at philosophy as a childish amusement (484c5-8) which, if continued into adulthood, renders the philosopher in need of a whipping (485a4-d3). Socrates' response to this invective is not merely mild, it is actually enthusiastic:

> Socrates: If my soul had happened to be made of gold, Callicles, do you not think I should have been delighted to find one of those stones with which they test gold, and the best one; which, if I applied it, and

> it confirmed to me that my soul had been properly tended, would give me full assurance that I am in a satisfactory state and have no need of other testing?
>
> Callicles: What is the point of that question?
>
> Socrates: I will tell you. I am just thinking what a lucky stroke I have had in striking up with you.
>
> Callicles: How so?
>
> Socrates: I am certain that whatever you agree with me in any view that my soul takes, this must be the very truth. (486d2-e6)

Socrates' enthusiastic response to Callicles derives precisely from the fact that Callicles is so forthright in his opposition. Callicles contends that Polus ended up agreeing with Socrates only out of a sense of shame. But if Callicles himself ends up agreeing with Socrates, given his willingness to be completely frank — not allowing shame to interfere at all — then Socrates will have more complete assurance that the views he had attributed to *everyone*, in the discussion with Polus, really do belong to everyone, for even the shameless Callicles will prove to hold those same positions.

It is clear from the outset of their confrontation, however, that this is precisely what Socrates thinks will happen, for in his very first words to Callicles, Socrates accuses his new adversary of contradicting himself (481d5-e1), and of living a life marked by internal discord and contradiction within himself (482b7-c3). Had we not already witnessed the exchange between Socrates and Polus, we might have wondered why Socrates would characterize Callicles in this way — why, in other words, Socrates would be so confident, about one who only just now joined the conversation, that Callicles' disagreement with Socrates was an indication that, as Socrates puts it, Callicles does not agree with Callicles (482b5-6). But having already seen how Socrates induces his interlocutors to testify for the very view they begin by disavowing — doing so by insisting that they answer his questions only by stating their own beliefs — it comes now as no surprise to see Socrates contradicting Callicles about precisely what Callicles himself believes. So it is that, just as he had done with Polus, Socrates confidently makes predictions about what Callicles will say — stating his own sincere beliefs — when Callicles is given a Socratic inducement to think more deeply about what Callicles himself actually believes.

> Socrates: Come now, let us be sure to remember this, that Callicles the Acharnian said pleasant and good were the same, but knowledge and courage were different both from each other, and from the good.
>
> Callicles: And Socrates of Alopece refuses to grant us this; or does he grant it?
>
> Socrates: He does not; nor, I believe, will Callicles either, when he has rightly considered himself. (495d2-e2)

4 Summary of Conclusions from Test Passages and Brief Mention of Other Texts

In Socrates' debates with Polus and Callicles, we find him quite explicitly making claims about what his adversaries believe and prefer, and also what he thinks every one on earth believes and prefers. The beliefs and preferences he identifies, moreover, are beliefs and preferences concerning the very ideals that we hold and live by — the very sorts of life-shaping ideals that Moravcsik discussed in *Plato and Platonism*. What we find in these debates clearly indicates that Socrates believes we have fixed natures with regard to beliefs and preferences about how we should live. Despite these fixed natures, it is not only possible for us to fail to know ourselves, and thus not to realize that we have the beliefs and preferences that we do, but also to hold beliefs and preferences that are contradictory to those we hold as a part of our natures. It is possible for us to be like lyres that are out of tune and discordant, as Socrates says of Callicles (482b7-c3) and not to realize that we are in such a state.

The upshot, I take it, looks much like the way Moravcsik characterizes Plato's view. Polus and Callicles certainly do need to engage in a drastic reorientation of their lives, based upon very different ideals, and very different beliefs and preferences, from those they (sincerely) defend in their debates with Socrates. The ideals, beliefs, and preferences they defend are presumably ones that now shape their lives and inform their actions; whereas the ideals, beliefs, and preferences that Socrates defends do not presently have much effect at all upon the ways Polus and Callicles live. These other ideals and such, however — the ones Socrates defends — have at least enough of a grip on Polus and Callicles to lead them to give the answers they do, answers that also express what they believe and prefer. Indeed, when forced either to retain these other ideals, beliefs, and preferences, or those they had initially avowed, Polus and Callicles find themselves abandoning those that before had shaped their lives. But at the heart of the sort of conversion experience Moravcsik noted is a shift from ideals we only hold in some shallow way, to ones we hold so deeply that we will always maintain them over any rivals, once the alternatives are clear to us. So Moravcsik is quite right to characterize people like Polus and Callicles as in need of reorientation around a new set of ideals, relative to the ones that had been shaping their lives. But it also seems that the new set of ideals is, in actual fact, not really *new* at all, but were there all along, fixed and stable within all of human nature, and thus within Polus and Callicles as much as they are in all the rest of us. So Polus and Callicles really have miscalculated their good, by mistaking what they really believe, prefer, and desire.

I do not mean to suggest, of course, that either Polus or Callicles should be seen as very much improved as a result of their single discussion with Socrates. It is more likely that — rather than see the way in which the argument worked as providing a significant insight into themselves — they will suppose only that Socrates is such a clever logic-chopper that he somehow manipulated the outcome in such a way as to confuse them (examples of this very reaction can be found at *Euthyphro* 11b and *Meno* 80a). Moreover, given the views Polus and especially Callicles originally express, it seems more than possible that they have already suffered significant damage to their souls from past wrongdoing — perhaps so much, indeed, as to be beyond all help from Socrates or even the gods.[5] Even so, Socrates manages to find within these aggressive proponents of tyranny, beliefs and preferences entirely contrary to the lives they sought to defend at the beginning of their discussion with Socrates. Depending upon how damaged their souls are, however, it may be difficult or even impossible now for them to allow the beliefs and preferences Socrates showed they had, to bring about the radical reorientation these beliefs and preferences would require.

At any rate, I doubt that when Moravcsik wrote this section of *Plato and Platonism* he had these passages in the *Gorgias* in mind. And it is easy enough to find other passages in which it might well appear as if the ideals around which we should shape our lives, according to Plato, appear to be wholly external ones. So, when Plato bids us to strain every nerve to the end of making a kind of cognitive contact with the Form of the Good, in the *Republic*, for example, it certainly does not appear that he is really bidding us only to find what is already within us, as opposed to finding and adjusting to something other and external to ourselves. But this impression of the externality of Platonic ideals, I think, should in important ways be qualified, even in the dialogue or dialogues Moravcsik probably did have in mind when he presented Platonism in his book.

For the purposes of brevity, I do not propose in this section to provide anything like a complete survey of the evidence provided by dialogues other than the *Gorgias*, so much as to indicate only briefly several of the places in which such evidence might be provided. So first, consider the doctrine of recollection in any of its various depictions. In the *Meno*, recollection is characterized as informational — we are there said to be able to recall propositions or information, as the slave-boy is said to be recalling certain truths of geometry. In the *Phaedo* and *Phaedrus*, we recall Forms, and by doing so may come to have in us cognitive states (which presumably have propositional or propositionalizable content), but these states or their content are not themselves what is recalled, as in the *Meno*, but are instead the products of recollection, rather than the actual constituents of recollection. But such differences, interesting and important as they may be to those who wish to formulate likely stories of Plato's philosophical development, make no difference whatsoever to the question of whether or not our natures are fixed vis-à-vis the ideals, beliefs, and preferences that should guide our lives. For if all that we need, cognitively speaking, is good access to what we *already* know (or knew in a former life), then at least in terms of what we should *believe*, in order to live well, once again, our cognitive natures are fixed by our very natures, and all that is needed is for us to gain the appropriate sort of access to the fixities of our natures in order to make the correct calculations required for good lives. Moreover, as Plato

---

[5] For a discussion of Socrates' theory that wrongdoing can eventually result in the ruin of the soul, see Brickhouse and Smith 2007.

had Socrates also insist in the *Gorgias*, in the *Meno* we find Socrates showing — or perhaps I should say "reminding" — Meno that the difference between good and bad people cannot be that good people desire good things whereas bad people desire bad things, because, as they quickly agree, everyone, good and bad, desires good things and does not desire bad things (77b6-78b2).[6] But this indicates that not only are our most basic cognitions fixed and stable, so, too, is our most basic conative condition.

The same case can be made for the cognitive and conative psychology of *erōs* that we find in Plato's *Symposium* and *Phaedrus*. Although the Beautiful Itself certainly does seem to be external to us in a way that would make it seem more congenial to Moravcsik's rendering of the implications of moral change, the actual psychology of our relationship with the Beautiful Itself is entirely fixed and innate — even those whose expressions of eroticism seem to us to be the most bestial and wrong-headed *really are* compelled by the same divine power that drives the most philosophical person to the top of the "ladder of love." By merely settling for intimate contact with other bodies, however, the failed Platonic lover simply falls short of what he really craves, which is why Plato is convinced that such ways of expressing the *erōs* within us can never be truly satisfying.

The same fixity and innateness, I claim, can also be found in the *Republic*. The Form of the Good, like the Form of Beauty, surely is something other and external to us. But the *dunamis* of knowledge by which we can make the fullest possible cognitive contact with the Good is a fixed and stable part of human nature.[7] Not all human beings are constructed in such a way as to be able to bring this *dunamis* into fullest realization, it is true; only the philosophers can reasonably hope for this, and even they can only hope to achieve such a goal through decades of tightly controlled education. But Plato never suggests that non-philosophers are born without the power altogether. So even here — where recollection is never mentioned — we find that the most basic cognitive structure required to live well is present innately, and also innately tuned and aimed at what we need to know in order to live well, if only we can have the right sort of opportunity to allow this part of our nature to become fully realized.

So, too, although the *Republic* seems to provide a motivational psychology that would threaten to fragment our nature by presenting distinct and incompatible sets of aims (via the tripartite division of appetite, spirit, and reason), recent careful study has shown that Plato provides us sufficient evidence for thinking that even here, the distinctions between motivational forces should still be understood in terms of our having a single aim (the Good), where the operations of the so-called "lower parts of the soul" should be understood not as providing utterly different and competing aims, but rather as the same aim, only characterized by the specific

---

[6] In saying that I count the argument of the *Meno* to be making the same point as what Socrates also argues for in the *Gorgias*, I indicate my agreement with Penner and Rowe 1994, and my disagreement with Santas 1979, ch. 6.

[7] For a discussion of Plato's characterization of knowledge as a *dunamis* and its implications, see Smith 2000.

conceptions of this aim appropriate to each part. In other words, the appetitive part of the soul conceives of the good as pleasure, and pursues pleasure *as good*, whereas the spirit conceives of the good as honor, and pursues honor *as good*. Only reason can take an all-things-considered view, which is why our pursuit of the good — which is in this way actually common to all of our psychic operations — must be managed by reason, for only reason is likely to calculate our *real* good in a way that is reliably correct.[8] So, rather than emphasizing the plasticity of human nature, the *Republic* is just like the other dialogues I have surveyed in holding that our pursuit of the good derives from stable fixities in our natures, whose cognitive and conative conditions simply need to be made salient to us, for us to make the right decisions. Accordingly, the change from faulty to correct ideals will always be a change that reflects and realizes cognitions and preferences we not only have already, but which are fixed parts of our natural endowment.

Nowhere in Plato's later works is the contrast between those who embrace different ideals made more starkly than in the *Theaetetus*, in which the lack of commonality between the lives of orators and philosophers is so great that the two can barely communicate with each other. But even here, the inferior life is one that Plato is careful to characterize as contrary to human nature: The iniquities of the orator's life result in his having an *unhealthy soul* — one that is "small and warped" (173a-b). Moreover, here in the *Theaetetus*, lack of self-knowledge is again shown to lie at the heart of wrongdoing: "they [wrongdoers] are just the sort of people they don't think they are, and all the more for not thinking so" (176d5-6).[9] So here, too, we find that to hold the right ideals requires us to know ourselves, with the clearest implication that there is something fixed within us for us to come to know.

5   The Ultimate Question

One advantage of Platonic moral psychology, according to Moravcsik, is that it allows for a clear and compelling answer to what has been called the "ultimate question" of ethics. Here is how Moravcsik puts it in *Plato and Platonism*:

> Within this theory, the question Why be moral? boils down to the question Why have an adequate ideal for ourselves? This assumes that there are objective, rational ways of assessing ideals which give these at least a partial ordering. If this is so, then the question about morality in the modern sense loses its bite. Once we have an adequate ideal, our reply will be: Why not? (300-301)

---

[8]Those who have read the recent essay by Carone 2001 will readily discern her influence on my characterization of Platonic moral psychology here. Although I agree with her that all motivation in Plato's *Republic* is good-dependent, I do not agree with her view that the *Republic* continues to deny the possibility of *akrasia*. This, however, is a topic for another argument.

[9]I am indebted to Zina Giannopolou for calling my attention to these passages in the *Theaetetus*.

As I understand the point Moravcsik is making here, the idea seems to be that the sort of radical transformation one would go through, in becoming a fully realized Platonist, would be one in which all of the reasons why such a reorientation is objectively preferable will be immediately and entirely *salient* to the one so reoriented. To those who have achieved a clear understanding of the correct ideal, the question, 'why be moral?' would simply make no sense, and could not even be sincerely framed.

But Moravcsik's depiction of what he calls Plato's plasticity of human nature thesis seems to make the rationality of the correct ideal inaccessible to those not already in a position to witness it — to those, that is, who have not already undergone the radical reorientation Moravcsik sees Plato as requiring of those who hold the wrong ideals. Those now inclined to regard hedonism, or the pursuit of unlimited political power, as the best policy plainly do not *now* have the right sort of access to the reasons why the different ideal Plato advocates is much preferable to those they now favor — if they did, they would not be inclined to hedonism or tyranny. Unless and until whatever reasons there may be for the likes of Polus and Callicles to change their ways become *salient* to them, it is difficult to see how any of whatever reasons there may be for such flawed specimens to undergo radical reorientation — however objective these reasons may be in fact — might be motivating. So in Moravcsik's version of what is required for moral change, it would seem that the only reasons that could motivate moral change must be inaccessible to those who most need to undergo such change, and would only be available to those who have already (somehow) undergone the change. To one who might sincerely ask the question 'why be moral?' then, there can be no satisfactory reply — except to those who would never ask the question and would never need it answered.

But in dialogue after dialogue Plato depicts Socrates confronting those for whom the ultimate question *does* require an answer, and Plato has Socrates lead his interlocutors towards that answer, by showing them that their own sincere answers to his questions will reveal the answer to them. If I am right about what lies behind Socrates' way of examining people, then to the cognitive version of the ultimate question — why should I *believe* that some ideal other than pleasure or tyranny is actually choiceworthy? — Socrates would, in effect, be leading them to see that they *already* believe this, if only they will attend more carefully to what they really believe. Socrates' arguments do not attempt to get people to change from what they now believe to what they do *not* believe; instead, he argues as he does in order to bring into a condition of salience beliefs they *already* have — or else they would not find themselves led to answer Socrates' questions in the ways they do. This sort of change actually transforms us from what we really *are not* — despite what we may *think* we are — into what we really *are*.

And to the motivational version of the ultimate question — why should I *want to* become a fully realized Platonist, rather than a hedonist or tyrant? — Plato reveals how Socrates leads his interlocutors to the recognition that they actually *already do* want precisely this, and *do not want* to lead lives of wanton pursuits of pleasure or political power. Moravcsik is right to see that the ultimate question is moot, for a fully realized Platonist. What Moravcsik seems to miss, if I have understood him at all correctly, is that the ultimate question is moot *for all of us*, by our very nature. And we would all realize this, if only we attended, by leading an "examined life," to what we actually do believe and want. In Moravcsik's version, we cannot see the mootness of the ultimate question until we are in a condition to reason well. I do not entirely disagree with this, but in the version I have given here, Plato would say that what renders the ultimate question moot is not simply the product of our innate intellectual interest finding its way to objective first principles, but also a result of the very structure of our *selves*.

In my understanding of Plato, then, human nature is actually not at all plastic, as Moravcsik had it, but rigid. To make this clear, let us return to what Moravcsik has to say on page 299 of *Plato and Platonism*:

> The difference between the more rigid and the more plastic conceptions of our appetitive nature can also be illustrated with respect to planning one's life. One can say, "Given that I have these likes and dislikes, these talents, these preferences, desires, and needs, what kind of life will give me the greatest satisfaction and enjoyment?" Alternatively, one can ask, "What things in life are really worth pursuing? Which of these are such that, with some effort, I can orient my life around them and let such orientation structure the objects for desires and attitudes and determine utility for me?" The second is the Platonic approach. The first seems more appropriate for contexts in which we are already fairly well settled and are considering more short-range goals.

I have claimed, in my discussion today, that the second question Moravcsik gives here — the one he regards as "the Platonic approach" — is actually to be understood as *the very same question* as the first one. What distinguishes the fully realized Platonist from the hedonist or tyrant is not a matter of what is or is not settled in us, for Plato regards all that matters to these questions, within us, as already settled by our very natures. The difference, instead, is the degree to which fully realized Platonists actually know themselves, and how little those inclined to live hedonistic or tyrannical lives know themselves, by contrast. In Plato's dialogues, Socrates confronts would-be hedonists or tyrants *with their own desires, preferences, and beliefs* and seeks to make these desires, preferences, and beliefs salient to his interlocutors, thereby indicating and motivating very different lives than those they have been leading.

One way to understand the difference between Moravcsik's characterization of the Platonic view and my own, then, is to see it as a difference about the degree of plasticity in Plato's conception of the *self*. In Moravcsik's depiction, ethical transformation would appear to require one to change one's self — those transformed change from what they *are* (now) into what they *are not* (now). In my view, those transformed must be true to themselves, must actually *become* themselves, changing from what they really *are not* (despite what they may think about themselves) into what they truly *are*. I do not deny, then, Moravcsik's quite accurate understanding of the ideals that would change lives as both objective and as discoverable by and sustained in reason. I have emphasized, however, that much of the objective basis for the correct ideals, and the goal at which reason should aim, may be found within every soul — even those of people who seem dedicated to lives wholly at odds with the right ideals. To put it in a way I hope Plato would approve, the attraction of our souls to the Form of the Good is an attraction of "like to like." To put ourselves in a position to know the Good requires coming to terms with what is divine in all of us.

Acknowledgements

I have greatly benefited from comments on earlier drafts of this paper given to me by Zina Giannopolou and Joel Martinez. All remaining errors, of course, are mine alone.

BIBLIOGRAPHY

[Benson, 2000] Benson, Hugh H. 2000. *Socratic Wisdom The Model of Knowledge in Plato's Early Dialogues*. New York: Oxford University Press.
[Benson, 2002] Benson, Hugh H. 2002. "Problems with Socratic Method." In Scott, 2002, 101-113.
[Brickhouse and Smith, 1994] Brickhouse, Thomas C. and Smith, Nicholas D. 1994. *Plato's Socrates*. Oxford and New York: Oxford University Press.
[Brickhouse and Smith, 2002] Brickhouse, Thomas C. and Smith, Nicholas D. 2002. "The Socratic *Elenchos*?" In Scott 2002, 145-157.
[Brickhouse and Smith, 2007] Brickhouse, Thomas C. and Smith, Nicholas D. 2007. Socrates on How Wrongdoing Damages the Soul. *Journal of Ethics* 11: 337-356.
[Carone, 2001] Carone, Gabriela Roxana. 2001. "*Akrasia* in the *Republic*: Did Plato Change His Mind?" *Oxford Studies in Ancient Philosophy* 20, 107-148.
[Irwin, 1993] Irwin, T. H. 1993. "Say What You Believe." *Apeiron* 26: 1-16.
[Lamb, 1925] Lamb, W. R. M. 1925. *Plato III*. Cambridge, MA: Harvard University Press (Loeb Classical Library).
[Moravcsik, 1992] Moravcsik, J. M. E. 1992. *Plato and Platonism: Plato's Conception of Appearance and Reality in Ontology, Epistemology, and Ethics, and Its Modern Echoes*. Oxford and Cambridge, MA: Blackwell.
[Penner and Rowe, 1994] Penner, Terry, and Rowe, Christopher 1994. "The Desire for the Good: Is the *Meno* Inconsistent with the *Gorgias*?" *Phronesis* 39, 1-25.
[Santas, 1979] Santas, Gerasimos. 1979. *Socrates: Philosophy in Plato's Early Dialogues*. London and Boston: Routledge and Kegal Paul.
[Scott, 2002] Scott, Gary Alan, ed. 2002. *Does Socrates Have a Method?* University Park, PA: The Pennsylvania State University Press.
[Smith, 2000] Smith, Nicholas D. 2000. Plato on Knowledge as a Power. *Journal of the History of Philosophy* 38, 145-168.
[Vlastos, 1991] Vlastos Gregory, 1991. *Socrates: Ironist and Moral Philosopher*. Cambridge: Cambridge University Press.
[Vlastos, 1994] Vlastos, Gregory, 1994. *Socratic Studies* (ed. M. F. Burnyeat). Cambridge: Cambridge University Press.

Part E
Greek Science

Plato by the Numbers
HENRY MENDELL

In *Republic* vii, Plato has Socrates introduce an elaborate educational plan for the guardians of his city. Before shimmying up to the top of the divided line to the world of dialectical investigation, they are to study five kinds of reasoning (a.k.a. sciences) that are supposed to lead the student to the study of the Forms and the Good itself. These are in order, arithmetic and calculation, geometry, stereometry, astronomy, and harmonics. Most readers of the *Republic* assume both that they know the content and styles of these sciences, something familiar from their readings of ancient texts, almost all later than Plato. Their perplexity starts when they attempt to match Socrates' descriptions of sciences to what they know. Some of the difficulty lies in the obscurity of Plato's views on science, some in the importation of later scientific conceptions into Plato's world. There is some justification in the fact that we are in many ways profoundly ignorant of scientific texts from the time of Plato. This facile matching is much too hasty and ignores other possible aspects of ancient mathematical practice. Careful attention to what Socrates says in the *Republic* and to what we do know of ordinary, contemporary scientific practice, I believe, can illuminate both. My discussion here is preliminary to a general survey of Plato's treatment of mathematical sciences. Here, I am going to focus exclusively on Socrates remarks on arithmetic and calculation. To put my issues in a more general context, here are two of the many questions that I think many of us ask:

1. Is Plato a revisionist when it comes to science? We can put this question in many ways. Where there is a distinct common practice, Glaucon thinks he knows what the common practice is but is perplexed by the description of the special versions of the science for the guardians. Presumably, the same could be said of Plato's intended audience's knowledge of the common practice. Can we also assume that when Socrates announces the different way of proceeding that the different way is also different from what any contemporary scientist does, or is Socrates' protestations that people need to do things in the different way merely an announcement of what the more recondite scientists are in fact doing? Or is the different way something that is similar to a recondite version of the science, but with a Platonic twist? Conversely, if neither Socrates nor Glaucon indicates anything unusual about a scientific practice, except perhaps for the Platonic interpretation of the practice, can we assume that the characters are indicating an ordinary

mathematical practice familiar to mildly sophisticated, contemporary readers of the *Republic*. Is Plato's intended audience well educated readers or the small handful privy to the more recondite mathematical works of Archytas or Theaetetus? To review the different types of sciences that Socrates lists, in arithmetic and calculation there is an ordinary and an expert arithmetic. Both are taught. In the case of geometry, there is only the expert version, but it can be applied to military arrangements (the guardians are not to be trained in temple construction). Stereometry also only has the expert version, which is supposed to be unpracticed. In astronomy, there is an ordinary version and an unpracticed expert version. Harmonics has an ordinary version and a practiced, almost expert version, but which fails to be truly expert, so that there is also an unpracticed truly expert version. Although it lies outside my discussion here, in fact, it is arguable that except for an anti-empirical, Platonic twist, the claim that the last three expert sciences were not a part of advanced Greek scientific practice would apply at most to the dramatic date of the dialogue, but certainly not to the time of Plato's writing of the *Republic*.[1]

Furthermore, there are many different ways in which a philosopher can be revisionist. Alternatively, the philosopher might advocate a different interpretation of the science from the way its practitioners typically understand it. Without thereby advocating a change in the language, the philosopher might criticize the ontological or epistemological commitments of the language of the science. Or the philosopher might advocate a change in the language to correct the wrong commitments. Or the philosopher might advocate a completely different way of practicing the science. In some cases, the philosopher might be revisionist without realizing it, as when the philosopher thinks that the revision is innocuous. Certainly, in claiming that the mathematician does not need the infinite because he does not use it, Aristotle (*Phys.* iii 7.207^{b}27-34) thinks he is not being revisionist in the strongest sense, but may very well be.

We can put our problem in a different way. What is the common science that Plato presumes his audience will recognize? What is its practice? The question is not as trivial as it might seem. We do not have very much in the way of direct evidence for how arithmetic was taught or what geometry looked like. For arithmetic, we extrapolate from the dozen or so extant abaci and the myriad of inscriptions, standard weights, and so forth, as well as the

---

[1] There are some caveats required here. For example, on the reasonable assumption that the stereometry described here involves the problem of doubling the cube, already reduced by Hippocrates of Chios (late 5th cent.), the solution of Archytas is the only one that could have been discovered before the writing of the *Republic*, and we have no evidence that it was. Although the double circular motion model of the sun and fixed stars, probably of Oenopides, had already been applied to all planets, presumably much as we find it in *Rep.* x, Socrates indicates some avenues of research that are unlikely to have been studied seriously in the 4th cent. These points require a fuller treatment that I hope to provide elsewhere.

traces of calculations in Greek literature, and we also extrapolate backwards from papyri and, most comfortably, from Euclid, *Elements* vii-ix. For geometry the situation is perhaps worse, here we have the obvious choice of taking later Greek geometry, later reports of the grand successes of Greek mathematics, all perhaps based on Eudemus,[2] and the styles of mathematics in Aristotle, but we can also extrapolate from Egyptian papyri, backwards from later Greek papyri, or the hazy evidence in Aristophanes, Euripides, Plato, and Aristotle, as well as other the occasional odd items that pop up. Was ordinary geometry more like Greek geometry in the grand style (qualitative and demonstrative and concerned with procedures of construction) or more like the papyri (quantitative, algorithmic, and concerned with procedures of calculation), or something of both, or were one, the other, or both appropriate in different contexts? Clearly, Socrates implies something that has crucial features of the grand style, namely constructions, but is it the grand style or something more between the two styles? It is even less clear what the astronomy should be, but Autolycus, *On Rotating Spheres* or better *On Risings and Settings*, are popular candidates in the literature. The difficulty is that these are very much later works (ca. 300-270 BCE), and we have no idea of the extent to which Plato could have a vision of Autolycus or that contents of Autolycus go back to the time of the writing of the *Republic*. For harmonics, the *Sectio Canonis* gets occasional mention. Yet, although it is common to attribute the mathematics in it to Archytas, no one doubts that the actual text is also later. All we can do is see what Socrates and Glaucon say in the text and try to match it up with a reconstruction of 4th century BCE high science.

In each case where Socrates discusses two or more practices that are appropriate for the guardians, are we to consider them as two different approaches to a subject, or one as an application of the other, where one is legitimate and one not, or what? How should this affect our answer to the question of what the ordinary science is supposed to be? For example, if a little geometry is enough for the military needs of the guardians (526D), is this a little of algorithmic geometry or a little of applied demonstrative geometry? Or is the little geometry that the guardians would need if they were to use geometry only for military purposes algorithmic and the little that they would use for military purposes given their higher training something else?

2. What are the objects of these sciences? Are they Platonic Forms or what Aristotle labeled 'intermediates'? In an insightful discussion of Plato on number, Julius Moravcsik [2000] poses a challenge to those who believe that Aristotle is correct in attributing to Plato the view that arithmetic uses so-called intermediate numbers, the objects of a semantic interpretation of Greek arithmetic, i.e. numbers composed of pure units that are multiple and can be

---

[2]Cf. Zhmud [2006, 166-213].

combined to form different numbers, as many as we need to do arithmetic. He shows that one can construct an interpretation of Form arithmetic that is free of such a notion. Now, it is plausible that Plato conceives of the relations between Forms in a way like the one Moravcsik describes, e.g., that "7+7 = 14" expresses a relation between double-of-seven, equal, and fourteen.[3] Since I shall focus on arithmetic, my concern will be an indirect answer to Moravcsik's challenge. What sorts of treatments of arithmetic does Plato actually suppose?

If the objects of arithmetical statements are a classical version of Platonic Forms where there is just one instance of each number and reasoning in mathematics treats of these objects, then Platonic arithmetic had better look more like Peano arithmetic than like Euclidean arithmetic, where there are many sevens and each one is an aggregate of different seven units. That would imply that Plato is a revisionist in a very deep sense. Yet, it is also possible that the question for Plato of how mathematical statements are about relations between Forms is completely distinct from the semantics of the statements by which we reason, e.g., we use sevens to talk about Seven. I will not address this issue directly in my discussion, since I shall be primarily concerned with the role of numbers in calculations. However, I hope to provide enough foundation to show that since, in Platonic arithmetic, common or expert, we use multiple units (hardly surprising, given the account of reasoning in the Divided Line), the question of what the correct Platonic interpretation of sentences in a science is cannot proceed from a view that the sentences do not use aggregates of units. Rather, the correct question must be whether Plato thinks that the diagrams used in reasoning represent perfect objects, i.e., intermediates (or that the sentences used are to be understood in a natural semantics) or that the diagrams are the objects of the natural semantics of the sentences, but in the respect that the sentences are about Forms they are not to be interpreted semantically.

Finally, in any discusion of the sciences in *Republic* vii, we must presuppose the assumptions of the Divided Line. In the discussion of the Divided Line (510B-11A), it is agreed that the reasoning faculty (a) uses diagrams and (b) reasons from hypotheses to conclusions in order (c1) to reason about the

---

[3]Cf. Moravcsik [2000, 192], as well as Moravcsik [1979] and Mohr [1981]. Part of the difficulty in constructing such an interpretation of arithmetic lies in our understanding how Plato would treat arithmetical operations and relations. I think it more likely that he would think of equal as a property of something that is equal (to-n) than as a relation between two entities. I also suspect that a Platonic version of "7 added to itself is equal to 14" should be parsed as a property of seven. Beyond that, there are too many possibilities to speculate about and too little evidence that Plato treated arithmetic in this way to make deeper rumination profitable. Moravcsik only needs the claim that such an approach to statements of arithmetic is historically possible. In this regard, try to imagine how Aristotle would treat statements of arithmetic within the confines of his theory of predication, while keeping in mind that relations for him are genera of qualities (double is a genus of double-three).

things that the diagrams are imitations of, (c2) to make their arguments about and for the sake of these, and (c3) to see things that can only be seen by reasoning.[4] We should expect these to apply to each of the sciences, including arithmetic.

And as a word of caution, we tend to write the history of science from our interests, the big stories. So in the age of Plato, we delight in the development of proportion theory, the geometrical modeling of planetary motion, solutions to doubling cubes, and so forth. The main concern of scientists (and dare we professionalize a very motley crowd) is not always so interesting to us and so may play second fiddle in our histories. One ordinary concern is the public need for good systems of measurement, a primary concern of this paper. However, I shall approach the issue of measurement through Plato's *Republic* vii and Plato's contrast between the ordinary practice of arithmetic and the advanced practice advocated for students in the ideal state that is to lead the guardians towards the Forms and the Good. Because I suspect that the audience for the *Republic* was not exclusively afficionados of recondite studies, my methodology will be to look to the minimum that satisfies the text.

1 Arithmetic

Let's consider one famous passage in Plato, *Republic* vii 525D5-E3, where Plato draws a contrast between the ordinary calculator and the expert:

> Τοῦτό γε, ὃ νυνδὴ ἐλέγομεν, ὡς σφόδρα ἄνω ποι ἄγει τὴν ψυχὴν καὶ περὶ αὐτῶν τῶν ἀριθμῶν ἀναγκάζει διαλέγεσθαι, οὐδαμῇ ἀποδεχόμενον ἐάν τις αὐτῇ ὁρατὰ ἢ ἁπτὰ σώματα ἔχοντας ἀριθμοὺς προτεινόμενος διαλέγηται. οἶσθα γάρ που τοὺς περὶ ταῦτα δεινοὺς αὖ ὡς, ἐάν τις αὐτὸ τὸ ἓν ἐπιχειρῇ τῷ λόγῳ τέμνειν, καταγελῶσί τε καὶ οὐκ ἀποδέχονται, ἀλλ᾽ ἐὰν οὐ κερματίζῃς αὐτό, ἐκεῖνοι πολλαπλασιοῦσιν, εὐλαβούμενοι μή ποτε φανῇ τὸ ἓν μὴ ἓν ἀλλὰ πολλὰ μόρια.
>
> Ἀληθέοτατα, ἔφη, λέγεις.

---

[4]For c1-3 cf. 510E3-11A1, "But making its arguments concerning those things which these (the diagrams) resemble for the sake of the triangle itself and diameter itself, but not for the sake of this which they draw, and the others similarly, these things themselves (or: these same things) which they shape and draw, for which there are shadows and images in waters, while seeking to see those things themselves which someone could not see in any way other than by reasoning (ἀλλ᾽ ἐκείνων πέρι οἷς ταῦτα ἔοικε, τοῦ τετραγώνου αὐτοῦ ἕνεκα τοὺς λόγους ποιούμενοι καὶ διαμέτρου αὐτῆς, ἀλλ᾽ οὐ ταύτης ἣν γράφουσιν, καὶ τἆλλα οὕτως, αὐτὰ μὲν ταῦτα ἃ πλάττουσίν τε καὶ γράφουσιν, ὧν καὶ σκιαὶ καὶ ἐν ὕδασιν εἰκόνες εἰσίν, ζητοῦντες δὲ αὐτὰ ἐκεῖνα ἰδεῖν ἃ οὐκ ἂν ἄλλως ἴδοι τις ἢ τῇ διανοίᾳ." The list of things themselves includes the square itself and diameter itself. There are two standard possibilities of interpretation, that Socrates refers to Forms or to intermediates however understood. However, as Burnyeat [2000, 35-7] has argued, the addendum 'itself' is constrastive. In this case the contrast is with the drawn square and drawn triangle. So the text is genuinely indeterminate in distinguishing one kind of entity or the other, so that a decision between the two must depend either on other considerations in the text or on one's interpretatation of Plato, but not on the mere use of the addendum.

This, what I was just now mentioning, leads the soul as much as possible upwards and compels it to discuss numbers themselves, in no way allowing it if anyone should propose discussing numbers that have visible or tangible bodies attached to them. For you know, I suppose, if someone should attempt to divide the one in a ratio, how experts in these things would laugh at him and not accept it, but if you break it up, they multiply, taking care lest the one should ever appear not one but many portions.

You speak most truthfully, he (Glaucon) said.

The ordinary calculation will attach numbers to visible things, to speak of six cows or three feet, and will readily break up a unit. The sophisticated will do neither. Our difficulty arises when we try to go further in characterizing the sophisticated calculation. So it is normal to attempt to give more content to Socrates' distinction, e.g. to look to Euclid, *Elements* vii-ix for the content of such a mathematics.[5] More sophisticated modern accounts connect the ordinary calculations with 'applied calculation (λογιστική)' and the advanced calculation with the theory of ratios,[6] and even with a rich theory of ratios based on anthuphairesis, the Euclidean procedure for finding the greatest common measure.[7] While I think it nigh impossible to show that any of these views are wrong, and there must be some truth in these claims in that the calculation mentioned involves division in a ratio and that anthuphairetic methods were important in working with ratios in Plato's time, I suspect that a much less sophisticated story is perhaps more consistent with what Plato says in the *Republic*. Certainly, the one clear example in Plato that we have of the art of calculation is quite ordinary but makes no reference to visible or tangible bodies (*Hippias Minor* 366C5-D1):

ΣΩ. Λέγε δή μοι, ὦ Ἱππία, οὐ σὺ μέντοι ἔμπειρος εἶ λογισμῶν καὶ λογιστικῆς· -ΙΠ. Πάντων μάλιστα, ὦ Σώκρατες. -ΣΩ. Οὐκοῦν εἰ καί τίς σε ἔροιτο τὰ τρὶς ἑπτακόσια ὁπόσος ἐστὶν ἀριθμός, εἰ βούλοιο, πάντων τάχιστα καὶ μάλιστ᾽ ἂν εἴποις τἀληθῆ περὶ τούτου·

Socrates: So tell me, Hippias, aren't you experienced then in calculations and the art-of-calculation? Hippias: Most of all, Socrates. Socrates: And so if someone were to ask you how thrice seven hundred, how much the number is, if you should be willing, you would speak truly about this faster and better than anyone?

There is a long history of elaborate interpretations of the science of calculation in Plato. If we dismiss the neo-Platonic view that the science of calculation is the common calculation and arithmetic in the manner of *Elements* vii-ix the higher science, as we certainly should,[8] we are left with a world of speculation based on

---

[5]Indeed, the neo-Platonic interpretation, for which cf. Klein [1968, 37-45].
[6]Klein [1968, 24ff.].
[7]Fowler [1999].
[8]Cf. Klein, op. cit., note [] above.

one obscure passage in Plato, *Gorgias* 450D-1C, supported perhaps by one other (*Charmides* 165E-6A, cf. *Philebus* 56E with *Laws* 817E). Here, Socrates says that arithmetic, i.e. numbering, and calculation both concern the same thing, the even and odd, but that calculation examines how in multitude they are both in relation to themselves and to one another (καὶ πρὸς αὐτὰ καὶ πρὸς ἄλληλα πῶς ἔχει πλήθους ἐπισκοπεῖ τὸ περιττὸν καὶ τὸ ἄρτιον ἡ λογιστική). There is nothing in this passage to indicate how Plato would describe arithemetic, but Klein [1968, 17-21] is probably right that arithmetic is just counting and calculation, well, just that. There is no hint of a distinction between ordinary and expert science, and there is no reason to think that Gorgias is expected to know more than the learned Hippias.

It is a reasonable question to ask whether 'arithmetic' or 'the counting craft' in Plato means the art of counting. This shocks us only because it seems so trivial. Surely, Plato must mean something more sophisticated. My following Klein in reading 'counting craft (ἀριθμητική)' in this trivial way is not to maintain that it must always mean that, but merely to see how far such a reading will go. It does go far. No passage in Plato ever requires more.[9]

In fact, the only serious puzzle of the text, I suspect, is why Plato identifies the subject as the odd and the even (for arithmetic at *Prot.* 357 A2-3, *Theat.* 198 A5-7) instead of number (as at *Rep.* vii 525 A9, *Theaet.* 198 B8-10, and possibly *Ion* 531 D12-E8). Of course, it is most obvious to take it as an allusion to the analysis of numbers we find in Euclid, *Elements* ix 21-34 (or 36)[10] or to its fundamental use in early proofs about irrationals or even to a more trivial fact that there was a Pythagorean tradition that treated these as the two species of number.[11] It is

---

[9] 'Arithmetic' occurs at *Theaetetus* 198AE (in providing a definition of arithmetic, it involves knowing all numbers, counting, and, how large each is, cf. B9-C5, E2-3), Polticus 258D (to be studied for knowledge and not practice), 299E (a list), *Philebus* 55E-57D (to be discussed later, but there is no need for the many's arithmetic and the philosophical arithmetic to be other than counting in the appropriate way), *Protagoras* 356E-7A (arithmetic is the art of the odd and even for measuring the excess and deficient; this is the strongest passage for reading arithmetic as the determination of anthyphairetic ratios), *Gorgias* 450D-453E, Ion 531CE (the arithmetician is best at judging discusions of number), 537E (arithmetic teaches us to recognize 5 fingers), *Republic* vii 525A (it and calculation concern number). None of these texts require that we think of arithmetic as other than counting. For substantially the same argument, cf. Mueller [1991]. However, we can imagine somewhat sophisticated things one can do with counting, of which anthyphairetic ratios are certainly among the most sophisticated. However, my point is that there is a reasonable minimalist interpretation.

[10] Cf. Mueller [1981, 101-6] for a discussion of whether ix 35-36, the perfect number theorem, might have originally depended on ix 21-34.

[11] My point here is that we see in Plato and Aristotle a treatment of odd and even as the two divisions or species of number. There is no need to recount the way the division plays out in the technical literature and in proofs about incommensurability, for which see Knorr [1975], but we can also look elsewhere. The division pops up in the Pythagorean list of opposed principles which Aristotle attributes, inter alios, to Alcmaeon (Arist., *Met.* A 5.986^{a}22-9). If Epicharmus, fr. 170 (Guillén [1996], fr. 248, Diog. Laert. iii 10-1, cf. 9-10) is genuine and hence also from the early to middle 5th cent, the division will have been part of the ordinary, intellectual joking about numbers. The source, Alcimus, via Diogenes Laertius, is arguing for Plato's dependence on Epicharmus, which may suggest that they are, quite the contrary, influenced by Plato and hence no earlier than the 4th cent. Burkert [1972], 438 n. 64, provides a fine defense of the

enough that we do not know why Plato identifies the kind in this way, but that we have too many explanations.[12] Of a different status, however, is the claim that the calculator hypothesizes the odd and even (*Rep.* vi 510 C3-4), an issue I will take up later.

In fact, if we are just interpreting the *Republic*, we can shove the issue aside, as Plato does not fuss over a distinction between arithmetic and calculation, where the issue is common and expert use of numbers. As difficult as it may be to prove it, I think that Plato's distinction between common and expert arithmetic/calculation involves just the two pairs of criteria that Socrates mentions, whether or not one calculates with tangible or visible bodies and whether or not one is allowed to divide the unit.

What I am curious about is Socrates' description of what the expert calculator will not accept (this is a contemporary practitioner and not the philosophy teacher in the ideal state). What is he supposed to mean in saying that you multiply if someone tries to divide? The most literal interpretation of this just doesn't make sense. I want to break up the 1 in a ratio of 1 : 5 and so multiply 1 by 6 to get 1 and 5 as the portions. Isn't this the wrong answer? Shouldn't the right answer be that you cannot do the operation at all? Yet, Socrates' interlocutor, Glaucon, takes Socrates' claim as obvious. Shouldn't we assume the same of Plato's intended audience, perhaps even seeing the situation as a typical lesson between a harsh teacher and an inattentive student. Clearly, the restriction should occur at a step in a problem where whole numbers are required for the solution.

2   Digression on Numerals and 'Arithmetic' in the time of Plato[13]

---

authenticity of the fragment, however, in the context of a conclusive argument that the origins of the distinction cannot be Pythagorean (ibid. 437-8), and Guillén [1996] includes it as genuine. By the end of the 5th cent. it is part of common discourse about numbers (e.g. Xenophon, *Hipparchicus* 2.6; Hippocratic Corpus, *De morb. pop.* 1.2.12, for odd and even ordinal days, *De semine* 4.46, 47, *De humoribus* 6). So, regardless of how the division in Plato is related to the mathematics of *Elements* ix 21-34, e.g., as a metaphysical interpretation of the importance of the theorems about odd and even or as motivating the study of odd and even, much less technical issues could have influenced Plato to think of number as odd-and-even. An argument that it would be strange for Plato to adopt this way of thinking without the theorems is just the sort of a priori argument I want to avoid, even if one allows that some (perhaps even sophisticated) understanding about odd/even must have justified Plato's adopting the Pythagorean conception, and even if Plato would have employed a richer classification system such as *Parmenides* 143D-4A with its arguments about even even-times, etc.

[12]However, least plausible is Fowler's suggestion [1999, 112-3] that odd and even are to be taken as the ordinal ranking of an antyphairetic expansion of a ratio, where if a > b then the odd'th expansions = a : b and the even'th expansion = a : b. This would be to make a property of the expansion of the ratio the subject of all counting and calculation. On the other hand, ordinal numbers can be divided into odd and even (cf. note 11).

[13]This section summarizes a longer paper in progress. For detailed discussions of numerals, cf., inter alia, Tod [1979], and Threatte [1980] and [1996], Lang [1956] and [1976], and Johnston [1979].

Let's turn to what the ordinary Athenian calculator does ca. 367 BCE, one who does not try to separate numbers from the tangible and visible. What sorts of numerals would our 4th century BCE calculator use and what systems for representing fractions would he use, where by 'fraction' I mean any amount between whole numbers? There are basically four ways of representing numbers in this period. They may be represented naturally, by an appropriate number of strokes or other markers, including pebbles in Pythagorean work on number and other counters;[14] they may be represented by the alphabetic or Ionic system; they may be represented by acrophonic numerals and its many variants; and they may be written out, as is common in non-mathematical literary texts. Additionally, numbers may be represented in a calculating device, usually employing pebbles, such as an abacus.[15] Occasionally, Greeks also used 24 letters of the Greek alphabet to indicate ordinal numbers, e.g., the first book of the Iliad, the fourth law court.[16] Associated with the Ionic system are two methods for representing fractions, combined non-iterative parts or unit fractions and a later system that is similar two our own common fractions (n/m). Associated with the acrophonic system is a system of sub-units and a written out system of multiple or iterative parts, or so I shall claim. There may have been other systems of fractions, but these are unknown.[17]

The most common form of numerals in later Greek is the alphabetic or Ionic system. Using an extended version of the Greek alphabet, the Ionic system uses 27 digits to represent numbers 1, ..., 9 (A, B, Γ, Δ, E, ⊏, Z, H, Θ); 10, ... 90 (I, ... Π, ϙ, and 100, ..., 900 (P, ..., Ω, ⊤). To represent numbers less than 1000, letters are normally placed higher to lower, e.g., PΠ⊏ = 186. In later Greek, a line is often placed above the number to warn the reader that it is a number, e.g., that $\overline{\text{MH}}$ is 48 and not 'not'. For numbers 1000 to 9000, a line may be placed below the letter A̩ or later to the left of it. Sometime after 300 BCE, higher numbers are placed above M (for myriad or 10000).

The standard representation of a fraction is as a part or a non-iterative combinations of parts, where a part is an nth portion of a unit, where for n > 2, the symbol is the corresponding letter with a slash above it: Γ́ is 1/3, which we will write 3′. Parts may then be combined, but must always be different and not iterate, i.e., 2 divided by 5 is never ÉÉ or 5′5′. Instead, 2 divided by 5 is typically Γ́ΙÉ or 3′10′5′, i.e. 1/3 + 1/15. Note that even if the numerals are written together, as here, they

---

[14]Cf. Netz [2002].

[15]There are also methods for counting and calculating with fingers. Cf. Williams and Williams [1995].

[16]Cf. Arist., *Ath. Const.* 63-4. In this regard, it is significant that the ranking comes from the order of the alphabet, not necessarily starting from A, given that the law courts are numbered from Λ, while the jury pool from each tribe is divided into 10 groups lettered A, ..., K, so that the boxes involved in a jury selection will still be A, ..., K, Λ, ..., depending on how many juries are needed. Obviously, this system presupposes the Ionic alphabet, officially adopted in 403/2. The system is obviously very limited and should hardly be considered a system of numerals. For the issue of such representations of ordering, cf. Threatte [1980, 117-9], as well as Tod [1954].

[17]Johnston [1979, 30-1] reports some dots following strokes on some of his Types 5D and 8D and cautiously suggests that they might be fractions. If they are, they are uninterpretable.

are unambiguous, since the larger part normally precedes the smaller part, so that the example cannot be $1/3 + 1/10 + 1/5$.[18] For clarity, we might better write it as $3'15'$. The exceptions in the system are that half gets a special sign, ⊂ or ∠, and Ḃ represents $2/3$. There is also a ligature for $3/4$, as well as other variations, which need not concern us here.[19] I shall call such combined parts, non-iterative. Later, we also find instances of a non-standard form, common fractions (n/m) but with the denominator on top,[20] e.g. $\frac{\acute{E}}{B}$ as $2/5$.[21]

Although the Ionic system goes back at least to the early 6th century, it seems to have fallen into disuse about 475 BCE and appears but rarely until its revival in Egypt in the late 4th cent. BCE, when it appears on a marriage contract P. Eleph. 1, ca. 311/10 BCE, as ⊢Ạ (drachmas 1000). Afterwards, it dominates in Egyptian papyri (are there non-Egyptian papyri with numbers from the 4th and 3rd centuries BCE?) and contemporary literary mathematical texts. It then appears in inscriptions primarily as representing ordinal numbers until it becomes, towards the end of the Hellenistic age, the standard form for representing numbers in all media. We should be cautious, however. Early Hellenistic papyri are basically Egyptian papyri, so that it would be more accurate to say that the Ionic system reemerges as the system of Egypt and literary circles influenced by Egypt.

That said, it might be more reasonable to conclude that Egyptian Greeks from some time before 311 BCE., their first Ptolemaic appearance in P. Eleph. 1, chose to use Ionic numerals instead of acrophonic ones and that from there the custom spread. This possibility is supported by the fact that one of the oldest published Egyptian Greek papyri, an expense account of travelers on the Nile from before 300 BCE and two unpublished papyri of the same period have acrophonic numerals.[22]

---

[18] Hibeh i.27 (Grenfell et al. [1906]) has at least two clear exceptions to this, where $45'$ is written $5'40'$ (lns. 89, 123, cf. also 153 for $3'10'40'5'5'$, clearly an error that was poorly corrected — it should be $3'10'5'40'5$, i.e. $3'15'45'$).

[19] Cf. Fowler [1999, 224-9]. Fowler uses $2'$ for $1/2$ and $3''$ for $2/3$, where I use ∠ and $2'$, which are closer to the original, if less clear to the modern reader.

[20] Here I use the terminology of Fowler [1999, 227].

[21] Cf. Fowler [1999, 255-7] and Vitrac [1992, 162-4]. Certainly, by the 3rd cent. CE, such fractions are not uncommon, as in Diophantus. Metrodorus (ca. 300 C.E.) writes out in his poems even unreduced fractions, cf. *Greek Anthology* xiv 117 (ἕκτα ... δοιά or 2/6), 119 (δύο τέτρατα or 2/4), 140 (δύ' ἕκτα or 2/6), 143 (δύ' ὄγδοα or 2/8). Although he normally will use written out common fractions, I note that Metrodorus once (xiv 121) writes out a unit fraction for 2/15 as "eighth and twelfth of one tenth (ὄγδοον ἠδὲ μιῆς δωδέκατον δεκάτης)", but this way of writing $120'$ may be due to metrical constraints.

[22] The papyrus is from Saqqara, labeled Sak GP.9 No. 5676, and was found during in an expedition of 1971/2. Cf. Turner [1975]. To make this argument that it predates 300 BCE, we must ignore the fact that one basis for Turner's dating is the fact that the numerals are acrophonic. Fortunately, Turner uses other criteria for the dating. Turner also implies that other papyri found in the expedition had acrophonic numerals. However, the bulk of the collection has never been published and may never be published since the negatives are lost and some of the papyri stolen (communications of John Tait and Harry Smith). Prof. Smith and the Egypt Exploration Society kindly supplied me with photographs of S.H5-GP.1 n. 1909 and S.H5-GP.2 n. 1910, found in 1966/7. GP.1 on the recto has writing in a language other than Greek. On the verso, it has ⊄⊄III, probably 4+4+3 = 11 drachmas (Cyrenian). GP.2 has, inter alia, acrophonic representations of

We could as easily infer that it is in the first decades of Macedonian rule that Ionic numerals became common. In other words, the papyrological and literary evidence says very little about the use of Ionic numerals before 300 BCE. The full history of Ionic numerals has yet to be written; however, if we are merely interested in the numerals that Plato would have used, it is highly likely that he would have used the acrophonic system.

Whether or not the Ionic system was revived and not just hidden from our view, it is also reasonable to ask when the Ionic system of fractions was also invented. The system of parts and non-iterative compound parts emerges like Athena, fully formed, in P. Hibeh i 27, a parapegma from about 300 BCE, providing times of night and daylight in equinoctial hours, and adding or subtracting 45′ hours per day, to a maximum and minimum of 14 and 10 hours, respectively.[23] The use of Ionic numerals is consistent with its being a literary text engaged in a play of numbers. However, is P. Hibeh i 27 part of an aged tradition of Ionic fractions, or is it at the beginning of the tradition?

Clearly, the system of fractions was invented before P. Hibeh i 27; the question is rather how much earlier. Given the close connection between the common or Demotic Egyptian system of fractions and the Ionic system, even if there are minor differences,[24] it is almost certain that the Ionic system of fractions derives from the Demotic system.[25] That said, we could tell many stories about how and when it was derived. Perhaps it was derived when the Ionic system itself was invented. Against this is the fact that there is, apparently, no occurrence of the Ionic fractional notation in any of the texts that employ Ionic numerals prior to 300 BCE.[26] Furthermore, the author of Hibeh i.27.37-39 hints that the use of fractions at the level of Hibeh is at least very onerous, so that he will refrain from a diurnal account. Of course, Ionic notation is rare in any case, and the context might just never have been appropriate. However, the lack of earlier examples and the testimony of the author should lead one to doubt that the notation goes back very far. Another possibility, then, is that the new Macedonian rulers of Egypt simply adopted local accounting and taxation practices and so adapted the Demotic system. There is yet a third possibility, since we are inventing stories, that Eudoxus learned about

---

13 drachmas and 2 drachmas, and 3 drachmas (I⊢I). It should be noted that there is a great difference between the informality of these texts, and the formality of the marriage contract, P. Eleph 1, where each occurence of the numeral, ⊢A (1000 drachmas), is separated off and written differently from the other alphas.

[23] One might misreada preliminary report by Threatte [1996, 448] as indicating a non-iterative fraction on a then unpublished inscription on grain taxation from 374/3 BCE, but the text is, in fact, a description of two separate taxes, a twelfth tax and a fiftieth tax. Cf. Stroud [1998, 4, 6, 9, 26-39], lns 6-8 of the inscription.

[24] A Fowler observes [1999, 258-62], P. Cair. 89127-30, 37-43 from the 3rd cent. BCE uses a symbol for 5/6, which he describes as a ligatured 2′6′. The question is how one conceives a ligature.

[25] Cf. Chrisomalis [2003]. Chrisomalis also derives the Ionic system from Demotic; however, even if he is right, there is still no necessity that both systems, the whole number system and the fractional system, derived from Demotic at the same time.

[26] Communication of Prof. Alan Johnston.

the Demotic system while visiting Heliopolis, adapted it to his Ionic system (itself akin to the Demotic system), and introduced it to members of the Academy (say, 370-360), whose political and scientific heirs introduced it back into Egypt. I conclude that we should be sceptical as to the origins of the Ionic system of fractions. This does not mean that the concept of treating fractions as non-iterative parts did not exist earlier. For this, we need to turn to the two other ways of representing numbers. However, the evidence strongly suggests that when Plato wrote the *Republic*, he would not have used the Ionic system of fractions.

The other general way of representing numbers is the so-called acrophonic systems, since there are many variations both between cities and within each system– the Roman numeral system is a one such variation.[27] Although it is apparently as old as the Ionic system, it only becomes the standard method of representing numbers in Athens in the 5th cent.[28] The standard form of the acrophonic system is to have symbols for 1 (I), 5 (Γ), 10 (Δ), 50 (Ᵽ), 100 (H), 500 (Ᵽ), and 1000 (X), etc. As in the Roman numeral system, 1's, 10's, 100's, 1000's, are repeated up to four times and are written in descending order. So 2476 might be written XXHHHHᵽΔΔΓI. Nine is always ΓIIII and never IΔ, as it is in late versions of the Roman system. There are many practical differences, as we shall see, between the acrophonic whole number system and the Ionic system. Given our interests in Plato, here are the more significant.

1. Ionic numerals can be used to represent ordinals; in fact, after their revival and throughout the 3rd cent. BCE, this is possibly the most common use of Ionic numerals in inscriptions, to indicate dates, and mirrors the use of ordinary Greek letters to represent ordinals. On the other hand, acrophonic numerals are never used to represent ordinals. This may be conceptually related to the next point.

2. In an important sense, not only are Ionic fractions non-iterative, but so are the numerals for whole numbers. In any Ionic numeral, each numeral can only appear once. Note that Ạ (1000) is, strictly speaking a different numeral from A (1). The Acrophonic system is not iterative throughout (5's, 50's, etc. do not iterate), but it is iterative in the 1's, 10's, 100's, etc.[29]

3. In addition to representing ordinals, Ionic numerals are numerically neutral.

---

[27]To call the Roman numeral system a variation, we need to attend more to the structure of the system than to the feature of having the first letter of the word for the number being the representation, a feature that leads to ambiguity and which is not always strictly followed.

[28]Threatte [1980, 112] says that it appears in Attic inventories just before the middle of the 5th century although outside Attica it appears in the first half of the sixth century BCE, while Lang [1956, 20-21] gives one example, no. 86, of acrophonic numerals as a graphitto from the turn of the 6th cent. BCE. In other words, it was invented about the same time as the Ionic system but was introduced earlier into Attica.

[29]Similarly, in the systems of Archimedes and Apollonius, the numberals do not iterate in the sense of having the same values in their iterations. For example, in the Apollonian system, Δ in the second myriad has the value 4,0000,0000, and in the first myriad 4,0000.

The same symbol is used whether we are talking about drachmas or dogs. So, in P. Eleph. 1, the symbol for 1000 was preceded by a drachma sign: ⊢Ạ. The drachma sign ⊢ is actually the standard Attic symbol for 1 drachma in the acrophonic system. If I am writing 12 drachmas, I will write Δ ⊢⊢, if 12 staters, ΔΣΣ, if 12 talents (weight/money) ΔΤΤ, if 12 khoes (volume) ΔXX (note too the potential ambiguity), but if I am writing 12 dogs, I will write ΔII. So different units of currency/weight/volume will be written as different units. It is as if we were to use the Roman system in giving prices and wrote that the movie cost X$$ or hybrids of the form X$I, instead of $XII.[30]

4. Since the words for ordinals larger than second in Greek are the same as the words for n'th parts (as in English), it is natural that Ionic numerals, conceived ordinally, be adapted to a Demotic system of parts. So far as I can tell, there is no general system for writing out fractional parts in the acrophonic system. There are, at best, symbols for certain privileged fractions, 'half', 'fourth', 'eighth', 'twelfth'. The norm in ordinary arithmetic is to do just what we normally do, only more so. I am a buying a mina of a medley of pork lung and womb at 2 obols 3 coppers a mina to grill up some nice mezedhes (to use modern Greek). Since my neighbor is making a small contribution to the party, I want to divide the purchase in a ratio of 5 : 1. We multiply 1 mina (a half-stater[31]) by 6 and change the unit to twelfth-staters and ask my butcher to lay aside 5 twelfth-staters. I also want to separate out the expenses and so take 1 sixth of my 2 obols 3 coppers (at 8 coppers to the obol). To find my share of the expenses I have the usual choices, but will certainly borrow my butchers abacus. I might multiply 2 obols 3 coppers by 5 to get 11 obols 7 coppers. To divide by six, I see that I get 1 obol with a sixth of 5 obols 7 coppers.[32] This is trivial, if tedious, certainly easier with the abacus, and almost what we do. Greeks using the acrophonic system treated fractions as subunits.[33]

I said that the Greeks of Plato's time would do what we do, only more so, because I suspect that the halves, quarters, and twelfths, of these texts are barely, if at all, conceived as our common fractions and certainly not as non-iterative combined parts. They are more like units, just as a quart for us is a unit that is one quarter

---

[30] Threatte [1980, 112] points out that in inscriptions the use of alternative symbols for the unit and higher units almost exclusively occurs in the case of currency, but that the other measures, X (choes) and K (kotyl) are mainly graffitti on vases. This is unimportant to my argument, since both will have been a part of ordinary representations of 'perceptible numbers'.

[31] The stater in currency is less than a mina, but having a different value in different states (2 and later 4 drachmas in Athens). However, the weight system is different, with 1 stater = 2 minae. Cf. Lang and Crosby [1964, 4-5].

[32] The example is obviously a fiction but is based on two early 1st century BCE inscriptions SEG 47.196A and B, which in fact use a combination of a variant acrophonic numeral for obols and Ionic numerals above a X for coppers or chalkeioi. Cf. Steinhauer [1994] as well as Pleket et al. [2000].

[33] Vitrac [1992, 164].

of a gallon, where unit symbols are frequently symbols for that kind of unit, the symbol for 1 obol differs from the symbol for 1 drachma. Or rather, users need not have made a tight distinction between parts and subunits. We all know that a quart is a quarter of the next unit up, but usually don't think about it.

Normally in commerce one multiplies to get a smaller unit. In the acrophonic system, fractions are normally handled by getting new units and treating the fractions as multiples of the smaller units. Larger numbers can be treated in the same way.[34] One shifts quickly from one sort of unit to another as one sets up different parts of the calculation, a task easily handled on abaci whose columns could shift values on the basis of need, now a talent, now a drachma, now ten drachmas, etc. So the fact that we find 'half quarter obols', for example, is not more surprising than the other sorts of divisions, e.g., the sixther (ἕκτευς) or a unit that is 1/6 medminos (dry volume), the difference being that, just as one does not write out more than one five-sign (Π), one does not normally write out more than one half-sign (often C, a symbol also of the Ionic system) or one quarter sign (often T), while one can write up to five sixthers, or other multiples of halves, i.e., three halves or five halves.[35] Most fractions in extant texts are really subunits.

One takes some part and because the acrophonic system cannot handle more arcane fractions, fractions would have been written out. That said, we do not find complicated non-iterative fractions written out in the 5th or 4th centuries of the form, "third fifteenth." We do find, however, the equivalent fraction treated as iterative parts:

> two portions of the five (τῶν πέντε τὰς δύο μοίρας) — Thucydides, *Hist.* i 10.2.5, on the portion of the Peloponnesus that Sparta rules.
>
> the two of five parts (πέντε μερῶν τὰ δύο) — Aristotle, *Politics* II 9.1270^{a}24, on the portion of Spartan land owned by women.

The land is divided into five parts, and then two parts are taken.

This way of conceiving fractions always deals with a determinate amount. It says nothing about how we are to conceive of the fraction of an indeterminate amount.

---

[34]Cf. Lang [1957] for a suggestions that Herodotus calculates with large numbers by treating myriads (10000) as units.

[35]I suspect that the primary reason we don't find CC is a matter of standard form and not conceptual. Lang [1956, 8], discusses an amphora with ΙΙΗΗ, which she interprets as 2 half half and argues that the owner was measuring out choes and marking them down on the way. One does find unreduced fractions in late antiquity. However, the Hippocratic corpus can speak of "cooked flower of copper half-portion, of myrrh *two half-portions*, of saffron three portions, a little honey cooked with wine (ἄνθος χαλκοῦ ὀπτὸν ἡμιμοίριον, σμύρνης δύο ἡμιμοίρια, κρόκου τρεῖς μοῖραι, μέλι ὀλίγον, σὺν οἰνῳὀπτώμενα)" at *De ulceribus* 12.27-30 for swellings and inflamations around an ulcer. The use of 'two half-portions' is appropriate because one is doubling a half-portion. Cf. notes 21 and 40 for other examples of unreduced fractions. Netz [2002, p. 11], regards the use of half, third, drachmas, etc. as evidence for unit-fractions. However, it is not uncommon to find three-halves and five-halves in late 5th-3rd cent. BCE inscriptions. Cf. Threatte [1996, 447], as well as Didyma 84, 85, 86, 87 (all 217/6 BCE), Delos ID 500 (297 BCE), and IMT Kyz Kapu Dag 1486 (Mysia, 4th cent. BCE). Since I am distinguishing iterative and non-iterative parts, one can say that Greeks used parts as their basic fractional units.

An Attic inscription, IG II² 1675 lns. 17-20, from 337/6, providing specifications for the dowels and dowel receptors of column drums for a portico in Eleusis, shows how this conception of iterative parts can be conceived abstractly and connected to a conception of subunits.

> He will work on copper of Marion mixed with regard to the twelfth [portion], the eleven parts of copper, the twelfth of tin (χαλκοῦ δὲ ἐργάσεται Μαριέως κεκραμένου τὴν δωδεκάτην, τὰ ἕνδεκα μέρη χαλκοῦ, τὸ δὲ δωδέκατον καττιτέρου).[36]

A twelfth is taken as an indeterminate portion of a unit mixture, with the mixture made up of 11 portions of copper and 1 portion of tin.

Empedocles, DK 33 B96, likewise uses the language of parts to describe a mixture with an unreduced fraction, where bone is consitituted by eight parts, two for Nestis (air and water?), four for Hephaestus (fire?) and the remaining two of earth.[37] Here the parts are not reduced, i.e., one, two, and one parts of four, perhaps because the two for Nestis are one part each for air and water. For our purposes, it is enough that the fraction is given in the same language of parts and, interestingly, in unreduced parts.

Whether or not these two examples illustrate the common language of mixture, it should be obvious that it is much easier to work with than a system of Ionic fractions which might ask the user to take two-thirds quarter of the total for one and twelfth of the other. This holds true for any sort of mixture of ingredients,

---

[36] The inscription uses χαλκός to mean both bronze and copper (as clearly in the second occurrence here). The first occurrence here specifies that the χαλκός should be from Marion (a city in Cyprus), whose copper was valued for its purity. Given that the contractor would be expected to smelt the bronze and that the auditor would have little means of determining whether imported bronze was 1/11 tin or 1/14 tin (say that less than 2% change in the mixture is not observable), it would be odd to say that the bronze should be from Marion. However, it is possible that "Marion bronze" was a name for bronze made with copper from Marion. So the first occurrence is probably, but not necessarily, 'copper'. For these and other details on the chemical and economic issues, cf. Varoufakis [1975]. 'The twelfth', an internal accusative, is feminine without a modified noun. It is difficult to know what noun should be supplied, whether μοῖραν (cf. Thucydides above) or μερίς (e.g. Stroud [1998, 4-5] lns. 8, 28, 30, 32; Agora 16.75), perhaps the word understood in the feminine of a tax amount, ἡ δωδεκάτη (the twelfth). Clearly, the author assumes we know what is to be supplied, which suggests that the phrase is formulaic.

[37] ἡ δὲ χθὼν ἐπίηρος ἐν εὐστέρνοις χοάνοισι / τῶν (all mss. of Aristotle, Themistius, Asclepius, Philoponus, and Sophonias; Alexander, ps.-Alexander (In Met.), Syrianus: τὰς; Simplicius: τὰ; Steinhart for Aristotle (ap. Ross) τὼ) δύο τῶν ὀκτὼ μερέων λάχε Νήστιδος αἴγλης, / τέσσαρα δ' Ἡφαίστοιο· τὰ δ' ὀστέα λευκὰ γένοντο/ Ἁρμονίης κόλλῃσιν ἀρηρότα Θεσπεσίηθεν (Grateful earth in her broad-chested melting-pots gets possession of two of the eight parts from the gleam of Nestis and four from Hephaestus. They became white bones, divinely fit together by the gluings of Harmony.). In De anima i 5 410ᵃ4-6, Aristotle quotes the first three lines. Simplicius, In Physica 300.21-4 adds the fourth line. The variations in the Aristotelian commentator's quotations, especially the feminine in Alexander, In Met. 135.16, etc., shows that there is no basic conception of what the supplied word is to be for 'the two of the eight parts'. For the meaning of the text, cf., for example, Wright (1981), 208-10. In fact, Aristotle, De partibus animalium i 1 642a18-22 calls these parts a ratio, which ties the notion of parts to the the notion of ratio (see my subsequent discussion above).

whether in metallurgy, pharmacology,[38] or cooking,[39] and even taxation.[40] We can also see the system of iterative parts as closely akin to the system of subunits. In the example, the twelfth is, in effect, a subunit of the whole. The difficulty is to find the appropriate part that constitutes the division one wants to make.

The system of iterative parts also ties in neatly into the language of ratio.[41] It is easy to forget in the hunt for the earliest occurrence of the word 'ratio (λόγος)' (Heraclitus fr. 31), that the language of ratios goes back to the beginning of Greek literature (Homer, *Odyssey* ix 209-10[42]). In fact, were it not for specifying the base portion as a twelfth, we could not tell whether IG II^2 1675 were specifying the ingredients of the alloy in the language of ratios or the language of multiple parts. In this regard, there is little difference conceptually between the two prior to the discovery of incommensurability and hence in the language of numbers. Yet, it is easy to see why Greeks would keep the two notions separate. If a fraction is essentially a portion of a whole, the fraction would only be functionally the same as a ratio if the second term of the ratio is the whole. So when the metallurgist prepares the alloy, the ratio of 11 : 1 would be conceived as relating parts of single unit, which is the sum of the terms of the ratio.

We can see this connection in yet one more occurance of two-fifths, Herodotus viii 129 (perhaps describing a small tsunami that engulfed a Persian army attacking Potidaea through a shallow lagoon during a 'flowing back' of the sea):

Ὡς δὲ τὰς δύο μὲν μοίρας διοδοιπορήκεσαν, ἔτι δὲ τρεῖς ὑπόλοιποι ἦσαν τὰς διελθόντας χρῆν εἶναι ἔσω ἐν τῇ Παλλήνῃ, ἐπῆλθε πλημμυρὶς τῆς

---

[38] Many recipes in the Hippocratic corpus do not specify amounts at all, and some others specific measures; however, there are recipes that are given purely in terms of portions. Cf. *De ulceribus* 12.27-8, 28-33, 33-37, 15.4-6, 9-10, 21.18-21, as one would expect where dosage is irrelevant. I have not made a careful survey of Egyptian medical texts, but a perusal of the Papyrus Ebers [Joachim/Bryan, 1930], ca. 1500 BCE, yields the following: either measures are equal and listed as 1 for each or the measures are in parts, where the parts do not need to add up to one, the only parts not n'ths are 2/3 (2 times) and 5/6 (3 times), otherwise, all measures are 3′, ∠, 4′, 8′, 16′, 32′, or 64′ (recall that teaspoon = 96′ cup, and that a pinch is less than 8′ teaspoon). Note that it would also be lunatic to take 64′ as the common part and then to measure out 16 units. Contrast this Egyptian measure with the Hippocratic *De morbis* ii 55.21-2: a drachma-ish (handful) of oregano, about what you can hold with three fingers (ὀριγάνου δραχμίδα ὅσην τρισὶ δακτύλοισι περιλαβεῖν).

[39] It is tempting to think that Aristophanes, *Equites* 1187 (with the explanation of Suda, *Lexicon* κ 1262), "you have to drink it [wine] mixed three and two (Ἔχε καὶ κεκραμένον τρία καὶ δύο)," in other words three parts water and two wine, reflects the same language of parts. Of course, we can read it as a ratio, 3 : 2, but that is not the idiom, or rather we may ask how the language of ratios and of parts are distinguished.

[40] Cf. a tax collection of two tenths, Agora I 7557, lns. 58-9 (Athens, 374/3 BCE), also Stroud [1998, 80-1, cf. 27-8] for the difficulties in interpreting 'two tithes'.

[41] That a late writer, such as Iamblichus (cf. *In Nic. arith. intro.* 64.1-14), might call a 'triple ratio' the triple of a number may be dismissed as coming from a period when the distinction between multiple and ratio was already eroding. So my arguments will not depend on these sorts of texts.

[42] ἐν δέπας ἐμπλήσας ὕδατος ἀνὰ εἴκοσι μέτρα χεῦ (Maron would pour filling one goblet [of his private reserve wine] for twenty measures of water).

θαλάσσης μεγάλη, ὅση οὐδαμάκω, ὡς οἱ ἐπιχώριοι λέγουσι, πολλάκις γι-
νομένη. (As they marched through two portions, while there further
remained three needed for those crossing to be there on the Pallene
(the peninsula of Potidaea), a great rise of the sea came up on them,
such as had never before, although it is frequent, as the inhabitants
say.)

One could read this merely as providing a ratio of 2 : 3 for the amount crossed to the amount not crossed, but it is not expressed in that way. The fraction is provided by giving portions of the amount and the portions of the remainder, which we can then add up to five if we want.

It is to be expected that use of iterative parts and of subunits also ties neatly into the most fundamental theorems of Euclid, *Elements* vii–ix. So if we think of a calculation where we need to find the appropriate subunit for comparing two amounts, we naturally need the greatest common part (or greatest measure of the two). This is just what the opening, anthuphairetic propositions of Euclid, *Elements* vii 1-3, do. They do not involve the notion of ratio, which is built up gradually out of these propositions, first by working out conditions under which two numbers are the same parts of other numbers (4-10), before we get the first proposition on proportions (11). We can see these early propositions of *Elements* vii-ix 20 as setting up deteriminate cases, namely of a part, what measures a whole, then paired with propositions expanding these cases to indeterminate cases, treating iterated parts of a whole (cf. Mendell [2007]). The *Elements* shows no trace of non-iterative parts, but much of it is about iterated parts.[43]

So we could look at *Elements* vii 1-10 out of their context as building an account of subunits, with the theory of ratios of whole numbers as built on it. We want to find a common unit for two measures, say 3 parts of 14 parts and 7 parts of 10 parts. So using the procedure of *Elements* vii 2 we find the greatest common measure of 14 and 10, namely 2, and find that 2 is a seventh of 14 and a fifth of 10. This gives us the unit 70, and that one part of 14 parts is 5 parts of 70 parts and that one part of 10 parts is 7 parts of 70 parts. Hence, 3 parts of 14 parts will be 15 parts of 70 parts and 7 parts of 10 parts will be 49 parts of 70 parts. We can now add or subtract the 15 and 49 parts since they have a common unit.

I admit that this account may contain some mythology. We have only indirect evidence for it. Yet it is a wealth of indirect evidence, a sense of how to manipulate

---

[43]There is an implicit philosophy of number in Euclid involving three types of numbers, ἀριθμοί, πλήθη, and μέρη (parts). It is sometimes suggested that vii 37-9 reflect a system of non-iterative parts. In fact, the theorems 37-8 concern a single part, that n has an mth part iff m measures n, while 39 concerns a class of problems for finding the least whole that has an m_1th part, an m_2th part, etc. Of course, this can be used to find a least whole for a non-iterative fraction, but, as is clear from its application in the *Greek Anthology* xiv, e.g., 116, 119, 123, the technique used in the scholia to solve these sorts of problems, *Elements* vii 39 has a broader application which can include iterative parts, namely that of finding a least whole number with an m_1th part, an m_2th, where it is allowed that some m_ith = some other m_jth. These issues, however, are far from my present concern.

division on a Greek abacus, a sense that Greek calculators used subunits and thought in terms of multiples of subunits, and the snippets of their discourse of parts that surely fit what they did on abaci. I could go further to examine how it fits with other snippets of Greek mathematics on number problems or deeper concerns in the theory of ratio.[44] It is a curiosity that the Greeks developed number theory, while the Egyptians and Babylonians, each with a rich system of fractions, did not. Of course, Egyptians and Babylonians used subunits, but within the context of their system of fractions. If I am right that the Greek system of fractions was primarily a system of subunits with associated systems of iterative parts and ratios of numbers, then the development of number theory is much more comprehensible.

3 Digression on Calcution after the time of Plato

The verb λογίζω just means 'to calculate', and so we expect logistikê to be a science or craft of calculation. Our difficulty in knowing what this could be is partly a matter of divining Plato's intent and partly a matter of rediscovering Greek mathematical pedagogy. At the very least logistikê is the art of calculation, of learning how to perform the four basic mathematical operations in the acrophonic system or on an abacus. It will also include learning how calculate in the different measurement systems and how to use subunits. Let's arbitrarily call this basic logistikê. Beyond are basic arithmetical problems of a sort that I shall be discussing in this section, puzzle logistikê, as 'problem' has been preempted by the next group. Demonstrative logistikê should be distinguished by two subjects, the theory of arithmetical problems and the study of special properties of numbers such as even/odd or of interesting classes of numbers such as perfect or prime numbers. The distinction is only partly artificial, since it is relatively uncontroversial that *Elements* ix 21-34 on odd/even constitute a departure from what precedes,[45] while even the prime number theorem, *Elements* ix 20, a capstone theorem ending the previous discussion, might be seen as having, nonetheless, a very different interest from what precedes it.

Elements vii-ix 19 may be seen as an elaborate treatise providing the foundation for solving arithmetical problems and for determining when they have a whole number solution. We can think of the basic strategy outlined in these books as providing procedures for finding the least whole number solutions to a part of a problem if such exist and under what conditions such exist. As in the case of geometry, the difference with the metrical tradition is not simply that there are two traditions, one that tells you how to solve a metrical problem by examples and one

---

[44]One arena of play is the treatment of certain quantitative relations where the mathematician keeps one relatum fixed in order to compare the other. For example, if I want to say that A is faster than B, I might find a common distance that they both travel to compare the time or find a common time to compare the distance. This is the basic conception of Aristotle in *Physics* vi 2. This should be contrasted with the more general treatment of speeds in Autolycus (*On Rotating Spheres*, defs.) who just compares the ratio of distances traveled with the ratio of times of travel. Cf. Mendell [2007].

[45]E.g., Becker [1936].

that proves a theorem or tells to how to construct/find a figure/number or ratio with a justification. Each, arguably, feeds the other, the metrical providing procedures to be translated into the language of construction and proof, the demonstrative providing justified procedures. Certainly, *Elements* vii-ix 19, whatever else it is doing, is providing this.

Consider the puzzle logistikê. Iamblichus mentions a procedure, the bloom of Thymaridas (5th cent. BCE?), for finding an undefined quantity if its sum with n other quantities is a certain amount (i.e., the amount is given) and its sum with each of them is also a certain amount.[46] The problem clearly reflects an interest in number games, which find their highest (or at least largest) expression in the Cattle Problem of Archimedes. Nonetheless, one can also connect it with a tradition of teaching number/mensuration problems in arithmetic and geometry. It is curious, perhaps even deliberate, that Iamblichus presents the bloom abstractly, i.e. as a general rule about numbers written out, in the manner of propositions in Euclid's *Elements*, while the Cattle Problem is a piece of 'common calculation' and concerns counting the cattle of the sun.

We have almost no knowledge of either pedagogy or arithmetical play in the 5th and 4th centuries. However, it would be surprising if it were very different, in a general way, from pedagogy elsewhere the non-Greek world, where problems are often given concretely, i.e. with actual numbers of perceptibles, to use Plato's terminology. The bloom of Thyrmaridas can easily be constructed as an applied problem, e.g., in mixing an alloy. It would certainly be natural for a later writer, influenced by Plato, to extract the pure arithmetic out of a method presented concretely.[47] Iamblichus goes on to show how one can get many solutions, even those with "divided units." However, the application of the bloom that Iamblichus next provides illustrates exactly what Socrates says in *Rep.* vii. He sets up an application of the bloom to a problem, to find 4 numbers, a_1, a_2, a_3, a_4, such that $a_1 + a_2 = 2(a_3 + a_4)$, $a_1 + a_3 = 3(a_2 + a_4)$, $a_1 + a_4 = 4(a_2 + a_3)$, although Iamblichus expresses these values as the first, the second, etc. His solution involves taking the sum of a_1, a_2, a_3, a_4 to be $2 \cdot 3 \cdot 4 \cdot 5$. Thus, instead of having a result where, e.g., $a_1 = 1$, but the others are iterations of 73^{rds}, the results are the least whole numbers satisfying the conditions. For his second example of the same class of problems, namely where $a_1 + a_2 = 3/2(a_3 + a_4)$, $a_1 + a_3 = 4/3(a_2 + a_4)$,

---

[46] Iamblichus, *In Nic. arith.* 62.18-63.2, with the application, 63.2-68.26. Cf. Heath [1921, 94-6] with cautions about his algebraic presentation. Basically, if $a_1 + ... + a_n = s_0$, and $a_1 + a_2 = s_1, ..., a_1 + a_n = s_{n-1}$, then $a_1 = [(s_1 + ... + s_{n1}) - s_0]/(n-2)$.

[47] In the *Greek Anthology* xiv, poem 49 looks as if it is set up to be solved by the bloom of Thymaridas. One is asked to mix gold, bronze, tin, and iron to make a crown so that the total amount is 60 minae (not light). The gold + bronze = 2/3 the total, the gold + tin = 3/4 the total, the gold + iron = 3/5 the total. One calculates these amounts and proceeds to apply the bloom, namely one adds them up to get: $40 + 50 + 36 = 121$, subtracts 60 minae to get 61 minae, and finally divides by 2 (the total number of ingredients less 2) to get 30 $1/2$ minae of gold, and finaly calculates 9 $1/2$ minae of bronze, 14 $1/2$ minae of tin, and 5 $1/2$ minae of iron. However, it should be noted that it is unknown when this poem was written; the anthology ascribes it to one Socrates. Cf. Vitrac [1992, 155-8] for a brief survey of these types of texts in Greek mathematics.

$a_1 + a_4 = 5/4\ (a_2 + a_3)$, where '3/2' stands for 'half again', etc., he takes the sum of a_1, a_2, a_3, a_4 to be $2 \cdot 5 \cdot 7 \cdot 9$.[48] One multiplies to avoid dividing a unit. Now, even if the bloom of Thymaridas goes back to the fifth century BCE,[49] there is no reason to think that the application does nor that it is a class of problems that Plato would have thought about. However, unless one means by the claim that a subject is the study of ratio if it involves multiplication and division, the bloom of Thymaridas and Iamblichus' application are not directly about ratios, although the generalization does require applying some facts about the ratios of numbers. Yet, the application does fit the description of Socrates in *Rep.* vii.

Even if *Elements* vii-ix 19 are primarily concerned with finding least whole number solutions to problems, they can be thought of as the first step in solving a slew of problems. For example, suppose that I have a problem set up involving a collection of unknowns, $x_1, ..., x_n$, where the set-up involves a number a, and I notice that by ignoring a, I can get an indeterminate problem that has a least whole number solution. I now calculate a number a_0 that plays the same role as a. My solution can now be derived by multiplying each false solution by a and by $1/a_0$. Without the requirement that the false value be a least whole number solution, this method of single false position pervades Babylonian and Egyptian mathematics.

Many of the problems of *Greek Anthology* xiv naturally fall into this class of single false position procedures.[50] Typically, we are given n unknowns with $n-1$ unknowns given as (iterative) parts of a whole, and the n'th as a determinate amount. For example, xiv 116, from the group ascribed to Metrodorus, divides an unknown whole of nuts, here S, into 8 portions, $2/7\ S$ (ἕβδομα διὰ in the poem and written $\zeta'\zeta'$, i.e. $7'7'$ in the scholion to it), $1/12\ S$, $1/6\ S$, $1/3\ S$, 20 nuts, 12 nuts, 11 nuts, and 1 nut.[51] The scholiast takes the least number that divides into the parts (the LCM of the numbers coordinate with the parts, of 7, 12, 6, 3, to use the language of Iamblichus), a false sum of 84 nuts. Since this

---

[48]In fact, if we think of the coefficients as $n_i : m_i$, the multiplier is $n_i + m_i$ for each coefficient, as Iamblichus makes clear when he turns to his second example (where the coefficients are epimoric), in other words, for 2:1, 3:1, 4:1, one multiplies $3 \cdot 4 \cdot 5$ to get the sum of the terms in the bloom, and if they are 3:2, 4:3, 5:4, one multiplies $5 \cdot 7 \cdot 9$ to get the sum. However, given p as the number of terms in the bloom, if the sum is not divisible by $p-2$, i.e., the number of coefficients -1, one then needs to increase the sum by multiplying it by some appropriate factor of $p-2$, in order to make the value of the first term whole. Heath, op. cit. note 46, explains this only for the case of 3 coefficients, namely that one may need to multiply by 2. However, Iamblichus is less than pellucid, if not deeply confused over for the reason for the selection of the multipliers in each example (cf. *In Nic. arith.* 64.1-14, 66.16-67.1). Incidentally, it is a sufficient condition for the sum to be divisible by $p-2$, that there be two terms $n_i + m_i$ and $m_j + n_j$, each divisible by $p-2$, although more refined tests are easy to find.

[49]Iamblichus names a Thymaridas in the Pythagorean cult from Paros (*De vita Pyth.* 128.19, 145.5) and another Pythagorean from Tarantum, cited by one Androkydos (*De vita Pyth.* 81.11-18). However, it is equally possible that the bloom is a later discovery merely named after some Thymaridas. For doubts, cf. Zhmud [2006, 179].

[50]For a classification of the problems, cf. Tannery [1894].

[51]For this scholion, cf. Diophantus, *Opera Omnia*, vol. 2, ed. Tannery (Leipzig: Teubner, 1895), 53-4.

divides into $2/7 \cdot 84 = 24$, $1/12 \cdot 84 = 7$, $1/6 \cdot 84 = 14$, $1/3 \cdot 84 = 28$, the sum of these parts will be 73, so that the remainder is $84 - 73 = 11$. Now the actual remainder needs to be $20 + 12 + 11 + 1 = 44$ nuts. If we multiply the total and each part by 4, we will get the corrected amount, 96 nuts + 28 nuts + 56 nuts + 112 nuts $+(20 + 12 + 11 + 1)$ nuts = 336 nuts. We can anachronistically describe the problem as $(xn_1/m_1 + \ldots + xn_p/m_p) + c = x$. By finding the least number which has these parts, in effect, the LCM of $m_1, \ldots, m_p = m = x_{false}$, we find the sum of $(n_1/m_1 + \ldots + n_p/m_p) \cdot m = n$, a whole number, so that $c_{false} = m - n$. Hence $x = m \cdot (c/(m-n))$, which can, if one wishes, be trivially verified algebraically. The choice of m fits with the tenor of *Elements* vii-ix 19 of laying out techniques whose basis is the finding of the least whole solutions to problems, and it seems to me a natural development out of the conception of fractions as subunits and iterative parts. In fact, the scholia to *Gr. Anth.* xiv 2 and 3, which Tannery plausibly attributed to Metrodorus,[52] base the strategy on *Elements* vii 39, "To find a number which is least of those having the given parts," and v 15, "Parts taken in relation to one another have the same ratio as their multiples."[53]

So far as I know, there is no such drive in Babylonian and Egyptian uses of the technique to keep the numbers whole up to the end, where the choice does not rule out fractions in the steps.[54] In fact, for the problems in question it makes no difference to the procedure what one takes as an initial value, so that seeking the least whole number is significant. All this does not imply that the strategy is as old as Plato. Yet, it is consonant with what Socrates says in the *Republic*.

---

[52]Cf. Tannery [1894] and Tannery's note in Diophantus [1895, v. 2, 44 n. 1].

[53]The scholion to *Gr. Anth.* xiv 2, a distribution of gold talents (Diophantus [1895], v. 2, p. 44): " 'I Pallas ....' To find a number which leaving out 8′ 10′ 20′ will have remainder 9 units. This happens if we find a number which is least that will have the proposed parts, that is according to the 39th of the seventh book of the *Elements* of Euclid. And so there is found according to the methods of Euclid a least number, 40, having 8′ 10′ 20′, where, with these taken away from 40, 9 remains and the problem is solved. But if initially, instead of 9 units, any number, 6, were given, then taking the ratio which 6 has to 9 units and finding some number that's in the same ratio to 40, e.g. 26 2′, we find the sought for number and the problem is solved. But one must do the same in the case of every number." Note that 2′ is 2/3.

The scholion to *Gr. Anth.* xiv 3, a distribution of apples (Diophantus [1895], v. 2, p. 45): " 'Kypris...' To find a number which leaving out a part of it 5′ 12′ 8′ 20′ 4′ 7′ will have a remainder 600 units. And this is similar to the previous ones and is accomplished though the same procedure. For we find a number which is least that will have the proposed parts, and is 840. And if this is left out, a part of it, 5′ 12′ 8′ 20′ 4′ 7′, a remainder remains 125. And since 600 is four-times 125, if 840 is quadrupled, it will make 3360 and the problem is solved. This is for this reason: as already 600 is to 125, so is 3360 to 840, because the parts taken in relation to one another have the same ratio as the same multiples, according to the 15th of the 5th of Euclid's *Elements*."

[54]Cf. Høyrup [2002, esp. 101-3 and the texts cited] for Babylonian use of single false position. As an Egyptian example, *Rhind Papyrus* Prob. 40 (Chace [1927-9, 84-5]), a division of 1000 loaves into 5 portions in arithmetic progression where 7 times the lower two equal the upper three, seems to start with the first value as 1 loaf and from there infers that the steps will be 5 1/2 loaves (this is outside the written solution), so that the false total of loaves will be 60. A whole number solution would have reasoned that 2 should be the first portion with 11 loaves as steps and 120 as the total. For my purposes, it is not important that the final result be a whole number. E.g., in *Greek Anth.* xiv 119, two of the girls get 3 1/2 apples.

My third example is the nuptial number from Plato (*Republic* viii 546BC).[55] Of course, this involves a calculation of years and mentions a square of an irrational and so will not be separate from perceptibles and hence cannot be an example from the expert's manual of logistikê. Nonetheless, as worded, albeit obscurely, the conditions could be seen as a puzzle, to find the first, i.e. least, number such that certain conditions are set down and a second number built on it. Now, it is very likely that the resulting number is 1296 myriads (1296,0000),[56] and that it is the only number that satisfies the conditions. Socrates only expresses these through calculation puzzles, the larger is a square of a multiple of 100 (36), the product of 100 times the square of the square root of 49 minus 1 or the square of 100 times the square of the square root of 50 minus 2 (4800), by 100 times the cube of three (2700), perhaps $3 \cdot 4 \cdot 5$ multiplied by itself three times, perhaps the last term of the continuous ratio 60 : 3600 : 21,6000 : 1296,0000, and perhaps other properties one might cull from this text. It is even possible that finding puzzles is part of the exercise. My point is that Plato presents the puzzle in a way that is consistent with posing a calculation problem, even if it is not of the form that requires multiplying to avoid dividing. We may presume that he wants the adventurous reader to take a stab at finding the number.

Moving to demonstrative logistikê, so far as I know, there is only one place in *Elements* vii-ix, where one explicitly multiplies to avoid dividing a unit, namely viii 4. This is the complicated 'recursive' procedure for finding the least numbers in a 'continuous' proportion where each ratio is distinct, i.e., where $x_1 : x_2 = a : b$, $x_2 : x_3 = c : d$, $x_3 : x_4 = e : f$, etc., where a, b, ... are least numbers in the given ratios. Employing a type of false position, the procedure involves finding b_1 as the LCM (least common measured number) of b, c. If M(x/y) is the number of times y measures x, assuming that y does measure x, then $a_1 = a \cdot M(b_1/b)$ and $d_1 = d \cdot M(b_1/c)$. We now have as temporary values for x_1, x_2, x_3, numbers a_1, b_1, d_1. We then repeat the procedure, except for the fact that Euclid divides up the case where e measures d_1 and does not require new values for x_1, x_2, x_3 and the case where it does not and so does require new values for x_1, x_2, x_3. If e measures d_1, then $f_1 = f \cdot M(d_1/e)$, and we have as temporary values for x_1, x_2, x_3, x_4, numbers a_1, b_1, d_1, f_1. Now, one might say that here we are multiplying to avoid dividing, but 'dividing' is not an operation here. On the other hand, if e does not measure d_1, taking $d_1 : x = e : f$ would involve dividing a unit. So we multiply to avoid dividing. Of course, Euclid does not say this and just proceeds to the case where e does not measure d_1. Here we take for d_2 the LCM of d_1 and e and have as the new temporary values for x_1, x_2, x_3, x_4, numbers $a_2 = a_1 \cdot M(d_2/d_1)$, $b_2 = b_1 \cdot M(d_2/d_1)$, d_2, $f_1 = f \cdot M(d_2/e)$. And so we proceed by multiplying to avoid dividing. What

---

[55] Cf. Adam [1902, 263-86], with reservations, in particular with regard to Adam's derivation of a first number 216 as $3^3 + 4^3 + 5^3 = 216$. I also omit various standard points such as the relation of the passage to the general rule for approximating the square root of two: $p^2 \pm 1 = 2q^2 \Rightarrow (p + 2q)^2 \mp 1 = 2(p+q)^2$.

[56] The number is cleaner in a sexagesimal notation: 1 (or rather 1,0,0,0,0), whether or not Plato would have known this.

seems to me distinctive about this step just is the separation of two cases, a case where the previous values for x_1, x_2, x_3 are unaffected by the next step and the case where all the values must be adjusted to avoid dividing a unit.

So one could argue plausibly that in other parts of the argument one is also multiplying to avoid dividing, in which case many problems of *Elements* vii-ix might seem to fit Plato's description, at least implicitly. In fact, however, that is not what the other steps do. If e measures d_1, it is given that there is an x such that $d_1 : x = e : f$. The only difficulty is to find x, which one does by multiplying. A similar point can be made about the finding of least numbers in continuous proportion equal to a single given ratio, i.e., where $a : b = x_1 : x_2 = x_2 : x_3 = \ldots x_n : x_{n+1}$. Whatever the heuristics may have been, the problem itself proceeds from taking $x_1 = a^n$ and $x_{n+1} = b^n$ and finding the numbers in between. There is no subtext indicating that we are dividing anything.

I see two objections one might make against these attempts to find the sort of mathematics that Plato has in mind. The easier to resolve is that the types of problems involve taking halves, thirds, etc. Aren't these fractions and so involve dividing up units. In response, one can note that the halves, thirds, etc. are not numbers. They function more like ratios (as in the language of Iamblichus, for which cf. note 41) or operational numbers to be understood contextually. A third-of-n is n divided into three equal parts. We can see this in the penultimate propositions of Euclid's *Elements* vii, 37 and 38, where, assuming that it exists, the mth part of n is conceptually tied to (literally: is homonymous with) the number m, which measures n. So it is wrong to think of the mth as a number in the same sense that m is a number, or, to be more precise, it is not an ἀριθμός. This is quite different from the use of 'third' in the expression 'two thirds', where two thirds must be an amount less than one.

The other objection is just that I have relied on late Roman and early Byzantine texts to explain something in Plato, texts that are perhaps five hundred years more removed from Plato than Euclid is. Why didn't I use the equally remote Diophantus or papyri or the less remote Cattle Problem of Archimedes? My reasons are just that the chosen texts work with whole numbers, they use a simple procedure that starts with least whole numbers, while we know that procedures of finding least whole numbers with given properties are an important aspect of mathematics in Plato's time, and that single false position is already a very old technique in two neighboring cultures. Finally, they work with a concept of fraction closer to the one that I am attributing to Plato's time. The nuptial number in Plato is used primarily to show that numerical puzzles are a part of Plato's conception of mathematical pedagogy.

Indeed, if we divide Archimedes' Cattle Problem into two parts, one difficult to solve, the numbers of eight different herds given certain rules, and one nigh impossible, that the sum of two herds of bulls should be square and that the sum of the other two herds of bulls should be triangular, the solvable part sticks also to these methods.[57] In this regard, it is notable that the one known ancient attempt at the easier part of the problem, the scholion printed in Heiberg's text, comes up with values 80 times the actual minimal solution.[58] In fact, the Cattle Problem differs in one important way from from these other texts, in that it essentially uses non-iterative fractions. This is hardly surprising given that Archimedes' numeral system in the Sand Reckoner is based on the Ionic system. The first part could well be intended as a puzzle for learners of the system, and the second part a tease which, even if unsolvable, would suggest the magnificent possibilities of Archimedes' system.

I emphasize that I am not claiming that Plato is at all aware of all these particular procedures, only that they fit very precisely the sort of procedure that Socrates describes and are at a level of mathematics consonant with his time, in their use of the technique of finding least whole numbers with given parts, established in *Elements* vii 39 but not necessarily in a way personally known to Plato. What sorts of problems Plato actually has in mind is unknowable.

Let me summarize the argument so far. The Greeks represented numbers in several ways, strokes, by letters of the Ionic alphabet, acrophonic numerals, abaci, and Ionic numerals. I argued that it is unlikely that Ionic numerals play much of role in $5^{th} - 4^{th}$ century BCE philosophical discussions, because they play little role in Greek numeracy at this time. Acrophonic numerals differ, depending on what is counted, and cannot express ordinality. They also do not provide, as far as we know, a general treatment of fractions. Hence, fractions must be written out. However, they do provide a notion of subunit that can be used in lieu of a general representation of fractions. This generalization involves the taking of parts. So fractions may be treated as iterative parts. Just as Ionic fractions can be thought of concretely, as an n'th of some established unit and abstractly as the n'th of any unit, the generalization of a system of subunits is a system where a part is found that is a 'common denominator', and which can then be treated as a subunit. When we remove the unit part, the twelfth in the Eleusinian inscription, what is left is a ratio. These two conceptual features, the differing representations of numbers depending on what is counted and the treatment of fractions as multiple parts and as subunits, I shall argue, form much of the basis of Plato's remarks on arithmetic. Finally, I considered examples from late antiquity where the structure of the puzzles involve finding a collection of least whole numbers, taken abstractly, and as satisfying a set of conditions or equalities and looked to some parts of Euclid as a demonstrative version of the same tradition. Although the nuptial number is an example of these sorts of problems, it illustrates the more general type of difficult puzzle that might have been a part of his conception of logistikê.

---

[57] Cf. Dijksterhuis [1987, 398-401].

[58] Or 8 times if we take all the parts separately. For example, $1/3 + 1/4$ the black bulls and cows gives a whole number, but taken separately requires half a bull and half a cow. However, the poem seems to require taking a herd of black cattle together for this part of the calculation, and the scholion's description of the problem does not differ from the poem on this point.

4 After the Digressions: Plato on calculations

Socrates begins his discussion about number with a contest between Palamedes, who claims in tragedies to be the inventor of numbers and so to be able count ships of the fleet and soldiers of the army, and Agamemnon, who wouldn't then have been able even to count his feet (Rep. vii 522D). Although Socrates only mentions counting as examples, he claims that both counting and calculating are important. Whereas Socrates implies no great sophistication here in the arithmetical abilities of a good general, Xenophon (*Hipparchicus* 2.6) at least points out that an even number of decarchs, commanders of units of 10 knights, is better than an odd. So, at least one other Socratic writer on military matters looks to simple arithmetic properties as important for the arrangement of troops. Nonetheless, the question is what Socrates presupposes. Not much!

Counting soldiers is applied arithmetic and need not concern us. Socrates proposes an advanced curriculum of arithmetic and calculation. What does he require? What is the minimum plausible curriculum that would instantiate Socrates' proposal. There are six operational conditions that Socrates' lessons in arithmetic and calculation must satisfy. Two are from the Divided Line, that mathematical activities proceed by reasoning (διανοεῖσθαι) from hypotheses to conclusions and that they involve diagrams, here understood in the most general and Platonic sense, namely as any perceptible that represents a number, a geometrical or stereometrical figure, an astronomical entity, or a harmonic entity, whether Form, intermediate or even perceptible. Even the most minimal interpretation of Socrates' account of arithmetic and calculation will satisfy these. Two more (vii 525D5-E3) are peculiar to the account of arithmetic and calculation, that they dispense with embodied numbers and avoid fractions. Here too, the most minimal interpretation of Socrates' account will satisfy these two. Additionally, the Divided Line and Socrates' discussion of arithemetic and calculation puts another, psychic restriction on the lessons, their purpose in seeing what cannot be seen except by reasoning (*Rep.* vi 510E3-1A1). Finally, we need to make minimal sense of why people working with calculations (λογισμοί) in the discussion of the Divideed Line (*Rep.* vi 510C4-5) suppose the odd and the even (ὑποθέμενοι τό τε περιττὸν καὶ τὸ ἄρτιον).

First, any of the three levels of logistikê certainly starts with hypotheses and proceeds to conclusions. Even the supposition of 700 and its tripling, which Hippias is quick at, as trivial as it may seem, is still supposition and reasoning from a supposition to a conclusion. Nor is it quite as trivial as it might seem to us, e.g., in acrophonic numerals, ΓΗΗ by III is the sum of HHH and HHH and ΓΓΓ, which will equal XXH, and accomplished without an abacus.

Readers are sometimes divided about what Plato means when Socrates claims that the reasoner hypthesizes the odd and even, figures, and three kinds of angles. I do not wish here to enter into this discussion except to point out that a hypothesis is nothing more than what is set down at the beginning of a discussion. A fortiori, if mere calculation from two numbers is a case of reasoning from a hypothesis to a conclusion, so will any of the more advanced logistikê. We can certainly imagine Plato as alluding to proofs of incommensurability or to the contents of *Elements* ix 21-36, and in any case to contemporary Pythagorean interest (cf. Philolaos 44A13, 14, 20, 44B5; Archytas A21, B5). However, if thinking of numbers as odd/even has filtered into popular conceptions in the hundred years since Epicharmus, assuming Epicharmus fr. 170 as genuine (cf. note 11), then the minimum just is that odd numbers and even numbers, i.e., numbers, are assumed. I should concede, however, that this passage constitutes what seems to me the strongest evidence for one of the more sophisticated alternatives. My point, however, is that we should be sceptical about which alternative.

As to diagrams, we can imagine four calculations. In one case, the general lines up his men and says, "700 knights;" or, using an abacus, where each pebble represents some aggregate of men, he says, counting two pebbles in the hundred slot and one in the five hundred slot, "700 knights;" or he just looks at the three pebbles and says, "700;" or the very diligent calculator lays out 700 pebbles and says "700." I emphasize these ways of looking at the calculations because even the expert calculator will not dispense with the diagram. The use of lines representing numbers is obvious to any reader of Euclid, *Elements* vii-x, even if we have little reason to put this form of representation back to the time of the writing of the *Republic*. But any representation of numbers will constitute the use of a visual object used as an image of a number if the visual object really is so used, whether knights, fingers, pebbles representing units, or pebbles representing higher values, or even acrophonic numerals. The point is only that they are so used. The general counting his knights to array them for a cavalry attack is using numbered knights as numbered knights, as is the user of an abacus or some counter; the only issue is what is actually being counted or calculated. This leads us to the first of the two conditions from Rep. vii.

Whereas the common calculator discusses numbers with visible bodies attached, that is so-many-perceptible-somethings, the expert does not. In the acrophonic system, this point is deeper than Socrates indicates. The very notation can be affected by what is counted. The intended audience would understand the contrast as not just two fingers, the example Socrates has just used, but also two-men or two-minas, two-feet (the stuff of tradesmen and soldiers), with just two by itself. Nonetheless, the general numerals, where I represents one, allow exactly what Socrates requires. There is no need for a conception of numbers beyond this simple point, and we may presume that the intended audience understood the point perfectly.[59] Put another way, the pebbles on an abacus can represent knights, the pebbles themselves, or just numbers.

The other distinction was in the refusal of the expert calculator to divide the unit in a ratio so that one multiplies instead of dividing. We have seen that in a sense the ordinary calculator does the same. To calculate with subunits one must multiply

---

[59] Of course, one could construct a story where Socrates is advocating Ionic numerals over acrophonic, and it could even be true, but there is no need for such a story.

the super-unit by the appropriate conversion. However, there is an important difference. A sub-unit is still a part of its supra-unit. We can easily imagine the types of problems that Plato has in mind, that are built out of calculations with subunits and supra-units. So the expert calculator's avoidance of dividing a unit might just be switching units to a subunit and multiplying appropriately.

At a more sophisticated level, the difference between the calculations of Plato's expert and the ordinary calculator may involve a different wording of problems and an emphasis on certain Diophantine problems with whole number solutions. The example of the application of the Thymaridas' bloom in Iamblichus and single false position procedures illustrate the type of problem well. It is here that we may need to think that Plato has in mind at least something of the puzzle tradition. We need not go beyond this.

As an incidental point, there is no reason to think that Greek mathematicians in the time of Plato distinguished two sciences of calculation. Even though Plato has Socrates in the *Philebus* (56D-7A) distinguish by name 'the measuring craft (μετρική)' in construction and commerce from the higher measuring craft, i.e., 'philosophical geometry (τῆς κατὰ φιλοσοφίαν γεωμετρίας)' and in the case of calculation the lower 'calculative craft (λογιστική)' from the higher 'calculation (λογισμός)', very likely a nonce distinction in terminology,[60] Socrates goes on (57CD) to imply that people normally treat the respective two levels of each science as having a common name (ὡς ὁμώνυμον at D9-10) and as a single craft (ὡς μιᾶς at D10). Socrates wonders whether these should not be thought of as two distinct crafts, but having a twin nature (τὴν διδυμότητα ἔχουσαι ταύτην at D7-8). So even if Plato thinks we should make some formal distinction in the demarcation of crafts, he certainly does not suggest that his contemporaries in fact did so. To put this point more specifically, Plato implies, if anything, that people do not distinguish demonstrative calculation from puzzle calculation nor puzzle geometry from demonstrative.

Furthermore, if we return to the *Republic*, there is no indication that we should treat what the common and expert teachers teach as two crafts or sciences. At most, Plato suggests that advanced lessons in calculation are more abstract and consider only whole numbers. By having Glaucon affirm that this is 'most true', he indicates that he expects his audience to recognize the lessons, but that is all. It is important that Glaucon and presumably Plato's intended audience recognize both the ordinary and the advanced teaching, i.e. if it truly is more advanced. For one might suspect some irony, if, in Plato's world, working with fractions requires more training than working without.

Socrates and Glaucon now turn to the pedagical value of studying arithmetic and calculation (*Rep.* vii 526 A1-7):

Τί οὖν οἴει, ὦ Γλαύκων, εἴ τις ἔροιτο αὐτούς· "Ὦ θαυμάσιοι, περὶ ποίων ἀριθμῶν διαλέγεσθε, ἐν οἷς τὸ ἓν οἷον ὑμεῖς ἀξιοῦτέ ἐστιν, ἴσον τε ἕκαστον

---

[60]Cf. Fowler [1999, 148-51] for the uses of λογιστική and λογισμός to refer to calculation.

> πᾶν παντὶ καὶ οὐδὲ σμικρὸν διαφέρον, μόριόν τε ἔχον ἐν ἑαυτῷ οὐδέν;" τί ἂν οἴει αὐτοὺς ἀποκρίνασθαι;
>
> Τοῦτο ἔγωψε, ὅτι περὶ τούτων λέγουσιν ὧν διανοηθῆναι μόνον ἐγχωρεῖ, ἄλλως δ' οὐδαμῶς μεταχειρίζεσθαι δυνατόν.
>
> And so, what do you think, Glaucon, if someone were to tell them, "O wonderous people, about what sorts of numbers are you discussing, in which the one (or: unity[61]) which you consider proper occurs, every individual (or: each whole) being equal to to every one (or: whole) and differing not even in a small way, but having in itself no portion?" What do you think they would answer?
>
> I think this, that they discuss those numbers that alone admit reasoning, and that they can get a handle on in no other way.

Socrates has someone pose a question to the expert calculators, and Glaucon proposes an answer on their behalf. It is, of course, perfectly possible that Plato would construct this conversation in a way that only a Platonically trained expert calculator could answer as Glaucon does. In fact, his answer echoes Socrates on the Divided Line 510E3-A1:

> ζητοῦντες δὲ αὐτὰ ἐκεῖνα ἰδεῖν ἃ οὐκ ἂν ἄλλως ἴδοι τις ἢ τῇ διανοίᾳ (seeking those things themselves which someone could not see in any other way than by reasoning)

Yet, the account of calculation should be something that expert calculators would recognize as their own activity and as one that Plato's intended audience could recognize as a part of Greek mathematical pedagogy. So at least the representation of numbers has not changed from the previous speech. Nor have the basic operations involved in the mathematics lessons. We may presume, as I have argued, that the expert does not use the symbol for a drachma, ⊢, but instead uses the neutral, I.

There are two ways in which a single thing may be unequal. One is the fact that fingers are typically of different sizes, and this is the most obvious interpretation, as it is based on *Rep.* vii 523D-4D. So too, if the expert is using just a pile of Pythagorean pebbles, the pebbles may differ in size, but that is irrelevant to the expert's activities. On the other hand, in the discussion of the finger, it is crucial that the same thing appear as one and many (esp. 525A). In the case of an abacus, the same pebble may be used to represent 1, 5, 10, 50, etc., but the units that it represents don't change. So the pebble now used for five and soon to be used for 1 or 10, represents units that are simply equal. Similarly, the symbol used in working with acrophonic numerals is one Γ representing 5 units. What are those units? I am not here claiming that Socrates makes these points in the dialogue; however, they are observations that any thoughtful, contemporary reader, Plato's intended audience, is likely to make.

---

[61] Cf. Cherniss [1935, 518], where the numbers are Forms, and Mohr for an extension of the interpretation to the *Philebus*.

Socrates focuses on the one, not typically called a number, but which, he says, occurs in numbers. I can imagine at least three different interpretations of the passage, where the one is a constituent of numbers, where the one is among the numbers (speaking loosely), and where the one is the unity of Form-numbers (a view of Cherniss, see note 61). This last interpretation is implausible. Socrates has just said that the expert calculator will not divide the one, and we can fit that claim into a standard discourse on numbers. But it would have been very strange if Socrates had said that the expert calculator would not divide numbers. No contemporary reader would have understood that, and Plato would have to have been making a bad joke if he had his protagonist suggest it. So a suggestion that the numbers used by the expert are Forms, and hence have a unity that is equal to the unity of every other Form, would, at the very least, be a non sequitur, and, at worst, a presumption that our expert already accepts Platonic views on Forms. Weirder yet to our expert would be the claim that each whole is *equal* (ἴσον) to every other, even if they were Platonists, that Five-itself would be *equal* to a Six-itself. Instead of Glaucon's answer, the expert calculators' response would be perplexity that anyone would suggest that their numbers are anything like those numbers Socrates attributes to them. Quite the contrary, the numbers must be numbers that the expert calculators would recognize in calculations, and these are concatenated units.[62] We can save the interpretation only by making the numbers ordinal, but then we would get back the non-sequitur, since the numbers Socrates is discussing are subject to standard arithmetic operations.

It is probably undecidable which of the other two interpretations Plato intends. If Plato intends every one to be equal to every other one, there will still be a plurality of ones, which are then elements of numbers, while every element of a number is also a one. So it is also unimportant. That said, it is useful to note that in the parallel passage in the *Philebus* (56D9-E3), Socrates contrasts counting differing units (μονάδας), two camps, two bulls, two very small things, two of the biggest things, with counting units that do not differ at all (cf. also *Theaet.* 195E-6B). If the two camps are two units, then either the pure units are counted in the same way or Socrates has omitted some facts about counting pure numbers unfamiliar to his Protarchus and Plato's readers. But what is counting?

Obviously, an important difficulty for interpreting Plato is that Greeks and we ordinarily conceive of numbers two very different ways. There is the herd, ten bulls, and there is the counting off of the herd according to a series, matching the each bull to a number in our series. Conceived in this way, the herd has an albeit arbitrary ordering. So it is conceivable that one think of the black bull as one and the white bull as two, etc. Similarly, there will be the one unit and the two unit that will not be different except for their order. Counting bulls and Form-numbers might not be so distinct, except that the ordering of Forms is not arbitrary. It is ironic perhaps, that this reading of the *Philebus* is only possible if we think that Plato only intends counting.

---

[62] Cf. Pritchard [1995, 119-36] for this last argument.

When Aristotle speaks of numbers as ordered units in *Met*. M 7, it is appropriate to look to the practice of using the alphabet to represent ordinal numerals, something he knows about, and something similar may even be the case in the rare use of Ionic numerals in the period 475-320 BCE.[63] Ordinal numerals conceived in this way are used for counting, but not for calculating. And this is the difficulty.

According to Socrates' description in the *Republic*, the expert calculators are well aware that they are talking about numbers that are separate from perceptibles—it would be hard to see how not. In this speech, Socrates is drawing an inference about those numbers, and it must be a recognizable inference. The expert calculator is not yet a Platonist or a student of dialectic, so that the argument would not be a very effective argument if it required of the expert calculator to hold that the numbers are unlike what the representations suggest. Yet, they are not perceptible numbers qua number, either. The expert calculators have not yet met Aristotle.

So the question before us may be put this way: is there enough ambiguity in how Socrates describes the question posed to the expert calculators to allow that even if the expert calculators misunderstand what they are doing and so conceive of their numbers as divisible, whence the form of the question, in reality that is not how Plato conceives of the numbers used by the expert calculator, and, furthermore, is there evidence for such a reading? Either the expert calculator's pure numbers are aggregated units or the numbers of the expert calculator differ profoundly in their structure from the perceived numbers treated as diagrams and imitations of them and despite the expert calculator's complete ignorance of this. The first alternative must result in some doctrine of intermediates, since it is crucial to the expert calculator's activity that 2 may be over here and added to 2 over there (by merging the pebbles in whatever sense conceived), but that they represent two pure units that are concatenated with two pure units. The second alternative does not

---

[63] All four occurrences of Ionic numerals cited by Lang [1956, 5], nos. 11-14, all from the last quarter of the 5th cent. or the early 4th cent., involve writing n-1 strokes with the Ionic numeral for n. So it appears that the user counted out the volume and wrote strokes as he counted and then wrote an Ionic numeral for the last stroke, e.g. (no. 13, P11387), E||||. In this case, the Ionic numeral might very easily be conceived as ordinally as the 5th measure. This would be awkward in the acrophonic system for numbers greater than 5, but compare Lang [1976, 22] E9, which, she suggests, might be a tally of 6 drachmas, ├─├─├─├─├─├─, while such tallies are commonly given as just strokes (cf. Lang [1956, 3-5]. Of course, any conclusion from this is very weak. I should point out other early instances of Ionic numerals in Attica. Tod's [1950, 137-8] example of numerals from ca. 450-440 BCE, IG I^2 760 = I^3 1387, is an unexplained table from the Periclean age (cf. also Threatte [1980, 117]). If these are Ionic numerals, as is probable, they are non-standard in several interesting ways. Threatte [1980, 23] suggests that it is also possible that some of five known abcdaria with digamma are actually lists of numerals, for which cf. Lang [1976, 7], A1, A2, A3 (all before the mid-5th cent. BCE) and Young [1940, 6-8] nr. 9, and especially Pervanoglu [1867, 75] for a lead plaque with qoppa and sampi from the Acropolis, which Pervanoglu places after Olymp. 94, though probably, as Threatte suggests, merely on the basis of its having Ionic letters. The sampi rightly suggested to Pervanoglu that these are numerals. However, it would be odd if all of these abcdaria were lists of numerals. Lang [1976, 22] E15 (ΟΛΚ M, 40 drachmas in weight), a grafitto on a sherd from a vase of the late 4th cent. BCE, but found in a 3rd cent BCE context, is likely to be outside our period. Cf. also Threatte [1996, 695], 5.022 for an Ionic numeral for 95 from 500 BCE and further discussion.

require intermediates but requires that there is no structual likeness, isomorphism if you like, between the diagrams and the objects they are copies of. "2+2=4" might be represented by this ** aggregated with this **, but it is about the two, the four, and maybe the equal and the adding. In this case, one may well conclude that the pre-Platonic expert calculators have no idea what they are doing. So is this possible?

My goal in this discussion extends as far as laying conditions for an account of Plato's metaphysics of number but not so far up the divided line to determine what that account must be, whether Form numbers are unities of partially incomparable units or are units, whether there must be intermediates between Forms and perceptibles in Plato's ontology. Glaucon's answer on behalf of the experts, especially as an echo of Socrates' earlier remark, makes clear where disputes on these hoary issues need to be played out. These things are themselves what artifacts (e.g., diagrams) and other ordinary perceptible objects are imitations of. These are the object of reasoning that cannot be seen except by reasoning and which someone could not get a handle on except by reasoning. Hence, it would be very difficult to argue that Glaucon's answer is wrong and in so representing Socrates' own view remains uncorrected. Glaucon and Socrates agree that whatever numbers these are, they are grasped through diagrams and by reasoning and that expert calculators would recognize that this is the case.

Again, you might think that even if their representations are pebbles, symbols, whatever, which are conceived through the aggregative and separative operations, the numbers of the expert are not aggregates at all, so that they could be Forms. On this view, much to the surprise of the pre-Platonic expert calculator, what she studies are not structured as the representations are. But you would also have to explain why Plato thinks (1) that these numbers cannot be seen or gotten a handle on except by reasoning and (2) why the expert still uses the representational system that she does. In response to (1), one could argue that to get to dialectic, we still need to do arithmetic, so that reasoning is a necessary first step in seeing Forms and hence that one cannot apprehend numbers without reasoning. Contra, this is not quite what Socrates seems to say anyway, rather that reasoning is the ONLY way to get a handle on this and to see them. Once we have climbed the line a little more, we will see Form-number in another way. Against (2) one might argue that the pebbles and numerals just are the representational systems that we have. Contra, we should not then expect that Plato has in mind any non-diagramatic arithmetic. Whatever is accomplished in dialectic, we have no reason to think that it includes an alternative arithmetic that eschews all available representational systems, or even that it doesn't, for that matter. For there is no dialectical calculation anywhere in the Platonic corpus except, perhaps, in the *Parmenide*.

We could put these points another way. Plato does not give to Socrates any claim other than that the expert calculator uses perceptible numbers, but treats them as representations of numbers detached from perceptibles and that the numbers so discussed are composed of equal units. The numbers used by the expert calculator, not the numbered pebbles, are at least treated as composed of iterative units and as being themselves iterated. This three is composed of three units and there is also the three I am adding to it. If the expert calculator knows what she is doing, her answer to Socrates' question should be an answer she could give.

The representation of numbers in calculation is not a trivial or discardable matter, since it goes to the core of how calculation is conceived. However the numbers are represented, most standard representations all involve representations of iterative units. In the acrophonic system, the abacus, the Athenian way of counting votes, the Pythagorean pebbles, and the lines composed of unit lengths in Euclid, all differ from the Ionic system and the limited alphabetic system, where each numeral occurs but once. Recall that Ionic numerals were commonly used in the 3rd cent. as ordinals, as were ordinary letters in the 4th, but that acrophonic numerals were never so used.

Of course, it is always possible that an ancient author has invented a way of looking at a technical subject that is both potentially fecund but nonetheless never makes it into the technical literature for centuries, if at all. In general, however, it is better to look to practice for the origins of philosophical views on these matters. That is the difficulty for seeing Plato as a profound revisionist. In other words, the hurdles in denying that the expert calculators use numbers that are aggregates separate from perceptibles are many and high. This is not to say that they must be intermediates in the sense that Aristotle maintained, as separate from perceptibles and fully distinct from Forms. That is a separate issue. Yet, it raises anew the question of which interpretation of Plato's ontology, one tripartite and one bipartite, requires more leaps and bounds and more sacrifices to the text.

5 Conclusion

Plato wrote for a contemporary audience, one that is very difficult for us to reconstruct. This intended audience, we may presume, was literate, intelligent, and versed in some mathematics. While it is possible that Plato snuck in tidbits that would be appreciated only by the most elevated thinkers of his time, the crucial philosophical points would be poorly received if the mathematics were completely obscure. In any case, the intended audience certainly could not know of mathematical discoveries or practices even from the time when Eudoxus first leapt onto the Academic stage. I have tried to ask what that audience and Plato himself would think about counting and calculation, what sorts of numeral systems they would use, how they would calculate, with what sorts of puzzles teachers would challenge their students, and what sorts of proofs they would try out.

It is probable that Plato plays games of mathematical erudition with his audience in *Republic* vi, vii, viii, and x, such as Lloyd [1992] sees in the *Meno*. It has not been a part of this discussion to work out what those games might be, although perhaps it ought to have been. For example, I suspect that they certainly would involve games of abusing mathematical language. It is enough for my investigation to examine what they need not have involve. So even in the *Meno*, any account that involves Plato challenging his readers to learn about conic sections probably goes beyond contemporary mathematics, especially if he wrote the *Meno* before the *Republic*.

I have downplayed Euclid's *Elements* vii-ix, not because I wrongly think that its contents were unknown to Greek mathematicians nor because I think it too recondite for the intended audience, although it probably was, but because it is unlikely that it was the sort of mathematics that the audience would think of immediately in reading the *Republic*. Additionally, as I suggested, *Elements* vii – ix 19, in particular, fits into the puzzle tradition all too well and can be read as a formalization or enrichment of puzzle solving techniques. Of course, we could look to the rest of *Elements* vii-x and the history of number problems and more of proportion theory, and we could go on to speculate about lost mathematics, at best alluded to in Aristotle or manifested in the subtext of *Elements* ii and in passages in Plato's *Parmenides*.[64] If there is a reasonable interpretation of the *Republic* which does not presume such a rich mathematics, then it is reasonable to pursue the less presumptive interpretation. Single false position puzzles and others like them fit Socrates' description very well. It is even arguable that mere simple arithmetical operations do. We are, after all, describing the education of the guardians, who need to know enough to study astronomy and harmonics. How much is enough for that?

I began with a problem posed by Julius Moravcsik, what sort of notions of calculation are presupposed by Plato's metaphysics. From the assumption that Plato's numerals were acrophonic and his fractions iterative parts, that his calculations were on abaci, that he could use simple counters, and even that he understood the numbering of books and law courts, I argued that his advanced calculators pose problems to their students that treat numbers as aggregates within the context of manipulating units and subunits. Their activities presume four things that the average teacher would know well. They start from the hypothesis of certain numbers that need to used in calculations (at whatever level of sophistication), they use numerals and other representations of numbers such as pebbles on abaci; the numbers they talk about, however, are so-many simpliciter and not so-many perceptibles, and they set problems that require avoiding dividing up units but allow multiplying to do it. One might argue that even if this is the right approach to Plato's discussion of arithmetic and calculation, an argument based on Euclid's *Elements* would have done as well. There is, I think, a virtue to getting the intellectual setting of the *Republic* right and in attending well to its intended audience, but the advantage may be cultural and not philosophical. After all, although *Elements* vii-ix does not avoid fractions, it does avoid fractions of units. The difficulty, I would suggest, lies with the *Elements* itself. We assume from the *Elements* that it presents a Greek concept of number (ριτμς) and that Plato reflects the same conception. The conception is barely motivated, and this is especially problematic in the realm of a rich system of fractions, such as the one that the Ionic system of non-iterative parts

---

[64] As most notably Fowler [1999].

provides. By seeing the origins instead in a weak system of iterative parts that is reduced to a whole number system for the purposes of calculation, we can see, completely separately from issues of irrationals, why the *Elements* developed as a system of whole numbers and why Plato might also think that arithmetic should be conceived in that way. I realize that this remark is programmatic, but it should alleviate some of these worries.

Now if the numbers just are the numbers of the pure calculator, either Socrates is reinterpretating what they are and doing it on the sly, or they are the ordinary numbers of 4th cent. BCE Greek calculation. Someone who wants to argue that Plato believed in intermediate units and numbers, distinct units that are essentially identical and aggregates composed of them (twos, threes, etc.), may find in this passage food for the thesis and strong motivation. The numbers that the expert calculates with cannot be Forms, since the expert calculator will identify two distinct threes corresponding to the threes on the abacus, each represented by three distinct pebbles. In other words, if the expert calculator is using Forms to calculate, she is remarkably unaware of the fact. On the other hand, it is still open to the opponent of this view, who maintains that Plato did not require intermediates, to argue that, for Plato, this just is the case, namely that the expert calculator is unaware of what she is talking about. How wonderous this might be, I leave to the litigants over intermediates.

Acknowledgements

I should first like to thank various members of the Egypt Exploration Society, Karen Exell, John Tait, and Harry Smith, who made available to me photographs of the two unpublished papyri discussed here. Prof. Smith also provided an account of the ill fate of the collection. Alan Johnston was extremely helpful in discussing the history of Ionic numerals in the 5th and 4th cent., as was Leslie Threatte on epigraphical issues. Bernard Vitrac and Reviel Netz challenged me to think about some issues on which I had been far too glib. Jens Høyrup was a fount of knowledge on types of problem texts. His talk, "Which kind of mathematics was known by and referred to by those who wanted to integrate mathematics in 'Wisdom' — Neopythagoreans and others?" presented at the conference on Science and Philosophy in the Greco-Roman World, Budapest, 2007, approached many of the same issues from very different directions but, to my delight, came to similar conclusions on several central issues. Most of all, I thank my teacher, Julius Moravcsik, especially for his efforts as my dissertation advisor and for a 30 year companionship in the exploration of texts in that most wonderful discussion group the West Coast Aristotelian Society.

BIBLIOGRAPHY

[Adam, 1902] J. Adam. *The Republic of Plato*. 2 vols. Cambridge: Cambridge University Press, 1902.

[Becker, 1936] O. Becker. "Die Lehre vom Geraden und Ungeraden im Neunten Buch der Euklidischen Elemente." *Quellen und Studien zur Geschichte der Mathematik, Astronomie und Physik*, abt. B (3): 533-553, 1936.

[Benoit et al., 1992] P. Benoit, K. Chemin, and J. Ritter, eds. *Histoire de fractions, fractions d'histoire*. Basel: Birkhäuser, 1992.

[Burkert, 1972] W. Burkert. *Lore and Science in Ancient Pythagoreanism*. Trans. Edwin L. Minar, Jr. of *Weisheit und Wissenschaft: Studien zu Pythagoras, Philolaos, und Platon* (Nürnberg, Verlag Hans Carl, 1962). Cambridge: Harvard U. Press, 1972.

[Burnyeat, 2000] M. F. Burnyeat. "Plato on Why Mathematics is Good for the Soul." In Timothy Smiley, *Mathematics and Necessity: Essays in the History of Philosophy. British Academy* 103: 1-81, 2000.

[Chace, 1927-9] A. B. Chace. *The Rhind Mathematical Papyrus*. Oberlin: Mathematical Assoc. of America, 1927-9.

[Cherniss, 1935] H. Cherniss. *Aristotle's Criticism of Plato and the Academy*. Vol. 1. Baltimore: Johns Hopkins Press, 1935. (reprint: New York: Russell & Russell, 1962).

[Chrisomalis, 2003] S. Chrisomalis. "The Egyptian Origin of the Greek Alphabetic Numerals." *Antiquity* 77, 485-96, 2003.

[Dijksterhuis, 1987] E. J. Dijksterhuis. *Archimedes*. Trans. by C. Dikshoorn. Forword (this edition) by Wilbur Knorr. Princeton: Princeton University Press, 1987.

[Diophantus, 1895] Diophantus. *Opera Omnia*, vol. 2. Ed. by Paul Tannery. Leipzig: Teubner, 1895.

[Fowler, 1999] D. H. Fowler. *The Mathematics of Plato's Academy*. 2nd ed. Oxford: Oxford University Press, 1999, (1st ed. 1987).

[Grenfell, Hunt et al., 1906] B. P. Grenfell, A. S. Hunt, et al.. *The Hibeh Papyri*, vol. 1. London: Egypt Exploration Society, 1906.

[Guillén, 1996] L. R.-N. Guillén. *Epicarmo de Siracusa. Testimonios y Fragmentos. Edición crítica bilingüe*. Oviedo: Universidad de Oviedo, 1996.

[Heath, 1921] T. L. Heath. *Greek Mathematics*. Vol. 1. Oxford: Oxford University Press, 1921.

[Høyrup, 2002] J. Høyrup. *Lengths, Widths, Surfaces: A Portrait of Old Babylonian Algebra and Its Kin*. New York: Springer, 2002.

[Joachim and Bryan, 1930] H. Joachim and C. P. Bryan, trans. *Ancient Egyptian Medicine: The Papyrus Ebers*. Intro. G. E. Smith, (intro.) Translation of H. Joachim, *Papyros Ebers: das älteste Buch über Heilkunde* (Berlin: Reimer, 1890). New York: Appleton, 1930 (reprint: Chicago: Ares, 1974).

[Johnston, 1973] A. Johnston. "Two-and-a-half Corinthian Dipinti." *Annual of the British School at Athens*, 68: 181-9, 1973.

[Johnston, 1979] A. Johnston. *Trademarks on Greek Vases*. Warminster: Aris and Phillips, 1979.

[Klein, 1968] J. Klein. *Greek Mathematical Thought and the Origin of Algebra*. Trans. Eva Brann of "Die griechische Logistik und die Entstehung der Algebra," *Quellen und Studien zur Geschichte der Mathematik, Astronomie und Physk*, Abt. B *Studien* 3 (1934): 18-105; 2 (1936): 122-235. Trans. J. Winfree Smith. Cambridge: MIT Press, 1968.

[Knorr, 1975] W. R. Knorr. *The Evolution of the Euclidean Elements: a Study of the Theory of Incommensurable Magnitudes and its Significance for Early Greek Geometry*. Synthese Historical Library, vol. 15. Dordrecht: Reidel, 1975.

[Lang, 1956] M. Lang. "Numerical Notation on Greek Vases." *Hesperia* 25: 1-24, 1956.

[Lang, 1957] M. Lang. "Herodotus and the Abacus." *Hesperia* 26, 271-288, 1957.

[Lang, 1976] M. Lang. *Graffiti and Dipinti. The Athenian Agora*, vol. 21. Princeton: American School of Classical Studies at Athens, 1976.

[Lang and Crosby, 1964] M. Lang and M. Crosby. *Weights, Measures and Tokens. The Athenian Agora*, vol. 10. Princeton: American School of Classical Studies at Athens, 1964.

[Lloyd, 1992] G. E. R. Lloyd. "The *Meno* and the Mysteries of Mathematics." *Phronesis* 37: 166-183, 1992.

[Mendell, 2007] H. Mendell. "Two Traces of Two-Step Eudoxan Proportion Theory in Aristotle: A Tale of Definitions in Aristotle, With a Moral." *Archive for History of Exact Sciences* 61: 3-37, 2007.

[Mohr, 1981] R. D. Mohr. "The Number Theory in Plato's *Republic* VII and *Philebus*." *Isis* 72: 620-627, 1981.

[Moravcsik, 1979] J. Moravcsik. "Forms, nature, and the good in teh *Philebus*." *Phronesis*, 81–104, 1979.
[Moravcsik, 2000] J. Moravcsik. "Plato on Numbers and Mathematics." In Suppes, et al., 177-196, 2000.
[Mueller, 1981] I. Mueller. *Philosophy of Mathematics and Deductive Structure in Euclid's Elements*. Cambridge: MIT Press, 1981.
[Mueller, 1991] I. Mueller. "Mathematics and Education: Some Notes on the Platonic Program." In Ian Mueller (ed.), Περὶ τῶν Μαθήματων, *Apeiron* 24 (1991) no. 4, 1991.
[Netz, 2002] R. Netz. "Counter Culture: Towards a History of Greek Numeracy." *History of Science* 40: 1-32, 2002.
[Pervanoglu,] P. Pervanoglu. "Scavi sull' Acropoli d' Atene nel 1866." *Bullettino dell'Instituto di Corresponenza Archeologica per l'anno 1867*: 72-82
[Pleket et al., 2000] H. W. Pleket, R. S. Stroud, A. Chaniotis, and J. H. M. Strubbe. SEG II2 196. *Supplementum Epigraphicum Graecum* 47: 73-6, 2000.
[Pritchard, 1995] P. Pritchard. *Plato's Philosophy of Mathematics*. Sankt Augustin: Academia Verlag, 1995.
[Steinhauer, 1994] G. Steinhauer. "Inscription agoranomique du Pirée." *Bulletin de Correspondance Hellénique* 118: 35-49, 1994.
[Stroud, 1998] R. Stroud. "The Athenian Grain-Tax Law of 374/3 B.C." *Hesperia Supplements* 29, 1998.
[Suppes et al., 2000] P. Suppes, J. Moravcsik and H. Mendell, eds. *Ancient & Medieval Traditions in the Exact Sciences: Essays in Memory of Wilbur Knorr*. Stanford: CSLI Publications, 2000.
[Tannery, 1894] P. Tannery. "Sur les épigrammes arithmétiques de l'Anthologie palatine," 1894. Reprinted in *Mémoires scientifiques*, vol. 2 (Toulouse: Édouard Privat and Paris: Gauthier-Villars, 1912), 442-6.
[Threatte, 1980] L. Threatte. *The Grammar of Attic Inscriptions*, vol. 1: *Phonology*. Berlin: De Gruyter, 1980.
[Threatte, 1996] L. Threatte. *The Grammar of Attic Inscriptions*, vol. 2: *Morphology*. Berlin: De Gruyter, 1996.
[Tod, 1911/12] M. N. Tod. "The Greek Numeral Notation." *B.S.A.* 18: 98-132, 1911/12. Reprinted in [Tod, 1979].
[Tod, 1950] M. N. Tod. "The Alphabetic Numeral System in Attica" *B.S.A.* 45: 126-39, 1950. Reprinted in [Tod, 1979].
[Tod, 1954] M. N. Tod. "Letter-Labels in Greek Inscriptions" *B.S.A.* 49: 1-8, 1954. Reprinted in [Tod, 1979].
[Tod, 1979] M. N. Tod. *Ancient Greek Numercial Systems: Six Studies*. Preface by Joseph Breslin. Chicago: Ares, 1979.
[Turner, 1975] E. G. Turner. "Four Obols a Day Men at Saqqara." In Jean Binen, Guy Cambier, and George Nachtergael (eds.), *Le Monde Grec: Hommage à Claire Préaux* (Brussels, Éditions del L'Universitaire de Bruxelles), 573-77, and Pl. X, 1975.
[Varoufakis, 1975] G. Varoufakis. "Materials Testing in Classical Greece: Technical Specifications of the 4th Century B.C." *Historical Metallurgy* 9: 57-63, 1975.
[Vitrac, 1992] B. Vitrac. "Logistique et fractions dans le monde hellénistique." In Benoit, etc. [1992], 149-72.
[Williams and Williams, 1995] B. P. Williams and R. S. Williams. "Finger Numbers in the Roman World and the Early Middle Ages," *Isis* 86: 587-608, 1995.
[Wright, 1981] M. R. Wright. *Empedocles, the extant fragments*. New Haven: Yale University Press, 1981.
[Young, 1940] R. Young. "Excavation on Mount Hymettos, 1939." *American Journal of Archeology* 44: 1-9, 1940.

Part F
Greek Philosophy

The Epicureans on Anger and the Desire for Revenge

VOULA TSOUNA

Like other Hellenistic philosophers, the Epicureans held views about anger and defended them in the broader context of debates concerning the emotions or passions in general. Epicurus and the early authorities of the school appear to have said little on the subject of anger,[1] and the same applies to Lucretius. Our principal source on the topic is a long fragment of a treatise *On Anger* (Περὶ ὀργῆς; *De ir.*, PHerc. 182) by Philodemus of Gadara, a prolific Epicurean author of the first century BC.[2] In fact, this is the earliest classical monograph on anger that survives in part to our day.[3] From a cultural point of view, it reflects a widespread ancient preoccupation with the nature, use, and control of anger from Homer onwards.[4] From a philosophical perspective, Philodemus' *On Anger* is a major contribution to the relevant literature and occupies an important place in ongoing controversies about anger both between the Epicureans and other schools and between competing factions within their own tradition.

Philodemus' *On Anger* is a rich and complex work and I do not aspire here to do justice to its contents. My main purpose is very limited. It concerns mainly an intriguing distinction that Philodemus draws between natural anger (ὀργή) and unnatural anger (θυμός), and also the three analogical arguments (ἐπιλογισμοί, sing. -ός; translit. *epilogismoi*, sing. -*os*) at the end of the treatise, which Philodemus attributes to some anonymous opponents and which he undertakes to answer one by one. Commentators have claimed that these arguments are baffling, incoherent, or at best lame, and that they make it virtually impossible to tell who is saying

---

[1] Epicurus makes the puzzling remark that the wise man is more susceptible than other men to some passions without this impeding his wisdom (D.L. X.117), and he asserts that the gods feel neither anger nor gratitude (*KD* 1) — which might imply that lesser beings feel both. According to Philodemus, Epicurus also claims that the wise man will experience θυμός; similar statements are found in the writings of Metrodorus and Hermarchus as well (*De ir.* XLV.5-15).

[2] I have looked at the earlier editions of *On Anger* by Gomperz 1864 and Wilke 1914, but mainly have used the edition of Indelli 1988 as well as the unpublished edition and translation of *On Anger* by David Armstrong which, with characteristic generosity, he made available to me. For cols. XLVII.18 - L.8 I have also consulted unpublished work by Kirk Sanders, whom I also wish to thank. For discussion of parts of the treatise, see Annas 1992, Erler 1992, Fillion-Lahille 1984, Fish 2004, Harris 2001, Nussbaum 1994, Procopé 1993, and Sorabji 2000.

[3] Two intact monographs on anger survive as well, by the younger Seneca and by Plutarch.

[4] Harris 2001 explains the rise and persistence of the concern to control or eliminate intense anger by drawing on a vast number of ancient texts from Homer to early Christianity.

what against whom. In my paper, I shall revisit the three arguments as well as the counterarguments that Philodemus offers in reply. I do not wish to deny that some aspects of the debate are scholastic and pedantic. However, I shall suggest that the *epilogismoi* play a crucial role to the full development of Philodemus' position, which is defended by Philodemus as the orthodox Epicurean position; they address a major theoretical issue — the last to be examined in the treatise; and they also touch on larger themes in moral psychology. In the first place, then, I shall sketch out the dialectical context of *On Anger* and indicate what might be the role of the authors of the *epilogismoi*. In the second place, I shall briefly outline Philodemus' position regarding anger — especially the technical distinction that he introduces between natural anger (ὀργή) and unnatural or empty anger (θυμός) and his related claim that the sage will feel the former kind of anger but not the latter. The *epilogismoi*, I shall suggest, strike at the heart of that distinction since, if they are accepted, its point becomes moot. In the third place, I shall turn to the *epilogismoi* themselves and shall try to reconstruct and reinterpret them. I hope to provide a better understanding of the controversy and to indicate the philosophical merit of Philodemus' replies to his critics.

1

The main protagonists of Hellenistic discussions about anger (and of Philodemus' treatise as well) are the Peripatetics, the Stoics, and the Epicureans. Interpreting (rightly or wrongly) what Aristotle says about anger,[5] and especially his classic treatment in the *Rhetoric* (*Rhet.* II.2-4), his later followers[6] view anger as 'the desire accompanied by pain or distress (λύπη) for what is seen as retaliation (cf. τιμωρίας) for some perceived slight (cf. ὀλιγωρίαν) directed towards oneself or

---

[5] Aristotle provides the necessary philosophical background for Hellenistic and Roman analyses of anger, including Philodemus' own. In the treatise *On the Soul*, in the context of an argument for the thesis that the affections of the soul involve the body and are λόγοι ἔνυλοι, formulas in matter, Aristotle gives two different definitions of ὀργή, the one physical and pertaining to the domain of the natural philosopher, the other intentional and appropriate for the dialectician. While for the natural philosopher ὀργή 'a surging of the blood [or heat] around the heart' (cf. Renehan 1963), the dialectician will call it 'a desire for revenge (ὄρεξιν ἀντιλυπήσεως or something like that' (*De an.* I.1.403a16-32). Perhaps not inconsistently (cf. Nehamas 1992), in the *Rhetoric* Aristotle elaborates this second approach (cf. *Rhet.* II.2.1378a31 ff.). There are enormous complexities related to these passages, but for present purposes it suffices to note that, according to Aristotle, anger admits of physicalistic as well as non-physicalistic approaches; in the second case, we should think of anger as being *about* something (a perceived slight) and as including an open desire *to act* seeking retaliation. Most later writers follow Aristotle on these points, although with modifications.

[6] Philodemus distinguishes between two different groups of Aristotle's followers who appear to hold essentially the same position, namely that anger is necessary in order to fight bravely and, in general, is useful for purposes of self-defence. Moreover, at least one of these groups seems to have emphasised the justice achieved by revenge and the pleasure to be derived from it (XXXII.26-29). If Philodemus accurately reports their views, they have misinterpreted or overinterpreted Aristotle's own. We do not know anything about the identity of these Aristotelian philosophers. Philodemus says that he has named them in the lost part of his treatise (cf. XXXI.25-27) and he refutes them in the extant remains.

one's own, the slight not having been deserved' (*Rhet.* II.2 1378a31 ff.). And they approve of the emotion: it cannot and ought not to be eradicated, but is beneficial provided that it is measured by reason.[7] Moreover, according to the Peripatetics, revenge is the best cure for rightful anger. Indeed, anger and the desire for retaliation are the natural and honourable reaction to intentional offence. The magnitude of one's revenge should be proportional to that of the harm to which one has been subject. This is important, if one is to redress fully one's injuries and regain peace of mind.

Lying at the opposite extreme is the orthodox Stoic position. Very roughly, it is that we should eliminate excessive and irrational impulses, which we develop as ordinary emotional responses and which are, in fact, false judgements about value. In a perfected human life, one's relevant impulses are compatible with normative reason and never disobey or exceed it. On the other hand, ordinary, familiar emotions are aberrations of the commanding faculty in precisely that sense.[8] Both earlier and later Stoics claim that anger in particular arises because one misjudges factors relevant to a given situation, notably the intentions of the offender, the magnitude of one's injury, and the desirability of revenge. It is an excessive impulse to pursue the objectives set by that passion, an urge far beyond the limits of normative reasoning which has a momentum of its own and triggers violent psychosomatic movements. In short, there is no room for ὀργή or *ira* (the main Latin equivalent

---

[7]Moreover, later Peripatetics attribute to anger many of the characteristics that they read (rightly or wrongly) in Aristotle. Anger (ὀργή) involves both pain and pleasure: pain because of the perceived offence, pleasure because one hopes for revenge or dwells on it in one's thoughts. Typically, the offence is some kind of slight directed at something to which one attaches value. Disdain, spite, and insult all imply that the offender inflicted or intended to inflict harm of that sort. Depending on the magnitude of the harm and also on other factors (for instance, the offender's social status and his relation to the victim, the victim's expectations, and who else witnessed the slight), one can be more or less angry and express one's anger in more or less uninhibited ways. In fact, Aristotle seems to make the assumption spelled out by both earlier and later writers that, barring exceptional cases, anger cannot be hidden but must find an outlet in behaviour. Moreover, the Peripatetics maintain that anger usually has an individual person as its target, and also that the angry person 'wishes to see what happens', i.e., he wants to witness (or at least to make sure) that the offender feels the full measure of the revenge and knows why he is being punished and by whom. When the slighted man is satisfied that the offender has suffered in his turn, his anger is appeased and eventually disappears. However, I think that it would be a mistake to think that Aristotle approves of anger without qualification. For on the one hand, he can be read as reinterpreting the Platonic legacy according to which anger belongs to the spirited part of the soul, secures victories on behalf of reason (cf. *Rep.* IV 440a ff.), and provides necessary protection against wrongdoing (cf. *Leg.* V 731b). On the other hand, he also elaborates Plato's intuition that anger ought to be restrained and controlled (cf. *Rep.* IX 572a, X 606d). Irascibility is a vice, an excess of anger that should be avoided. The same holds for its opposite extreme, the habitual or complete absence of the emotion (*NE* II.7.1108a4-9). The virtue that stands in between these two extremes (let us call it even temper) implies that the person who possesses it will be angry, but only with the right people, for the right reasons, in the right way, at the right moment and for the appropriate length of time. Thus, the virtuous person can get very angry and desire maximal retaliation when circumstances warrant it. Nonetheless, his natural inclination is towards deficiency of the emotion, and he is not vengeful (*NE* IV.5 1125b28-1126a3).

[8]Chrysippus' view does not entail that a perfected human life will be almost emotionless.

of ὀργή) in the ideal life.

As I mentioned, the authorities of the Epicurean school said little that has survived about anger, but they appear to have held that some sort of anger is unavoidable and that some sages are more prone to it than others. However, they evidently did not clarify just what kind of anger is ineradicable or whether the wise man is susceptible to every form of anger. Later Epicureans debate these issues, each group giving a different interpretation of the canonical texts and citing scripture to defend it. The position that Philodemus advocates in *On Anger* (which probably reflects the line of Zeno of Sidon and his school) is one such view: the sage never experiences an unnatural kind of anger, but is liable to feeling a natural kind of anger compatible with moral perfection. Thus, Philodemus can be perceived as striking a wise compromise between the Peripatetics and the Stoics, and also as holding a middle ground between competing Epicurean factions.[9]

These latter are the principal targets of *On Anger*, but it is often extremely difficult to determine their philosophical affiliations and views. Philodemus mentions by name two of them, Nicasicrates and Timasagoras (cf. Νικασικ[ρατ —]: fr.7.15; Τιμασαγόρας: VII.7)[10] and suggests that they maintain contrasting views. Nicasicrates is a minimalist about anger: one ought to try to feel as little anger as possible and, ideally, no anger at all. On the other hand, Timasagoras has been thought to be a maximalist who believed that the sage may feel intense and prolonged anger as well as moderate and brief forms of the emotion.[11] What is the position of the authors of the three *epilogismoi* closing Philodemus' treatise? It is very difficult to tell. Their stated position is pro-anger: 'the wise man will feel rage [no less than] the common man' (XLVI.13-16). But I think that they could equally well be minimalists with Stoic leanings (cf. Seneca, *De ir.* II.6.3), who try to reduce to absurdity the idea that the sage will feel any kind of anger at all.[12] In either case,

---

[9] See Procopé 1993.

[10] They have been thought to be Peripatetics (so Croenert 1906, pp. 89 ff., Wilke 1914, pp. xxi ff.), but the evidence strongly suggests that they are Epicureans (cf. Longo Auricchio and Tepedino Guerra 1982, Indelli 1988).

[11] There are two main arguments in support of that suggestion. First, Timasagoras denies the usefulness of Chrysippus' and Zeno's diatribes, because he believes that to quote from such writings promotes the Stoic goal of eradicating almost all familiar emotions including anger: Ringeltaube 1913 argues this point. Second, Philodemus may imply that Timasagoras is pro anger when he makes the following gibe at his expense. 'He himself (sc. Timasagoras: the name is not mentioned but is almost certainly implied) was not clear about the misfortunes that were to follow from his anger against Basilides and Thespis, although he had set limits, as he thought, upon its sharpness' (*De ir.* V.18-25). Indeed, if Timasagoras is associated with 'those who want to be faithful to the books' (cf. βυβλιακοῖς: XLV.16-17) and who attribute to 'the Great Men' the belief that any kind of anger is compatible with sagehood, then he may be a maximalist just as they are. However, we should bear in mind that there is no decisive evidence associating Timasagoras with these thinkers. Also, Timasagoras believes that '[anger] is entirely an evil' (VI.28-29) and, in this respect, he appears to approach the position of Nicasicrates who is a minimalist.

[12] Again, we do not know who the βυβλιακοί are or whether they are the same as the authors of the three arguments in the form of *epilogismoi* towards the end of *On Anger*. Perhaps these authors do not belong to the same group, but represent two different factions of Epicurean max-

the *epilogismoi* entail the rejection of Philodemus' thesis that the wise man feels natural anger but not unnatural rage. For if the wise man is subject to maximal anger, there is no motivation for differentiating further between two different kinds of the emotion; and the same holds if the wise man should not experience any anger at all.

2

For the Hellenistic philosophers anger is a moral disease that, in order to be properly treated, must be analysed and understood. Borrowing material from Chrysippus and Bion of Borysthenes,[13] Philodemus undertakes at the outset to lay out the nature and symptoms of the passion, the beliefs and feelings that it involves, and its terrible consequences; thus he hopes to convince the irascible that their disposition and its outbursts are a great evil, and motivate them to seek remedy. While up to a point he speaks about anger generically (cf. cols. VIII.16 - XXXI.23), however, in the remainder of the fragment he lauches an attack against his professional rivals which he structures by means of asking and answering a series of theoretical questions. Is anger a good or a bad thing? Will the sage ever experience it? If he does, is he ever shaken by great anger? And if he is, what kind of anger is this and how does it compare with the anger of the common man? Philodemus' technical distinction between natural and empty anger serves, precisely, to settle these problems.

'Since there is false reasoning of some sort induced by the word (sc. 'ὀργή'), we do not make any simple pronouncement (sc. as to whether anger is a fine or an evil thing), but we claim that the emotion itself taken in isolation is an evil because it is painful or close to painful, whereas taken in conjunction with one's disposition it can even be called a good, as we think. For it results from our understanding of the nature of things and from our holding no false beliefs in the matter of measuring the offences and of punishing the offenders. As a result, in the same way in which we called empty anger (cf. κ[ενὴν ὀρ]γήν: XXXVIII.1) an evil because it arises from a thoroughly corrupt disposition and brings on countless troubles, we must call natural anger (cf. φυσική[ν]: XXXVIII.6) not an evil - but, in so far as it is something biting, [it lasts a very short time]' (XXXVII.20 - XXXVIII.9). In this passage, Philodemus models his own account of two different kinds of anger after Epicurus' distinction between natural and empty desires.[14] Drawing attention to the ambiguity of 'ὀργή', he distinguishes between anger *per*

---

imalists, the βυβλιακοί maintaining the weaker position that the sage will experience rage as well as milder forms of anger.

[13] As mentioned, Chrysippus' Θεραπευτικός may well be Philodemus' source for the diatribe section of *On Anger*. Chrysippus' use of vituperation, involving the vivid depiction of evils caused by the passions, suggests that he considers it peculiarly suited to correct the aberrant judgements that constitute a given passion and, in this case, anger. However, there is no reason to believe that Chrysippus belongs to those who '*only* censure but do little or nothing else about it (sc. the disease)' (I.13-16), as Philodemus seems to suggest.

[14] To my knowledge, Procopé 1993 (p. 173) was the first to point out that the hallmark of Philodemus' account is not the distinction between moderate and excessive anger, but rather

se and anger in connection with the disposition from which it derives.[15] In the former sense, anger is an evil because it is intrinsically painful or sort of painful. In the latter sense, anger can be a good or an evil depending on whether one's disposition is good or bad. Moreover, assuming that one's disposition is good, we should not refuse to accept natural anger (XXXVIII.18-22). Feeling its 'bite' may be bad because it hurts, but not feeling it would be worse. For it would suggest that we do not function properly as moral beings.

Just how does natural anger (which Philodemus calls ὀργή) differ from empty anger or rage (θυμός)? First of all, there are four senses in which ὀργή is natural whereas θυμός is not: ὀργή is advantageous (XXXIX.26-29; cf. also XXXIX.29-38); accords with a correct understanding of the nature of things (XXXVII.20 - XXXVIII.9); is a sound, unperverted reaction to intentional offence serving purposes of self-defense (cf. Epicurus, *KD* 7); and it is unavoidable (XL.17-22). In fact, as Philodemus reminds us, Epicurus calls anger, gratitude, and other such things weaknesses (*KD* 1) in the sense that they are natural drives to which all human beings are subject, not least the wise man (XLIII.14-41).[16] The point is important for present purposes because, as we shall see, it bears on two of the three *epilogismoi* that we shall try to figure out.

Equally important for the study of the *epilogismoi* (especially of the third one) are the ways in which ὀργή and θυμός differ as cognitive and affective events.[17]

---

that between natural and empty anger. The analysis below gives support to this claim.

[15] Philodemus does not clarify here what precisely is the relation between the angry people's disposition and their true or false beliefs, but he probably assumes that one's disposition is, among other things, one's inclination to hold certain beliefs and react in certain ways to certain circumstances on the grounds of these beliefs. The beliefs involved in anger are judgements about how things are and comparative judgements about the magnitude of the perceived offence and the severity of an appropriate punishment (cf. κολάσεσι: XXXVII.38-39) for the offender. When people have a corrupt (i.e., irascible) disposition, they tend to hold empty beliefs about these matters and Philodemus consequently classifies their emotion as empty anger and calls it an evil. On the other hand, persons who have a good disposition hold true beliefs about how things are, correctly appraise the nature of the offence and the magnitude of the damage and, on that basis, seek the offender's due punishment.

[16] The naturalness of ὀργή bears on the issue whether ὀργή involves natural and necessary desires or merely natural desires. On the one hand, the inescapability of natural anger would seem to entail that the desire to get even with one's offender is natural and necessary (cf. Annas 1989). On the other hand, while we feel pain if our natural and necessary desires are unsatisfied, we normally do not suffer if our desire to punish those who have deliberately harmed us remains unfulfilled (cf. Procopé 1993, p. 178). If we do, this is a sign that our anger is not natural but empty. Moreover, although the desire for security is a natural desire, and although natural anger does provide a kind of security through self-protection and deterrence, showing ὀργή is not always the easiest or the most expedient way to achieve these goods. But perhaps it would have to be, if ὀργή involved desires both natural and necessary.

[17] As in the cases of other emotions, beliefs play an important role in the generation of anger and appear to have both causal and temporal priority with regard to other elements of the emotion, notably feelings. The way in which different aspects of a given emotion are related to each other could be this: both beliefs and feelings are essential components of the emotion, the beliefs persisting as the intentional content of the emotion, the feelings corresponding to its affective content. Believing oneself slighted and lusting for revenge occur together only when, and

Cognitively, natural anger is based on exclusively true beliefs, whereas empty anger is consequent upon false opinions (ψευδοδοξία; these mainly concern what the irascible person perceives as the intention of the offender, the magnitude of the offence, and the revenge that would be commensurable with it.[18] Affectively, ὀργή and θυμός have each its own distinct experiential quality (cf. XLIII.41 - XLIV.35, XLV.34-37) — they are felt as different kinds of emotions. There are other related differences as well. Natural anger is self-contained, whereas unnatural rage has the tendency to escalate, precisely because of the empty beliefs which are added to it (XL.6-12). The 'bite' of ὀργή is brief (XXXVIII.8-9), whereas the pain of empty anger appears small at the beginning ([μ]ικρόν: XL.7) but later on becomes sharp ([ὀξύ]: XL.10).[19] Moreover, even on occasions when the sage feels great anger (cf. 'is profoundly alienated and indeed hates' his offender),[20] his tranquillity remains almost unaffected. We may put it in this way. The sage's anger is a natural and automatic response to the hostility coming from the outside.[21] He cannot avoid that feeling but, on the other hand, he does avoid assenting to the belief that truly great harm was done to him. For anger-provoking harm typically has to do with external goods to which the Epicurean sage does not attribute much value.[22] This

---

precisely because, one is irascible.

[18]Typically, an irascible man believes that the supposed offender has acted with the intention to harm him, that the harm is greater than it really is, and that the offender must suffer considerable harm in turn. When enraged, one is unwilling to accept the offender's explanation or apology, partly because he has false beliefs about the situation (XXIII.20-24).

[19]The text is restored. However, it is certain that Philodemus draws a contrast between the time when anger is first aroused and a later time when the emotion has escalated, and that he opposes the small pain of anger in its early stages ([μ]ικρόν in XL.7 is a fairly safe conjecture) to the pain of violent anger.

[20]'We shall tell our opponent that the sage will be profoundly alienated from, and indeed hates, the person who inflicts on him such great [injuries] or will obviously cause him [great] damage in the future — for this is a fitting consequence (ἀκ[όλο]υθον: XLII.3-4) - but he does not suffer great mental disturbance. [Neither is any] external thing [all that important], since the sage is not even susceptible to great mental disturbance in the presence of great physical pain, let alone in the presence of angry feelings. For [to be in a state of dreadful suffering] derives from folly. So if one is a fool, this suffering can be [inevitable]. Indeed, there are infinite misfortunes both involved in his folly and consequent upon it, into which the wise man, having a completely clear vision of them (θεωρῶν: XLII.19-20), would never fall' (XLI.39 - XLII.20). Philodemus' general strategy will be to concede that the wise man may feel very great anger, but also insist that his anger remains within natural bounds and is different in kind from the anger of the fool.

[21]Consider also the following passage. 'When the wise man has been intentionally harmed by someone or gets the impression that he will be harmed, will he experience a feeling of indifference (ἀδιάφορον: XL.35-36) as for instance when someone has looked at him, or will he experience an alien or inappropriate one (ἀλλότριον: XL.36-39), since calling it appropriate (οἰκεῖον: XL.39-40) would certainly be bizarre? Now, to call it indifferent does violence to our ordinary way of speaking. On the other hand, if it is alien, and he knows that when he (sc. the offender) is punished he will be calmed and will be a deterrent to others, then he would not again come against him in his madness, causing him pain in any way whatsoever. It is this feeling that we are calling anger' (XL.32 - XLI.9).

[22]Compare the sage's attitude towards intense physical suffering. As Epicurus showed on his deathbed, the sage can cope with such pain without losing his serenity and happiness. Surely, it is much easier to safeguard one's peace of mind against the assault of natural anger no matter

last point too is relevant to one of the *epilogismoi*, as we shall see promptly. Finally, ὀργή and θυμός differ in the attitudes that they dictate towards punishment. The natural anger of the sage does not make him desire the punishment of the offender as something pleasurable, but rather as a necessary and unpleasant thing (XLIV.5-8, 15-22, 32-35).[23] On the other hand, crises of empty rage (cf. μεγάλαις ὀργαῖς: XLII.24) involve seeking retaliation as though it were enjoyable;[24] but in that case, according to Philodemus, the greatest vengeance that one takes is on his own self (cf. XLII.21-39).

Before moving on, it is important to stress a controversial point. According to my account, ὀργή and θυμός, the 'bite' caused by the former and the acute pain caused by the latter, are both genuine emotions. In fact, ὀργή is a representative member of a special category of emotions that even the wise man has, and that Philodemus often calls 'bites' or 'pangs'.[25] Like other such 'bites', ὀργή is the natural and healthy counterpart of a harmful passion, θυμός. As I mentioned, it consists of beliefs and ways of experiencing, comparably to θυμός and every other Epicurean emotion. The difference is that, in the case of ὀργή and other benign 'bites', the beliefs are true and the painful feelings are usually mild and of short duration.[26] To understand the *epilogismoi* at the end of *On Anger*, we must bear in mind this. Philodemus is willing to concede that there are circumstances in which any decent person would feel 'bites' of anger. To the extent that they arise from our human nature, he acknowledges and accepts them. For he sees them as forgivable and even appropriate reactions to aggression: feeling them is bad, but not feeling them is worse — in fact, it would imply that we do not function properly as moral beings. What Philodemus shall not concede to his opponents is that a good person, let alone the sage, can ever experience θυμός — the harmful kind of anger plaguing most men. The debate in the final colums of his treatise turns on

---

how intense it may be.

[23] Contrast Aristotle, who counts the prospect of vengeance among the pleasures of anticipation (*Rhet.* 1370b9-16, 1378b1-10). Also, according to Philodemus, some of the Peripatetics emphasize the usefulness and pleasure of revenge (*De ir.* XXXII.23-29).

[24] This attitude can only derive from a vicious disposition (XLIII.30-32) and involves empty beliefs (XLII.21-30).

[25] Philodemus' concept of the 'bite' of natural anger and of other emotions too may be traced back to members of Zeno's school.

[26] Compare the fear of death, where Philodemus repeatedly contrasts 'bites' of distress with deep grief (λύπη) and treats them as distinct but conceptually related kinds of πάθη. For example, he compares pain that one naturally feels at the approach of premature death with 'the part about how one's enemies will rejoice' (XX.4), and he argues that the former is forgivable (συγγνωστόν: XX.3), whereas the latter is unforgivably vain (XX.4-5). Any thoughtful and sensitive person would be likely to shed tears and feel 'a truly natural bite' (φυσικώτατον δηγμόν: XXV.8) at the thought that his loved ones will face material hardships because of his death (XXV.2-10). This 'bite' differs in kind from the unnatural distress that people feel, e.g., because they leave their property to heirs other than their children (XXIV.5-10). The prospect of death in a foreign land brings naturally 'pangs' of grief (νύττειν: XXVI.3), especially if one has family back home. Philodemus contrasts them with 'great grief' (λύπην μεγάλην: XXVI.4) that makes the difficulties of living and dying in a foreign country even harder. Dying is painful anyway, therefore its pain and distress (πόνους: XXXIII.34-36) should not become worse by the prospect of dying at sea.

precisely that point.

3

We are now ready to broach the theoretical question to which the *epilogismoi* of Philodemus and of his rivals are supposed to give an answer: will the sage feel no less anger than the common man? As we saw, Philodemus advances as canonical the view that the wise man will never be very angry because he will never be very hurt.[27] The authors of the three *epilogismoi* (cf. XLVI.16 - XLVIII.3) deny this, although their own position on anger I think remains uncertain.[28] Philodemus responds also by means of three arguments each countering an *epilogismos* of his rivals. Despite the textual and interpretative difficulties surrounding the relevant passages, it is clear that both sides defend their cases by relying systematically on comparison and analogy[29] and by pointing to experience. I shall now try to reconstruct the debate at least in general outline.

The first *epilogismos* is this. 'If the wise man will feel gratitude towards those who have treated him well by their own initiative, he will also feel anger (ὀργισθήσεται) towards those who have voluntarily harmed him. On the other hand, if he will not feel angry (ὀργισθήσεται) at the latter, he will not feel grateful towards the former either. For the one emotion in each case is the opposite correlative (ἀντίστροφος)[30] of the other, and the element of voluntariness moves us to anger (cf. ὀργήν) just as it moves us to gratitude. For just as we do not feel gratitude towards inanimate objects that produce some good effect, nor towards those animate ones that unintentionally provide us with some good, so we do not feel indignant against them either. But these people claim that we are naturally moved to anger (ὀργήν) just as we are to gratitude by the opposite correlative cause' (XLVI.18-35). The argument contains or alludes to several features which might be considered canonical. Epicurus pairs anger and gratitude and asserts that neither of these emotions affects the gods (*KD* 1), whereas probably both affect the wise man in so far as he has the vulnerability of a human being (cf. XLIII.14-41, XLIV.41 - XLV.15). In fact, Epicurus seems to have held that *only* the wise man is capable of gratitude (D.L. X.118), presumably because only he will feel it for the right reasons and towards the right persons.[31] And although Philodemus and his opponents have disagreements on the subject of anger, they both accept that the sage will experience gratitude. Moreover, Philodemus would unquestionably agree with his rivals that the voluntary or

---

[27]This view was probably sanctioned by Zeno of Sidon, Philodemus' teacher and the scholarch of the Garden in Athens.

[28]I suggested that they may be maximalists or, alternatively, minimalists.

[29]On the substance of the three *epilogismoi*, see Annas 1989, Procopé 1993, Schofield 1996 and, most recently, Sanders (see n. 2 above).

[30]Not only can anger and gratitude be co-present in a person, but also they are extremes of the same range and are necessarily correlated: if a person is susceptible to the one, then he must be susceptible to the other as well.

[31]This position is not found in the remnants of Philodemus' work *On Gratitude* (*De grat.*, PHerc. 1414). Philodemus focuses on the gratitude that the sage receives from those whom he has taught Epicurean philosophy (cf. *De grat.* I.5-6), and also he describes the way in which persons of good character both bestow and receive favours (cf., for instance, IV.6, V.6-14, VIII.1-2, IX.14 ff., and XVI.11-12).

intentional element (τὸ ἑκούσιον: XLVI.30) lies at the basis of the analogy between gratitude and anger and is important in order to understand in what sense these emotions and their causes are ἀντίστροφοι (XLVI.25-26, 39-40). They are similar to the extent that we are naturally impelled to them by someone's voluntary action, but opposite in so far as the voluntary action in question is beneficial in the one case, harmful in the other.

The argument essentially consists of two conditionals emphasising the relationship between gratitude and anger, and a suppressed premise asserting that the sage feels gratitude. Paraphrasing, if the sage feels gratitude towards those whom he perceives as having intentionally benefited him, he also feels anger towards those whom he perceives as having done him intentional harm. Equivalently, if he does not get angry towards his offenders, he is not grateful towards his benefactors. But he does feel gratitude towards the latter, therefore he also feels anger towards the former. Philodemus has no reason to object to this form of the argument. Assuming that 'ὀργή' and its cognates refer to anger generically, he accepts the premises as well as the conclusion that the sage experiences anger *of some sort*. However, he presents and refutes another version of the same argument defending the thesis that the sage feels, not some sort of anger, but intense anger. This version too relies on the analogy between anger and gratitude and, despite the facts that the text is heavily supplemented and that there is a lacuna of about five lines (c. XLVIII.13-18), the point is quite clear. 'If we are naturally impelled to feel intense gratitude (cf. συντόνως εὐχ[αρις]τεῖν: XLVIII.6-7) towards those who have voluntarily [benefited us], then we are also naturally provoked to intense anger (cf. συ[ν]τόνω[ς ὀρ]γίζεσθαι: XLVIII.10) against those who [by choice] have harmed us' (XLVIII.5-12).[32] If this is true, the wise man feels *as much anger as* the common man. Philodemus, however, denies this. The wise man is not intensely grateful, because he does not attribute great value to externals, whether goods or evils, but the benefits bestowed upon him are such goods: '... since he considers also external favours to be unimportant; for it is posited that nothing external is important not only with regard to evils, but also to goods' (XLVIII.18-24). Towards those who provide him with pleasurable things the wise man will of course be grateful. But in so far as these things are externals, he will not feel intense gratitude, as in the converse case he will not feel intense anger.

Unlike external goods, however, wisdom and certain other things (for instance, the goods of friendship and of a proper relation with the gods)[33] are of the greatest value. It would seem to follow that the wise man will be intensely grateful for such gifts and, by analogy, intensely angry for evils of a corresponding magnitude.

---

[32] It is very likely that Philodemus' fictional interlocutor (cf. XLVIII.3-5) affirms the antecedent whereas, in the missing part of the text, Philodemus denies it. According to Indelli 1988, p. 247, Philodemus imagines that an objection of this sort could be raised by his rivals. The same holds for the interjection in XLVIII.24-28.

[33] Armstrong (cf. n. 2) suggests that these 'certain other things' (XLVIII.26-27) are the goods that we receive from the standard list of our greatest benefactors, notably the gods, our parents, and the πόλις.

Again, Philodemus presents this counterexample as an interjection by an imaginary interlocutor who argues on behalf of his opponents. Philodemus' bare outline of a reply suggests that, while he concedes that the sage will feel profound gratitude towards his teachers, he refuses to accept the inference that the sage will also feel intense anger. An obvious reason is that the analogy between gratitude and anger does not hold in respect of philosophical wisdom, since it is a uniquely valuable gift to which no harm can correspond. Moreover, no other good can be compared with it in terms of value. Philodemus ends his reply with sarcasm. "But he (sc. the sage) is enormously thankful, not just to those who made him wise, but also to those who procured certain other things for him". But if someone will claim that the wise man acts in this manner thinking chiefly of their (good) intentions, then obviously he will accept the same conclusion in respect of anger' (XLVIII.24-32). The benefactor's intent (cf. προαίρεσιν: XLVIII.29) is of course important, since we do not normally feel gratitude for unintentional benefits resulting from accident or chance. But it is less essential than the value of the gift itself, at least regarding the intensity of our response. The sage feels deeply grateful to his teachers not so much for their intention to give him wisdom as, mainly, for the wisdom itself and other great goods, such as friendship and community life. Perhaps Philodemus suggests that the benefactor's intent is a necessary but not a sufficient condition for (great) gratitude. If so, he adumbrates his line of response against the third *epilogismos* as well.

The second *epilogismos* is not preserved in its entirety, but on the basis of the extant remains it can be reconstructed as follows. Assuming that drunkenness is comparable to anger, if the sage is susceptible to getting drunk, he is also susceptible to feeling angry. But he is naturally susceptible to the former, therefore he is naturally affected by the latter. 'Just as we encounter many people who, whenever they drink wine, get drunk — [not] just fools but sensible people too, and the former no more than the latter — we come to understand that getting drunk happens not only in a folly, but, if even the wise [get drunk], [in wisdom as well];[34] [so also it is obvious] that not only [worthless people], when they are intentionally injured by someone, [are liable ⟨to anger, but also⟩ wise men]. [For this reason], we shall claim that [just as the wise man] can get drunk according to nature, so also [anger] must happen to him [because of the same] cause' (XLVI.40 - XLVII.18). Like the previous *epilogismos*, this too has elements that Philodemus seems unwilling to challenge. Several ancient authors employ the analogy between drunkenness and anger for different purposes,[35] and Philodemus does not object to its use by his

---

[34] From this point onwards, the text is terribly damaged. I provisionally follow Indelli, who prints Philippson's restoration of XLVI.10-17.

[35] For instance, Aristotle appeals to both drunkenness and anger in order to illustrate the point that acting *through* ignorance seems different from acting *in* ignorance (*NE* III.1 1110b24 ff.). Cicero says that, if he has acted bravely in public life, he certainly has not acted in anger, for anger is as irrelevant to bravery as drunkenness and insanity are (*Tusc.* IV.52). Seneca makes a similar point: anger does not make people brave for, by that reasoning, drunkenness too would (*De ir.* I.13).

Epicurean opponents. Moreover, the argument as it stands rests on a premise first accepted by Epicurus, that the sage will get drunk, and reaches the conclusion that Philodemus has defended in his own right, namely that the sage will get angry. On the other hand, Philodemus' rivals state also that sensible people (cf. συνετοῖς: XLVII.3) get drunk *no less* than fools (XLVII.2-5), and they suggest that the same holds for the sages: according to nature (κατὰ φύσιν: XLVII.15), sages get drunk *just as much* as other people or even more so (XLIX.19-22) and they get drunk in the same manner as other people do (XLIX.25-26).

In fact, Philodemus appears to address a stronger version of the original *epilogismos*, which incorporates these theses and runs roughly along the following lines. If the sage gets drunk *to the same degree and in the same way* as the fool, then he gets angry *with the same intensity and in the same manner* as the fool, i.e., he experiences the kind of anger that Philodemus calls θυμός, empty anger. This version too can draw support from Epicurus' writings, and in particular from his claim in the *Symposium* that the wise man will be uninhibited when he is drunk (D.L. X.119).[36] Part of Philodemus' reply is contained in the following passage. 'Indeed, we should consider this second argument stupid. For regarding the claim that even the wise man will get drunk, if by the phrase the good men too get drunk they mean Epicurus, they are talking nonsense, but if they mean themselves, [obviously] it is absurd to reason from them to the wise man. One could go on in a similar fashion to demonstrate that the wise man will also seek glory and will [fall in love] and [be liable to] countless other passions, [if indeed others among truly good men experience continual troubles] ... and we would have to accept that the wise man is more prone to outbursts of anger than some fools are, and that he feels them no less than the fools, since he gets drunk no less than they do according to the sense in which they use the expression "to get drunk"' (XLVIII.36 - XLIX.26).

Although part of this passage is heavily restored and part of Philodemus' reply is missing (XLIX.13-19), the main argument seems to go as follows. First of all, the opponents do not clarify who the good men are (cf. χα[ρ]ίεν[τας]: XLIX.1) when they contend that even good men get drunk. If they refer to Epicurus and his associates, their claim is absurd. On the other hand, if they speak about themselves, they merely project their own passions onto the sage. Philodemus' attack is *ad hominem*. For he intimates that his adversaries are not only ignorant about how to construe a valid argument, but also susceptible to many passions including outbursts of violent anger (cf. ὀργάς: XLIX.22), i.e., the emotion that they attribute to the sage on fallacious grounds.[37] Furthermore, they fail to distinguish

---

[36] Concerning the MSS reading of this passage, I follow Usener. However, on any of the proposed readings, one could interpret Epicurus as saying that the sage will get *very* drunk (e.g., he talks as foolishly as non-sages, or acts as insolently as they do, or surrenders his vigilance as they do, etc.). I have learned a lot from Sanders' discussion of different MSS readings.

[37] Philodemus' *ad hominem* argument may indicate that his opponents are maximalists: self-indulgence like theirs could justify anything including violent anger. Compare his sarcasm against the minimalist Nicasicrates who thought that, although anger was natural, it could be prevented: 'he himself, to the extent that he shares in human nature, cannot escape anger entirely, but is

between different senses of the expression 'to get drunk' and, consequently, taint with ambiguity the analogy between drunkenness and anger. Presumably, Philodemus' point is that, if 'getting drunk' means getting tipsy and behaving in the way in which a sage would, one could infer that the sage will also get angry in the same way, namely he would experience natural anger (XLVII.15), usually in moderation. However, if 'getting drunk' means drinking as much as fools would and behaving in the way in which they would, the sage will probably drink less than they do and act differently from them; likewise, he will get angry both less and differently than fools do. So, Philodemus turns the tables on his opponents. He exploits the analogy between drunkenness and anger both to refute them and to reinforce his own claim that the sage will experience only natural anger.

The third *epilogismos* once again turns on an analogy[38] and involves comparative judgements concerning the anger experienced, respectively, by the fool and the sage. 'Of course, it is not because he has been hit by lightning that the fool is subject to foolish outbursts of anger, but rather because of antecedent beliefs. One man is convinced that he has been harmed, another (that he has been harmed) and greatly, [getting from some (circumstances)] no such beliefs but getting them from other (circumstances), he is unangered in the one case but beside himself in the other. So that if being roused to anger quite generally follows on beliefs, and if the wise man, having been harmed by someone, believes (correctly) that he has been harmed [intentionally] but only to the extent to which he has actually been harmed, then he will certainly become angry, but briefly, because he never receives an impression of suffering great harm since he does not consider any external thing very important. But some (philosophers) have also used these same considerations in connection with the claim that the wise man will experience rage' (XLVII.18 - XLVIII.3). According to this passage, Philodemus' opponents argue that if anger requires the presence of antecedent beliefs, and if even the fool gets angry not unaccountably but only when he has formed the belief that he has been intentionally injured, the sage too will be angry (ὀργισθήσεται: XLVII.36-37) only when he believes that he has been harmed to the extent to which he has in truth been harmed. Yet again, Philodemus does not take issue with either the premises or the conclusion of the original argument, since they accord with his own position. However, after presenting his opponents' reasoning, he stresses that the wise man will not be angry for long, because he will not believe himself to be very much harmed (XLVII.37-41); in this respect, he differs from the fool, who will occasionally think that he has suffered great harm (cf. XLVII.24-25). In the final sentence of the passage cited above, Philodemus alludes to a stronger version of the original *epilogismos*. If the sage perceives himself as being harmed greatly, he will be angered greatly (θυμωθήσε[ς]θαι: XLVIII.1-2), just like the fool (cf. ματαίοις ὀργαῖς: XLVII.19); and since the antecedent holds, the conclusion follows. At first, Philodemus appears inclined to reply that if the sage will not believe himself to be greatly injured, he

---

certainly susceptible to some form of it' (XL.22-26).
[38]Cf. Schofield 1996, p. 227.

will not be greatly angry. Assuming that the former is the case, the latter is also the case: the sage only feels a brief and, presumably, mild form of anger, not great anger (θυμός) also experienced by the fool.

However, when Philodemus undertakes to give a detailed answer to the third *epilogismos*, he does not pursue that line of attack. Instead, he concentrates on the issue whether the beliefs concerning an anger-provoking situation are both necessary and sufficient conditions for the sage to feel ὀργή.[39] 'The last argument is inconclusive because from the premises 'anger (ὀρ[γ]ήν: XLIX.29) does not occur without the belief that one has been harmed' and 'the sage is intentionally harmed' it infers 'the sage does also feel angry' ([ὀ]ργίξεσ[θ]αι: XLIX.32-33). For just as one cannot become wise without learning the alphabet, but it will not follow that if someone has learned the alphabet that person is also wise, so the philosopher who has postulated that anger (ὀργήν: L.1) is consequent upon the belief of having been harmed and cannot occur otherwise is not in a position to infer that the man who has got the impression that he has been harmed will [necessarily][40] become angry (ὀ[ργ]ισθήσεσ[θ]αι: L.3), unless one can demonstrate [also][41] that the belief that one has been harmed is an efficient cause of anger (ὀργῆς: L.7)' (XLIX.27 - L.8).

There is disagreement concerning the interpretation of this argument, and especially the meaning of ὀργή and its cognates. One possibility is that 'ὀργή' here means natural anger as opposed to θυμός, empty anger. If so, Philodemus argues that the sage's belief that he has been harmed is a necessary but not sufficient condition for the sage to feel natural anger. Does this contradict Philodemus' claim that natural anger is unavoidable? I do not think so. For, in fact, Philodemus does not hold the view that antecedent beliefs are *always* sufficient conditions for anger, and in particular of natural anger. Indeed, the alphabet analogy indicates that they are not. Just as lots of other things besides learning the alphabet are required for wisdom, so lots of other things besides the belief that one has been harmed are involved in the arousal of the sage's anger. Natural anger is inescapable for the sage in the sense that the sage is bound to experience it *sometime* — he cannot avoid it altogether. But it does not follow that the sage will feel it *every time* that he correctly believes himself harmed. In fact, many things may impede the sage from anger on such an occasion: for instance, the triviality of the offence, the unworthiness of the offender, and also elements of his disposition, temperament, and upbringing (cf. *De lib.dic.* Va.3-10, VIb.8-15). Generally speaking, the sage's occasional outbursts of natural anger should be assessed in the light of several factors which are jointly sufficient for an emotion of this kind. Truly believing oneself to

---

[39]Most recently, Sanders has read the papyrus and has made a new proposal concerning the text and the content of Philodemus' answer to the last *epilogismos*. I am very grateful to him for sending me the last version of his work on that subject (cf. n. 2). However, since Sanders' text is not yet published, and since I have not checked his proposed readings against the papyrus, I prefer to use Indelli's text, who restores the disputed passages following Gomperz and Wilke.

[40]L.2-3 τὸ [πά]ντως Indelli following Wilke and Gomperz.

[41]L.6: κ[αί] Indelli following Gomperz.

have been harmed is one of these factors and, moreover, is a necessary condition of natural anger. Another possible interpretation of Philodemus' answer to the third *epilogismos* is this. Philodemus uses 'ὀργή' in the same sense as his opponents to mean θυμός, empty anger.[42] He bypasses the issue whether belief is both a necessary and sufficient condition of *natural* anger, but remarks that his opponents have not demonstrated belief to be a condition both necessary and sufficient of *empty* anger. Therefore, they have failed to establish their desired conclusion, that the sage will be angry as much and in the same way as the common man.

Scholars are perhaps right to complain that the close of *On Anger* leaves us with the feeling that we have been let down. It is true that Philodemus gives the *epilogismoi* a rather summary treatment and writes in a hurried and slap-dash prose. However, as I hope to have shown, we can gain much from a closer examination of the form as well as the content of the *epilogismoi*, especially in connection with what precedes them in the treatise. As I suggested, these arguments occupy an important place in the elaborate dialectic of *On Anger*. As examples of the procedure of *epilogismos*, they throw considerable light on the Epicurean conception of argument and reason. And also, especially the last *epilogismos* invites us to think harder about central questions in moral psychology: for instance, what conditions are logically equivalent to an occurrence of anger; what role do beliefs play in the arousal of anger; and, more generally, what are the relations between emotion and belief.[43]

BIBLIOGRAPHY

[Adkins, 1969] A. W. H. Adkins. Threatening, Abusing and Feeling Angry in the Homeric Poems, *Journal of Hellenic Studies* 89: 7-21, 1969.

[Annas, 1989] J. Annas. Epicurean Emotions, *Greek, Roman and Byzantine Studies* 30: 145-64, 1989.

[Annas, 1992] J. Annas. *Hellenistic Philosophy of Mind*, Berkeley and Los Angeles, 1992.

[Armstrong, unpublished] D. Armstrong. Text and translation of Philodemus *On Anger*, unpublished.

[Braund and Gill, 1997] S. M. Braund and C. Gill, eds. *The Passions in Roman Thought and Practice*, Cambridge, 1997.

[Brunschwig and Nussbaum, 1993] J. Brunschwig and M. C. Nussbaum, eds. *Passions and Perceptions*, Cambridge, 1993.

[Considine, 1966] P. Considine. Some Homeric Terms for Anger, *Acta Classica* 9: 15-25, 1966.

[Croenert, 1906] W. Croenert. *Kolotes und Menedemos*, Leipzig, 1906.

[De Lacy and De Lacy, 1958] P. De Lacy and E. De Lacy, Epicurean ἐπιλογισμός, *American Journal of Philology* 79: 179-83, 1958.

[De Lacy and De Lacy, 1978] P. De Lacy and E. De Lacy. *Philodemus: On Methods of Inference*, 2nd edition, Naples, 1978.

[Erler, 1992] M. Erler. Der Zorn des Helden: Philodems 'De ira' und Vergils Konzept des Zorns in der 'Aeneis', Grazer Beiträge XVIII: 103-26, 1992.

[Fillion-Lahille, 1984] J. Fillion-Lahille. *Le de Ira de Sénèque et la philosophie stoicienne des passions*, Paris, 1984.

---

[42]This interpretation is based on Indelli's text.

[43]I presented earlier versions of this paper at Stanford University and at the University of Texas at Austin. I wish to thank warmly both audiences for their comments and criticisms.

[Fish, 2004] J. Fish. 'Anger, Philodemus' Good King, and the Helen Episode of *Aeneid* 2.567-589: A New Proof of Authenticity from Herculaneum', in Armstrong, D. *et al.* (eds.) (2004): *Vergil, Philodemus, and the Augustans*, Austin Texas: 111-38.
[Fortenbaugh, 1970] W. W. Fortenbaugh. Aristotle's *Rhetoric* on Emotions, *Archiv für Geschichte der Philosophie* 52: 40-70, 1970.
[Fowler, 1997] D. Fowler. Epicurean Anger. In Braund and Gill 1997: 16-35.
[Frede, 1987] M. Frede. The Ancient Empiricists. In Frede, M. (1987): *Essays in Ancient Philosophy*, Minneapolis: 243-60, 1987.
[Frede and Striker, 1996] M. Frede and G. Striker. *Rationality in Greek Thought*, Oxford, 1996.
[Gigante and Indelli, 1978] M. Gigante and G. Indelli. Bione e l'epicureismo, *CErc* 8: 124-31, 1978.
[Gomperz, 1864] T. Gomperz. *Philodemi Epicurei De ira liber*, Leipzig, 1864.
[Harris, 2001] W. V. Harris. *Restraining Rage. The Ideology of Anger Control in Classical Antiquity*, Cambridge Mass, 2001.
[Indelli, 1988] G. Indelli. *Filodemo, L'ira*, Naples, 1988.
[Longo Auricchio and Tepedino Guerra, 1982] F. Longo Auricchio and A. Tepedino Guerra. Chi è Timasagora?, in *La regione sotterrata dal Vesuvio: Studi e prospettive*, Naples: 405-13, 1982.
[Nehamas, 1992] A. Nehamas. Pity and Fear in the *Rhetoric* and the *Poetics*. In Rorty, A. O. (ed.) (1992): *Essays on Aristotle's Poetics*, Princeton: 291-314, 1992.
[Nussbaum, 1994] M. Nussbaum. *The Therapy of Desire*, Princeton, 1994.
[Procopé, 1993] J. Procopé. Epicureans on Anger. In Sihvola and Engberg-Pedersen 1998: 171-96, 1993.
[Renehan, 1963] R. Renehan. Aristotle's Definition of Anger, *Philologus* 107: 61-76, 1963.
[Ringeltaube, 1913] H. Ringeltaube. *Quaestiones ad veterum philosophorum de affectibus doctrinam pertinentes*, Göttingen, 1913.
[Rorty Oksenberg, 1980] A. Rorty Oksenberg. *Explaining Emotions*, Berkeley, 1980.
[Sanders, unpublished] K. Sanders. The conclusion of Philodemus *De ira*, unpublished.
[Schofield, 1996] M. Schofield. 'Ἐπιλογισμός: An Appraisal', in Frede and Striker 1996: 221-37, 1996.
[Scully, 1984] S. Scully. The Language of Achilles: The ὀχθήσας Formulas, *Transactions of the American Philological Association* 114: 11-27, 1984.
[Sihvola and Engberg-Pedersen, 1998] J. Sihvola and T. Engberg-Pedersen, eds. *The Emotions in Hellenistic Philosophy*, Dordrecht, Boston, and London, 1998.
[Sorabji, 2000] R. Sorabji. *Emotions and Peace of Mind*, Oxford, 2000.
[Sullivan, 1993] S. D. Sullivan. Person and θυμός in the Poetry of Hesiod, *Emerita* 61: 15-40, 1993.
[Tsouna, 2001] V. Tsouna. Philodemus on the Therapy of Vice, *Oxford Studies in Ancient Philosophy*, 21: 233-58, 2001.
[Tsouna, 2007] V. Tsouna. Philodemus on Emotions. In Sorabji, R. and Sharples, R. (eds) (2007): *Greek and Roman Philosophy 100 BC to 200 AD, Bulletin of the Institute of Classical Studies*, volume 1: 213-241, 2007.
[Wilke, 1914] K. Wilke. *Philodemi Epicurei De ira liber*, Leipzig, 1914.

Philoponus' Account of Theses, Hypotheses, Postulates and Definitions in his Commentary on Aristotle's *Posterior Analytics*

RICHARD MCKIRAHAN

Aristotle's *Posterior Analytics* was the subject of several ancient commentaries. Those of Theophrastus, Galen, and Alexander have perished; Philoponus's is the first to survive. Its title says that Philoponus based it on lectures on the *Posterior Analytics* given by Proclus's student Ammonius, which he supplemented with some of his own observations.[1] He wrote it in the early sixth century of our era, perhaps eight and a half centuries later than the composition of the original text by Aristotle.

Philoponus' work is a commentary in the tradition of the other authors in the *Commentaria in Aristotelem Graeca* series, going back to Alexander. It proceeds by explaining, rarely criticizing Aristotle from other perspectives, but aiming to make sense of his dense and difficult text. On most points it proceeds by explicating Aristotle *through* Aristotle, presupposing that Aristotle's philosophy as a whole is coherent so that something obscure in one text can be correctly understood by showing its relation to other texts that are better understood. Philoponus also presupposes that a given work, in this case the *Posterior Analytics*, is coherent and consistent. He is more reluctant than modern interpreters to admit inconsistencies and his efforts to avoid them sometimes lead to strange interpretations.

My project in this paper is to consider the particularly interesting and instructive case of this interpretive approach that is found in Philoponus' treatment of the structure of demonstrative sciences and of the nature of their principles. Philoponus' interpretation is importantly different from modern interpretations and contains elements not found in the *Posterior Analytics*. Since the commentary has been well known since the beginning of printed books,[2] the fact that his interpretation has not been followed on these points means that it has not been ignored or

---

[1] Philoponus, 1,1-3.

[2] The Aldine editio princeps of 1504 was followed by a second edition in 1534 and a third in 1558. The first translation, by Theodosius, was first published in 1539 and was reprinted nine times. The second, by Rota, was published in 1559 and reprinted in 1560. For references, see C.B. Schmitt, "Philoponus' Commentary on Aristotle's *Physics* in the Sixteenth Century," in R. Sorabji ed., *Philoponus and the Rejection of Aristotelian Science*, London/Ithaca, N.Y., 1987, pp.216, 228.

overlooked but rejected. I will not focus here on the question whether his interpretations of the relevant points are correct or incorrect, so much as on how he arrived at them. I believe that there is clear evidence in his text (and in related texts) to reveal the sources of his (mis)interpretations and of the interpretive methods (different from our own) that led him to the conclusions he reached.

I will begin by listing some basic features of demonstrative sciences found in the *Posterior Analytics*. I next will present and discuss the principal passages for Aristotle's claims about theses, hypotheses, postulates and definitions, as well as what I take to be a defensible interpretation of the nature of those kinds of scientific propositions, showing how that interpretation is grounded in the Aristotelian text and how it deals with some difficulties and with some conflicting passages — since Aristotle's remarks do not appear entirely consistent. Third, I will present Philoponus' claims about theses, hypotheses, and postulates, calling attention to places where his interpretation differs significantly from the interpretation outlined above. Afterwards, fourth, I will give a similar discussion of his statements about definitions. Fifth, I will list some of the examples he uses to illustrate his interpretations and show how they account for some of his divergent views. I will then give evidence that the most significant remaining differences are due to the influence of two post-Aristotelian works: Euclid's *Elements* and Proclus's commentary on that work. I will end with some conclusions about Philoponus's methods and his conception of his work as a commentator.

1   Some claims of the *Posterior Analytics*

I begin by stating without discussion several basic features of demonstrative science that Aristotle treats in the *Posterior Analytics*. They are familiar to modern students of the *Posterior Analytics* and most if not all of them are accepted as correct interpretations of the text.

S1   Every demonstration has one conclusion and at least two premises.

S2   All premises and conclusions are in subject-predicate form.

S3   The premises and conclusion are *per se* predications.

S4   The premises of a demonstration are either conclusions of prior demonstrations or indemonstrable principles; the ultimate premises of any conclusion are indemonstrable.

S5   The distinction between indemonstrable principles and demonstrable conclusions is basic to demonstrative sciences.

S6   The principles are better known (more intelligible) in nature than the conclusions; the conclusions are better known (more familiar) to us.

S7   Demonstrations explain their conclusions by showing how they follow from the principles; a demonstration not only proves *that* the conclusion is and must be the case, but also shows *why* it is and must be so. The principles are the real grounds of the conclusions.

S8 Each science studies a unique subject genus, which is variously described as including all the subjects and attributes the science studies, all the subjects it studies, or the primitive subjects.

S9 Aristotle distinguishes between primitive subjects (whose existence is posited in the principles of a science) and derivative subjects (those that are proved to exist given the existence of the primitive subjects).

S10 There are three types of principles: axioms, definitions, and hypotheses.

S11 Axioms are common principles: "common" in that they are common to (apply in) more than one science; some axioms are common to all sciences.

S12 Definitions and hypotheses are "proper" principles: unlike axioms they apply only in one science and make assertions about its subject genus.

S13 The principles include definitions of all the subjects and attributes the science studies.

S14 Definitions state the essence of the definiendum.

S15 Hypotheses assert that certain entities (primitive subjects) studied by the science exist.

S16 A proof that attribute A belongs to subject S presupposes that we know what the terms "A" and "S" signify and that S exists.

2 The *Posterior Analytics* on Theses, Hypotheses and Postulates

I shall begin by translating and commenting on the most important passages.

> **A1** Among immediate deductive principles I call a thesis one that cannot be proved and that a person does not need in order to learn anything no matter what. But one which a person does need in order to learn anything at all I call an axiom. There are some things of this kind, for it is especially to these things that we are accustomed to apply the name. An hypothesis is a thesis that assumes either part of the contradiction, (alternate translation: a thesis that assumes either part of *a* contradiction), namely that something is or that something is not. One that does not do this is a definition. A definition is a thesis, since the arithmetician posits that a unit is that which is indivisible in quantity. But it is not an hypothesis; for what a unit is and that a unit is are not the same. (72a14-24)

This passage contains a classification of immediate deductive principles. It first divides them into theses and axioms, the difference between them being that axioms are needed in order to learn anything at all, while theses are not. He next divides theses into two kinds: hypotheses and definitions. Here the difference is that hypotheses assume "either part of the contradiction, namely, that something is or is not," while definitions do not. On another translation, they assume either part of *a* contradiction, namely that something is or is not, while definitions do not. Which reading of the passage we adopt has important consequences for our understanding of the nature of hypotheses and definitions. I note in anticipation that Philoponus favors the second interpretation, while I believe that the *Posterior Analytics* as a whole favors the first.

> **A2** I call principles in each genus the ones that it is not possible to prove that they are. Now what both the primary things and the things derived from them signify is assumed, but that they are we must assume for the principles and prove for the rest, for example we assume what a unit is or what straight is or what a triangle is, but we assume that the unit is and that magnitude is, and prove the rest. Of the things employed in demonstrative sciences, some are proper to each science and some are common, but common by analogy since they are useful only as far as they apply to the science's genus. Examples of proper principles are that a line is such and such and that straight is such and such; an example of a common thing is that if equals are subtracted from equals, the remainders are equal. Each of these is sufficient as far as it applies to the genus, for it will do the same even if the geometer does not assume it for everything but only as applying to magnitudes, and an arithmetician assumes it only as applying to numbers. Things that are assumed to be, whose *per se* attributes the science considers, are proper things, as arithmetic assumes there to be units and geometry points and lines. For regarding these they assume that they are and that they are this. As to their *per se* attributes, they assume what each signifies, as arithmetic assumes what odd, even, square and cube signify, and geometry assumes what irrational, bent and verging do; but that these things are they prove through the common principles and on the basis of results that have been demonstrated. And likewise in astronomy. For every demonstrative science is concerned with three things: things that are posited to be (these are the genus whose *per se* attributes it considers), the common things that are called axioms, from which as primary they demonstrate, and third, the attributes of which it assumes what each signifies. (76a31-b16)

In this passage Aristotle again divides scientific principles, this time into common principles and proper ones. Proper principles apply to the subject genus of a single science, while common principles are common in that they apply to the subject genus of more than one science. He illustrates this kind of principle with the principle that if equals are subtracted from equals the remainders are equal, which holds in both geometry and arithmetic. He then distinguishes two kinds of proper principles, this time without giving them names. One kind assumes that something is and the other kind assumes what something is ("that they are and that they are this").

I agree with modern commentators who believe that the three kinds of principles identified in **A2** coincide with those identified in **A1**. The proper principles of **A2** are **A1**'s theses and the common principles of **A2** are the axioms of **A1**. Where **A1** speaks of axioms and says that they are needed in order to learn anything, **A2** speaks of common principles that hold in more than one science, and mentions "the common things that are called axioms". This does not prove that all common principles are axioms. For that we would expect **A2** to say that the common principles are common to all sciences, and we would expect him to offer an example that is more general than the mathematical one he gives. I will return to this issue below.

Where **A1** speaks of hypotheses and definitions, **A2** works mainly through examples. In arithmetic we assume what a unit is, in geometry we assume what straight is and what a triangle is. In geometry we also assume that points and lines are, in arithmetic we assume that units are. More generally, **A2** at the beginning speaks of assuming what things signify and what things are, and at the end speaks of assuming that things are and that they are this. The best way to reconcile this information is to take **A2**'s assumptions that things *are* to be **A1**'s hypotheses and to take **A1**'s definitions to be identical with what **A2** calls assumptions that things *are this* or assumptions of what things are or signify.

Some further work still needs to be done to identify the kinds of principles found in **A2** with those identified in **A1**. I will sketch what out what I think is a reasonable way to make this case for hypotheses and definitions, leaving the question of axioms for discussion in connection with the next passage (**A3**). **A1** concludes by distinguishing definitions and hypotheses with the following example: 'what a unit is and that a unit is are not the same.' Clearly Aristotle here describes definitions as stating "what something is" (τί ἐστι), which is one of his formulations in **A2**. In addition to speaking of "what something is" **A2** also speaks of "what something signifies" (τί σημαίνει), and apparently uses these two expressions interchangeably.

Later on we will find a difference. What something is is a question that applies only to things that are. Goat-stags, which do not exist, are not anything. And since they do not exist, it makes no sense to ask what they are. On the other hand it does make sense to ask what goat-stag signifies. And here it is not a non-existent thing we are asking about, but a λόγος or ὄνομα (92b6-7). Aristotle may be on the verge of distinguishing between definitions of things and definitions of words, but it is not important for present purposes to go further into this interesting point. In the passages cited, there is no question of definitions of nonentities. Further, at the beginning of the presentation of a science, prior to constructing any demonstrations, we set out the principles including the definitions of all the subjects and attributes in the science's subject genus (76a32-3) — even though it is only the primitive subjects of which we know "that they are" (76a33-4), and only later will we go on to prove from the fact that these primitive subjects are that it follows for other subjects "that they are" (76a33-6), and also that both the primitive and the derivative subjects have *per se* attributes, thus establishing for those attributes "that they are" (76b9-10). Since Aristotle does not discuss in **A2** situations where we might want to define subjects or attributes which we go on to prove *are not*, he can reasonably use the expressions "what it is" and "what it signifies" indifferently.

So much for definitions. Two important questions arise in connection with hypotheses. First, whether **A1** presents "that something is or is not" as an example of what an hypothesis might say, or as what an hypothesis must say. In the Greek, this comes down to the question whether to translate τῆς ἀντιφάσεως as "the contradiction" or "a contradiction". Both are possible translations, so the answer must depend on what makes better sense in the context.

What is at stake is first, whether Aristotle has one or more than one contradiction in mind, and second, what the contradiction is. If he intends only one contradiction, then hypotheses will have the form either "x is" or "x is not". Alternatively, if he intends more than one, then presumably they will have the form either "x is y" or "x is not y." These formulations strongly suggest that the two readings contain different syntactical uses of "is" — the former requiring only one term to complete, the latter requiring two. On the two-place reading, an obvious way to understand the claim "x is y" is as a subject-predicate statement in which "x" is the subject, "y" is the predicate, and "is" is the copula. The principal attraction of this interpretation is that Aristotle conceives scientific demonstrations as syllogistic arguments whose premises and conclusions have exactly this form. On the two-place interpretation it is not immediately apparent what room is left for definitions as a separate category of principles. On the one hand we might suppose that hypotheses include all indemonstrable propositions that can serve as premises of demonstrations in a science, so that there is no need for definitions. Alternatively since definitions are the source of immediate *per se* predications, as *APo* 1,4 makes clear, and since demonstrative premises state *per se* predications, we may equally wonder what other premises there remain to be classified as hypotheses.

On the one-place reading, the obvious way to understand the claim "x is" is as asserting the existence of its subject. This is not the place to give a fuller account of what "existence" might mean in the context of demonstrative science, or to consider whether it is a coherent notion. I will simply leave the interpretation at that. On this reading the problem identified above does not arise. The *per se* predications that are immediate premises of demonstrations will come from the definitions, and the hypotheses will play a different role in science.

I have elsewhere[3] presented my account of the roles that the three kinds of principles play and will not go through it here in detail. Roughly speaking, sciences treat subject genera of existing things that have certain natures. The definitions specify the natures and the hypotheses specify that some of those things exist. Not all of them, but enough to entail the existence of the rest. Demonstrations proceed from what is already known. At the outset, only the principles are known. The first demonstration establishes that they (or some of them) entail a certain conclusion, and once that conclusion is demonstrated, it is known and can be used as a premise in later demonstrations. Some demonstrations prove that subjects known to exist have *per se* attributes not present in their definitions, while others prove that the subjects known to exist entail that other subjects exist. The role of axioms in demonstrations is as major premises that allow us to move from things already known to something else. For example, in inferring if A=A′ and B=B′ then A-B=A′-B′, the axiom that if equals are subtracted from equals the remainders are equal is the major term, and A-B and A′-B′ (namely, an individual instance of equals subtracted from equals) is the minor term. This is not strict syllogistic form, but there is ample evidence in the *Posterior Analytics* that Aristotle admitted this kind of "syllogizing" reasoning in his demonstrations.

On this account both definitions and hypotheses have important and distinct roles in the theory of demonstration. And this account is supported by a number of passages, which talk of assuming (or investigating) "what it is" (τί ἐστι) and "if it is" or "that it is" (εἰ ἔστι, ὅτι ἔστι), prominently the following passage taken from the opening chapter of the work.[4]

> **A3** There are two ways in which it is necessary to have prior knowledge. For some things it is necessary to assume in advance that they are, for others it is necessary to understand what the thing being said is, and for some both.... For example, regarding the principle that everything may be truly asserted or denied, it is necessary to assume in advance that it is. Regarding the triangle, it is necessary to assume in advance that it signifies this. Regarding the unit, both — both what it signifies and that it is. (71a11-16)

A3 fits well with my interpretation of **A1** and **A2**. In the second sentence, "assume in advance" means "posit as an indemonstrable principle". "That they are" means "that they exist" and refers to hypotheses. "What the thing being said is" refers to definitions. The examples in the last two sentences bear this out. Triangle is a derivative subject whose existence follows from the existence of straight lines. Units are primitive subjects. In the former case we posit the definition ("that it signifies this"); in the latter we posit both the definition ("what it signifies") and the existence ("that it is").

---

[3] R. McKirahan, *Principles and Proofs. Aristotle's Theory of Demonstrative Science*, Princeton: Princeton University Press, 1994, see the entries for "axioms", "definitions", and existence-claims" in the General Index.

[4] Also *APo* 2,1-2.

The remaining example, the principle that everything may be truly asserted or denied, better known as the law of the excluded middle, is one of the three examples of axioms or common principles found in the text. The other two are the principle of non-contradiction and the example of a common principle found in **A2**: if equals are subtracted from equals the remainders are equal. As for **A3**'s assertion that regarding this principle it is necessary to assume in advance "that it is", I follow most commentators in thinking that here "that it is" means "that it is the case".[5] I think that the example is not to be taken specifically as an example of axioms; it is true for the other principles too that we have prior knowledge (that is, undemonstrated knowledge, prior to any demonstrations within the science) that they are the case. Instead I take it just as an example of a principle. Thus **A3** is distinguishing among the kinds of "prior knowledge" we have of a science's primitive subjects, of the other items in its subject genus, and of its principles.

The final thing I want to mention about Aristotle's views on axioms and common notions in the three passages so far discussed is the conflict between **A1**'s statement that an axiom is an immediate deductive principle "which a person does need if he is going to learn anything at all" and **A2**'s treatment of the common principle that if equals are subtracted from equals the remainders are equal, which applies in geometry and arithmetic but not outside mathematics. It is universally recognized that this example does not fit **A1**'s description, and it is generally accepted that the basic fact about axioms is that they are common in **A2**'s sense: they are employed in more than one science. As it happens, two of Aristotle's three examples of common principles (the law of the excluded middle and the principle of non-contradiction) are common not only in the way specified in **A2** but also in the way demanded by **A1**, and I agree with most commentators that Aristotle wrote **A1** with cases like these in mind, but that **A1**'s claim of universality for the axioms should be discounted in favor of **A2**'s account, so as to make room for the example involving the subtraction of equals as a legitimate axiom.

The final Aristotelian passage that bears on our topic makes different claims about hypotheses and also introduces a new term: postulate.

> **A4** What must be and must seem to be on account of itself is not an hypothesis or a postulate. For the demonstration is not directed at external discourse but at the discourse that takes place in the soul (since deduction is not either). It is always possible to raise objections against external discourse, but not always against our internal discourse. As for everything that is provable and that a teacher assumes without proof, if he is assuming things that seem true to the student he is hypothesizing them and this is not an hypothesis without qualification, but relative to him only. But if he assumes the same thing when the student either has no view on the subject or in fact has the contrary opinion, he is

---

[5] E.g., W.D. Ross, *Aristotle's Prior and Posterior Analytics*, Oxford: Oxford University Press, 1949, p.505. Philoponus disagrees on this point; see below.

postulating it. And hypotheses and postulates differ in this. For a postulate is opposite to the opinion of the student or alternatively it is anything demonstrable that anyone assumes and puts to use without proving it. (76b23-34)

The most important thing to note about this passage is that it is not about indemonstrable principles, which "must be and must seem to be on account of themselves," but about propositions that are provable (δεικτά). Second, it distinguishes different kinds of hypotheses and postulates and is mainly concerned to distinguish between one type of hypothesis and one kind of postulate. The hypotheses mentioned here are called hypotheses relative to an individual and whether something is an hypothesis of this kind or a postulate in the corresponding sense depends entirely on whether or not it seems true to the person in question; the same thing can be an hypothesis relative to one person and a postulate relative to another. (Aristotle takes care to point out that this includes cases where the individual believes that it is false and also cases where he has no view as to whether it is true or false.) This kind of hypothesis is contrasted with hypotheses in the strict sense, a reference to the hypotheses of **A2**. On the other hand, in addition to postulates that are provable propositions put forward without proof that do not seem true to an individual, Aristotle specifies another application of the term, which includes both postulates of the first kind and hypotheses relative to an individual: namely, "anything demonstrable that anyone assumes and puts to use without proving it". Since **A4** spends so much time expounding different senses of "hypothesis" and "postulate", Aristotle's purpose must be to situate **A2**'s use of the term "hypothesis" in relation to other current uses of the term, in order to avoid confusion. And since "hypothesis" and "postulate" were used in closely related ways, Aristotle goes on to distinguish them from one another as well, even though he does not use "postulate" as a technical term in his analysis of the nature of demonstrative science.

In the next section we will see that Philoponus understands these texts very differently.

3 Philoponus on Theses, Hypotheses and Postulates

Where Aristotle characterizes theses as immediate deductive principles that we do not need to know in order to know anything whatever (**A1**) and (since they are identical with the "proper" principles of **A2**) as restricted to a single science, Philoponus describes them as follows:

ΦT1 A thesis is an immediate premise that is indemonstrable or needs very little explanation. (34,13-14)[6]

ΦT2 Some theses are self-guaranteeing axioms because they are evident, but they need some attention because they are not evident without qualification.

---

[6] A translation of the Philoponus passages referred to is given in the Appendix to this paper.

(34,18-19)

ΦT3 Theses are not put forward from ourselves, but are taken from the teacher of the science. (34,21-2)

ΦT4 Immediate premises that are not natural to all but to some are called theses. (127,24-5)

The difference is huge. Philoponus acknowledges that theses are immediate premises, but he introduces them in terms that have to do with the state of the person who knows them, or rather who is learning them. They require little explanation (**ΦT1**), they are evident, but not evident without qualification (**ΦT2**), they are taken from the teacher and not put forward by the student on his own (**ΦT3**). I suppose that "self-guaranteeing" amounts to "immediate", but the assertion that theses are axioms is very unexpected in a commentary on the very passage that distinguishes theses and axioms as different kinds of principles. (**ΦT4**) is Philoponus' way of making this distinction: axioms are natural to all people and theses are natural only to some — in a sense of "natural" that is not found in the Aristotelian text.[7] So already we see that Philoponus has a very different way of looking at theses than a straightforward reading of Aristotle's text warrants.

Where Aristotle classifies hypotheses as theses that state that primitive subjects are (namely, exist), Philoponus gives the following information:

ΦH1 Hypotheses are a species of thesis. (35,1-2)

ΦH2 Hypotheses are always true. (129,23-4)

ΦH3 An hypothesis predicates something of something. (35,4; 127,26-7; 131,30-1)

ΦH4 Hypotheses say things that belong or do not belong to the substance *per se* or accidentally. (35,17-19)

ΦH5 Hypotheses are always "in the premises". (132,1)

ΦH6 Axioms are common since they appear true to everyone and they have their truth from within ourselves, while hypotheses do not appear to true to everyone. (130,14-16)

ΦH7 An hypothesis does not appear to be so by necessity since it does not appear true to all. (130,28-9)

ΦH8 Hypotheses are not natural notions but are posited by the teacher. (35,21-2)

---

[7] Philoponus says that axioms are natural to all people in common because we have conviction in them from within ourselves. (127,12-15)

ΦH9 Even if some hypotheses are in some way self-guaranteeing because they are apparent just as the axioms are, nevertheless not everyone can bring them to hand from within himself, but they need to hear something about them from the teacher, even though when they have heard them they do not always need an argument to prove them since they have their truth in evidence. (129,28-33)

ΦH10 Hypotheses appear true to the learner. (127,27-30; 128,16-17; 130,3-4)

The first five of these claims have to do with the classification of hypotheses among scientific principles, their content, and their role in demonstrations. The rest reveal Philoponus' views on how evidently true they are. I will go through all ten briefly, raising some questions as I go along.

ΦH1 and **ΦH2** agree with Aristotle's account. **ΦH3** shows that Philoponus understands the expression "that something is or is not" in **A1** to mean "something is or is not predicated of something" — an interpretation which is possible in the immediate context, but which I have shown is difficult to reconcile with other passages in the *Posterior Analytics* and which also seems to imply that all immediate demonstrative premises are hypotheses, a conclusion that puts into question the roles that axioms and definitions play in demonstrative sciences. The claim in **ΦH4** that some hypotheses are accidental predications is another surprising statement to find in a discussion of Aristotelian demonstration, since Aristotle is so insistent that the premises and conclusions of demonstrations are *per se* predications. **ΦH5** indicates that hypotheses are premises of demonstrations. It does not specify whether they are all or only some of the premises.

ΦH6 distinguishes between axioms and hypotheses differently from Aristotle. While for Aristotle the axioms are "common" in that they hold in more than one science, Philoponus interprets this claim as meaning that they are the common property of all people — that is, they are so evident that everyone thinks they are true. So, since hypotheses are not "common" they must be less evident than axioms are. As Philoponus puts it here, they do not seem true to everyone. **ΦH7** makes the same point, but in doing so seems to take the expression "appear to be so by necessity" as meaning "necessarily appear to be so" rather than taking "by necessity" as modifying "to be so" as at *APo*76b23-4. The "natural notions" referred to in **ΦH8** are the axioms, which are natural in the sense that we have conviction in them from within ourselves (127,23-4) and as **ΦH9** says, everyone knows them without needing to be taught. Hypotheses need to be taught, but when the teacher presents them we immediately understand them and accept them as evidently true. This the point of **ΦH9** and **ΦH10**. This way of thinking about the immediate principles that are hypotheses is foreign to the *Posterior Analytics*. It has its roots in passage **A4**, which distinguishes hypotheses from postulates on the grounds of whether or not the student believes them. But as I pointed out in connection with **A4**, the hypotheses of that passage are provable (δεικτά) and therefore are not the indemonstrable hypotheses of **A1**, so Philoponus' attempt to bring in material from **A4** to explain **A1** and **A2** is misconceived. Many of Philoponus' unexpected claims about scientific principles, particularly claims having to do with how evidently true the different kinds of principles are and with the belief attitudes different people have towards them can be understood as stemming from this misinterpretation.

A similar problem is found in Philoponus' distinction among several kinds of hypotheses. In the first place he subsumes the discussion of **A4** under that of **A2** by saying that the hypotheses and postulates of **A4** are species of the hypotheses of **A2** (35,19-36,2; 127,27-31) and are in turn divided into subclasses, as follows.[8]

> hypotheses in a general sense: predicate one thing of another (Philoponus' interpretation of **A2**)
>
> A. hypotheses in the proper sense ("homonymously with the genus"): are taken from a person who knows and are true
>
>> 1. hypotheses in the strict sense: appear true to the learner and do not require much attention for their truth to be seen
>> 2. hypotheses relative to the learner: appear true to the learner but require demonstration and further investigation
>
> B. postulates: are taken from a person who knows but do not appear true to the learner
>
>> 1. postulates in the strict sense: true and require little explanation
>> 2. postulates relative to the learner
>>> (a) false and opposite to the learner's opinion
>>> (b) true but require more demonstration

This division distinguishes postulates from "hypotheses in the proper sense" but classifies them both as species of "hypotheses in the general sense" — the immediate principles discussed in **A2**.

This is what Philoponus has to say about postulates.

ΦP1 Postulates are a species of hypotheses. (35,19-20)

ΦP2 With some postulates the student does not have an opinion of whether they are true or false, while with others the student believes that they are false. (36,6-13)

ΦP3 Hypotheses that are assumed though they do not appear true to the interlocutor, and are true and require but little explanation are called postulates in the strict sense, while those that are false and are opposite to the opinion of the interlocutor, or are true and require more demonstration are called postulates relative to the learner. (129,5-11)

---

[8]What follows is taken from 127,27-129,25. A somewhat different account is found in 35,2-36,13.

ΦP4 Hypotheses that are not clear or known, but need proof, and are taken from the teacher without demonstration are called postulates. (35,25-36,2)

ΦP5 Postulates are granted even though they do not yet appear true. (130,13-14)

ΦP6 Postulates are not always true, but are granted by the person at whom the reasoning is directed. (129,24-5)

All these claims except **ΦP1** and **ΦP6** are reasonable ways to understand what **A4** says about postulates. They largely repeat **A4**, except that **ΦP3** interprets **A4**'s references to two uses of the word "postulate" as a classification into two kinds: postulates in the strict sense and postulates relative to the learner. **ΦP1** classifies postulates under the heading of immediate deductive principles, which is certainly something Aristotle does not say. The explanation for this aberration is the same as in his treatment of hypotheses: in his effort to make **A4** consistent with **A2**, he overlooks the fact that the hypotheses and postulates of **A4** are demonstrable. The claim in **ΦP6** that postulates are not always true is something not clearly suggested by Aristotle. One way to account for it is to say that Philoponus understood **A4**'s statement "a postulate is opposite to the opinion of the student" to include cases where the student's opinion is correct, so that the postulate will be false. But this is not a natural way to understand the Aristotelian text, which must refer to the only postulates so far mentioned, which are true. I will offer another explanation below.

4 Philoponus on Definitions

Aristotle informs us that definitions are theses (thus, indemonstrable scientific principles located in a single subject genus), that definitions state "what it is" (τί ἐστι), and that the things (typically genus and differentiae) found in definitions belong *per se* to the definiendum. Philoponus makes the following claims about the nature of definitions.

ΦD1 Definitions give the being of a thing; they state the essence of a thing not its attributes; they determine what the definiendum is, they report the nature of a thing. (35,2-3; 35,6-8; 35,12-13; 127,25-6; 128,31-2)

ΦD2 A definition is no different from the definiendum. (35,10)

ΦD3 Definitions are neither universal nor particular, neither affirmative nor negative, but only indicate the being of each thing in accordance with what it is. (130,18-21)

ΦD4 Definitions do not predicate one thing of another. (35,4-5; 130,16-18; 131,31-2)

ΦD5 Genera and differentiae are predicated of the definiendum. (35,15-17)

ΦD1 combines a number of statements that give familiar Aristotelian accounts of definitions. The best way to take ΦD2 is as using "definition" in the sense of definiens. Thus in the definitional statement "man is a rational animal", "man" is the definiendum and "rational animal" is the definition. ΦD2 then says that rational animal is no different from man. It is just "what man is". Accordingly ΦD3 makes the point that "rational animal" is neither universal ("every rational animal") nor particular ("some rational animal") and is neither affirmative or negative (only propositions can be so).[9] ΦD4, then, means that the definition does not predicate rational of animal, or either rational or animal of man, although, as ΦD5 recognizes, rational and animal are in fact predicated of man (however, the propositions that do so are not definitions). This is an important point, although Aristotle does not make it in the *Posterior Analytics*. I shall return to it shortly below.

In classifying definitions among scientific principles, Philoponus says the following:

ΦD6   Definitions are theses: in the definition of man we posit what a man is. (37,8-9)

ΦD7   Definitions are not hypotheses. (35,1-19; 37,7)

ΦD8   Definitions whose truth is evident are hypotheses. (128,4-5)

ΦD9   A definition is an hypothesis — it is the same as the subject, but different in its relation as are affirmation and negation... For when the definition is assumed as a part of a premise, it is an hypothesis and not a definition. (128,23-7)

ΦD10 Hypotheses are always "in the premises" while definitions are not in the premises but are merely like utterances, supplying understanding of what the thing said is. (132,1-3)

ΦD11 If definitions are ever employed in premises they no longer remain definitions, but become premises that have the definiendum as subject and the definition as predicate and then these too become hypotheses. (130,21-3)

ΦD12 Definitions that have their conviction from within ourselves and also appear true to the learner are called hypotheses in the strict sense. (128,16-17)

ΦD13 dDfinitions that do not have their conviction from within ourselves but require demonstration are called hypotheses relative to the learner. (128,17-23)

ΦD14 Some hypotheses are not definitions (128,32-3)

---

[9] Aristotle, *De Int.* 5-6.

ΦD6 agrees with **A1** and gives an explanation of the terminology: the word "thesis" (θέσις) is connected with the verb translated "posit" (τίθεσθαι). ΦD7, which comments on **A1**, agrees with **A1** on this point. However ΦD8 contradicts ΦD7 and Aristotle as well. ΦD8 occurs in the commentary on **A4** and forms part of Philoponus' misguided attempt to combine **A4** with **A1**, and not the soundest part at that. For shortly after specifying how definitions are different from hypotheses (definitions declare what each thing is, while hypotheses predicate one thing of another) he goes on to define hypotheses "in the strict sense" as those that "both appear true to the interlocutor and are true, and do not require much attention for their truth to be seen". He then says that some definitions are like this (namely, their truth is evident)[10] and shortly afterwards he recurs to this point, saying that "all definitions that have their conviction from within ourselves and also appear true to the learner are called hypotheses in the strict sense as we have already said". Philoponus' focus on similarities between definitions and hypotheses has caused him simply to forget that he has just marked them apart from one another. On the other hand, ΦD9 makes an important point for Philoponus' interpretation of principles. Since definitions do not predicate one thing of another they cannot serve as the premises of demonstrations. (Also ΦD10.) However, they are the source of some premises. If "rational animal" is the definition of man, it follows that all men are rational and that all men are animals, and these are immediate *per se* propositions that can be used as premises in demonstrations. The way Philoponus sees it, these propositions are hypotheses. He expresses this view somewhat roughly in ΦD9 and more clearly in ΦD11, although he would have done better to say that the predicate is not the entire definition (i.e., definiendum) but one of the terms found in it. ΦD12 and ΦD13 then go on to divide definitions into two kinds by applying the division of hypotheses in the general sense into hypotheses in the proper sense and postulates. Some definitions are immediately understood once stated (such as the definition of triangle as a figure surrounded by three straight lines[11]) — these are hypotheses, while others are not so easily understood (such as the definitions of point, line, and surface[12]) — these are hypotheses relative to the learner. Finally, ΦD14 raises another problem. If definitions are the source of immediate *per se* propositions and immediate *per se* propositions are the premises of demonstrations, then what other scientific principles can there be? I will take up this question in connection with my discussion of the examples Philoponus offers of hypotheses.

5 Philoponus' Examples

Much of Aristotle's exposition in the *Posterior Analytics* is conducted through examples. The same holds for Philoponus's exposition of this text. In both cases

---

[10] Here he is thinking of definitions as propositions: "man is a rational animal", not just "rational animal".

[11] ΦHe15, below.

[12] ΦHe9, below.

the examples frequently throw more light on the doctrines than Aristotle's general and frequently obscure formulations do. Philoponus gives the following examples in connection with his discussions of hypotheses and postulates.

Examples of hypotheses

ΦHe1 Motion occurs in things. (35,22)

ΦHe2 Nothing comes to be from what in no way or manner is. (35,22-3)

ΦHe3 To draw a straight line from any point to any point. (35,23-4)

ΦHe4 To describe a circle with any center and distance. (35,24-5)

ΦHe5 Let this be a unit. (37,10)

ΦHe6 The unit is. (37,12)

ΦHe7 The soul is self-moving. (127,35)

ΦHe8 Opposites come to be from one another. (127,35)

(ΦHe7 and ΦHe8 are hypotheses in the strict sense)

ΦHe9 The definitions of point, line, and surface. (128,18-19) (hypotheses relative to the learner)

ΦHe10 The sun is larger than the earth. (128,20)

ΦHe11 The earth is in the center (or has the relation of the center). (128,20)

(ΦHe10 and ΦHe11 are hypotheses relative to the learner)

ΦHe12 Saying in a theorem "the lines falling from the center to the circumference are equal to one another". (128,28-9)

ΦHe13 Saying in a theorem "when a straight line standing on a straight line makes the adjacent angles equal to two right angles". (128,29-30)

(ΦHe12 and ΦHe13 are cases where definitions that appear true to the interlocutor are employed in premises and thus are hypotheses and not definitions)[13]

ΦHe14 The moon is illuminated by the sun (an hypothesis, if it is assumed and appears true to the interlocutor). (129,1-2)

ΦHe15 A triangle is enclosed by three sides. (129,33)

---

[13] ΦHe13 is derived from Euclid's definitions of circle and center: "a circle is a plane figure contained by one line such that all the straight lines falling upon it from one point among those lying within the figure are equal to one another" (Def. 15) "and the point is called the center of the circle" (Def. 16).

ΦHe16 A quadrilateral is enclosed by four sides. (129,34)

ΦHe17 What has a right angle is a right-angled figure. (129,34)

ΦHe18 What has an acute angle is an acute-angled figure. (130,1)

(ΦHe15-ΦHe18 are hypotheses in the strict sense)
  Examples of postulates

ΦPe1 Straight lines produced from less than two right angles meet. (36,2-3; at 129,13-17 this is given as an example of a postulate that is true but requires more explanation)

ΦPe2 Right angles are equal to one another. (36,7-9)

ΦPe3 Two straight lines do not enclose a space. (36,10-12)

ΦPe4 A point is without magnitude. (36,12)

ΦPe5 A line has no breadth. (36,13)

ΦPe6 To draw a circle with any center and distance. (129,6-7)

ΦPe7 To draw a straight line from any point to any other point. (129,7-8)

(ΦPe6 and ΦPe7 are postulates in the strict sense and are also postulates which the teacher asks to be granted and which do not in all cases appear true)

ΦPe8 If one of the followers of Democritus or of Anaxagoras should ask that it be granted to him that atoms or homoeomeries are the principles of things. (129,11-13) (a false postulate)

ΦPe9 If someone who believes that there is no void should grant that there is void in order to know to what purpose the hypothesis will be used. (129,17-20) (a postulate that is contrary to the opinion of the interlocutor but he grants it in order for some conclusion to be reached)

ΦPe10 If someone has no opinion whether the stars are even or odd in number, but grants the person doing the deduction what he wants to assume in order to see what follows. (129,20-3) (a postulate where neither of the contradictory pair appears true)

Most of these examples straightforwardly illustrate Philoponus's claims about hypotheses and postulates. I will not go through them, but I will call attention to a few that help solve some outstanding problems. The last examples given of postulates account for one of the questions that remain: Philoponus asserts (ΦP6) that some postulates are not true, whereas Aristotle states that they are provable entails that they are true. This is the case of example ΦPe8. (ΦPe9 and ΦPe10 are similar.) As a good Aristotelian, Philoponus did not believe in the existence of homoeomeries or atoms, the principles of Anaxagoras and of Democritus, respectively. If an Anaxagorean or an atomist is expounding his physical theory, Philoponus is willing to accept for the purpose of the discussion that they exist, and he calls such cases postulates. In such cases the student does not believe the claim, so they have the property that distinguishes postulates from hypotheses. This approach, however, is open to the objection that it neglects the fact that hypotheses in the generic sense are true, and therefore so are hypotheses in the specific sense and postulates as well.

Next, geometrical examples are prominent in the *Posterior Analytics*, and so it is not surprising to find some in Philoponus, in fact many of his examples of hypotheses and most of his examples of postulates are drawn from mathematics. We find references to Euclid's definitions as well as his Postulates and Common Notions.

Definition of point:	ΦHe9 (cf. Euclid, Definition 1)[14]
Definition of line:	ΦHe9, ΦPe5 (cf. Euclid, Definition 2)
Definition of surface:	ΦHe9 (cf. Euclid, Definition 5)
Definition of circle:	ΦHe12 (cf. Euclid, Definition 15)
Definition of right angle:	ΦHe13 (cf. Euclid, Definition 10)
Definition of triangle:	ΦHe15 (cf. Euclid, Definition 19)
Definition of quadrilateral:	ΦHe16 (cf. Euclid, Definition 19)
Definition of right-angled figure:	ΦHe17 (cf. Euclid, Definition 21)
Definition of acute-angled figure:	ΦHe18 (cf. Euclid, Definition 21)
Postulate 1:	ΦHe3, ΦPe7
Postulate 3:	ΦHe4, ΦPe6
Postulate 4:	ΦPe2
Postulate 5:	ΦPe1

Common Notion 9 ("two straight lines do not enclose a space"): ΦPe3

Significantly he calls some definitions in geometry hypotheses and others postulates according as how obvious they appear to students. That two items on this list are identified as both hypotheses and postulates need not cause surprise. Philoponus calls Euclid's Postulates 1 and 3 hypotheses in a context that can be taken as talking about hypotheses in the generic sense that includes postulates, rather than hypotheses in the specific sense, which excludes them. That only one of Euclid's Common Notions is mentioned is easily explained as well. By Philoponus' lights, the others are evident to everyone and therefore count as axioms, as opposed to theses. They are mentioned as axioms elsewhere.[15] On the other hand the fact that

---

[14] ΦPe4 is not Euclid's definition. Philoponus takes it as a fact about points that is difficult to accept.

[15] Philoponus cites C.N. 1 ("Things equal to the same things are equal to one another"), C.N. 3 ("If equals are subtracted from equals the remainders are equal") and C.N. 4 ("Things that

the definition of line is once called an hypothesis relative to the learner (**ΦHe9**) and once a postulate (**ΦPe5**) is surprising, but no more surprising than that the very passage that identifies it as an hypothesis says that it (along with the definitions of point and surface) requires demonstration — that is, they are not principles but theorems. It is hard to see anything here but confusion.

The fact that Euclid's Postulates figure so prominently among Philoponus' examples of postulates points to the solution of some remaining puzzles. In contrast to Aristotle's postulates, which are provable, Euclid's postulates are unproved principles. I think that this fact contributed decisively to Philoponus' classification of postulates as immediate scientific principles. Having made this decision, he simply applied to Euclid's Postulates Aristotle's criterion in **A4** for distinguishing postulates from hypotheses. Students either have no opinion whether or not a postulate is true or they believe it is false. As a matter of fact Euclid's fifth Postulate *is* difficult to understand and many students might well have no view on whether or not it is true. But Philoponus' confident assertion that the same holds for Euclid's fourth Postulate (All right angles are equal) is less plausible, and one might think it is implausible for the first and third Postulates as well.[16] It is worth noting that Philoponus believes that the fifth Postulate can be proved (35,25-36,5; 129,13-17), which is in line with Aristotle's assertion that postulates are provable (although Philoponus does not claim that the other Euclidean Postulates can be proved as well). The price for doing so is not small, however, since it leaves the status of the other Euclidean Postulates in doubt — are they provable or not? — and it undermines Philoponus' taxonomy of hypotheses and postulates as species of immediate principles.

So far we have located the source of some of Philoponus' discrepencies from Aristotle in Philoponus' interpretations in his desire to make Aristotle's text coherent — a desire that runs to excess when it leads him to misunderstand the text he is commenting on. Another source is his use of Euclid to understand Aristotle. This is not in itself a bad thing — or if it is bad, I have been seriously guilty of it myself. But it needs to be done carefully and critically, since the resemblance between the three kinds of principles Aristotle discusses and the three kinds found at the beginning of the *Elements* is by no means exact.

The truth is that there are many odd features in Euclid's principles, which leaves serious doubt as to why he groups them as he does. In a previous publication I studied this question in detail and concluded that Euclid's choice of three kinds of principles was influenced by Aristotle's discussion, and that for the good of his own presentation he would have done well to add at least one more kind.[17] One of the oddities is that while most of the Common Notions are usable in other branches of mathematics in addition to geometry, some are not. This is what led Philoponus

---

coincide with one another are equal to one another") at 10,32-11,3, for example.

[16] I do not mention the second Euclidean Postulate because Philoponus does not mention it.

[17] R. McKirahan, "Η Φιλοσοφία, η επιστήμη και τα μαθηματικά στον τέταρτο αιώνα π.χ." ("Philosophy, Science and Mathematics in the fourth century B.C.") Deukalion 18 (2000) 5-25.

to attribute to Aristotle the view, unwarranted by the text, that some axioms hold in only one science.[18] Another is that while the first three Postulates involve the construction of straight lines and circles, the fourth and fifth Postulates state properties of certain lines and angles, and so seem to be more like theorems.

The ancients recognized some of the problems and offered a number of attempts to account for them. There is a record of several attempts in Proclus' *Commentary on the First Book of Euclid's Elements*, none of them wholly successful.[19] Even the solution Proclus eventually adopts contains some of the same flaws for which he faulted previous accounts.[20] As to the fourth and fifth postulates, as a matter of fact they cannot be proved to follow from the other principles of Euclid's geometry, and Euclid was right to place them in his principles. But they look as if they might be proved. We know that many people in antiquity and afterwards tried to prove the fifth Postulate, and Proclus tells us that some believed that the fourth Postulate needs to be demonstrated as well (Proclus, 183,23-4). Philoponus is aware of attempts to prove the fifth Postulate — he tells us that Ptolemy and Proclus wrote treatises on the topic,[21] but he erroneously supposes this to show that Postulates are demonstrable. This shows that some of Philoponus' faulty interpretations come from his use not only of Aristotle and Euclid, but of the later mathematical tradition, in which I include commentaries as well as strictly mathematical works. In fact Philoponus himself wrote a commentary on Nicomachus' *Introductio Arithmetica*.[22]

We must not forget that Philoponus' commentary advertises itself as a reworked version of lecture-notes of Ammonius, and that Proclus was Ammonius' teacher, which means that there may well be a close connection between what we find in Philoponus' commentary and in Proclus. I believe that this is the case and that some of Philoponus' unexpected interpretations of the *Posterior Analytics* can be traced to Proclus' attempts to make sense of Euclid's *Elements*.

First, Proclus surprisingly refers to Euclid's principles not as Definitions, Postulates and Common Notions, as we find in our texts of the *Elements*, but as hypotheses, postulates and axioms (Proclus, 76,4-6, 178,1-2), and he makes it clear that the hypotheses he is referring to are what we know as definitions ("hypotheses, or what are called definitions" — Proclus, 178,7-8). He also incorrectly attributes this terminology to Aristotle (Proclus, 76,24-77,1). This view (in combination with Philoponus' interpretation of 72a20 as indicating that hypotheses are subject-predicate statements and with his views on definitions that imply that they cannot

---

[18] I discuss this issue in "Philoponus' Account of Scientific Principles in his Commentary on Aristotle's *Posterior Analytics*," forthcoming in *Documenti e Studi* 20 (2009).

[19] Proclus, *sulla tradizione filosofica medievale* (PIsa) 182,21-184,10.

[20] Proclus says that belonging to the common genus of mathematics is characteristic of axioms (Proclus, 195,23-196,14), although earlier he had recognized axioms proper to geometry and to arithmetic (Proclus, 184,12-22).

[21] Philoponus, 129,16-17.

[22] Recently edited by G. R. Gardina, *Giovanni Filopono Matematico tra Neopitagorismo e Neoplatonismo. Commentario alla Introduzione Aritmetica di Nicomaco di Gerasa*, Catania: CUECM, 1999.

be demonstrative premises) may well be an ingredient of Philoponus' view that in some sense definitions are hypotheses, a view which we saw is impossible to reconcile with what Aristotle says. That Philoponus was uncomfortable with simply identifying Aristotle's hypotheses and definitions is reflected by his insistence that some hypotheses are not definitions (ΦD14) and is justified by several of his examples (ΦHe1–ΦHe8, ΦHe10, ΦHe11, ΦHe14). He considers these propositions to be immediate principles that are not extracted from definitions, without seeming to recognize the problems that such principles raise.

Second, Proclus distinguishes Euclid's kinds of principles from one another in terms of their evidence:

> When what is employed as a principle is something both familiar to the student and self-guaranteeing, such a proposition is an axiom: for example, that things equal to the same thing are equal to one another. When the student does not have a self-guaranteeing notion of the assertion proposed but nevertheless posits it and concedes the point to his teacher, such an assertion is an hypothesis. That a circle is a figure of such-and-such a sort we do not know by a common notion in advance of being taught, but upon hearing it we grant it without a demonstration. Whenever, on the other hand, the statement is unknown and nevertheless is taken as true without the student's conceding it, then, he says, we call it a postulate: for example, that all right angles are equal. (Proclus, 76,9-21)

So according to Proclus, the student does not know whether the postulates are true (this corresponds to one of Philoponus' species of postulates). He does not reveal the student's attitude to hypotheses, but since he holds them to be distinct from postulates, he presumably holds that the student believes or even knows that they are true. This suggests the following taxonomy:

axioms: familiar to the student and self-guaranteeing
hypotheses: familiar to the student but not self-guaranteeing
postulates: not familiar to the student and not self-guaranteeing

If this is right, then Philoponus is broadly in agreement, holding that the distinguishing features of axioms are that they are natural to all men in common (127,22-4), appear true to everyone (130,14-15) and are self-guaranteeing (23,1-3), and that the main difference between hypotheses and postulates is that students think that the former are true, but either think that the latter are false or have no view either way. And it is reasonable to see Proclus behind Philoponus' interpretation, particularly since Proclus concludes his account of Euclid's principles by saying that "This is how axioms, postulates and hypotheses are distinguished according to Aristotle's teaching" (Proclus, 76,24-77,1). Here at least Philoponus is adopting (or rather adapting) an earlier interpretation of Aristotle (itself doubtless colored by reflection on Euclid's principles) rather than interpreting Aristotle through Euclid or through interpretations of Euclid.

Conclusion

In this paper I have presented material from a work of late antiquity that is no longer well known. In studying it I found a number of interpretations that are strikingly different from modern interpretations and which stray far from the text it is commenting on. Some of them can be seen to come from putting Aristotle together differently from the way we now do — giving more prominence to some passages than we do and paying less attention to some words and phrases. And some of these differences I think amount to mistakes. Sorting them out is a project of a certain amount of interest but not, perhaps of much importance. More provocative are the cases where the interpretations are based on nothing or next to nothing in the Aristotelian text. It is natural to suppose that they came from elsewhere — either from lost earlier commentaries that did a better job than Philoponus does of justifying them, or from works that have survived. The fact that Philoponus uses many mathematical examples to illustrate Aristotle's points is not surprising; Aristotle did the same. But this fact has proved to be the key to understanding much in Philoponus that would otherwise have remained unclear.

In the first place, Philoponus did not simply use mathematical examples; most of the mathematical examples are drawn specifically from Euclid's *Elements*, which is the only mathematical text that divides its principles into three kinds, a division that corresponds closely (though not exactly) to Aristotle's division of the kinds of principles required by any demonstrative science. In addition, we are blessed by the survival of Proclus's lengthy, learned and philosophically-oriented commentary on the very part of the *Elements* (book 1) that contains the threefold Euclidean division of the principles of geometry. This commentary extensively discusses the nature of Euclid's principles and bases its discussion in part on Aristotle's treatment of the same topic. Further, Philoponus' teacher Ammonius had associated with its author, and had also given lectures on the *Posterior Analytics* which are the basis of Philoponus' commentary. This combination of circumstances makes Proclus' commentary on Euclid a plausible candidate to be the actual source of some of Philoponus' ideas. An examination of the text of Proclus has supported this hypothesis by making it possible to account for some of Philoponus' interpretations that would otherwise be difficult to explain. In going through this material I believe that I have provided some new insight into Philoponus' method as a commentator. I will conclude this paper by reflecting on one feature of his method.

Mathematics very early became a specialized discipline. Philosophers as early as Plato found important philosophical lessons in mathematics, but in general, ancient mathematicians were not serious philosophers and few ancient philosophers are regarded as serious mathematicians. Philosophers tended to refer to other philosophers, and mathematicians (except in commentaries on other mathematicians) tended not to refer explicitly to anyone.

I have argued elsewhere[23] that Aristotle's threefold division of scientific princi-

---

[23] See above, n.17.

ples owes a good deal (though not everything) to earlier mathematical practice and that Euclid's threefold division of geometrical principles owes something (though again not everything) to Aristotle's similar division. About eight centuries later we see Philoponus drawing on both the philosophical and the mathematical traditions. To begin with, he is commenting on a philosophical text. In doing so he refers to other philosophers and especially to other commentators on the same work. But he also refers to the primary mathematical text of antiquity and to the primary commentary on that text. How unusual a practice this is I do not know. We do not find it in other surviving ancient commentaries on the *Posterior Analytics* (although this may not mean much since they are much shorter and less detailed than Philoponus' commentary). And it is important to keep in mind that Proclus too draws on the philosophical as well as the mathematical traditions in his Euclid commentary. How good a job Philoponus did of deploying the mathematical material is another question, and my analysis has suggested an unencouraging answer. But even if we have reservations on this score, we should perhaps take a broader look at what he was doing and acknowledge the importance of his willingness to employ non-philosophical material in interpreting Aristotle. This is one way to avoid the sterility of simply repeating, rearranging, and choosing among what others have already said, and it may be the best way to spark new interpretations and ideas.

Appendix of Passages from Philoponus, *On Aristotle's Posterior Analytics*[24]

10,27-11,3

It is also necessary to know that some of the axioms are in the foundations of all sciences universally, others in some, and others in only one. For example, "in every case either the affirmation or the negation" will be relevant to every science, since we employ such an axiom even in the ordinary arts and in conversations. However, "things that are equal to the same thing are also equal to one another" and "if equals be subtracted from equals, the remainders are equal" (11) apply to several sciences, since music, geometry, and arithmetic employ them. On the other hand, "things which coincide with one another are equal to one another" belongs to geometry alone.

22,26-23,3

There is (23) also another kind of knowledge which is not demonstrated but is self-guaranteeing and without deduction, for example knowledge of the axioms, for this does not come to be present in us through demonstration but is self-guaranteeing.

34,7-36,13

---

[24] The translations of the first four passages are taken from *Philoponus, On Aristotle, Posterior Analytics 1.1-8*, in the series Ancient Commentators on Aristotle (London: Duckworth and Ithaca, N.Y.: Cornell University Press, 2008). The translations of the remaining passages are drafts of the translation that will appear as *Philoponus, On Aristotle, Posterior Analytics 1.9-18* in the same series.

Since "immediate premise" has different meanings, he now makes a division of it and says that of immediate premises some are theses and others are axioms and common notions. Axioms are those that we know from within ourselves and without demonstration, some of which contribute to every science, as has been said, others contribute to several—for example, those concerned with quantity—and some to one. I have given examples. A thesis too is indemonstrable or needs very little explanation—for example, "the straight lines extending from the center to the circumference of a circle are equal to one another", "to draw a straight line from any point to any point", "a point is without parts", and "every triangle is contained by three straight lines". These are self-guaranteeing axioms because they are evident, but they need some attention because they are not evident without qualification.

And so a thesis differs from an axiom in this way, but it differs in another way too, because we put forward axioms or common notions from within ourselves, as was said, but the theses we take from the teacher of each science. For the arithmetician posits that the unit is indivisible, the geometer posits the things previously mentioned, the doctor posits that bodies are composed of four elements, and the natural philosopher that all natural things are composed of matter and form and that (35) nature is a principle of motion and rest.

These are the species of thesis: hypothesis and definition. A definition is one that gives the being of the thing, for example "man is a mortal rational animal", while an hypothesis is one that predicates or denies something of something. Clearly of course, predicating one thing of another is not a characteristic of definitions, since they do not predicate mortal rational animal of man, but say what the subject is. Definitions state the essence of the thing, not its attributes, for what is predicated must be different from the subject, since nothing is predicated of itself: no one says that man is man. But the definition is not different from the definiendum, for mortal rational animal is nothing different from man. "Mortal rational animal" is an explanation and explication of man. Therefore definitions are not predicated of the definienda, but determine what the definiendum is, while genera and differentiae are predicated, because they are different from the species. For it is not the same thing to say man and animal or man and rational; when we say that man is an animal or rational, we are predicating them of man as being things that are different from man. On the other hand, hypotheses and generally every affirmation and negation say things that belong or do not belong to a substance *per se* or accidentally.

Hypothesis in turn is divided into two species, of which one is called an hypothesis homonymously with the genus, and the other is called a postulate. Something that every hypothesis has in common is that it is not based on a natural notion but is posited by the teacher. For example, "motion occurs in things", "nothing comes to be from what in no way or manner is", "to draw a straight line from any point to any point", and "to describe a circle with any center and distance". But all that are not clear or known, but although they need (36) proof are taken from the teacher without demonstration, are called postulates. For example, "straight lines produced from less than two right angles meet", which is taken from the geometer without demonstration, even though it needs a good deal of argument for its demonstration. In fact Ptolemy devoted a whole monograph to its proof.

And while at this point he stops with this division, further down he divides postulates into those known in neither way and those known contrarily. What do I mean? That when the geometer says that right angles are equal to one another, the student who does not know geometry does not have an opinion in either way, either that right angles are equal or that they are unequal; however, the geometer takes this as something that has been granted. Further, when the geometer says "two straight lines do not enclose a space", the student will think the contrary, that they will enclose some narrow area. Also concerning a point, he believes that it is not without magnitude, and concerning a line he has the opinion that it has breadth.

37,7-13

He shows in these words that a definition is a thesis but not an hypothesis. That it is a thesis is clear, since in fact we posit, for example, man as a mortal rational animal, and a unit as that which is indivisible in respect of quantity. But it is not an hypothesis. For if we say "let this be a unit", then we state an hypothesis. However, in definitions we declare only what the thing is. And it is different for it to be posited that there is a unit and, once the unit has been hypothesized in respect of its being, to say precisely what it is.

127,1-5

In every science there are three things on which every demonstration is based: the genus concerning which the science demonstrates the things that belong *per se* — which is the given; the very affections that belong to it *per se* — which is the sought; and third, the axioms from which the affections are proved as belonging to the subjects.

127,21-130,29

Some immediate premises are self-guaranteeing and are natural to all people in common, and some are not natural to all. Those that are natural to all in common because we have conviction in them from within ourselves, are called axioms and common notions. Those that are not natural to all but to some are called theses, and of theses those that declare what each thing is are called definitions, while those that predicate one thing of another are called by the common term hypotheses. Some hypotheses are true and appear to the learner to be true and are taken by the learner from the expert, while others are taken by the learner from the expert although they do not appear to the learner to be true. Those that are taken and appear to the learners to be true are called hypotheses in the proper sense, homonymously with the genus, and those that are taken although they do not appear to the learners to be true are called postulates. All hypotheses that are taken in circumstances where they both appear true to the interlocutor and are true, and do not require much attention for their truth to be observed, are called hypotheses in the strict sense. For example if someone wants to establish that the soul is immortal, he will ask his interlocutor if the soul appears to him to be self-moving, or if opposites come to be from one another. If (128) the interlocutor agrees to the question, he will say that it is so. For even if these things require some attention, still they are true and it immediately becomes clear that they are so to a person who thinks about them for even a little. These are called hypotheses in the strict sense. Of this kind too are definitions whose truth is evident. For example, a triangle is a figure surrounded by three straight lines, and a circle is a figure surrounded by one line such that all the straight lines falling on it from one point within the circle are equal to one another. For that the circle is surrounded by one line and that the lines from the center are equal is evident to anyone who only understands that the distance from the center, where one point of the compass is placed, to the other end is a straight line which generates the circle by being turned completely around. And in similar cases it likewise requires but little attention. But all that appear true to the interlocutor and are true but require demonstration and further investigation are hypotheses relative to the learner but not in the strict sense. For example, the definitions. All of them that have their conviction from within ourselves and also appear true to the learner are called hypotheses in the strict sense as we have already said. But all those that do not have their conviction from within ourselves but require demonstration — for example the definitions of point, line, and surface, and also that the sun is larger than the earth and that the earth is at the center of the *kosmos* or has the relation of a center — or whatever appears true to the interlocutor and is taken, since these require demonstration but are taken without being demonstrated, they are called hypotheses relative to the learner. And clearly a definition is an hypothesis that the definiens is the same as the subject, but it is different in its relation as are affirmation and negation, and premise and problem and conclusion. For when the definition is assumed as a part of a premise, it is an hypothesis and not a definition, as when, for example, we employ the definition of circle in a premise, saying in the course of proving a theorem "the lines falling from the center to the circumference are equal to one another" or "when a straight line standing on a straight line makes the adjacent angles equal to two right angles" and the like. But when it is not employed as a premise but as reporting the nature of the thing as that very thing, then it is a definition, not an hypothesis. However, it is not true that in every case an hypothesis is a definition. For example, that opposites are generated from one another (129) is an hypothesis, but not a definition, and that the moon is illuminated by the sun is an hypothesis but not a definition, if they are taken and appear true to the interlocutor. Now all hypotheses that appear true to the learner or the interlocutor are called hypotheses in a specific sense as has been said, homonymously with the genus. But all that are taken though they do not appear true to the interlocutor, but are true and require but little explanation, are called postulates in the strict sense. For example, that it is possible to draw a circle with any center and distance and to draw a straight line from any point to any other point and the like. But if they are taken without appearing true, on the one hand if they are false and opposite to the opinion of the interlocutor, or even if they are true and require more demonstration, they are called postulates relative to the learner. Examples of false ones: if one of the followers of Democritus or of Anaxagoras should ask that it be granted to him that atoms or homoeomeries are the principles of things. An example of ones that are true but require more explanation: the one that says that lines extended from less than two right angles meet. For the geometer assumes this without demonstration as a postulate, although Ptolemy and Proclus devoted entire books to it. Often the postulates are in fact opposite to the opinion of the interlocutor but he grants it in order for some conclusion to be reached. For example if someone who believes that there is no void should grant that there is void in order to know to what purpose the hypothesis will be used. Often neither of the contradictory pair appears true to him, for example, that the stars are even or odd in number, but again he grants the person doing the deduction what he wants to assume in order to see what follows. So both axioms and hypotheses are in all cases true, but postulates are not true in all cases, but are granted by the person at whom the reasoning is directed. This is the entire division.

But the things that have been discussed are different from one another. Axioms differ from natural hypotheses because, as we distinguished them in the beginning, axioms are naural to all and each person has them from himself and puts them forward even if the teacher does not state them. But even if some hypotheses are apparent and so in some way are self-guaranteeing like axioms, still not everyone can apply them from within himself, but some people need to hear something about them from their teacher, even though when they have heard they do not always need an argument to prove them since their truth is evident — for example that what is surrounded by three sides is a triangle and what is surrounded by four is a quadrilateral, and what has a right angle is a right-angled figure, (130) while what has an acute angle is an acute-angled figure, and all such cases. This is how axioms differ from hypotheses in the strict sense. Axioms and hypotheses differ from postulates in the strict sense: hypotheses because they are taken from the teacher and appear true to the learner, while postulates which the teacher asks to be granted do not entirely appear true. For example, if he were to say "let it be granted to me to draw a straight line from any point to any point and to draw a circle with any center and distance." And postulates differ from both axioms and hypotheses because axioms and hypotheses have conviction, while postulates require more or less explanation.

He presented the distinction among these at the beginning, and now he distinguishes axioms from both hypotheses relative to the learner and postulates, and distinguishes these from each other, on the grounds that postulates differ from hypotheses in that hypotheses appear true to the learner while postulates are granted even though they do not yet appear true, and axioms differ from both in that they are common since they appear true to everyone and they have their truth from within ourselves, while hypotheses do not appear true to everyone and neither do postulates. All of them differ from definitions in that they are all premises predicating one thing of another either universally or individually, and either affirmatively or negatively, while definitions do not predicate one thing of another either universally or individually, affirmatively or negatively, but only indicate the being of each thing in accordance with what it is. But if definitions are ever employed in premises they no longer remain definitions, but become premises which have the definiendum as subject and the definition as predicate and then these too become hypotheses.

"What must be because of itself and must seem to be because of itself is not an hypothesis or a postulate": he [Aristotle] says how axioms differ from both hypotheses and postulates: an axiom is that which necessarily is because of itself and appears to be so by necessity, which holds for neither hypotheses nor postulates. For an hypothesis does not necessarily appear to be so since it does not appear <true> to all, while a postulate does not appear <true> at all, as has been said.

131,30-132,3

Here he distinguishes definitions from hypotheses in that hypotheses affirm or deny one thing of another, while definitions neither affirm nor deny anything of anything, but only state what the (132) thing in question is. And so hypotheses are always "among the premises", but definitions are not among the premises, but are only like utterances, allowing us to understand what the thing said is.

Part G
Aristotle

Sophistic Elenchis 176^a 10-12: Many Questions for Julius Moravcsik[1]

JOHN WOODS

1 Aristotle on fallacies

Presocratic and sophistic philosophy brims with absurdities that try the very notion of proof. A proof is always welcome when it confirms something already known or believed. But it is easy to see that proofs are at their most powerful when they overcome antecedent doubts, or convictions to the contrary. But not every valid proof is a sound demonstration of something surprising or previously believed to be impossible. Some proofs are *reductios* of their premisses or of the rules applied to them. A hard question is whether there is a suitably principled way of marking this difference. The present difficulty generalizes to arguments of all kinds. Some good-looking arguments are bad arguments, whether in philosophy or public policy. The thinking that lands us in Gorgias' scepticism and the thinking that lands us on the losing side of the Peloponesian war is bad thinking which, in its time, looked good.

Aristotle wanted to recover the distinction between good and good-looking arguments. For this he sought, in the *Topics* and *On Sophistical Refutations,* a wholly general account of argument, at the theoretical core of which he would place the logic of syllogisms.[1] A syllogism is a valid argument satisfying additional constraints. One is that the conclusion not repeat a premiss. Another is that no premiss be redundant.[2] Also required is that syllogisms be constructed

---

*For helpful comments at the Moravcsik Symposium, I warmly thank Henry Mendell, Grigori Mints, and Julius Moravcsik and Voula Tsouna.

[1] "It is altogether absurd to discuss refutation without first discussing syllogisms; for a refutation is a syllogism, so that one ought to discuss syllogisms before describing false refutations; for a refutation of that kind is a merely apparent syllogism of the contradictory of a thesis" (*On Sophistical Refutations,* 10, 171^a, 1-5).

[2] "For a syllogism rests on certain statements such that they involve necessarily the assertion of something other than what has been state, through what has been stated" (SE 165^a, 1-3). See also *Topics,* 100^a, 25-27 and *Prior Analytics,* 24^b, 20-22. Some scholars, Julius Moravcsik among them, interpret "through what has been stated" as imposing on syllogistic premisses the burden of *explaining* their conclusions. This is a plausible construal when a syllogism is a demonstration from the first principles of a science. But I venture to say that this is not the right understanding of the "through"-clause for syllogisms that function as refutations.

from *propositions,* that is, from statements affirming or denying only one thing of only one thing (SE 169^a, 7).³ A further feature, derivable from the non-circularity condition, is that syllogisms not have inconsistent premiss-sets. This makes for an interesting-looking system. In fact it is the first-ever relevant, paraconsistent and nonmonotonic logic. And if we add the condition that syllogisms not have multiple conclusions, it also has an intuitionist cast about it.⁴, ⁵ Aristotle was drawn to the view that every good argument would embed, without necessarily being exhausted by, a syllogism. Accordingly, it would be the job of the syllogistic to furnish these core arguments.

In *On Sophistical Refutations,* Aristotle thought a fallacy was the confusion of a merely apparent syllogism with an actual syllogism. How disappointed he must have been to discover the fallacies! For what were syllogisms wanted for in the first place, if not to lift the murk that blotted the distinction between good-looking and good arguments? But if an argument can look like a syllogism without being one, the corrective promised by syllogisms is afflicted with the very misery that it was engaged to clear away. So now something more than a definition of fallacy is needed. We must have a theory of them.

In *On Sophistical Refutations* Aristotle develops this theory in the context of refutation arguments. In these cases, there is a thesis T advanced by one party, whose further role is to give Yes-No answers to questions put to him by his interlocutor. Aside from putting the questions, the role of the questioner is to construct a syllogism whose conclusion is the contradictory of the answerer's thesis T and whose premisses are drawn entirely from his answers. If successful, the questioner will have arranged it for T's defender to convict himself out of his own mouth.⁶

An important precursor of the Aristotelian refutation argument is the eristic

---

³See also *Posterior Analytics,* 72^a, 9. Cf. *Metaphysics,* 1006^a, 32; *On Sophistical Refutations,* 18^a, 13-14; *On Interpretation,* 18^a, 13-14; *Sophist,* 252 C ff., 262 D5-6.

⁴For the connection between non-multiple conclusions and intuitionism, see D.J. Shoesmith and T.J. Smiley, *Multiple-conclusion Logic,* Cambridge: Cambridge University Press, 1978, p. 4.

⁵It is a matter of contention as to whether in *On Sophistical Refutations,* Aristotle requires syllogisms to have multiple premisses. Suffice it to say that *On Sophistical Refutations* contains a great many examples of fallacies which are (non-enythememematic) single-premissed arguments. To take just one example, the fallacy of *secundum quid* emerges from single premisses at SE 166^b, 37; 167^a, 1, 7-9; 168^b, 11; 180^a, 23-24, 31-32, 33-34, 34-35, 35-36; 180^b 9-10, 11-12, 14-16, 18-19, 20-21, 21-23. (See here David Hitchcock, "Fallacies and formal logic in Aristotle", *History and Philosophy of Logic,* 21 (2000), 207-221). More generally, *On Sophistical Refutations,* Aristotle devotes fairly full discussions to sixty-four cases of arguments, which only appear to be syllogisms. Of these, forty-nine have, by the lights of the *Prior Analytics,* the wrong number of premisses, or premisses or conclusions of the wrong sort. A further fifty-five examples are alluded to briefly (L.-A. Dorion, Editor, *Aristotle,* "Aristotle's original work on *On Sophistical Refutations*", Paris and Québec: J. Vrin and Presse de l'Université Laval, 1995).

⁶"For to refute is to contradict one and the same attribute — not the name, but the object and one that is not synonymous, but the same — and to confute it from the proposition granted, necessarily without including in the reckoning [= syllogism] the original point to be proved, in the same respect and relation and manner and time in which it was asserted ... . Some people, however, omit one of the said conditions and give a merely apparent refutation." (*On Sophistical Refutations,* 167^a, 23-29).

argument, prominently on display in the *Euthydemus*. It is a refinement of the Socratic elenchus, found in such dialogues as *Euthyphro, Laches, Charmides* and *Lysis*. Bonitz identifies twenty-one different eristic arguments in the *Euthydemus* alone (Hermann Bonitz, *Platonische Studien*, Hildeschiem: Olms 1968; reprint of 3rd Berlin edition of 1886). The structure of these arguments considerably resembles that of Aristotle's refutations. Here, too, a thesis is attacked by questions and defended by answers to them. Most of the questions are Yes-No, to which the expected answer is nearly always in the affirmative. In some cases, questions have an either-or structure, and the answerer responds by picking one of the disjuncts. It is the job of the questioner to draw conclusions from the answerer's concessions. For the most part, but not invariably, the consequences are drawn deductively. The argument is successful when the questioner is able to derive from the respondent's concessions either a conclusion incompatible with the original thesis (though not necessarily its contradictory) or some absurdity whose derivation employs that thesis as premiss. For all their similarities,[7] it is easy to see that Aristotle's refutations are different from eristic arguments; they are a refinement of them.

2 Many questions à la mode Aristotelienne

Here is what Aristotle has to say about the many questions fallacy. He considers the question, "Are Coriscus and Callias at home or not at home?"[8], and writes as follows:

> For it is possible for it to be true to say "Yes" or "No" without qualification to countless different questions; but still one should not answer them with a single answer, for that is the death of the argument ($SE 176^a$, 10-12).

The death of the argument? How so? Aristotle points out that those fallacies

> that depend upon the making of several questions into one consist in our failure to articulate the account of a proposition. For a proposition predicates a single thing of a single thing .... Now since a syllogism starts from propositions and a refutation is a syllogism, a refutation, too, will start from propositions (SE 169^a 6-14).

Not very satisfying, is it? Aristotle excludes many questions on a technicality. It is the fallacy of building a would-be syllogism out of non-propositions, in this special sense of "proposition" that excludes compound statements.

Aristotle's preoccupation with propositions might strike us as ludicrous. In fact, however, there is something that might be said on his behalf. It has to do with a sweepingly reductionist claim that he makes at *On Interpretation* 16^a, 19-26, 16^b, 6-10, 19-25, 16^b, 26-17^a, 2. There he launches without proof the thesis

---

[7] See here Voula Tsouna, "Dialectical devices in the Socratic elenchus", forthcoming.
[8] Note that Aristotle does not intend this question as formulating a tautology. Its sense is preserved fully under suppression of the redundant "or not at home".

of propositional simplification, according to which everything stateable at all is stateable without relevant loss in the language of propositions. But if this is so, the use of a statement given in answer to a complex question is compensated for by the fact that every statement that is a non-proposition is re-expressible in the language of propositions. So it is difficult to see why Aristotle is so harshly disposed towards compound statements generally. And certainly, if we are to understand his passionate denunciation of statements given in answer to complex questions, something beyond this trivial-seeming technical glitch will need to be unearthed.[9]

In the interests of dramatic tension, let us switch our example of a complex question from the one questioning the whereabouts of Corisius and Callias to the old standby, "Have you stopped beating your dog?" Putting D for "I have a dog", U for "I used to beat it", and N for "I beat it now", a No-answer to our question gives

> Not-((D and U) and N).

Now there is nothing in Aristotle's rejection of many questions that requires him to deny that "not-((D and U) and N)" expresses a fact. However, we may take it that, in asking that question to which this is the No-answer, the questioner was intent on knowing whether I have a dog, whether I used to beat it and whether I still do. If I answer No, all of these questions are left unanswered. The No-answer gives my questioner none of the information he seeks. The mistake here is certainly the questioner's. But it is not the mistake of confusing a non-syllogism with a syllogism. This can be seen as follows. Suppose that our two parties are disputing about whether the answerer is virtuous. Suppose that it has already been agreed that anyone who is a dog-beater cannot be virtuous. It would be grist for the mill of the questioner's would-be refutation if he could get his interlocutor to admit that he is a dog-beater. If, with these goals in mind, the questioner asks

> ?((D and U) and N)

he will get nowhere if his respondent answers No. But the problem disappears entirely if the respondent's answer is Yes. For the Yes-answer decomposes to

> D
> U
> N

from which the questioner is free to select N as a premiss of his would-be refutation:

> Everyone who Ns is non-virtuous
> Everyone who is my present interlocutor Ns
> So everyone who is my present interlocutor is non-virtuous.

---

[9] Equally, we can take Aristotle's determination to regard many questions as a fallacy as renunciation of the thesis of propositional simplification. But this leaves unmet the burden of explaining the propositions-only constraint on syllogisms.

We learn from this a useful twofold lesson. One is that asking a complex question is not sufficient for denying to the asker what he seeks to know. The other is that asking such a question doesn't imply the slightest disposition to mistake a non-syllogism for a syllogism.[10]

Suppose again that the answer to ?((D and U) and N) is No. Then, as we have seen, the answer

   Not-((D and U) and N)

does not tell the questioner what he wants to know. But, given the standard presupposition of the case, which is that the poor fellow never beat a dog in his life, there is no repair of his questioner's defective question that will enable him (the questioner) to construct the syllogism that he has it in mind to construct. Let's be clear, he can *repair* the question, but he still can't get the premisses he seeks.

The repair is made, as before, by asking the component questions one by one:

   ?D
   Yes
   ?U
   No
   ?N
   No

Of course the problem of *many questions* is now removed, but this provides no premiss with which to construct the desired refutation. The relevant answer is the *negation* of the needed premiss.

What is the moral here? It is that irrespective of whether the question is asked complexly or non-complexly, i.e., one-by-one, if the answer is No, then the question of whether the resulting refutation is actually a syllogism doesn't arise. It doesn't arise because there are no premisses available for *that* refutation to be made. It remains the case that where an answer to a complex question doesn't decompose, it is clearly better to avoid complex questions. But there isn't the slightest plausibility to the suggestion that when you do ask a complex question whose answer does not decompose, you have landed yourself in the pickle of mistaking a non-syllogism for a syllogism.

Can we, even so, rescue Aristotle's claim that many questions represents the death of argument? No. For, again, if the question is ?((D and B) and N), a No-answer denies to the questioner a premiss he wants. The argument he seeks to construct is, as we might say, dead-in-the-water. The reason he can't get the premiss he wants is that his No-answer won't decompose. On the other hand, if the answer to this same question is Yes, it will decompose, and the questioner is free to syllogize away, with N now unfetteredly available to him as a premiss. The best

---

[10]Similarly for the question ?(X or Y). A No-answer gives not-X and not-Y, which effortlessly decomposes.

that can be said for Aristotle here is that sometimes, not always, asking a complex question will rule out — or if you like, kill — the argument the answerer is intent on producing. When we read SE 176^a,10-12, "the death of the argument" strikes us as a general indictment, suggesting that many questions kills any argument in which it is involved. In fact, it does no such thing. It kills a certain arguments that a questioner might wish to make. But it doesn't do this always. It depends on how the complex question is answered.[11]

3 From Many to Begging

It would be wrong to think that the trouble created by Aristotle's treatment of many questions creates is one-off. The failure to tie the actual wrong of many questions to the wrong of mistaking a non-syllogism for a syllogism is a difficulty that dogs (sorry!) each of the fallacies discussed in *On Sophistical Refutations*. The wrong of *petitio principii* is independent of the fault of confusing a non-syllogism with the real thing. The wrong of equivocation is independent of this same confusion, and so on; with the net effect of making Aristotle's account of the fallacies a systematic failure. Let us give this objection a name. Let us call it the Non-instantiation Thesis. The Non-instantiation thesis is a rather dramatic one. It accuses the founder of logic of a major confusion reflected in the fact that the fallacies on Aristotle's famous *list* fail to instantiate his equally famous *definition* of them. The Non-instantiation Thesis is a quite broad charge, for whose full defence I lack the space here. But I shall close with some remarks about the other great fallacy of questioning, *petitio principii*. Modern readers are likely to regard the term "begging the question" as somewhat unclear and perhaps a trifle theatrical. But "begging" in this context does not mean supplication. Rather it is what any questioner does when attempting to refute an opponent's thesis. Before refuting a thesis, the questioner must ask his opponent what premisses he or she agrees on. Begging the question is a mistaken way of questioning one's opponent on this matter. In other words, it is a mistaken way of selecting propositions that are eligible to serve as premisses in a would-be refutation. Aristotle recognizes not just one but five ways in which a question is begged. Here is what he says about the first two of these ways.

> People appear to beg their original question in five ways: the first and most obvious being if anyone begs the actual point requiring to be shown: this is easily detected when put in so many words; but it is more apt to escape detection in the case of different terms, or a term and an expression, that mean the same thing. A second way occurs whenever any one begs universally something which he has to demonstrate in a particular case ... (*Topics* 162^b 34ff).

---

[11] For an impressively detailed examination of the related issue of compound terms in Aristotle's logic, see Henry Mendell, "Making sense of Aristotelian demonstration", *Oxford Studies in Ancient Philosophy*, 16 (1998) 160-225.

For Aristotle, the *original question* of a refutation is the respondent's thesis, T. A question is then "begged in the first way" if the questioner begs the point that he himself must try to derive, namely, not-T. Even if, says Aristotle, you get your opponent to admit that the argument

> Not-T
> Not-T.

Now, it is perfectly true that

> Not-T
> Not-T

is an argument that fails the definition of syllogisms outright. But the error committed by this first form of begging the question is not that of producing a non-syllogism, but rather that of asking the respondent a question to which he is antecedently bound to answer in ways that confound the questioner's purpose in asking it. Even if, *in extremis*, the answerer were to give the questioner what he begged for, the argument would be over at that very juncture, without the need to produce a syllogism of any sort. Here is why. Irrespective of whether it is a syllogism the argument question is valid. Its premisses necessitate its conclusion, which if the contradictory of the questioner's thesis. The answerer's defence of that thesis fails at this juncture, irrespective of whether the argument is a syllogism.

In the second way of begging the question, Aristotle calls into question arguments in which the conclusion follows from a single general premiss, as with

> All humans are mortal
> Therefore, some humans are mortal.

Interestingly enough, Aristotle is in no doubt that the premiss implies or necessitates the conclusion. What he does not like is the idea that this argument is a syllogism. Here his reasoning turns on a technicality in the definition of refutation that we have not yet called up to do some work for us. As we noted at the beginning, Aristotle requires that in a successful refutation every premiss must be consistent with the respondent's original thesis, T. Thus it is only the premisses *collectively* that imply the thesis' contradictory, not-T.[12] Suppose, then, that the original thesis was "No man is mortal," and that the holder of this thesis has conceded that all men are mortal. Now this proposition clearly implies that some men are mortal, which is the contradictory of the original thesis. This being so, the premiss "All men are mortal" is not consistent with the original thesis. So it cannot be used to refute that thesis by drawing the immediate implication that contradicts it.

---

[12]See here W.D. Ross: "And syllogism is distinguished from *petitio principii* in this, that while in the former both premisses together imply the conclusion in the latter the premise alone does so" (*Aristotle*, 5th edition. London: Methuen 1953; p. 38).

Here again we see that the fault that is committed here is that it violates a condition on refutations. It breeches the requirement that one not petition one's opponent for a proposition that delivers the failure of his own thesis by immediate inference. Arguer's who know their onions won't concede such a proposition, needless to say. The mistake made in asking for it is the mistake of inducing an answer that is the opposite of what the would-be refuter wants. Of course, here too there are stupid respondents. It is possible that the Yes-answer might be given. If so, the argument is over, by the necessitated inconsistency of that answer with the original thesis. There is no need to consider making a syllogism out of it.

The third way "is to beg particular cases of what has to be shown universally" (*Topics* 163^a6). It can be illustrated with the following argument:

> Socrates, who is Greek, loves to argue
> Therefore, all Greeks love to argue.

To modern eyes, this looks more like the fallacy of hasty generalization than begging the question. But Aristotle's thinking here appears to be that since the conclusion cannot be true unless the premiss is true, asserting the conclusion is a way of re-asserting the premiss. This is a special case. It is hard to see how a displayed argument begs the question in any sense. But suppose for now that it did. Then, again, consider the refutatory set-up in which this argument is assumed to arise. The questioner is seeking to over-turn the answerer's thesis "Some Greeks don't love to argue". Since a refutation requires that the answerer concede premisses that yield the contradictory of the thesis in question, it is clear that the questioner must establish "All Greeks love to argue". Asking for "Some Greeks love to argue" is unavailing, in this regard, even if its truth follows from the very proposition that this answer doesn't entail. Once more, the fault is that it is a stupid question - a rotten way of bringing about a refutation – irrespective of whether the contradictory of the opponent's thesis implies it.

But is it question-begging? If one concluded that all Greeks love to argue from the fact that some do, the inference fails. If it succeeded, then there would be a case of sorts that might be advanced to support the charge of question-begging. It is that the true premiss yields a proposition that entails it. This would give the equivalence of the premiss and conclusion, hence an argument that is circular. But since the premiss doesn't yield the conclusion, there is no occasion for question-begging in this sense to arise.

The fourth way of begging the question is a bit tricky. On the face of it, there appears to be nothing wrong with an argument of the form

> A
> B
> Therefore, A and B

Certainly, arguments of this form will be valid. Its premisses necessitate its conclusion. So perhaps the fault is that the conclusion violates the non-circularity condition on syllogisms twice over, by repeating both premiss in the conclusion. Curiously, this appears not to have been Aristotle's own diagnosis. Instead, he insisted that syllogisms must be constructed entirely from categorical propositions.Since, as we have already seen, no compound statement is a categorical proposition in Aristotle's sense, the fault is that the conclusion is not technically a proposition.

Case four (*Topics* 163^a 9-14) need not detain us long. Hamblin characterizes it as the fallacy of begging "a conjunctive conclusion piecemeal"[13]. Here the questioner's thesis is, say, "Either not-A or not-B" and its contradictory "A and B". If in his effort to have his opponent concede "A and B" he asks for A and B, then once again he has asked a question which any consistent arguer will answer in ways that do the questioner no good. But, as before, if a stupid respondent gives both A and B, the argument is over, by the necessitation by the premises of the contradictory of the answerer's thesis. It is true that the argument of "A and B" from A, B is not a syllogism, for the technical reasons that came up in our discussion of many questions. The offence to refutation given by the petition of A, B is present and complete entirely independently of what a syllogistically-minded refuter makes of stupid answers.

Finally, the fifth way of begging the question bans arguments of the form

A
B

Therefore, C

in which C is equivalent to A or to B. The fifth case is a blend of cases one and three, and is dispatched in the ways we have already described for them.

Before we finish, it is necessary to consider a sixth case. Let the original thesis be that some A aren't C. The refuter's task is to find premises that yield its contradictory, "All A are C". Suppose that the questioner helps himself to propositions which haven't arisen as answers to any question put to the respondent. If those unasked for and unventured propositions do the thesis some damage, then this is a "pure case" of question-begging. It attributes to the answerer propositions that kill his thesis, yet in a way that denies him occasion to deny them. Let those premises be "All A are B" and "All B are C". The inference to "All A are C" is a syllogism. It is a *perfect* syllogism. But its premises are a pure case of question-begging.

It is time to sum up. In Aristotle's five cases, we see that the embedded offence is that of asking a question to which the likely answer will be of no use to the questioner. This is so entirely independently of whatever syllogism the questioner gets around to constructing. As with many questions, it is true that a stupid answer — the Yes-answer — might be forthcoming. In which case, since necessitation is truth-preserving, the answerer has responded in ways that contradict his own thesis. But Aristotle's position is that this is a thesis-eliminator that the questioner can't accept, since doing so would involve him in the construction of a valid necessitation argument that failed to meet the further conditions on syllogisity. No one need

---
[13] C.L. Hamblin, *Fallacies*. London: Methuen 1970; p. 74.

doubt that this would be an extremely odd situation, one in which, although the questioner has refuted himself, the questioner cannot say so. The sixth case is arguably the most damaging to Aristotle's position. It gives us a clear case of a perfect syllogism that purely begs the question.

I conclude that in the case of many questions and question-begging the Non-Instantiation Thesis is confirmed.[14]

---

[14] Julius Moravcsik and I arrived in Ann Arbor in the Fall of 1959, he a freshly-minted Assistant Professor and I a callow Ph.D student. It was for me a particularly happy convergence. The large intellectual debt I owe to the University of Michigan flows in good part from Julius Moravcsik's tutelage and example. I have valued his colleagueship and friendship ever since. It give me great pleasure to dedicate this paper to Julius on the occasion of his retirement from the Stanford Philosophy Department.

Aristotelian Colors as Causes
ALAN CODE

For Aristotle the study of living things, speaking quite generally, takes place within the larger context of the study of objects that have their own intrinsic principles of change. These are the natural, or physical objects, and the intrinsic principle of change of such an object is its nature. It is the task of natural philosophy to explain the physical or natural activities and behaviors of these objects. Here the English terms 'natural' or 'physical' do not mark out a distinction between different respects in which they are to be studied or different sets of phenomena to be explained. The natural/physical is simply what pertains to a substance's nature. The explanation of physical changes treats them as hylomorphic composites, and the nature of a composite is identified with its form.

This is true quite generally of all physical objects. Living things are themselves a part of the natural world, and as such are compounds of matter and form, where the form of a living thing is its nature. Their study is incorporated into the larger project through the identification of their form, and hence their nature, with their soul. Since what is physical or natural for an object is what is due to or pertains to its nature, and what is psychological is what is due to or pertains to its soul, the psychological is thereby a special case of the natural. That is, for Aristotle psychological activity is a special case of physical activity. There are many types of physical processes, states and behaviors, and specifically different kinds of physical objects have specifically different natural behaviors.

It is from this perspective that Aristotelian science studies the distinctive aspects of the various inhabitants of the observable, changeable world. Some of its inhabitants, the animals, engage in a variety of forms of cognition and awareness as a part of their distinctive ways of life, and as such these activities are due to their natures. It was in relation to this observation that Julius Moravcsik and I have said:

> "Aristotle treats psychological activity as requiring definable structures, but does not hold that the elements that enter into the specification of the form and structure are properties, features, powers or relations that belong to matter that can exist outside of the realization of some enlivening potential."[1]

---

[1] Alan Code and Julius Moravcsik, "Explaining Various Forms of Living," *Essays on Aristotle's De Anima,* Martha C. Nussbaum and Amélie Oksenberg Rorty (eds.), Oxford (1992), p. 133.

Cognition involves both a structure on the side of the knower and a structure on the side of the known. In the article just cited, in connection with the structure on the knower's side we said that "it is a mistake to see these structures as arising from the powers of inanimate matter."[2] All cognitive functioning of animals presupposes perceptive capacities, and for the basic sense modalities he famously characterizes perceptive capacities as 'receiving form without matter'. About this we wrote:

> "In the context of describing perception, 'receiving form without matter' remains a basic, primitive notion. It points in the direction of what we would call 'content' or 'information' today."[3]

For instance, through the exercise of a capacity to receive visual information animals become aware of the colors that physical objects have. In order for this to be possible there must be on the animal's side a suitable condition of receptivity to this kind of information. However, the information is information that one physical object has about another. To have a suitable receptive capacity, the perceiver and what is perceived must be suited naturally to each other.

For Aristotle colors either are or possess causal powers. Colors have the capacity to cause themselves to be seen. Each color has an active power to change a transparent medium that is continuous between the surface having that color and the organ of sight.[4] Sight is a passive, or receptive capacity, and what has sight is acted on through the medium in such a way that the sighted organism perceives the color. This is a causal feature of color. In fact, this pretty much sums up the causality that Aristotle attributes to color. To be sure, there are various phenomena connected with the reflection of colors, such as rainbows, halos and mirrors of various sorts. However, in his treatment of them his concern is with the ways in which reflective devices, natural or manmade, enable one to perceive colors and colored shapes. In Aristotle's philosophy of nature colors are there to be perceived, but leave inanimate objects as well as plants alone.[5]

Unlike tangible qualities such as heat, moistness and their contraries, colors do not cook things, crumble them, rot them or make them wither away. Nonetheless animals that can be affected by them in such a way as to see them thereby receive a great deal of information about the world that they inhabit. This information enhances their ability to navigate their way around and support their activities. Like the other sense modalities, sight too provides "a means of preservation in order that, guided by antecedent perception, they may both pursue their food, and shun things that are bad or destructive."[6]

---

[2] ibid.

[3] Op.cit., p. 137.

[4] See *de An.* III.12, 434b27-29, for a general description of conditions on the media required for perception at a distance.

[5] *de An.* II.12 424b10-11: "Light or darkness, sounds and smells leave bodies quite unaffected." All translations of Aristotle are from *The Complete Works of Aristotle: The Revised Oxford Edition*, edited by Jonathan Barnes, Princeton (1984).

[6] *Sens.* 1, 436b20-437a1.

Indeed, for Aristotle visual information is the most useful sensory information for an animal when it comes to coping with the needs of life and survival. Physical objects are colored, and by seeing their colors together with the shapes and sizes and motions that accompany them animals are able to keep track of objects, and to distinguish by visual appearance food, water, predators and prey. Of course, in intelligent creatures the information acquired through sight and the other senses is the indispensable starting point for various sorts of knowledge, culminating ultimately in scientific understanding.

How can nature be like this? How is it that physical objects, both animate and inanimate alike, have properties or features in virtue of which they cause other physical objects to be aware of them? It is this topic that he takes up in *de Sensu* 3:

> "The point of our present discussion is to determine what each sensible object must be in itself, in order to produce actual sensation."[7]

In the *de Anima* Aristotle had explained how sensible forms such as colors act through various media on sense organs. In the case of sight, there must be a transparent, or 'diaphanous', medium such as water or air that is in contact with both the organ of sight and the color seen, and is continuous between the two. For the color to affect the organ, the medium through which it acts must at the time of acting be *actually* transparent. On his account that is another way of saying that there must be light in order for colors to be seen by acting on the organ of sight.

What Aristotle here calls 'the transparent' plays a central role in his account of colors and the awareness of colors. The transparent is not itself a physical body, but rather is described by him as a nature that is present to physical bodies. It is especially apparent in air, water and the like, but is in fact present to some degree in all bodies:

> "... but what we call transparent is not something peculiar to air, or water, or any other of the bodies usually called transparent, but is a common nature and power, capable of no separate existence of its own, but residing in these, and subsisting likewise in all other bodies in a greater or less degree."[8]

What Aristotle is here calling 'the transparent' is a power that is common to all physical bodies. For a body to be transparent is for it to be able to contain light, and light itself just is the exercise of this capacity. As he puts it in the *de Anima*:

> "Of this ... light is the activity — the activity of what is transparent *qua* transparent"[9]

For a physical body actually to be transparent is for light to be present to it. To some degree or other every physical body has the ability to contain light,[10] and

---

[7] *Sens.* 3, 439a16-17.
[8] *Sens.* 3, 439a21-25.
[9] *de An.* II.7, 418b9-10.
[10] See *Sens.* 3, 439b8-10 together with 439a21-25.

the presence of light in that body just is its exercise of this capacity. For light to be present in a body of air there must be fire, or, he says, something such as the 'upper body' (i.e., the fifth element). A predominant source of light is the sun, and when the sun is overhead it typically lights up the sky in all directions. Darkness is simply the absence of light, and when the sun is not present and there is no source of light in the vicinity (such as a fire), then a transparent body is dark.

However, transparency and its absence do not characterize only the medium. They also characterize the visible objects that are seen through the medium. In the former case, that of the medium, the body of air (or whatever) lacks a determinate boundary of its own. The body of air does at any given time have a finite spatial extension, and is bounded by whatever bodies contain it. However, it lacks a surface of its own. Insofar as it is actually transparent, its transparency is not a feature of its boundary. It is rather the case that its actual transparency is no other than light, the very condition required of a medium through which colors act on the organ of sight.

Such indeterminate transparent bodies often *appear* to have a color, though in fact the really do not have any color of their own. For instance, sometimes the sky appears blue or the sea appears a certain shade of purple. Nevertheless, Aristotle observes that when the body has no definite boundary of its own, it has no fixed color. In favor of this we might consider the fact that the part of the sky that is close to us does not look blue, and in general that the indeterminate bodies do not have the same color appearances from different distances.

On the other hand, a body that does have its own determinate boundary, and hence a surface, exhibits fixed colors:

> "...whereas in determinate bodies the colour presented is definitely fixed, unless, indeed, when the atmospheric environment causes it to change."[11]

Both indeterminate and determinate bodies appear colored, though only in the latter case is the color a property of the colored object. Even so, Aristotle states quite emphatically that:

> "...it is clear that that in them which is susceptible of colour is in both cases the same".[12]

According to the *de Anima*, light is the color of the medium of sight.[13] However, light just is the activity of the transparent, and as such it is the transparent itself that is 'susceptible of color'. When the sky looks dark blue at sunset this is not really its color, for being an indeterminate body it can have no color of its own. It merely appears to us to be dark blue at that time and from a certain perspective.

---

[11] *Sens.* 3, 439b5-6.
[12] *Sens.* 3, 439b6-7.
[13] "Light is as it were the proper colour of what is transparent" (*de An.* II.7, 418b11).

This is a transitional period between daylight and the darkness of night, and it is this resulting combination of light and dark that appears bluish.[14]

What Aristotle is claiming at 439b6-7 is that whatever it is that takes on the appearance of color is the same in all bodies, regardless of whether the body has or lacks a surface. This has important consequences for his account of colors. It is in virtue of the transparent and its absence that bodies appear colored. The difference between the case of the medium and that of a physical object that has its own color is simply that in the latter (i.e., when the color is fixed) there is a surface. Aristotle appeals to this fact to locate the color as a feature of the surface itself. The surface of a body is a fixed part of that body, and the particular combination of transparency and darkness in that surface is what we are seeing when we see the color of that body. The surface does not change depending upon our proximity or our angle of viewing, and neither does the color that we see when we look at it.

At this point it is worth repeating the well-known fact that unlike modern accounts of color, Aristotle's treatment of color does not distinguish hue from luminosity. This is relevant to the fact that the Greek adjective '*leukos*' that gets translated as 'white' in Aristotle's discussion of color, is also commonly used to mean 'bright' or 'clear'. Contemporary translators usually treat the latter as a different usage of the term. However, it is significant that for Aristotle the basic use[15] of '*leukos*' as a color term is for what is produced in a determinate body when whatever it is that produces light is present:

> "Now, that which when present in air produces light may be present also in the transparent; or again, it may not be present, but there may be a privation of it. Accordingly, as in the case of air the one condition is light, the other darkness, in the same way the colours white [*to leukon*] and black are generated in determinate bodies."[16]

Hence in his theoretical understanding of colors, there is a sense in which these two apparently different uses of the term are picking out the same phenomenon. For instance, fire produces light in an indeterminate transparent body; if the body is *determinate* what it produces is the primary color 'white', '*to leukon*'. In the case of an indeterminate medium the absence of fire or a like substance results in darkness, whereas the condition that results if the body has a surface is called 'black'. Just as light is the actuality of the indeterminate transparent medium, so too the color white is what fire produces at the extremity of a determinately

---

[14]In this regard it may be useful to consult *de Coloribus*. Although this treatise is not by Aristotle, its explanation of the apparent colors of the sea or the sky fits well with the account of colors as mixtures in his *de Sensu*.

[15]I say 'basic use' to indicate that here I am talking about his use of this term as a primary color in his theory. In ordinary language the term has a range of uses corresponding to a range of colors, "varying from the pure *white* of snow...to the *grey* of dust" (*A Greek-English Lexicon*, 9th revised edition, edited by Henry George Liddell and Robert Scott, Oxford: 1996).

[16]*Sens.* 3, 439b14-18.

bounded transparent object. Likewise the color black is produced at the surface of the object by the absence of fire or a kindred substance.

Accordingly, when at 439b5-6 (cited above) Aristotle states that determinate bodies have fixed colors he is including transparent solid bodies in this general statement. Ross's note on these lines indicates that Aristotle does not mean to include them, but this does not seem to be the case.[17] Such a restriction would go against Aristotle's attempt to characterize colors as features of the determinate boundaries of physical objects. Even a transparent body is visible if it has its own surface, and in order for it to be visible it has a color. As Aristotle is using the term '*leukon*', the primary color that characterizes a transparent glass sphere is *leukon*.

There is a similar use of the term in the Peripatetic treatise *de Coloribus* when it says:

> "Simple colours are those which belong to the elements, i.e. to fire, air, water, and earth. Air and water in themselves are by nature white [*leuka*], fire (and the sun) yellow, and earth is naturally white."[18]

Since here white, yellow and black are the primary colors, the text contradicts Aristotle's own view that there are just two primaries, and also does not easily square with his view that the sun in itself appears *leukos*, not yellow.[19] Nonetheless, the author feels no difficulty in applying *leukon* as a color term to the natural color of air, despite the fact that it is transparent and not what we would ordinarily classify as something that is colored 'white'.

Indeterminate bodies also appear colored[20] but for them the color they appear to have at any particular time is not properly speaking their color at all. Rather it is the result of a combination of its actual transparency at the time and the lack thereof in the body as a whole. In a way the indeterminate bodies are colored. In the sense in which they are colored it is their light that is their color. However, strictly speaking only the determinately bound physical objects have their own colors, and it is this idea that Aristotle captures in his definition of color:

> "Whence it follows that we may define colour as the limit of the transparent in determinately bounded body. For whether we consider the special class of bodies called transparent, as water and such others, or determinate bodies, which appear to possess a fixed colour of their own, it is at the exterior bounding surface that all alike exhibit their colour."[21]

---

[17] Ross comments as follows: "...of course transparent solids should be coupled with air and water, and he here means 'solids that are not transparent', *Aristotle: Parva Naturalia, A Revised Text with Introduction and Commentary*, Sir David Ross, Oxford (1955).

[18] *Col.* 1, 791a1-4.

[19] See *Sens.* 3, 440a10-11, for the latter.

[20] Though not, *pace* Beare and Ross, at their extremities. See note 21.

[21] *Sens.* 3, 439b11-14. Note that in this translation the punctuation follows Beare (and later

For Aristotle the primary colors are white and black; or *clear* and *dark*. They are contraries, and all other colors are intermediaries that are mixtures of these two primary colors. The simplest mixtures are whole integer ratios of clear to dark such as 3 to 2 or 4 to 3. These are the colors thought to be the most pleasing.[22]

The other colors are mixtures of white and black in which there is more of one and less of the other, but no whole integer ratio that obtains between the quantities of each. The majority of the colors will be those for which the excess of one and deficiency of the other is *asummetron*, or incommensurable:[23]

> "It is plain that when bodies are mixed their colours also are necessarily mixed at the same time; and that this is the real cause determining the existence of a plurality of colours."[24]

So, with the exception of the two primary colors, all other colors are mixtures of the two primaries.

What we see when we look at a determinately bounded body is the mixture of white and black at its surface. Such bodies are colored in virtue of the condition of their surface, their bounding limit. As the *de Anima* puts it:

> "Whatever is visible is colour and colour is what lies upon what is in itself [*kath hauto*] visible; 'in itself' here means not that visibility is involved in the definition [*logos*] of what thus underlies colour, but that that substratum contains in itself the cause of visibility."[25]

It is surfaces that are visible in their own right, or *kath hauto*, in the second of the two senses of the term distinguished in *Posterior Analytics* I.4. Although the surface of an object is visible this is not part of the essential nature captured by the definition of what it is to be a surface. Nonetheless, being visible is an intrinsic feature of surfaces due to the fact that the surface is mentioned in the definition of color. It is in this sense that a surface is colored in its own right. A color is a feature of a surface, and since color is the cause of visibility, it follows that the cause of visibility is a *per se* attribute of surface.

Ross) in putting a comma after *huparchein*, rather than after *eschaton*. Against this, I would note that the definition of color does *not* apply to the sense in which indeterminate bodies appear colored. Accordingly, I would propose translating "... which appear to possess a fixed color of their own at the limit, color belongs to all in a similar manner."

[22] *Sens.* 3, 439b31-33. As examples Aristotle gives *halourgon* and *phoinikoun* (440a1), purple and crimson. The former is literally 'wrought by the sea', from *hals* and *ergon*; the latter a variant of *phoinikeon* — red, purple-red, crimson. Cf. *HA* 592b23-4 for crimson as the color of the crest of the wren, and *Metaph.* X.7, 1057a24-6, on crimson being an intermediary between white and black; see also *Col.* 2, 792a9-26 on how various mixtures of clear and dark give rise to the appearance of crimson or purple.

[23] *Sens.* 3, 439b27-30.

[24] *Sens.* 3, 440b14-15.

[25] *de An.* II.7, 418a29-31.

The surface has many other features, but all that is relevant to its *visibility* is its specific mixture of white and black. On this theory, the color of the body is a feature that its surface possesses insofar as that surface is the limit of something transparent. The transparent has no separate existence from the body, and its limit is the limit of the body in which it is present, the body of which it is a power. The color is what this surface is insofar as it is the surface of the transparent.

Aristotle's Planetary Observations
ISTVÁN M. BODNÁR

Aristotle in *De caelo* II 12, in an argument about the relative position of the planets, that they are further away from the Earth — the centre of the universe — and closer to the periphery — the first celestial sphere of the fixed stars — than the Sun and the Moon are, corroborates his assertion by referring to an observation.

> This has become conspicuous to sight, too, about some of these. For we have seen the half Moon as coming before Mars from among the stars, which was occulted at its [the Moon's] black side and came [then] forth at its light and bright side. (292a3–6)

This, more personal observational report is immediately followed by a mention of the testimonies to the same effect about the other planets, handed down by the Egyptians and Babylonians, who had been conducting observations for many years. The formulation in first person plural clearly indicates personal involvement on Aristotle's part. Even if he had not been present at the occultation observation — although we have no reason to raise doubts against this — he reports on it in such vivid detail which make it beyond doubt that he is informed at first hand. Earlier commentators of this passage mentioned 4 April 357 BCE, the date computed by Kepler.[1] Since the late 20's of the last century, 4 May 357 BCE, the result of computations from the tabular data in Schoch has been available,[2] which then has been confirmed by the computations of Stephenson.[3] As we shall see, even though there was no occultation of Mars by the Moon on 4 April 357 BCE, Kepler's considerations for preferring the date he submitted as the result of his computations retain some interest.[4] On the other hand, the occultation on 4 May 357 BCE still remains the most likely candidate for the one Aristotle reports on in *De caelo* II 12, although it is not without contenders for this distinction.

---

[1] So Paul Moraux in his edition of *De caelo*. Aristote, *Du ciel*. Texte établie et traduit par Paul Moraux (Paris: Les Belles lettres, 1965), n. 1 to p.81 (on p.161), following Stocks' note to this passage in his translation of *De caelo* in: *The Works of Aristotle translated into English* vol. ii, Oxford: Clarendon 1930.

[2] So in W.K.C. Guthrie's edition in the Loeb series, Aristotle, *On the Heavens*, Cambridge, Mass.: Harvard University Press — London: Heinemann 1939, 204f., referring to K. Schoch, *Planeten-Tafeln für Jedermann*, Berlin–Pankow: Linser 1927, col. xx.

[3] F. Richard Stephenson, "A lunar occultation of Mars observed by Aristotle," *Journal for the History of Astronomy* 31 (2000), 342–44. Stephenson's result was announced much earlier, in a review by James Longrigg about Moraux' edition of the *De caelo* in the *Classical Review* 20 (1970), 170–74.

[4] See n. 11 below.

For the purposes of this note I checked the possible occultations of planets and the Moon with the Horizons system of the Jet Propulsion Laboratory (Pasadena, California). That system uses the long duration planetary and lunar ephemeris DE–406/LE–406, an ephemeris which is based on a numerical integration of all the major solar system bodies using the most accurate observational data currently available, and spans the time period from 3000 BCE to 3000 AD. The major source of uncertainty in the calculations is the value of ΔT for the difference between universal time (defined by the rotation of the Earth and non-uniform as a result) and ephemeris time which is a uniform, smooth time scale used in the ephemeris. As a result errors in this difference, which can only be estimated by analysis of ancient eclipse reports, determine the accuracy of the angle of rotation of the Earth about its axis at the time of the occultations. At the time of Aristotle, the uncertainty in ΔT is of the order of 1000 seconds. It should be noted that this uncertainty has no impact on whether an occultation occurred, or the latitude of where the event could have been observed, but rather the longitude.[5]

The list of occultations in the Appendix to this note suggests that Aristotle's observation report was typical in so far as from among the dozen or so occultations observable in his lifetime five or six were occultations of Mars. From among these five or six occultations of Mars there are two or three where the phase of the Moon cannot be claimed to match the details of Aristotle's description even with a huge amount of charity. The remaining three candidates (20 March 361 BCE, 4 May 357 BCE and 24 June 340 BCE) occurred during different periods of Aristotle's career: during the first two he was a disciple, or a junior member of the Academy, whereas in 340 if he still was the tutor of the young Macedonian Prince Alexander, he most probably was in Pella at the Macedonian court, otherwise he most probably was back in Stagira.

If we wanted to evaluate which of these three dates might be the most likely candidate, we may also take into account Aristotle's other planetary observation report, at *Meteorology* I 6, 343b30–32. There Aristotle mentions that he observed the conjunction of one of the stars of Gemini with the planet Jupiter. As we do not know which of the many stars within the constellation he speaks about, we cannot produce exact dates as for the occultation of Mars, we can only give the years when Jupiter spent several months in the constellation. As these follow each other in periods of twelve years, only three observational seasons could have been suitable: 360 BCE (at the Academy), 348 BCE (still at the Academy or already at Assos) and 337/6 BCE (still in Stagira, or perhaps in Pella).[6]

The most remarkable feature of the two reports, taken together, is their isolat-

---

[5] I am grateful for advice on the details of the DE-406/LE-406 ephemeris, and on the value of the clock error in Aristotle's time to Dr E. Myles Standish of the Jet Propulsion Laboratory.

[6] A fourth observational season, in 325 BCE may have been too late for inclusion in the *Meteorology*. Sheldon M. Cohen, "Aristotle and a star hidden by Jupiter," *Sky and Telescope* June 1992, 676–77 lists the following conjunctions: 24 April 360, 6 April 348, 22 July 337, 5 December 337, 14 March 336, 2 July 325, singling out the occultation on 5 December 337 as the most likely candidate.

edness: in whatever way Aristotle made these observations, he certainly was not conducting prolonged astronomical sightings on a regular basis. Had he done so, he in both cases could have referred to some more occasions of the Moon occulting a planet,[7] or a planet in conjunction with one of the fixed stars. This means that although Aristotle endorsed the idea of the scientific enterprise which should incorporate observational astronomy, he was not willing to spend his nights star-gazing on end: as soon as he saw with his own eyes an occultation, in confirmation of earlier Egyptian and Babylonian reports, he rested content with that single observation, almost like an *experimentum crucis* on his part, and did not seek further corroboration. He certainly did not need to collect further evidence in person — that had been already collected by the Egyptian and the Babylonian astronomers long before his life-time. Moreover, as I shall argue below, Aristotle's observations most probably also presupposed some sort of contemporary astronomical activity.[8] In this case, to amass even further evidence in corroboration of the relative position of the planets and the Moon would have been clearly unnecessary on his part.[9]

Indeed, the isolatedness of the two observational reports is something what one might be tempted to call the paradoxical nature of these observations: Aristotle made them in person, without conducting regular sightings. The two conjunctions are conspicuous events, anybody with a bare minimum of astronomical knowledge

---

[7] The distribution of planetary occultations is by no means even, as should be clear from the Appendix. Nevertheless, the late 360's and the 350's had a dependable series of occultations — weather permitting — from Athens,

[8] This could be compared to *Metaphysics* XII 8, 1073b13–17, where Aristotle submits that there are issues which he has to investigate himself, whereas other things need to be inquired about from those who do the investigation themselves, and in these cases the more exact (*akribesteroi*) astronomers should be given preference.

G. E. R. Lloyd has argued recently that Aristotle's amateurish dabbling in astronomy confirms in so many cases that "he [Aristotle] may be seriously out of his depth in a way that shakes one's confidence in his ability, indeed, to judge whose model [Eudoxus' or Callippus'] was more adequate. At that point we might object that, even if no practising astronomer himself, he owed it to his audience to have done more homework in the field if he wanted (as he did) to make use of some of its results." (G. E. R. Lloyd, "Heavenly aberrations: Aristotle the amateur astronomer," in *id.*, *Aristotelian explorations*, Cambridge: Cambridge University Press 1996, 182) But Aristotle could — rightly or wrongly — think that he can just skim what counts as astronomical research activity, and astronomical theory. Indeed, he did not need to possess any independent criteria in order to pass judgement on the adequacy of competing astronomical accounts: he could just rely on the assessments of the astronomers themselves (even when in some cases these might have contained some conflicting evaluations, e.g. about the need for the additional Callippan homocentric spheres for the Sun and the Moon).

In a similar fashion, he as a philosopher of nature could just rely on the context, background assumptions, overarching theoretical considerations of astronomers when he took part in the few and isolated sightings of planetary occultations and conjunctions reported in *De caelo* and in the *Meteorology*. (Note, furthermore, that the Egyptian and Babylonian observation records Aristotle mentions most certainly were known to him only through the intermediary of professional astronomers.)

[9] This remains true about the observation mentioned in *Meteorology*, even if we accept the variant reading of some manuscripts, that he already observed the occultation twice, as he clearly did not go out of his way to observe some of the other planets in conjunction with a fixed star.

— with a competence in identifying the two planets[10] and the constellation Gemini — can make them without any preparation. In principle it is not impossible that Aristotle just stumbled upon them, casting an inadvertent eye on the sky. Nevertheless, although these observations certainly do not require any elaborate planetary theory, it is fairly unlikely that one would just happen to stumble on them. Therefore, I would submit that Aristotle's planetary observations presuppose something close to an institutional background — a setup where celestial observations are conducted on a regular, indeed, on a day-to-day basis. Besides Aristotle's reports on these occultations, we have no further information about such observational activity, but it is more likely that they took place at the Academy than in Assos, Pella, or Stagira.[11]

If Aristotle was dropping in at some of the highlights of somebody else's observations at the Academy some time around the interval between 361 BCE and 360 BCE or between 360 BCE and 357 BCE, the most natural thing to ask is who was conducting these observations. Unfortunately we cannot answer this question with the same confidence as Kepler thought he could when he wrote that at that time Aristotle was an eager and diligent disciple of Eudoxus'. Eudoxus' biography with all the journeys and the founding of his own school at Cyzicus does not guarantee a constant presence at Athens during the late 360's or early 350's, and we are in no position to tell what impact, if any, his earlier visit to Athens in 366 BCE might

---

[10] I submit that the scholium in Codex Coislianus 166 to the observational passage in *De caelo* (as printed by Bonitz in his *Scholia in Aristotelem* (Aristotelis Opera vol. iv), Berlin: Reimer 1836, 497b13f.), which alleges that according to Alexander of Aphrodisias Aristotle did not observe an occultation of Mars, but rather one of Mercury by the Moon, is not meant to call into question Aristotle's competence in identifying the planets, it rather reports a variant reading *Hermou* instead of *Areôs* of the passage only. Note, however, that Alexander (or the originator of the variant reading) presumably did not realise that with this proposal they tacitly blamed a grave blunder on Aristotle, as there is no way for Mercury to be occulted by the half Moon, as the greatest elongation of the orbit of Mercury is much less than 90 degrees.

[11] This argument is analogous to, although not identical in its presuppositions with the one Kepler employs in his (unpublished) computations. Kepler's computations namely did not yield the single candidate, as he later claimed at *Astronomia nova* ch. 69, p. 323 (p. 408 of the modern edition, Johannes Kepler, *Astronomia nova* (Gesammelte Werke vol. III) ed. Max Caspar, Munich: C.H. Beck ²1990). Rather he made a choice between two possible dates, 5 (in the *Astronomia nova* 4) April 357 BCE and 7 August 336 BCE, with the following words: "Either of these two must have been it. The former is likely in that Aristotle at that time was young, and heard the astronomer Eudoxus in Plato's school very diligently and eager to know matters celestial. [...] The latter is likely, because Aristotle was already a man and wrote *De caelo* at that time, hence he could better remember the recent occasion. But the fact that he at that time was away from Athens militates against that occasion. [...]" (XIV, 299^v, on p. 505 of Johannes Kepler, *Manuscripta astronomica (II): Commentaria in theoriam Martis* (Gesammelte Werke vol. XX, 2), ed. Volker Bialas, Munich: C.H. Beck 1998.

Note further that even if Aristotle had made at least one of these observations from Assos, Pella, or Stagira, as we know of no indigenous schools of astronomers, the observational activity most likely would have been set up on the behest of Aristotle, and on the example of his home institution, the Academy. This then will again lead us back to the supposition that there must have been regular astronomical sightings conducted at the Academy.

have had on the Academy, or on Aristotle.[12] One should note, however, that we do not need an astronomer of Eudoxus' caliber for these observations. Other members of the Academy — e.g. Heraclides Ponticus or Philip of Opus[13] — also had a lasting interest in matters celestial, and certainly could have been able to conduct the observations themselves. Nevertheless, we do not need to attach a name to these observations. Aristotle's report is all the more interesting in its first person plural anonymity, as it attests that notwithstanding Plato's misgivings against empirical astronomy, as professed in *Republic* VII,[14] the Academy did house people engaged in this enterprise — even if they might as well have been after some more sublime, theoretical end while conducting these observations.

Acknowledgements

Work on this paper was supported by a grant (K 69217) of the Hungarian Scientific Research Fund. I am grateful for important comments and suggestions to Allan Gotthelf, Pavel Gregorié and Jim Lennox.

Appendix

List of occultations of planets by the Moon,
379–326 BCE, time: UT+ 1^h 35'

379-Oct–10 22:59–Oct–11 00:17, **Mars,** max: -10.8403 arc secs, at 23:37, Moon: **99.857%**, waxing — **Provides no information on relative distance of Mars and the Moon**

377-Feb–25 18:47–19:23, **Saturn,** max: -2.9483 arc secs, at 19:05, Moon: **99.927%**, waxing — **Provides no information on relative distance of Saturn and the Moon**

374-Feb–16 18:40:30–19:08:30, **Mars,** max: -0.90547 arc secs, at 18:54:30, Moon:

---

[12] For Eudoxus' bibliography see George de Santillana, "Eudoxus and Plato. A study in chronology," *Isis* 32 (1940, the issue was actually published in 1949), 248–62, François Lasserre, *Die Fragmente des Eudoxos von Knidos* (Texte und Kommentare, vol. 4), Berlin: de Gruyter 1966; Hellmut Flashar (ed.), *Die Philosophie der Antike, vol. 3: Ältere Akademie, Aristoteles — Peripatos*, Basel — Stuttgart: Schwabe 1983, 73f and Henry Mendell, "Eudoxos of Knidos," in Paul Keyser and Georgia L. Irby-Massie (eds.), *The Encyclopedia of Ancient Natural Scientists: The Greek Tradition and its Many Heirs*. London — New York: Routledge, forthcoming, 313.

[13] Especially if he is not only a second rate mathematician, pursuing mathematical problems which he deemed relevant for Platonic philosophy as Proclus reports about him in his catalogue of mathematicians at the beginning of his commentary to Euclid's *Elements* Bk I, or the editor of Plato's *Laws* and the author of the pseudo-Platonic *Epinomis,* but he is identical with the Philippus referred to in Hipparchus' Commentary on Aratus, in Ptolemy's *Phaseis,* or in Geminus' *Elementa astronomiae.* (The Philippan testimonies are conveniently collected in Leonardo Tarán, *Academica: Plato, Philip of Opus and the Pseudo-Platonic* Epinomis (Memoirs of the American Philosophical Society vol. 107) Philadelphia: American Philosophical Society 1975, 115ff).

[14] Note that the composition of *Republic* is generally presumed to be around 360 BCE, i.e. roughly around the time of the first observational season for the conjunction of Jupiter, and of the first two possible dates for the occultation of Mars.

74.633%, waxing

369-Feb-08 06:07:30–07:31:30, **Venus,** max: -15.27 arc secs, at 06:48:30, Moon: 15.2%, waning,

Sun rises at: 07:06:30

0365-Jan-30 17:12:30–18:19, **Venus,** max: -11.5625 arc secs, at 17:44:30, Moon: 1.157%, waxing

Sun sets at: 17:22, occulted Venus sets: 18:19 — Occultation cannot be observed

362-Sep-09 23:42–Sep-10 00:47, **Mars,** max: -10.29 arc secs, at 00:13:30, Moon: 71.132%, waning

361-Mar-20 22:31–23:18, **Mars,** max: -5.46252 arc secs, at 22:55:30, Moon: 34.195%, waxing

0360-Jul-19 04:01–04:56:30, **Saturn,** max: -4.04298 arc secs, at 04:29:30, Moon: 71.911%, waning

Sun rises at: 04:40:30 — Provides no information on relative distance of Saturn and the Moon

0360-Nov-04 04:36:30–00:40, **Saturn,** max: -9.5976 arc secs, at 00:08:30, Moon: 81.928%, waxing

0357-May-04 19:56–21:12, **Mars,** max: -11.6316 arc secs, at 20:35, Moon: 44.42%, waxing

0353-Jan-14 05:12–06:11:30, **Jupiter,** max: -8.03036 arc secs, at 05:41:30, Moon: 5.366%, waning

Moon rises at: 05:30, occulted Jupiter rises at: 05:31:30

0353-Mar-22 20:48:30–21:45, **Saturn,** max: -7.44072 arc secs, at 21:17:30, Moon: 38.648%, waxing

0346-Jul-25 19:20–20:09:30, **Jupiter,** max: -13.31 arc secs, at 19:45, Moon: 1.554%, waxing

Sun sets at: 19:19:30, occulted Jupiter sets: 20:09 — Occultation cannot be observed

0343-Jan-18 04:37–05:46:30, **Saturn,** max: -9.31688 arc secs, at 05:12, Moon: 48.363%, waning

0343-Dec-31 22:07–22:50, **Mars,** max: -2.47717 arc secs, at 22:28, Moon: **99.735%**, waning **— Provides no information on relative distance of Mars and the Moon**

0341-Dec-14 06:40:30–07:46, **Mars,** max: -7.24319 arc secs, at 07:14, Moon: 73.232%, waning

Sun rises at: 07:10:30 — Provides no information on relative distance of Mars and the Moon

0340-Jun-24 22:15:30–23:07, **Mars,** max: -6.6061 arc secs, at 22:41, Moon: 35.137%, waxing

0339-Feb-13 19:10:30–20:14:30, **Venus,** max: -14.6462 arc secs, at 19:43, Moon: 15.35%, waxing

0336-Apr-10 22:12–23:03:30, **Venus,** max: -9.73406 arc secs, at 22:40:30, Moon: 14.363%, waxing **Occulted Venus sets at: 22:14, Moon sets at: 22:16:30 — Borderline case, occultation starts too close to horizon**

0336-Jun-20 23:01:30–Jun-21 00:17, **Saturn,** max: -7.47894 arc secs, at Jun-20 23:49 Moon: **97.05%**, waning **— Provides no information on relative distance of Saturn and the Moon**

0335-Apr-27 19:27:30–20:06:30, **Mercury,** max: -3.45501 arc secs, at 19:47:30, Moon: 2.849%, waxing

0328-Jan-12 16:22–17:09, **Venus,** max: -2.23922 arc secs, at 16:46:30, Moon: 6.312%, waxing

Civil twilight starts: 17:05 — Provides no information on relative distance of Venus and the Moon

0326-Sep-06 04:29:30–05:27:30, **Mars,** max: -4.84535 arc secs, at 04:58, Moon: 29.785%, waning

Sun rises at: 05:26 — Borderline case (end of occultation cannot be observed)

0326-Oct-28 02:08:30–03:26:30, **Saturn,** max: -8.62498 arc secs, at 02:48, Moon: **94.121%**, waning — Borderline case, Moon very close to full

0326-Dec-27 01:42–03:02, **Mars,** max: -12.2759 arc secs, at 02:22:30, Moon: 89.531%, waning

TALLY:

Mercury: 1

Venus: 2 and 1 borderline case, and 1 not observable (but which can be used as evidence with comparison of sightings of preceding and following days)

Mars: 5 and 1 borderline case

Jupiter 1 and 1 not observable (but which can be used as evidence with comparison of sightings of preceding and following days)

Saturn: 3, and 1 borderline case

BIBLIOGRAPHY

[Aristote, 1965] Aristote, *Du ciel.* Texte établie et traduit par Paul Moraux, Paris: Les Belles lettres 1965.
[Aristotle, 1939] Aristotle, *On the Heavens*, Cambridge, Mass.: Harvard University Press — London: Heinemann 1939.
[Aristotle, 1930] *The Works of Aristotle translated into English* vol. ii, Oxford: Clarendon 1930.

[Cohen, 1992] Sheldon M. Cohen, "Aristotle and a star hidden by Jupiter," *Sky and Telescope* June 1992, 676–77.
[Flashar, 1983] Hellmut Flashar (ed.), *Die Philosophie der Antike, vol. 3: Ältere Akademie, Aristoteles — Peripatos*, Basel–Stuttgart: Schwabe 1983.
[Kepler, 1990] Johannes Kepler, *Astronomia nova*, in: Gesammelte Werke vol. III, ed. Max Caspar, Munich: C.H. Beck ^{2}1990.
[Kepler, 1998] Johannes Kepler, *Manuscripta astronomica (II): Commentaria in theoriam Martis*, in: Gesammelte Werke vol. XX, 2, ed. Volker Bialas, Munich: C.H. Beck 1998.
[Lasserre, 1966] François Lasserre, *Die Fragmente des Eudoxos von Knidos* (Texte und Kommentare, vol. 4), Berlin: de Gruyter 1966.
[Lloyd, 1996] G. E. R. Lloyd, "Heavenly aberrations: Aristotle the amateur astronomer," in *id.*, *Aristotelian explorations*, Cambridge: Cambridge University Press 1996, 160–83.
[Longrigg, 1970] James Longrigg, "Review of Aristote, *Du ciel.* Texte établie et traduit par Paul Moraux (Paris: Les Belles lettres 1965)" *Classical Review* 20 (1970), 170–74.
[Mendell, forthcoming] Henry Mendell. "Eudoxos of Knidos", in Paul Keyser and Georgia L. Irby-Massie, (eds.), *The Encyclopedia of Ancient Natural Scientists: The Greek Tradition and its Many Heirs*. London—New York: Routledge, forthcoming, 313–316.
[de Santillana, 1940/1949] George de Santillana, "Eudoxus and Plato. A study in chronology," *Isis* 32 (1940/1949), 248–62
[Schoch, 1927] K. Schoch, *Planeten-Tafeln für Jedermann*, Berlin–Pankow: Linser 1927.
[Stephenson, 2000] F. Richard Stephenson, "A lunar occultation of Mars observed by Aristotle," *Journal for the History of Astronomy* 31 (2000), 342–44.
[Tarán, 1975] L. Tarán, *Academica: Plato, Philip of Opus and the Pseudo-Platonic* Epinomis (Memoirs of the American Philosophical Society, vol. 107) Philadelphia: American Philosophical Society 1975.